Luther:
Letters of Spiritual Counsel

THE LIBRARY OF CHRISTIAN CLASSICS

Volume XVIII

GENERAL EDITORS

Luther:
Letters of Spiritual Counsel

Edited and Translated by
Theodore G. Tappert

REGENT COLLEGE PUBLISHING
VANCOUVER, BRITISH COLUMBIA

LUTHER: LETTERS OF SPIRITUAL COUNSEL
Copyright © 1960 by the Estate of Theodore G. Tappert

First published 1960 by The Westminster Press, Philadelphia

This edition published 2003 by Regent College Publishing
5800 University Boulevard, Vancouver, B.C. V6T 2E4 Canada
www.regentpublishing.com

The views expressed in works published by Regent College Publishing
are those of the author and do not necessarily represent the official
position of Regent College <www.regent-college.edu>.

National Library of Canada Cataloguing in Publication Data

Luther, Martin, 1483-1546
   Luther: letters of spiritual counsel / Theodore G. Tappert.

   Includes bibliographical references and index.
   ISBN 1-57383-092-5

   1. Consolation. 2. Pastoral theology. I. Tappert, Theodore G.
(Theodore Gerhardt), 1904-1973. II. Title.

BR332.L6T36 2003   253   C2003-910874-0

THE LIBRARY OF CHRISTIAN CLASSICS

Volume

GENERAL EDITORS' PREFACE

The Christian Church possesses in its literature an abundant and incomparable treasure. But it is an inheritance that must be reclaimed by each generation. THE LIBRARY OF CHRISTIAN CLASSICS is designed to present in the English language, and in twenty-six volumes of convenient size, a selection of the most indispensable Christian treatises written prior to the end of the sixteenth century.

The practice of giving circulation to writings selected for superior worth or special interest was adopted at the beginning of Christian history. The canonical Scriptures were themselves a selection from a much wider literature. In the Patristic era there began to appear a class of works of compilation (often designed for ready reference in controversy) of the opinions of well-reputed predecessors, and in the Middle Ages many such works were produced. These medieval anthologies actually preserve some noteworthy materials from works otherwise lost.

In modern times, with the increasing inability even of those trained in universities and theological colleges to read Latin and Greek texts with ease and familiarity, the translation of selected portions of earlier Christian literature into modern languages has become more necessary than ever; while the wide range of distinguished books written in vernaculars such as English makes selection there also needful. The efforts that have been made to meet this need are too numerous to be noted here, but none of these collections serves the purpose of the reader who desires a library of representative treatises spanning the Christian centuries as a whole. Most of them embrace only the age of the Church Fathers, and some of them have long been out of print. A fresh translation of a work already translated may shed much new light upon its meaning. This is true even of Bible translations despite the work of many experts through the centuries. In some instances old translations have been adopted in this series, but wherever necessary or desirable, new ones have been made. Notes have been supplied where these were needed to explain the author's meaning. The introductions provided for the several treatises and extracts will, we believe, furnish welcome guidance.

JOHN BAILLIE
JOHN T. McNEILL
HENRY P. VAN DUSEN

CONTENTS

General Introduction

MARTIN LUTHER (1483-1546) IS USUALLY THOUGHT of as a world-shaking figure who defied papacy and empire to introduce a reformation in the teaching, worship, organization, and life of the Church and to leave a lasting impression on Western civilization. It is sometimes forgotten that he was also—and above all else—a pastor and shepherd of souls. It is therefore well to remind ourselves that the Reformation began in Germany when Luther became concerned about his own parishioners who believed that if they had purchased letters of indulgence they were sure of their salvation.[1] And just as Luther's public activity of reform began in this pastoral concern, so the life of the Reformer ended in a pastoral ministry. In January, 1546, in the dead of winter, sixty-three-year-old Martin Luther traveled to his birthplace, Eisleben, to reconcile the quarreling counts of Mansfeld. After long and painful negotiations the noblemen were reconciled, and on the following day Luther died.[2] Between these two pastoral acts—the one that marked the beginning of the Reformation and the one that closed the Reformer's life—lay a rich lifetime of pastoral activity.

The spiritual counsel which Luther offered to contemporaries is not limited by any means to the letters he wrote to specific persons who sought his help or to the conversations he had with particular individuals who had burdened consciences. The

---

[1] Luther's letter to Archbishop Albert of Mayence, Oct. 31, 1517, with which he enclosed the Ninety-five Theses, posted the same day. *WA, Br,* I, 111; English translation in *Works of Martin Luther,* Philadelphia ed., I, 26.

[2] See letters of Feb. 7 and 10, 1546, in Chapter III.

13

pastoral concern of Luther is prominently revealed in his sermons.[3] It emerges again and again in long excursuses in his lectures and commentaries on books of the Bible.[4] It was the immediate occasion for the writing of many of his tracts and books.[5] Consequently a full treatment of Luther as pastor would have to take into account all that he is known to have written and said.

I

Such an examination of the collected works of Luther makes it clear that his spiritual counsel was not simply the application of external techniques. It was part and parcel of his theology. As for Luther himself, so for the people of his age generally, God was real and to be reckoned with. All men naturally know that there is a God, he wrote, but they do not know what his will is or what is not his will. True knowledge of God and his will can be found only in Christ.[6] Consequently Luther rejected the assumption of medieval scholastics that God can be known by means of reason or logic and the theory of medieval mystics that God can be known by means of self-mortification or ecstasy.

In the sight of God man is a sinner when he relies upon himself and what he does, without acknowledging his dependence on God and God's gifts. "Not to believe, trust, fear him, not to give him glory, not to let him rule and be God" is sin.[7] So sin is at bottom a turning away from God.[8] It is not believing.[9] Sin is not so much a matter of wrong acts (although it is this too) as it is a matter of wrong orientation. With this understanding the medieval distinction between mortal and venial sins of course collapsed. Man confesses, "I am a sinner," rather than, "I have committed a sin."

Man's fellowship with God is broken by sin, but God takes the initiative to restore this fellowship. In Christ, God graciously takes upon himself man's sin, compassionately suffers in man's behalf, lovingly gives of himself to reconcile man, gratuitously

---

[3] For example, the sermon of Dec. 1, 1538, reported by Anthony Lauterbach, in Chapter VIII.
[4] For example, his lectures on Isaiah (1532–1534), *WA*, XXV, 229–235.
[5] For example, "for weak and timid and doubting consciences" Luther wrote the tract "Whether Soldiers, Too, Can Be Saved" (1526), (*Works of Martin Luther*, Philadelphia ed., V, 32), and he wrote his tract "On Trading and Usury" (1524) in order that "some, if only a few, may yet be delivered from the gaping jaws of avarice" (*op. cit.*, IV, 12).
[6] Commentary on Galatians (1535), *WA*, XL[i], 607–609.
[7] *WA*, X[i], 25.   [8] *WA*, III, 28, 74.   [9] *WA*, III, 331.

INTRODUCTION 15

offers pardon and forgiveness. For Luther the word "forgiveness" embraces all of this. It is something positive rather than merely negative. It is God's acceptance of man in spite of his sin, and it is the eternal life that is such acceptance.

Man, for his part, can receive only what is thus given. He is not worthy of the gift, nor can he make himself worthy of it. He simply takes hold of what is offered, placing his confidence at once in the promise, and the Giver in God's Word and in God himself, who addresses man in his Word. "God gives you nothing on account of your worthiness," Luther wrote. "Nor does he establish his Word and Sacrament on your worthiness. But out of pure grace he establishes you, unworthy as you are, on his Word and sign."[10] The Word of God (more specifically, the gospel) is the means by which God comes to man with his offer of forgiveness and life. Because it is a promise, it can be received only in faith—not intellectual assent to doctrine, but personal trust in and commitment to God in Christ—which is itself a gift of God rather than an achievement of man. Faith is the assurance that God loves in his wrath and is gracious in his judgment. To have faith is to have God.[11]

The Christian life, then, is a life of faith, a life lived in and under God. A Christian does "good works," not to save himself, but to serve his neighbors in love. "To serve our neighbor is a service to God," is *Gottesdienst*.[12] A Christian does this freely, spontaneously, joyfully—not in order to secure salvation but because he is saved.

In Luther's eyes, therefore, spiritual counsel is always concerned above all else with faith—nurturing, strengthening, establishing, practicing faith—and because "faith cometh by hearing," the Word of God (or the gospel) occupies a central place in it. The aim is not to get people to do certain things—fasting, going on a pilgrimage, becoming a monk, doing "good works," even receiving the Sacrament—so much as it is to get people to have faith and to exercise the love which comes from faith.

The ministry to troubled souls is a ministry of the gospel. It is a ministry to those who have or who lack faith, and therefore it stops at death. What were considered superstitions associated with the administration of Extreme Unction and Holy

10 *WA*, II, 694.
11 Cf. Erich Seeberg, *Luthers Theologie in ihren Grundzügen* (Stuttgart, 1950), 126, 129.
12 *WA*, XXIII, 358.

Communion disappear[13] and vigils and Masses for the dead are discontinued.[14] Although the calling of clergymen is held in the highest esteem, the medieval distinction between clergy and laity largely disappears. Laymen as well as clergymen can minister to the spiritual needs of their fellow men, and nowhere is this more evident than in the encouragement of laymen to hear confession and pronounce absolution.[15] Moreover, help and guidance were always afforded in the context of the Church, in the fellowship of all believers.

This listing of salient features of Luther's theology can, of course, make no claim to completeness, but it may serve to indicate the relation that existed between his pastoral counsel and his theology. At the same time it may suggest both what was new in Luther's approach and what was old, for he continued throughout his life to employ terminology and techniques that he had learned in the monastery and in the priesthood before he became a Reformer.[16]

II

Sickness (see Chapter I) played a large part in the lives of people in the sixteenth century. It was then commonly believed that sickness could be induced by the practice of black magic. In a sermon that he preached in 1529, Luther referred in passing to sicknesses caused by sorcerers,[17] but as a rule he traced diseases to natural causes—not, to be sure, without reference to Satan's activity behind these natural causes. It would be possible to make a list of the specific diseases that assailed the people to whom he ministered. Tuberculosis took a heavy toll. Luther referred to outbreaks of ulcers, boils, and abscesses. Some of these may have been venereal diseases, but he also made direct reference to syphilis. Other ailments men-

13 See, for example, letters to the dean and canons of All Saints in Wittenberg, March 1 and Nov. 17, 1523, in WA, Br, III, 34–36, 375–377.
14 See Chapter II.
15 Cf. John T. McNeill, A History of the Cure of Souls (New York, 1951), 163–176.
16 See, for example, Walter Dress, "Gerson und Luther," in Zeitschrift für Kirchengeschichte, LII (Stuttgart, 1933), 122–161; A. W. Hunzinger, Das Furchtproblem in der katholischen Lehre von Augustin bis Luther (Leipzig, 1906); John T. McNeill, A History of the Cure of Souls (New York, 1951), Chapters V–VII.
17 Hermann Werdermann, Luthers Wittenberger Gemeinde wiederhergestellt aus seinen Predigten (Gütersloh, 1929), 105–109.

tioned by Luther were scrofula, smallpox, inflammation of the eyes, fever, dysentery, epilepsy, apoplexy, jaundice, colic, dropsy, and stone. The prevalence of such diseases, aggravated by poor sanitation and diet, was made worse by the fact that their origin and treatment were not so fully understood as they are today.

In his ministry to the sick Luther recommended physicians, barbers, and apothecaries. Resort to medicine is desirable, he said, and it is well that physicians and nurses do what they can. However, Luther went beyond most of these physicians in pointing to the mental and emotional origin of some physical ailments. "Our physical health depends in large measure on the thoughts of our minds. This is in accord with the saying, 'Good cheer is half the battle.' "[18]

There were also epidemics (see Chapter VIII) of the sweating sickness. Feared more, however, was the bubonic plague, which attacked the population of towns again and again and was fatal to large numbers of people. Whenever the plague struck, there was apt to be panic. Work came to a standstill as terror spread. Those who were able to do so fled from plague-ridden towns. The effects of diseases were then increased by want and hunger. Luther believed in using every reasonable precaution. "Use medicine. Take whatever may be helpful to you. Fumigate your house, yard, and street. Avoid persons and places where you are not needed or where your neighbor has recovered. Act as one who would like to put out a general fire."[19] Those who had responsibilities toward their neighbors were to remain in their calling. "Put your trust in the Lord," Luther declared from the pulpit on one such occasion. "Let everyone remain in his calling, for your neighbor needs your help and support. Do not forsake your neighbor."[20] In keeping with his own advice, Luther remained in Wittenberg during seasons of the plague, even when the university itself was moved temporarily to another town. Not only did he visit the sick, but he took some of them into his own home.

To those who were afflicted with illness of one kind or another Luther expressed warm sympathy. He did not minimize their distress. But he encouraged them to be calm and confident in the assurance that God is a gracious and loving Father. He is not forsaking those who suffer. He loves them more than they love

[18] Letter to Conrad Cordatus, 1537, in Chapter III.
[19] Letter to John Hess, Nov., 1527, in Chapter VIII.
[20] Report of sermon, Dec. 1, 1538, in Chapter VIII.

themselves. Accordingly the sick are admonished to remember and hold fast to what they have learned in church of the Word of God. They need have no fear of death, for in Jesus Christ, God has overcome death.

In the case of death (Chapter II) Luther's ministry was addressed to the surviving mourners. Grief is natural and proper, he insisted, as long as it is not excessive and is informed by faith. Loss of loved ones is not to be interpreted as punishment at the hands of a wrathful God since we know from God's revelation of himself that he is a gracious God. "If we are sure of God's grace, everything will be well with us."[21] Here again Luther's ministry revolved about the Word of God and faith.

III

Luther was called upon to minister not only to the sick and dying but also to those who were assailed by a variety of trials and temptations. Some of these assaults were physical and others were spiritual.

The most common physical temptations, especially for young people, were temptations of the flesh (see Chapter IX). "We see," wrote Luther, "that the whole world is full of shameful works of unchastity, indecent words, tales, and ditties. . . . The vice of unchastity rages in all our members: in the thoughts of our heart, in the seeing of our eyes, in the hearing of our ears, in the words of our mouth, in the works of our hands and feet and all our body. To control all these requires labor and effort."[22] As in the case of illness, so here Luther first recommended the use of material measures. One must avoid "gluttony and drunkenness, lying late abed, loafing, and being without work." It may also be desirable to avoid "soft beds and clothes," excessive adornment, and intimate association with members of the opposite sex. Luther also recommended early marriage as a constructive measure to overcome temptations of the flesh and consequent vices,[23] and sometimes, as in the case of Philip of Hesse,[24] he gave considerable play to impulses of the flesh.

In addition to such outward measures for combating unchastity, Luther recommended spiritual medicine. "The

---

[21] Letter to John Reineck, April 18, 1536, in Chapter II.
[22] "Treatise on Good Works" (1520), in *Works of Martin Luther*, Philadelphia ed., I, 275, 276.
[23] *Ibid.*, 267.   [24] See Chapter IX.

strongest defense," he once wrote, "is prayer and the Word of God, namely, that when evil lust stirs, a man flee to prayer, call upon God's mercy and help, read and meditate on the gospel, and in it consider Christ's sufferings. . . . In this work a good, strong faith is a great help. . . . For he who so lives that he looks to God for all grace takes pleasure in spiritual purity; therefore he can so much more easily resist fleshly impurity: and in such faith the Spirit tells him of a certainty how he shall avoid evil thoughts and everything that is repugnant to chastity."[25]

More than for such physical temptations, however, Luther was consulted in cases that involved what he called spiritual trials and temptations, or *Anfechtungen* (see Chapters III; IV). These were of many different kinds. Boys, he once remarked, are tempted by beautiful girls. But when they are thirty years old they are tempted by gold, and when they are forty years old they are tempted by the quest for honor and glory.[26] Worse than these are temptations of faith. They trouble some persons more than others and they take different forms. "To me," said Luther, "Satan casts up my evil deeds, the fact that I used to say Mass, or that I did this or that in the days of my youth. Others, again, he vexes by casting up to them the wicked life which they have lived."[27] Luther believed that Satan caused men to dwell on their sin. Melancholy and despair were induced. Men would doubt that God is gracious, they would become uncertain of the forgiveness of their sin, they would be persuaded that God hates them, they would despair of salvation. "I have myself learned by experience," Luther confessed, "how one should act under temptation, namely, when anyone is afflicted with sadness, despair, or other sorrow of heart or has a worm gnawing at his conscience."[28]

Here, too, some external remedies were first proposed. Avoid solitude, he advised as he pointed out that Satan seduced Eve in paradise when she was alone. The solitude of monks and nuns was an invention of the devil. Christ did not wish people to remain alone and so he gathered them into the Church. God created man for fellowship, not for solitude, and Christ promised that where two or three are gathered in his name, he would be in their midst. Whoever is tempted, therefore, should seek company. Get out of your room and house, Luther advised. Seek out your friends! Talk to anybody! "I too," he

[25] *Works of Martin Luther*, Philadelphia ed., I, 276, 277.
[26] *WA, TR*, II, No. 1601.   [27] *WA, TR*, I, No. 141.
[28] *WA, TR*, I, No. 122.

said, "often suffer from great temptation and melancholy. Then I seek out the company of men. Indeed, a simple maid with whom I have spoken has often comforted me."[29]

The proposal to seek companionship was accompanied by other recommendations. Do not fast, for a hungry man merely exposes himself to the fiery darts of Satan. Eat, drink, and be merry. Luther quoted with approval the words of Prov. 31:6, "Give strong drink to him that is ready to perish, and wine unto those that be of heavy hearts." Luther also suggested work as a remedy. "The human heart must have something to do," he said. "If it does not have the work of its calling to occupy it, the devil comes and casts in temptation, despondency, and sadness."[30]

There are also spiritual weapons with which to counteract spiritual trials and temptations. "Read something in the Holy Scriptures," Luther advised. "Although you may be disinclined (for Satan tries to hinder it and awaken aversion to it), still you should compel yourself to do this."[31] Like reflection on the Word of God, prayer will turn the heart and mind away from temptations to what we know of God and his mercy. The afflicted man will say, "I know nothing of any other Christ save him whom the Father gave and who died for me and for my sins, and I know that he is not angry with me, but loves me."[32] Melancholy, anxiety, fear, and despair can be overcome only by faith in a gracious God, only by reliance on God's Word, and it is most helpful when this Word is communicated to us by the living voice of a clergyman or neighbor.[33] Meanwhile it is also helpful to remember that trials and temptations can be a blessing when they undermine our pride and our reliance upon ourselves and teach us to put our trust in God's mercy and goodness.

IV

Luther once said of himself: "You know that Dr. Martin is not only a theologian and defender of the faith. He is also a supporter of the rights of poor people who come to him from near and far to secure help and overtures to governments. Taking care of such things would give him enough to do even

---

[29] WA, TR, III, No. 3754; cf. Table Talk, 1534, in Chapter III.
[30] Cf. WA, TR, II, Nos. 1299, 1349; letter to Jerome Weller, July, 1530, in Chapter III.
[31] Lectures on Isaiah (1532–1534), in WA, XXV, 230.
[32] WA, XXV, 231.   [33] See Chapter III.

if no other work rested on his shoulders, but Dr. Martin is happy to serve the poor."[34] The town of Wittenberg attracted multitudes of people who were in trouble and need (see Chapter VI), and Luther did what he could to relieve their distress or intercede with others who were in a position to do so.

Among those who appealed to him for help were needy widows and orphans, unemployed workers, underpaid clergymen, and monks and nuns who had abandoned monastic life and experienced difficulty in adjusting themselves to secular life. He interceded in behalf of those who had been justly or unjustly imprisoned, for persons whose property had been confiscated, and for people who had lost their means of livelihood in other ways. He was interested in the welfare of poor students and secured stipends and scholarships to enable them to continue their studies. He interceded with parents in behalf of their children and pleaded with men and women in behalf of their respective wives and husbands. He used his good offices to assist refugees and relieve the plight of people who were suffering from oppression or persecution (see Chapter VII), and he called upon the authorities to intervene in time of famine (see Chapter VIII).

Luther's counsel in such cases was often two-sided. On the one hand, he exhorted wrongdoers to reform and to redress the evil they had done. On the other hand, he admonished the wronged to bear their sufferings with patience. This simultaneous counsel to two or more parties is illustrated most clearly, perhaps, in Luther's counsel to rulers and subjects (see Chapter XI), where obedience is paralleled by bold criticism, submissiveness by zeal for reform. Long-suffering was not confused with timidity, for Luther believed that there were times to resist courageously and fight forthrightly (see Chapter V).

Of rather different character was the advice that Luther gave to fellow clergymen who approached him with problems (see Chapter X). These were many and varied. They touched upon religious liberty and the relations of Church and State. They concerned questions of conscience, doctrine, and practice. Is it permissible to baptize a stillborn child? Is Baptism valid when administered without water, or when administered with warm water? Is it a sin to receive Holy Communion under the form of bread alone? May Communion be celebrated privately in a house as well as publicly in a church? May a man put aside his leprous wife and marry again? Should the unbelieving be buried

[34] *WA, Br,* VIII, 237.

in a churchyard with the rites of the Church? Are suicides to be buried in the same fashion as those who die a natural death? What is to be said about women as preachers? Is the Last Judgment near at hand? Are the ceremonies inherited from the Middle Ages to be preserved or abandoned? Such questions as these were answered in terms of Luther's understanding of the gospel and in terms of the immediate situation.

V

Within a few years of Luther's death the first collection of his letters of spiritual counsel was gathered and published, and almost every generation since then saw the appearance of at least one new collection.[35] Each of these reflected the problems and tastes of the age as well as the interests of the compiler. Luther was held in such high esteem, moreover, that his opinions continued to be regarded as authoritative and were cited as such in Protestant works of casuistry and manuals for clergymen.[36]

Including dedicatory epistles, prefaces, open letters, and opinions, about 3,000 letters of Luther have come down to us, and we know from allusions elsewhere that he wrote many more. As a rule these letters were written by hand rather than dictated, and they were written in Latin when addressed to the learned and in German when addressed to the unlearned, although this was not an invariable rule. A comparatively small selection has here been made from the extant letters to illustrate various aspects of Luther's spiritual counsel, and it seemed best to make a fresh selection rather than attempt to reproduce the letters that have appeared in earlier collections.

Closely related to Luther's letters are his table talks.[37] The Reformer sometimes read his correspondence to friends and

---

[35] For an analysis of the five earliest collections of the sixteenth century see Johannes Haussleiter, "Luthers Trostbriefe," in *Allgemeine Evangelisch-Lutherische Kirchenzeitung*, L (Leipzig, 1917), 434–487. Available in English translation is August Nebe, *Luther as Spiritual Adviser* (Philadelphia, 1894). The most recent is a small collection by Paul Scheurlen, *Vom wahren Herzenstrost: Martin Luthers Trostbriefe* (Stuttgart, 1935).

[36] Among the best-known manuals is Conrad Porta, *Pastorale Lutheri, das ist nützlicher und nöthiger Unterricht . . . für anfangende Prediger und Kirchendiener*, 1582. Reprinted Nördlingen, 1842. See also Jakob S. Gotthold, *Manuale casuisticum* (Frankfurt, 1717).

[37] For an introduction see Preserved Smith, *Luther's Table Talk, a Critical Study* (New York, 1907).

students who gathered about his hospitable table. At other times he discussed subjects that had just been brought to his attention by correspondents or by those who were seated at table. Between 1524 and 1546 a number of Luther's friends and students made notes of such table conversations and later transcribed them. Occasionally they recorded what Luther said and did outside of his home, and notes were also made of many of his sermons. All these were set down in a curious mixture of Latin and German, partly because the participants in the conversations were bilingual and easily slipped from one language into another, and partly because the recorders, accustomed to taking shorthand notes in Latin, often put into Latin what was actually said in German. This is most apparent in the case of the macaronic notes of sermons which were unquestionably delivered in German.[38] Only a small selection has here been made from the voluminous table talks to supplement the spiritual counsel contained in the letters.

Often the selections from the table talks indicate the context in which Luther spoke, but it is not always possible to reconstruct the circumstances. In the case of the letters, on the other hand, the occasion for Luther's writing is usually apparent or can be pieced together from what is known of his correspondents, and such information as is necessary for an understanding of the letters has in every case been set down briefly. Since it proved impracticable to acknowledge indebtedness at every point, it deserves to be emphasized here that all studies of Luther inevitably rest heavily on the painstaking editorial labors of the several editors of the Weimar edition of Luther's works and on the many monographs that have been written. The most important of these are listed in the bibliography appended to this volume.

The translations have been freshly made from the original Latin and German. Many of the pieces have never before appeared in English, and most of them have not previously appeared in full. Some of the early letters have before been translated as a whole or in part by Preserved Smith and Charles M. Jacobs,[39] and the present translator gratefully acknowledges the help these translations have given him.

Even casual readers of Luther's letters will observe that they are redolent with Biblical atmosphere. In addition to conscious

38 See, for example, *WA*, XXXIV^{i}.
39 *Luther's Correspondence and Other Contemporary Letters*, 2 vols. (Philadelphia, 1913, 1918).

quotations, the letters are filled with unconscious allusions. Luther lived so intimately with the Bible that its phrases and imagery slipped easily and naturally into whatever he was writing or saying. This confronts a translator with thorny problems. Quotations and allusions were usually introduced by Luther from memory, and consequently they sometimes suggest a phraseology of the Latin Vulgate, sometimes reflect the wording of the Hebrew or Greek originals, sometimes approach the translations in his own German Bible, and sometimes bear little resemblance to any of these. For the purposes of this volume it seemed best to employ the familiar English of the King James version whenever this conformed with the sense which Luther was expressing and to depart from it only when slavish adherence would do violence to Luther's apparent intention. The problems confronting a translator have to do not only with Luther's language, however, but also with his loose practice in using references. In his time, Biblical citations (if given at all) were to chapters, not to chapters and verses, and chapter divisions in the Vulgate and in the German Bible were not in every instance like ours. Moreover, in quoting from memory Luther sometimes cited the wrong chapter, or even the wrong book of the Bible. It seemed best for the purposes of this volume to clarify the Biblical references, without undue pedantry and unnecessary annoyance to the reader, in the footnotes, where the location of passages is given in terms of modern English Bibles and where quotations are distinguished from allusions.

ABBREVIATIONS

(See Bibliographies for Details)

C.R.—Corpus Reformatorum, edited by C. G. Bretschneider and H. E. Bindseil, Vols. I-XXVII (Halle, 1834-1860).

De Wette—Luther's correspondence edited by W. M. L. de Wette (1825-1856).

EA—Erlangen edition of Luther's Works (1826-1857).

Enders—Luther's correspondence edited by E. L. Enders (1884-1923).

WA—Weimar edition of Luther's Works, main body of publications (1883-   ).

WA, Br—Weimar edition, Correspondence (1930-1948).

WA, TR—Weimar edition, Table Talk (1912-1921).

I

Comfort for the Sick and Dying

TO ELECTOR FREDERICK OF SAXONY

September, 1519

*The fifty-six-year-old Frederick the Wise of Saxony, for whose pro-
tection in the early years of the Reformation Luther had reason to be
grateful, was stricken with gout, kidney stone, and fever in the late
summer of 1519 and his court feared for his life. The elector's chaplain
and secretary, George Spalatin (1484-1545), who played the important
role of mediator between the prince and the Reformer, suggested that
Luther write something for the comfort of the sick man. Within a month
the devotional booklet* The Fourteen of Consolation for Those Who
Labor and Are Heavy Laden,[1] *was written. It was sent to Spalatin
in its original Latin form, with the request that he translate it freely into
German for the elector's use. Afterward, early in 1520, it was published.
Following is the dedicatory epistle that accompanied the original draft.*
[Text in Latin; *WA*, VI, 99-106.]

To the most illustrious prince and lord, Frederick, duke of
Saxony, archmarshal and elector of the Holy Roman Empire,
landgrave of Thuringia, margrave of Meissen, my very gracious
lord.

    Our Lord and Saviour Jesus has left us a commandment that
concerns all Christians alike, namely, that we should perform
humanitarian duties or, rather (as the Scriptures call them),
works of mercy in behalf of the afflicted and oppressed, visit
those who are sick, try to liberate those who are captives, and
do other things of this sort for our neighbors,[2] whereby the evils
of our time might be somewhat alleviated. Our Lord Jesus
Christ has himself given us a very clear example of this commandment when, out of his great love for humanity, he came

---

[1] English translation in *Works of Martin Luther*, Philadelphia ed., I, 103-
171.   [2] Cf. Matt. 25:34-46.

down from the bosom of his Father to share our miseries and captivity (that is, our flesh and wretched life) and took upon himself the penalty of our sins in order that we may be saved. It is as Isaiah wrote in ch. 43, "Thou hast made me to serve with thy sins, thou hast wearied me with thine iniquities."[3] Whoever remains unmoved by so clear an example, and whoever is not driven by the added authority of the divine commandment to perform such works of charity, will in the Last Judgment deserve to hear the voice of the angry judge saying: "Depart from me, thou cursed one, into everlasting fire, for I was sick, and thou visitedst me not.[4] Ungrateful as thou art for all the benefits which I have bestowed on thee and the whole world, thou wouldest not so much as lift a little finger to help thy brethren—nay, to help me, thy God and Saviour Christ, in thy brethren."

When, therefore, I learned, most illustrious prince, that Your Lordship has been afflicted with a grave illness and that Christ has at the same time become ill in you, I counted it my duty to visit Your Lordship with a little writing of mine. I cannot pretend that I do not hear the voice of Christ crying out to me from Your Lordship's body and flesh and saying, "Behold, I am sick." This is so because such evils as illness and the like are not borne by us who are Christians but by Christ himself, our Lord and Saviour, in whom we live, even as Christ plainly testifies in the Gospel when he says, "Inasmuch as ye have done it unto one of the least of these my brethren, ye have done it unto me."[5] Although it is our duty to visit and comfort in this fashion all those who are afflicted with ill-health, we are obliged to do so especially in the case of those who are of the household of faith, for Saint Paul clearly distinguishes between those who are of the household (bound to us by some necessity) and those who are not, Gal., ch. 6.[6]

I also have other reasons for performing this duty of mine. I am persuaded that, as one of Your Lordship's subjects in that great multitude of those who are subject to you, I ought to be affected by Your Lordship's illness and suffer with you as a member with the head on whom all our fortune, safety, and happiness depend. For we recognize in Your Lordship another Naaman through whom God is today delivering Germany as he once delivered Syria.[7] On this account the whole Roman Empire is turning its eyes to Your Lordship. It venerates and

[3] Isa. 43:24. [4] Cf. Matt. 25:41, 43. [5] Matt. 25:40.
[6] Gal. 6:10. [7] Cf. II Kings 5: 1.

regards Your Lordship as the father of the fatherland, as the pre-eminent ornament and guardian of the whole empire, and especially of the German nation.

We ought to do more than console Your Lordship as much as we can, more than sympathize with Your Lordship in the present affliction. Above all else we ought to pray God for your health and safety, and I trust that Your Lordship's subjects are doing this with all diligence and devotion. As far as I am concerned, being one whom Your Lordship's many benefits and signal benefactions have made your debtor before all other men, I acknowledge that I feel obliged to express my gratitude by performing some special service. Since by reason of my material and intellectual limitations I can offer nothing of value, I welcomed the suggestion of your chaplain, Mr. George Spalatin, that I prepare some kind of spiritual consolation and present it to Your Lordship, to whom such a service, he said, would be very acceptable. I did not wish to be so disagreeable as to reject his friendly advice, and so I have gathered these fourteen chapters, as it were in a numbered tablet, and have called them "The Fourteen."[8] They are to take the place of the fourteen saints whom our superstition has invented and called defenders against all evils.[9] This is not a silver tablet but a spiritual one. It is not intended to adorn the walls of churches but to uplift and strengthen a godly heart. I hope that it will prove to be very useful to Your Lordship in your present condition. It has two sections: the first contains the images of seven evils, in the contemplation of which present troubles may be lightened; and the second similarly presents the images of seven blessings, which have been gathered for the same purpose.

May Your Lordship accept this little work of mine in good part, and may it so please Your Lordship that a diligent reading and contemplation of these images will provide some comfort.

Humbly commending myself to Your Lordship, I am

Your Lordship's subject,

Martin Luther, Doctor.

---

[8] *Tessaradecas*, Greek for "fourteen."
[9] In late medieval Germany fourteen patron saints had been given special recognition, each of whom was believed to be a defender against a particular disease or danger: throat distemper, toothache, headache, plague, etc. See Theodor Heckel, *Martin Luthers Vierzehn Tröstungen* (Gütersloh, 1948).

TO GEORGE SPALATIN. July 10, 1527

*It is not known what the nature of George Spalatin's illness, to which
Luther referred in this letter, was, but his illness may have come from an
unhappy conflict in which he was engaged at the time (see Chapter XI).
On August 19, 1527, Luther again wrote to Spalatin and expressed
satisfaction that his friend's health had been restored.*[10] *Luther's own
illness at this time was reported in detail by Justus Jonas.*[11] *[Text in
Latin; WA, Br, IV, 221, 222.]*

To the esteemed gentleman, Mr. George Spalatin, servant of
Christ in Altenburg, my dear brother in the Lord: grace and
peace in Christ.

My dear Spalatin:

Oral and written reports have come here that you are ill. If
this is true, I pray the Lord Jesus that he may restore your
health and preserve you longer to the glory of his Word. Meanwhile, patiently bear the blows of his kindly hand, as you have
been taught to do, in order that you may know not only how
to do this yourself but also how to teach others to do likewise.
For with the temptation the Lord will also make a way of
escape.[12]

Three days ago I too was seized with such a sudden fainting
spell that I despaired of life and thought that I was about to
die before the eyes of my wife and friends, so suddenly was I
deprived of all strength. But the Lord was merciful and speedily
restored me. I beg, therefore, that you will pray the Lord for
me that he may not forsake his sinner. Farewell in the Lord.

It is rumored that the plague has broken out here, but the
report is empty and false; by the favor of Christ everything is
safe and quiet.[13]

Yours,

July 10, 1527.   Martin Luther.

TO FATHER JOHN LUTHER. Feb. 15, 1530

*Luther was a dutiful son who respected and loved his father. His parents
were present at his marriage to Catherine von Bora in 1525, and they*

---

[10] *WA, Br*, IV, 232, 233.

[11] *WA, TR*, III, No. 2922b; partially translated in Preserved Smith and
Charles M. Jacobs, *Luther's Correspondence and Other Contemporary Letters*
(Philadelphia, 1913–1918), II, 404–407.   [12] Cf. I Cor. 10:13.

[13] The epidemic turned out to be more serious. Cf. letter to George
Spalatin, Aug. 19, 1527, in Chapter VIII.

visited the Reformer and his wife several times in Wittenberg. Now that his parents were advanced in years and his father was in poor health, Luther proposed that they move to Wittenberg. The weakness of the father made this impossible, and he died on May 29, 1530, three months after this letter of consolation was written. On June 5, Luther wrote to Melanchthon: "John Reineck wrote me today that my beloved father, the senior Hans Luther, departed this life at one o'clock on Exaudi Sunday. This death has cast me into deep mourning, not only because of the ties of nature but also because it was through his sweet love to me that my Creator endowed me with all that I am and have. Although it is consoling to me that, as he writes, my father fell asleep softly and strong in his faith in Christ, yet his kindness and the memory of his pleasant conversation have caused so deep a wound in my heart that I have scarcely ever held death in such low esteem."[14] [Text in German; WA, Br, V, 238-241.]

To my dear father, John Luther, citizen in the valley of Mansfeld: grace and peace in Christ Jesus, our Lord and Saviour. Amen.

Dear Father:

My brother James[15] has written me that you are seriously ill. As the weather is bad and the season dangerous, I am very anxious about you, for though God has given you a strong, tough body, yet your age and the inclemency of the weather give me disquieting thoughts. None of us is, or should be, sure of his life at any time. I should have come to you personally with the greatest willingness, but my good friends advised me against it and have persuaded me not to, and I myself thought it better not to tempt God by putting myself in peril, for you know how lords and peasants feel toward me. It would be the greatest joy to me if it were possible for you and mother to come hither, which my Katie and all of us beg with tears that you will do. I hope we are able to take good care of you. Therefore I am sending Cyriac[16] to see whether your weakness will allow you to be moved. However in God's wisdom your illness turns out, whether you live or die, it would be a heartfelt joy to me to be with you again and with filial piety and service to show my gratitude to God and to you according to the Fourth Commandment.

In the meantime I pray from the bottom of my heart that

[14] WA, Br, V, 351.   [15] Luther's brother lived in Mansfeld.
[16] A nephew of Martin Luther, Cyriac Kaufmann, was matriculated as a student in Wittenberg three months before this.

our Father, who has made you my father, will strengthen you according to his immeasurable kindness and enlighten and protect you with his Spirit, so that you may receive with joy and thanksgiving the blessed teaching of his Son, our Lord Jesus Christ, to which doctrine you have now been called and to which you have come out of the former terrible darkness and error; and I hope that his grace, which has given you such knowledge, and thereby begun his work in you, will guard and complete it to the end of this life and to the joyous hereafter of our Lord Jesus Christ. Amen.

God has already sealed this teaching and faith in you and has testified to it by such marks[17] as that you have suffered much slander, abuse, obloquy, mockery, scorn, hatred, and odium for his name's sake, as we all have done. These are the true marks of our likeness to the Lord Christ, as Paul says, that we may be like him also in future glory.[18]

Let your heart be strong and at ease in your trouble, for we have yonder a true mediator with God, Jesus Christ, who has overcome death and sin for us and now sits in heaven with all his angels, looking down on us and awaiting us so that when we set out we need have no fear or care lest we should sink and fall to the ground. He has such great power over sin and death that they cannot harm us, and he is so heartily true and kind that he cannot and will not forsake us, at least if we ask his help without doubting.

He has said, promised, and pledged this. He will not and cannot lie; of that we are certain. "Ask," says he, "and it shall be given you; seek, and ye shall find, knock, and it shall be opened unto you."[19] And elsewhere: "Whosoever shall call on the name of the Lord shall be saved."[20] The whole Psalter is full of such comforting promises, especially Ps. 91, which is particularly good to read to the sick.

I wish to write this to you because I am anxious about your illness (for we know not the hour),[21] that I might become a participant of your faith, temptation, consolation, and thanks to God for his holy Word, which he has richly and graciously given us at this time.

If it is his divine will that you should postpone that better life and continue to suffer with us in this troubled and unhappy vale of tears, to see and hear sorrow and help other Christians to suffer and conquer, he will give you the grace to accept all

17 Cf. Gal. 6:17.   18 Rom. 8:29.   19 Matt. 7:7.
20 Acts 2:21.   21 Cf. Matt. 24:36.

this willingly and obediently. This life, cursed by sin, is nothing but a vale of tears. The longer a man lives, the more sin and wickedness and plague and sorrow he sees and feels. Nor is there respite or cessation this side of the grave. Beyond is repose, and we can then sleep in the rest Christ gives us until he comes again to wake us with joy. Amen.

I commend you to Him who loves you more than you love yourself. He has proved his love in taking your sins upon himself and paying for them with his blood, as he tells you by the gospel. He has given you grace to believe by his Spirit, and has prepared and accomplished everything most surely, so that you need not care or fear any more, but only keep your heart strong and reliant on his Word and faith. If you do that, let him care for the rest. He will see to it that everything turns out well. Indeed, he has already done this better than we can conceive. May our dear Lord and Saviour be with you so that, God willing, we may see each other, either here or yonder. For our faith is certain, and we doubt not that we shall shortly see each other in the presence of Christ. Our departure from this life is a smaller thing to God than my journey would be from here to Mansfeld or yours from Mansfeld to Wittenberg. It is only an hour's sleep, and after that all will be different. This is most certainly true.

I hope that your pastor and preacher[22] will point out such things to you in faithful service, and so you will not need what I say at all. Yet I write to ask forgiveness for my bodily absence, which, God knows, causes me heartfelt sorrow. My Katie,[23] little Hans, Magdalene,[24] Aunt Lena,[25] and all my household send you greetings and pray for you faithfully. Greet my dear mother and all my friends. God's grace and strength be and abide with you forever. Amen.

Your loving son,

February 15, 1530.   Martin Luther.

TABLE TALK RECORDED BY JOHN SCHLAGINHAUFEN.[26] Spring, 1532

I thank God that my father died a godly death. Before his end I wrote him a letter of consolation. The parish clergyman read

22 Martin Seligmann or Michael Cölius.
23 Catherine, nee von Bora, Luther's wife.
24 John, four years old, and Magdalene, one, children of Luther.
25 Magdalene von Bora, aunt of Luther's wife.
26 Macaronic text; *WA, TR,* II, No. 1388.

it to him and asked whether he believed what he had heard. He answered: "Of course! If I didn't believe it, I'd be a knave."

TO MRS. JOHN LUTHER. May 20, 1531

From his younger brother James, who was living in Mansfeld, near the Reformer's paternal home, Martin Luther received word of the serious illness of his mother. It proved to be a fatal illness, for on June 30, 1531, thirteen months after the death of her husband, the aged Margaret Luther died. Long before her illness Luther's mother had embraced the Evangelical faith, and in the following letter of consolation her son makes comparisons between the Catholic and the Reformation teaching about Christ which must have been especially meaningful to her. The major theme of the tender letter was taken from John 16:33. [Text in German; WA, Br, VI, 103-104.]

Grace and peace in Christ Jesus, our Lord and Saviour. Amen.

My beloved Mother:

I have received my brother James's letter[27] with its account of your illness. It grieves me deeply, especially because I cannot be with you in person, as I should like to be. Yet I shall be with you in this letter, together with all the members of my family, and I shall assuredly not be absent from you in spirit.

I trust that you have long since been abundantly instructed without my help, that (God be praised) you have taken God's comforting Word into your heart, and that you have been adequately provided with preachers and comforters. Nevertheless, I shall do my part too. I acknowledge that, as your child, I have a duty to perform to you as my mother, for our common God and Creator made us and bound us to each other with mutual ties. Accordingly I shall add myself to the number of your comforters.

First, dear mother, you are now well-informed about God's grace and know that this sickness of yours is his gracious, fatherly chastisement. It is quite a slight thing in comparison with what he inflicts upon the godless, and sometimes even upon his own dear children. One person is beheaded, another burned, a third drowned, and so on. And all of us must say, "For thy sake are we killed all the day long; we are counted as sheep for the slaughter."[28] Therefore, this sickness should not distress or depress you. On the contrary, you should accept it

[27] The letter is not extant.   [28] Ps. 44:22; Rom. 8:36.

L.L.S.C.—3

with thankfulness as a token of God's grace, recognizing how slight a suffering it is (even if it be a sickness unto death) compared with the sufferings of his own dear Son, our Lord Jesus Christ, who did not suffer for himself, as we do, but for us and for our sins.

Secondly, dear mother, you know the real basis and foundation of your salvation, on which you must rest your confidence in this and all troubles, namely Jesus Christ, the cornerstone,[29] who will not waver or fail us, nor allow us to sink and perish, for he is the Saviour and is called the Saviour of all poor sinners, of all who face tribulation and death, of all who rely on him and call on his name.

He says, "Be of good cheer; I have overcome the world."[30] If he has overcome the world, surely he has overcome the prince of this world with all his power. And what is his power but death, with which he has made us subject to him, captives on account of our sin? But now that death and sin are overcome, we may joyfully and cheerfully listen to the sweet words, "Be of good cheer; I have overcome the world." And we must not doubt that they are certainly true. More than that, we are commanded to accept their comfort with joy and thanksgiving. Whoever is unwilling to be comforted by these words does the greatest injustice and dishonor to the Comforter—as if it were not true that he bids us to be of good cheer, or as if it were not true that he has overcome the world. If we act thus, we only restore within ourselves the tyranny of the vanquished devil, sin, and death, and we oppose the dear Saviour. From this may God preserve us!

Therefore, let us rejoice with all assurance and gladness. Should any thought of sin or death frighten us, let us lift up our hearts and say: "Behold, dear soul, what are you doing? Dear death, dear sin, how is it that you are alive and terrify me? Do you not know that you have been overcome? Do you, death, not know that you are quite dead? Do you not know the One who has said of you, 'I have overcome the world'? It does not behoove me to listen to or heed your terrifying suggestions. I shall pay attention only to the cheering words of my Saviour, 'Be of good cheer, be of good cheer; I have overcome the world.' He is the Conqueror, the true Hero, who in these words, 'Be of good cheer,' gives me the benefit of his victory. I shall cling to him. To his words and comfort I shall hold fast. Whether I remain here or go yonder, he will not forsake me.

[29] Cf. I Peter 2:6.   [30] John 16:33.

You would like to deceive me with your false terrors, and with your lying thoughts you would like to tear me away from such a Conqueror and Saviour. But they are lies, as surely as it is true that he has overcome you and commanded us to be comforted."

This is also the boast of Saint Paul and his defiance of the terrors of death: " 'Death is swallowed up in victory. O death, where is thy sting? O grave, where is thy victory?'[31] Like a wooden image of death, you can terrify and frighten, but you have no power to destroy. For your victory, sting, and power have been swallowed up in Christ's victory. You can show your teeth, but you cannot bite. For God has given us the victory over you through Christ Jesus our Lord, to whom be praise and thanks. Amen."

With such words and thoughts, and with none other, you may set your heart at rest, dear mother. Be thankful that God has brought you to such knowledge and not allowed you to remain in papal error, by which we were taught to rely on our own works and the holiness of the monks and to consider this only comfort of ours, our Saviour, not as a comforter but as a severe judge and tyrant, so that we could only flee from him to Mary and the saints and not expect of him any grace or comfort.

But now we know differently about the unfathomable goodness and mercy of our Heavenly Father: that Jesus Christ is our mediator,[32] our throne of grace,[33] and our bishop[34] before God in heaven, who daily intercedes for us and reconciles all who call upon and believe in him[35]; that he is not a grim judge, except to those who do not believe in him and who reject his comfort and grace; and that he is not the Man who accuses and threatens us, but rather that he intercedes for and reconciles us by his own death, having shed his blood for us in order that we might not fear him but approach him with all assurance and call him our dear Saviour, our sweet Comforter, the true Bishop of our souls, etc.

To such knowledge, I say, God has graciously called you. In the gospel, in Baptism, and in the Sacrament [of the Altar] you possess his sign and seal of this vocation, and as long as you hear him addressing you in these, you will have no trouble or danger. Be of good cheer, then, and thank him joyfully for such great grace, for he who has begun a good work in you will

---

31 I Cor. 15:54, 55.   32 Cf. I Tim. 2:5.   33 Cf. Heb. 4:16.
34 Cf. I Peter 2:25.   35 Cf. I Tim. 4:10.

perform it until the day of Jesus Christ.[36] We cannot help ourselves in such matters. We can accomplish nothing against sin, death, and the devil by our own works. Therefore, Another appears for us and in our stead who can do better and give us the victory. He commands us to accept his victory and not to doubt it. He says, "Be of good cheer; I have overcome the world," and again, "Because I live, ye shall live also; and your joy no man taketh from you."[37]

The Father and God of all consolation[38] grant you, through his holy Word and Spirit, a firm, joyful, and thankful faith to overcome this and all other trouble. May you taste and experience that what he himself says is true: "Be of good cheer; I have overcome the world." Herewith I commit your body and soul to his mercy. Amen.

All your children[39] and my Katie pray for you. Some weep. Others say when they eat, "Grandmother is very sick." God's grace be with us all. Amen.

Your loving son,

Saturday after the Ascension of our Lord, 1531. Martin Luther.

TABLE TALK RECORDED BY CONRAD CORDATUS.
Autumn, 1531

A former Roman priest, Conrad Cordatus (1475-1546) became a bold and tenacious follower of Luther. He was involved in various controversies and was made to suffer for his faith. After being driven out of Zwickau (see Chapter X), he spent some time in Wittenberg, where he was a table companion of Luther. The following appears to be a circumstantial account based on Cordatus' observation of Luther's ministry to the sick. [Macaronic text; WA, TR, II, No. 2194b.]

When he [Luther] approaches a sick man he converses with him in a very friendly way, bends down as close to him as he can with his whole body, and first inquires about his illness, what his ailment is, how long he has been sick, what physician he has called, and what kind of medicine he has been using. Then he asks whether the sick man has been patient before God. When he has now assured himself that the sick man's will is inclined toward God, that he acknowledges that the illness, sent upon him by the will of God, is to be borne with patience, and that he is prepared to die in God's name, if this be his will,

[36] Phil. 1:6.   [37] John 14:19; 16:22.
[38] Cf. Rom. 15:5.   [39] Grandchildren.

Luther highly praises this disposition of his as a work wrought in him by the Holy Ghost himself. It is a great mercy of God, he says, when a man comes to a knowledge of the Word, his Saviour Jesus Christ, especially if he perceives in himself such a disposition and such a faith as the Word of God brings and if he thinks it excels all things that may be esteemed precious. Because he has such faith, he has an ever-present and gracious God. Luther commends such faith to others, at the same time admonishing the sick man to continue steadfast in his faith and promising to pray for him.

When the sick man begins to thank Luther and declares that he can never repay him for the blessing of his visit, Luther is accustomed to reply that this is his office and duty and that it is therefore not necessary to thank him so profusely. He also makes use of this consolation, that the sick man should not be afraid because God, who has provided him with a letter and seal (that is, with his Word and Sacrament), has also given himself for the man's redemption.

TO JOHN RUEHEL. June 29, 1534

A doctor of laws, John Rühel was chancellor to Count Albert of Mansfeld. He was related to Luther by marriage and served as sponsor at the baptism of Luther's son Martin in 1531. Luther learned of his illness and of his impatience in his illness from the tutor of Rühel's sons, Christopher and Martin, who were living in Luther's home and eating at his table. [Text in German; *WA, Br,* VII, 81-83.]

Grace and peace in Christ. Where these are, there is also life, and comfort.

My dear Doctor, my dear and kind Brother-in-law:

I am truly sorry to learn of your infirmity from your Justus'[40] letter and am even more sorry to learn that you take your infirmity so hard.

Are you not, together with us, a friend, member, and confessor of that Man who speaks to all of us in Saint Paul, "My strength is made perfect in weakness"[41]? The realization that you have been called by this Man, that you have been blessed by a knowledge, desire, and love for his Word, and that you have been sealed therein by his Baptism and Sacrament should surely make you more cheerful. What more do you expect of

---

[40] Justus Waldhausen was the tutor of Rühel's two sons.
[41] II Cor. 12:9.

Him who has inwardly given you such love toward him and has outwardly given you such seals and such a confession and testimony of his grace? Dear doctor, behold the good things you possess at his hands rather than what you suffer. The balance is tipped immeasurably in favor of the former.

Besides, he is able, if you give him time, to restore your health. To be sure, we are his at all times; as Saint Paul says, "whether we live or die, we are the Lord's."[42] Yes, indeed, *Domini* in the genitive and in the nominative—in the genitive (we are the Lord's) because we are his dwelling place, his members, and in the nominative (we are lords) because we rule over all things through faith, which is our victory, and because, thanks be to God, we trample the lion and the dragon underfoot. In short, he says, "Be of good cheer; I have overcome the world."[43]

Therefore, be of good cheer, my dear doctor,[44] and admit into your heart the words of your brethren through whom God himself speaks to you above and beyond his daily works, for he says, "Where I am, there shall ye be also."[45]

I shall treat your sons,[46] who are with me, as if they were my own. That you are not a false friend of mine I know and have sufficiently experienced. Accordingly I shall not deal falsely with you and yours as long as God gives me life. Amen.

God willing, Master Philip[47] will shortly have more to say to you in person. Greet all the members of your family for me.

Martin Luther, Doctor.

Saint Peter's and Saint Paul's Day, 1534.

TO CASPAR MUELLER. November 24, 1534

The friendly relationship that existed between Luther and Caspar Müller, chancellor of Mansfeld, is suggested by the fact that the Reformer addressed his "Open Letter Concerning the Hard Book Against the Peasants" (1525) to him.[48] Later, in 1526, he asked Müller to serve as sponsor at the baptism of his oldest child.[49] Now that Müller was sick, Luther wrote him the following letter of comfort. [Text in German; WA, Br, VII, 117-119.]

42 Rom. 14: 8. From here to the end of the paragraph in Latin.
43 John 16:33.   44 From here to the end of the paragraph in Latin.
45 John 14: 3.   46 Christopher and Martin Rühel.
47 Philip Melanchthon (1497–1560).
48 In WA, XVIII, 375–401; translation in Works of Martin Luther, Philadelphia ed., IV, 255–281.
49 Cf. Luther's letter to Müller, WA, Br, IV, 80, 81.

To the honorable and prudent Caspar Müller, chancellor of Mansfeld, my gracious lord and friend: grace and peace in Christ.

My dear Lord and Friend, Chancellor Müller:

I address you thus, and it is right that I do so, although this may displease some of your colleagues. I have received your letter, and also the pitchers. They please me very much, and I thank you heartily for them. One of them, especially, is beautiful; we are already worrying about who will break it, and where, when, how, etc.

I am sorry that God has heaped more sickness upon you, for I am certain that by God's grace you are one of those rare birds[50] who take the Word of God very seriously and are faithful to the Kingdom of Christ. I also know that your health and activity can be useful and comforting to us all, especially among so many addlepated persons. But if God wishes you to be sick, his will is surely better than ours. After all, even that noblest and most innocent will of our Lord had to be subject to the higher and supremely good will of his dear Father. Let us be cheerful, or at least patient, in submitting to his will. Amen.

In short, it is written, "Be of good cheer; I have overcome the world."[51] What should we do but glorify and bear in our bodies Him who gained the victory over the world, the devil, sin, death, flesh, sickness, and all evils.[52] His yoke is easy, and his burden is light.[53] The yoke and the burden which he bore for us was the devil—indeed, the wrath of God. May God defend us from these. In fact, he has already freed us from them, and in their place we bear his easy yoke and his light burden. We must continue to do so. The exchange is to be accepted cheerfully. He is a good merchant and a gracious tradesman who sells us life for death, righteousness for sin, and lays a momentary sickness or two upon us by way of interest and as a token that he sells more reasonably and borrows at more favorable rates than the Fuggers[54] and the tradesmen on earth. Well, then, our Lord Jesus Christ is the valiant man who fights for us,[55] conquers for us, triumphs for us. He is and must be the man, and we must be with him and in him. There is no other way, no matter how much the gates of hell rage.[52]

---

[50] *Der seltsamen Vogel einer; rara avis.*   [51] John 16: 33. Quoted in Latin.
[52] Part of this sentence is written in Latin.   [53] Cf. Matt. 11:30.
[54] The Fugger family controlled a banking house in Augsburg.
[55] Compare the words of Luther's hymn, "A Mighty Fortress Is Our God," stanza 2: "But for us fights the Valiant One Whom God Himself elected."

Accordingly, since you asked me to write you a letter of consolation, this is my comfort in Christ: Be cheerfully thankful to the Father of all grace, who has called you to his light and the confession of his Son, and who has given you enough of his abundant grace to oppose the enemy of his Son (that is, his designs)—unless it be that Cochlaeus,[56] Vicelius,[57] or Albert in Halle[58] please you more than, or at least as much as, Saint Paul or Isaac, which, I trust, is not the case. It matters little, then, that God has caused you to be sick and bedridden inasmuch as he has so abundantly blessed you, chosen you, and rescued you from the darkness of the devil and the rabble of hell. Offer God thanksgiving, give him the interest due him honestly, pay your vows.[59] It is as Ps. 116 declares, "I believed, therefore I was greatly afflicted."[60]

But how can I pay for what God has done for me? Well, I can drink of the cup cheerfully and can praise and thank the name of my Lord. That is to say, I can bear my suffering and misfortune with gladness, singing, "Alleluia!" "This do, and thou shalt live."[61] Christ our Lord, "which hath begun a good work in you," will perform it until the day of Jesus Christ,"[62] and he will do the same in all of us although we are poor sinners. "Likewise the Spirit also helpeth our infirmities; the Spirit itself maketh intercession for us."[63] Herewith I earnestly commit you to his keeping.

Have I not visited the sick long enough now? My Lord Katie greets you and hopes that you will soon be well and will visit us.

Martin Luther, Doctor

Tuesday, the vigil of Saint Catherine, 1534.

TO URBAN RHEGIUS. December 30, 1534

Urban Rhegius, or Rieger (1489-1541), a Roman priest who became an Evangelical clergyman through the influences of humanism, spent the years of his early public ministry in and near Augsburg. In 1531 he was made superintendent (bishop) in Lüneburg and from there extended his activity to Hanover. The following letter was sent by Luther to comfort him in an illness. [Text in Latin; *WA, Br*, VII, 147, 148.]

56 John Cochlaeus (1479–1552), a Roman opponent of Luther.
57 George Witzel (1501–1573), an adherent of Luther for several years, became dissatisfied and returned to the Roman Church but agitated for a reconciliation of the two religious parties.
58 Cardinal Archbishop Albert of Mayence, who then had his residence in Halle.   59 Cf. Ps. 50:14.   60 Ps. 116:10
61 Luke 10:28.   62 Phil. 1:6.   63 Rom. 8:26.

To the venerable brother in the Lord, Urban Rhegius, sincere and faithful minister of Christ in Celle, Saxony: grace and peace in Christ, who is our peace and solace.

My dear Urban:

Your report that you are buffeted by a messenger of Satan and are suffering from a thorn in the flesh[64] does not distress me too much, for I recognize in this that you are conformed to the image of God's Son[65] and all the saints. I believe that this trial comes to you, as it does to other brethren who occupy high stations, in order that we may be humbled. Therefore, be of good courage, let your heart be comforted, and wait on the Lord,[66] who said to Saint Paul, "My strength is made perfect in weakness."[67] God is faithful. By him we were called.[68] He will perform a good work in us until the day of Jesus Christ.[69] Amen. This Lord have I heard, and by him have I been comforted as much as the Lord has given it to me to be.

I have told you to be confident and to know that you are not alone when you are occasionally afflicted, for "the same afflictions are accomplished in your brethren that are in the world."[70] We must support one another and be supported. Even so, Christ supports all of us from the beginning of the world unto the end. We cannot always be strong and healthy, nor always weak and infirm. Our condition depends upon Him who bloweth where he listeth.[71] By these vicissitudes he teaches us not to be arrogant, as we might be if we were always strong, and not to despair, as we might if we were always infirm. "He knoweth our frame," said David; "he remembereth that we are dust."[72] We are best off when we ourselves acknowledge that we are framed of dust and are mere dust.

But why should I write all this to you, who are Christ's? Only because a brother must speak to his brother, and each must give the other his hand in this vale of tears, until that day comes for which we long.

Give my respectful greetings to your excellent prince.[73] I am very thankful (God is my witness) that he loves the Scriptures, and I pray that the Father of mercies may increase the great blessing in him and in us all. Amen.

64 Cf. II Cor. 12:7.
65 Cf. Rom. 8:29.
66 Cf. Ps. 27:14.
67 II Cor. 12:9.
68 Cf. I Cor. 1:9.
69 Cf. Phil. 1:6.
70 I Peter 5:9.
71 Cf. John 3:8.
72 Ps. 103:14.
73 Ernest the Confessor, duke of Brunswick-Lüneburg.

Farewell to you and yours in the same Lord, and pray for me who am also a sinner.

Saint David's Day, 1535.[74]   Martin Luther, Doctor.

TO BERNARD WURZELMANN. November 2, 1535

Bernard Wurzelmann had given up his position as cathedral canon to embrace the teaching of the Reformation. In 1533 he went to the imperial free city of Dinkelsbühl, in Franconia, as an Evangelical clergyman and quickly won the confidence of his parishioners. Among them was a woman who was believed to be possessed by the devil. No particulars concerning her condition are known, and it appears that Wurzelmann, who asked Luther for advice, did not report any. [Text in Latin; *WA, Br*, VII, 319, 320.]

To Mr. Bernard, sincere pastor of the church in Dinkelsbühl: grace and peace in the Lord.

My dear Pastor:

A brother in the Lord brought me your letter, and with it your question concerning a certain woman who is plagued by the devil. I am compelled to write briefly because I am burdened with a great number of other obligations. But since Theobald Diedelhuber,[75] who is to be the bearer of this letter, is here, I wish to reply, even if for no other reason than to commend him to you.

The first thing you and your congregation ought to do is this: Pray fervently and oppose Satan with your faith, no matter how stubbornly he resists. About ten years ago we had an experience in this neighborhood with a very wicked demon, but we succeeded in subduing him by perseverance and by unceasing prayer and unquestioning faith.[76] The same will happen among you if you continue in Christ's name to despise that derisive and arrogant spirit and do not cease praying. By this means I have restrained many similar spirits in different places, for the prayer of the Church prevails at last. Consequently you should have no doubt, if you pray in truth and with perseverance, that this wicked spirit will be humbled.

The second thing is this: Carefully investigate whether that woman might be practicing some fraud by means of which all of you could be made objects of ridicule. In my own experience

---

[74] The probable date is 1534.
[75] A former Cistercian who was at this time an Evangelical clergyman in Illingen.   [76] Cf. Mark 9:29.

(apart entirely from what I have read in books) I have encountered such frauds, and afterward I reproached myself for my simplicity. The evil spirit takes delight (as he did from the beginning with Adam) in using a woman to make a fool of a man—if he cannot make him godless, as he much prefers to do. In short, whatever it is, whether it be in this woman or in others whom you mention, whether it be in the form of an incubus, a succubus, or other monstrosities, we nevertheless know that it is the devil. Therefore, we should not be inattentive and casual with regard to his fabrications and deeds, his realities and apparitions, but should fight against him with faith and prayer. The One whom he crucified lives. And by his own power the crucified One again triumphed over his crucifier in order that in the former we too may triumph over the latter.

Farewell in the Lord.

Wittenberg, November 2, 1535.   Martin Luther.

TABLE TALK RECORDED BY ANTHONY LAUTERBACH. March, 1536

In 1532, Anthony Lauterbach (1502-1569) was made deacon in Leisnig, where he married a former nun. Later he served as deacon in Wittenberg for several years before going to Pirna, Saxony, where he was superintendent (bishop) from 1539 to his death. While in Wittenberg, Lauterbach was a frequent guest at Luther's table and made extensive notes of the Reformer's sermons as well as conversations. He sometimes accompanied Luther on pastoral visits, and the following is his account of Luther's ministry to a sick woman. [Macaronic text; *WA, TR,* III, No. 3612c.]

After he had preached, Dr. Martin [Luther] visited an honorable sick woman, Mrs. Breu, an exile from Leipzig.[77] On account of the death by drowning of her husband she was overcome by such great grief and sorrow that she became ill and fainted fifteen times the first night. When Dr. Martin Luther visited her, she said, "My dear doctor, how can I repay you for this kindness?"

Then he asked her how she was feeling and admonished her to submit to the will of God, who (as is his wont) was chastising

[77] On the persecutions in Leipzig, see Luther's letters to the Evangelicals in Leipzig, Oct. 4, 1532, and April 11, 1533, in Chapter VII. Among those exiled from Leipzig were Mr. and Mrs. John Breu. The former was drowned in March, 1536.

her after freeing her from all the evils of Satan and abominations of the pope.[78] "A daughter," he said, "should bear the
chastisements of her Father unto death or life. We are the
Lord's, whether we live or die.[79] The Lord says, 'Because I live,
ye shall live also.'[80] He has sent you a very precious gem when
he brought this suffering upon you, and he will give you the
strength to bear it. Pray, therefore."

She responded by saying many godly things. When he left
he committed her to the protection of our dear Lord.

TO ANDREW EBERT. August 5, 1536

*A clergyman in Frankfurt on the Oder, Andrew Ebert wrote to Luther at
the close of July, 1536,[81] to ask for advice concerning the treatment of a
girl who was believed to be possessed by the devil. The girl, Matzke
Fischer, had a long history of mental illness. After a period of apparent
convalescence she suddenly became much worse. It was reported that she
snatched small coins from tables or the sleeves, coats, or beards of people
who were standing nearby, placed them in her mouth, chewed and
swallowed them. It was also reported that she began to speak in a German
dialect that she had not known before. A Roman priest came from a
neighboring town and made use of consecrated herbs, holy water, and
exorcism, but he failed to cure her. What, asked Ebert, could be done to
help the poor girl? [Text in Latin; WA, Br, VII, 489, 490.]*

To the reverend gentleman, Mr. Andrew Ebert, preacher in
Frankfurt, on this side of the Oder River, my dear brother in
the Lord: grace and peace in Christ.

My dear Andrew:

What you write appears incredible to many. When, before
you wrote to me, this case was reported here, I too thought that
I was listening to a joke or a fable. But if things are as you write,
I believe that this is to be taken as a sign that God is permitting
Satan to imitate and portray the practice of certain princes who
are everywhere robbing and devouring wealth without accom-
plishing anything.[82]

Inasmuch as you have to do here with a jocular spirit who in
his leisure pokes fun at our security, we must first of all pray
earnestly for the girl who is compelled to suffer such things on
our account. In the second place, this spirit must in turn be

---

[78] In Leipzig.   [79] Rom. 14:8.   [80] John 14:19.
[81] Letter in WA, Br, VII, 482–487.
[82] Compare letters of Dec. 2, 1536, and Dec. 28, 1541, in Chapter XI.

ridiculed and derided, but he must not be attacked with any exorcisms or serious measures, for he laughs at all these things with diabolical scorn. We must persevere in our prayer for the girl and our contempt of the devil until finally, Christ permitting, he lets her alone. It would also be good if the princes who are accused by this sign would lay aside their vices, for the evil spirit indicates that he controls them mightily and securely.

I pray you, since the case deserves it, that you publish an account of it[83] and that you investigate everything carefully to discover whether any deception is being practiced, especially whether the money or coins which the girl takes feel hard in the hands of others and are of the kind that can be used in the market place. For I have before been harassed by so many dissimulations, artifices, frauds, lies, tricks, etc., that I am necessarily reluctant to believe everything and everybody; I must believe only what I know I have myself done and said. Such is the power of the devil, the wickedness of the world, and the impudence of men today! Wherefore watch and be careful lest you too are deceived and I am led astray by you. As the proverb puts it, "Let experience be your guide."

Farewell in the Lord, and pray for me.
Wittenberg, August 5, 1536.   Martin Luther.

TABLE TALK RECORDED BY ANTHONY LAUTERBACH. 1537

Among the permanent residents in Luther's home was Magdalene von Bora, an aunt of Catherine von Bora, who had followed Luther's wife from the convent in Nimbschen. She was a beloved member of the household and helped to care for and teach the Reformer's children. In 1537 she fell ill and died. The following is an observer's account of Luther's last ministry to her. [Macaronic text; WA, TR, V, No. 6445.]

When Dr. Martin Luther approached a certain honorable matron who was lying on her deathbed, he consoled her in this fashion:

"Aunt Lena, do you recognize me and can you hear me?"

When she signified that she could understand him, he said, "Your faith rests alone on the Lord Jesus Christ." Afterward he said: "He is the resurrection and the life.[84] You shall lack

---

[83] Ebert published such an account under the title *Wunderliche Zeitung von einem Geld Teuffel* (Wittenberg, 1538). See *WA, Br*, VII, 483, 484, for a summary.   [84] Cf. John 11:25.

nothing. You will not die but will fall asleep like an infant in a cradle, and when morning dawns, you will rise again and live forever."

"Yes, indeed," she replied.

Then he asked, "Is anything troubling you?"

"Nothing."

"Do you have pain in the region of your heart? The Lord will deliver you from all pain. You will not die."

Turning to us, he said, "It is well with her, for this is not death, but sleep." He went to the window to pray by himself, and at twelve o'clock he left her. At seven o'clock she fell asleep.

TABLE TALK RECORDED BY ANTHONY LAUTERBACH[85]. July, 1538

The elector [of Saxony] wrote to Luther to express his sympathy with him in his illness.[86] He knew, he wrote, that Luther was not always responsive to medicine, and by this he suggested diplomatically that he was an impatient patient.

"It is true," said Luther, "that the regimen prescribed by physicians should not be despised. But many physicians are so rash that they prescribe for the sick without discrimination. A new cemetery must be provided for them. On the other hand, others are too timid and undecided. They are uncertain about the illness and say, 'Diagnosis is difficult, the weather is treacherous, the disease is acute,' and they make the patient impatient with their many doubts.

"Physicians observe only the natural causes of illness and try to counteract these by means of their remedies. They do well to do this. But they do not understand that Satan is sometimes the instigator of the material cause of the disease; he can alter the causes and diseases at once, and he can turn fever into chills and health into illness. To deal with Satan there must be a higher medicine, namely, faith and prayer. It is as Psalm 31 says, 'My times are in thy hand.'[87] During this illness of mine I have learned really to understand this verse. [Hitherto I applied it only to the hour of death. But it means that my times—that is, my whole life, all my days, hours, and moments—are in God's hand. It is as if I should say, 'My health and sickness,

---

[85] Macaronic text; *WA*, *TR*, IV, No. 4784.
[86] This letter is not extant. During the summer of 1538 Luther suffered from dysentery and from the kidney stone which plagued him again and again.   [87] Ps. 31:15.

fortune and misfortune, life and death, joy and sorrow are in thy hand,' and experience bears this out. When we intend to be merry, gay, pious, healthy, etc., everything is turned about and the opposite happens.][88]

"I have nothing but praise for the physicians who adhere closely to their principles. But they should not take it amiss if I cannot always agree with them, for they wish to make a fixed star out of me when I am a roving planet. The responsibility of physicians, to whom human life is entrusted, is a great one. Since our bodies contain many mysterious vapors and internal and invisible organs, there are also various and unexpected dangers; our bodies can go to pieces in an hour. Therefore, a physician must be humble—that is, he must be God-fearing—and unless he practices with the fear of God, he is a murderer."

TO FREDERICK MYCONIUS. January 9, 1541

Frederick Myconius (or Mecum, 1490-1546), pastor in Gotha and known as the reformer of Thuringia, had for some time been suffering from a pulmonary infection. By the summer of 1540 he had the symptoms of tuberculosis, and soon afterward he lay down on what he thought was his deathbed. However, he recovered, and he survived Luther by a few weeks—as a result, he was persuaded, of the following letter of consolation and the prayers of Luther. Myconius wrote to George Rörer, "Although I had made up my mind that I would not rise from my bed again and that I would shortly give up the ghost there, I was so helped by the letter of that dear man [Luther] that, when I read it, I could not but think that I heard Christ say to me, 'Lazarus, arise!' "[89] [Text in Latin; WA, Br, IX, 301-303.]

To the illustrious gentleman, Frederick Mecum, bishop of the church in Gotha and of the churches in Thuringia, my beloved brother: grace and peace.

My dear Frederick:

I received your letter in which you report that you are sick unto death—that is, if you interpret it rightly and spiritually, sick unto life. I was singularly pleased to learn that you are unafraid of death, of that sleep which is the common destiny of all good men, and that you rather desire to depart and be with Christ.[90] We should have this desire not only on our sickbed but also in the full vigor of life. We should have it at all

88 Text in brackets from a variant version.   89 Cf. John 11:43.
90 Cf. Phil. 1:23.

times and in all places and circumstances, as befits Christians who have been quickened, who have been raised up, and who sit in heaven with Christ,[91] where we shall judge angels[92] and where the veil and dark glass will be removed.[93]

Although, as I say, I am singularly pleased that you feel as you do, yet I pray and beseech the Lord Jesus, who is our life, health, and salvation, that he may not add this to my other sorrows, that I should live to see you or any other friend of mine break through the veil and penetrate to the rest beyond while I am left outside, after your death, to continue suffering among the demons, inasmuch as I have already suffered so much and for so many years that I am most deserving and worthy of going before you. So I pray that the Lord will make me sick in your place and command me to put off this useless, outworn, exhausted tabernacle.[94] I am quite aware that I am no longer of any value. Therefore, I ask that you join in our prayers that the Lord may be willing to preserve you for a while longer to serve his Church and to spite Satan. You see—and Christ, who is our life, also sees—what men and gifts his Church has need of from time to time.

After having waited for five weeks and almost given up hope, we finally received several letters from Worms.[95] George Rörer[96] will send you portions of them. Our friends are acting firmly and wisely in all things. On the other hand, our opponents are acting childishly, foolishly, and ineptly and are employing absurd tricks and crass lies. You see, when the dawn appears, Satan becomes impatient of the light; he resorts in a thousand ways to subterfuge, evasion, and indirection; but everything turns out wrong, as inevitably happens when anyone tries to maintain and defend an open lie against the manifest truth, which is impossible. Why do we doubt? Glory, power, victory, salvation, and honor are worthy of the Lamb that was slain[97] and rose again—and, together with him, of us also who believe that he was slain and rose again. About this there is no doubt.

I hope that our friends will soon return.

Farewell, dear Frederick. The Lord grant that I may not

[91] Cf. Eph. 2:5, 6.   [92] I Cor. 6:3.
[93] Cf. I Cor. 13:12.   [94] Cf. II Peter 1:14.
[95] A conference was being held in Worms to reconcile the differences between the Roman and Lutheran parties. John Eck and Philip Melanchthon were the respective leaders.
[96] George Rörer, a skillful notary, often took notes of meetings, conversations, and sermons.   [97] Cf. Rev. 5:12.

hear of your departure while I am still living. May he cause you to survive me. This I pray. This I wish. My will be done. Amen. For it is not for my own pleasure but for the glory of God's name that I wish it.

Farewell again. I pray for you from my heart. My Katie and all the others, who are deeply moved by your illness, send their greetings.

Yours,

Sunday after Epiphany, 1541.   Martin Luther.

TO JUSTUS JONAS. May 15, 1542

After serving for ten years as dean of the theological faculty in Witten-berg, Justus Jonas (1493-1555) was active in the visitation and re-organization of churches. In 1541 he introduced Evangelical preaching in Halle, and while there he had a severe attack of kidney stone. Luther, who also suffered again and again from this malady, comforted his friend in the following letter. [Text in Latin; WA, Br, X, 64, 65.]

To the distinguished gentleman, Justus Jonas, doctor of sacred theology, apostle and ambassador of Christ in Halle, Saxony; my good friend in the Lord: grace and peace.

My dear Jonas:

I was very sorry to read that you too suffered from the illness which overtook me in Smalcald—namely, tenesmus[98]—and I thank God that he restored you to health. To prevent a re-currence of such an insidious evil you must observe a certain diet. I have a very trustworthy remedy for this: our beer is a diuretic, and the physicians indeed call it *diureticotate*. In this respect it is plainly the queen of all beers. Wine, however, must be used sparingly.

Thank you for the quinces.

There is no news except that Satan is beginning to feel secure because we are slumbering and are slothful in prayer. There are many things that suggest this, among them that the pastor in Ronneberg[99] has begun to teach that baptism with warm water (with which infants are baptized in cold weather) is not

---

[98] *Dysuria*, difficulty in passing urine. Luther suffered severely from this when he went to Smalcald in February, 1537.

[99] Melchior Frenzel, to whom Luther wrote on July 13, 1542, to protest against the novel teaching that warm water is not pure. Others may hold, Luther wrote, that "damp water is not pure because dampness is a proper quality of the air," etc. See *WA, Br*, X, 97.

true baptism because another element—namely, fire—has been added, and because water which is heated is no longer pure water. Behold the boldness with which our fearless foe[1] operates.

I expect little from the countless soldiers who have been sent against the Turk,[2] and just as little from the whole expedition, unless God chooses to perform miracles on account of our very cold prayers. Today the margrave[3] is reported to have set out with his horses so decorated as to suggest that he was going on parade or to a ball rather than against the Turk. Fate urges us on,[4] our sins oppress us, and we rage against one another with madness. I pray you, admonish your church to pray earnestly, fervently, constantly. The wrath of God is greater than even we who are godly readily believe. Nowhere is penitence to be found, but only untamed obstinacy. God have mercy on us. Amen.

Greet all our friends.

Yours,

Monday after Rogate, 1542. Martin Luther.

TABLE TALK RECORDED BY CASPAR HEYDENREICH. September, 1542

One of Luther's table companions in later years was Caspar Heydenreich (1516-1586), who returned to Wittenberg in 1541 to study. In this year he received his master's degree there, and in October, 1543, he again left to become chaplain to Catherine, widow of Duke Henry of Saxony, in Freiberg. Later he moved to Torgau, where he was superintendent (bishop) at the time of his death. During Heydenreich's stay in Wittenberg, Luther's fourteen-year-old daughter Magdalene took sick and after a brief illness died on September 20, 1542. The following circumstantial account was recorded by Heydenreich. [Macaronic text; WA, TR, V, Nos. 5494, 5491, 5496.]

When his daughter was very ill he [Luther] said: "I love her dearly, but if it is thy will, dear God, to take her, I shall be glad to know that she is with thee."

Later, when she was lying in bed, he said to his daughter: "Magdalene, my little daughter, you would gladly remain here with me, your father. Are you also glad to go to your Father in

---

[1] Satan.
[2] It was decided at the Diet of Spires that the empire should furnish 40,000 foot soldiers and 8,000 horses to drive the Turks out of Hungary.
[3] Elector Joachim II of Brandenburg.   [4] Vergil, *Aeneid*, XI, 587.

heaven?" The sick girl replied: "Yes, dear father, as God will."
The father said, "Dear daughter!"

[Turning away from her, he said:][5] "The spirit is willing, but
the flesh is weak.[6] I love her very much. If this flesh is so strong,
what must the spirit be?" And among other things he said: "In
the last thousand years God has given to no bishop such great
gifts as he has given to me (for one should boast of the gifts of
God).[7] I am angry with myself that I am unable to rejoice from
my heart and be thankful to God, although I do at times sing a
little hymn and thank God. Whether we live or die, we are the
Lord's[8] (in the genitive singular and not in the nominative
plural)."[9]

When his wife wept loudly, Martin Luther comforted her by
saying: "Remember where she is going. It will be well with her.
The flesh dies but the spirit lives. Children do not argue. They
believe what they are told. To children everything is plain.
They die without anxiety, without complaint, without fear of
death, without great physical pain, just as if they were falling
asleep."

When his daughter was in the agony of death, he fell upon
his knees before the bed and, weeping bitterly, prayed that God
might save her if it be his will. Thus she gave up the ghost in
the arms of her father. Her mother was in the same room but
was farther from the bed on account of her grief.

It was a little after nine o'clock on the Wednesday following
the fifteenth Sunday after Trinity in the year 1542.

TO SEVERIN SCHULZE. June 1, 1545

*Until shortly before the following letter was written Severin Schulze
was Evangelical pastor in Prettin, a village near Wittenberg. At this
time he was pastor in Belgern and appears to have been advanced in
years. This letter suggests how a case of mental illness might be
handled by Schulze.* [Text in Latin; *WA, Br,* XI, 111, 112.]

To the honorable Mr. Schulze, pastor in Belgern, my dear and
good friend: grace and peace in God and in Jesus Christ.

---

5 Words in brackets from a variant.   6 Matt. 26:41.
7 The great gifts to which Luther here refers are his wife and children.
8 Cf. Rom. 14:8.
9 The Latin word *Domini* in the expression *Domini sumus* may be rendered
  either "we are the Lord's" (genitive singular) or "we are lords"
  (nominative plural). Cf. letter to John Rühel, June 29, 1534, above.

Venerable Sir and Pastor:

The tax collector in Torgau and the councilor in Belgern have written me to ask that I offer some good advice and help for Mrs. John Korner's afflicted husband. I know of no worldly help to give. If the physicians are at a loss to find a remedy, you may be sure that it is not a case of ordinary melancholy. It must, rather, be an affliction that comes from the devil, and this must be counteracted by the power of Christ and with the prayer of faith. This is what we do, and what we have been accustomed to do, for a cabinetmaker here was similarly afflicted with madness and we cured him by prayer in Christ's name.

Accordingly you should proceed as follows: Go to him with the deacon and two or three good men. Confident that you, as pastor of the place, are clothed with the authority of the ministerial office, lay your hands upon him and say, "Peace be with you, dear brother, from God our Father and from our Lord Jesus Christ." Thereupon repeat the Creed and the Lord's Prayer over him in a clear voice, and close with these words: "O God, almighty Father, who hast told us through thy Son, 'Verily, verily, I say unto you, Whatsoever ye shall ask the Father in my name, he will give it you'[10]; who hast commanded and encouraged us to pray in his name, 'Ask, and ye shall receive'[11]; and who in like manner hast said, 'Call upon me in the day of trouble: I will deliver thee, and thou shalt glorify me'[12]; we unworthy sinners, relying on these thy words and commands, pray for thy mercy with such faith as we can muster. Graciously deign to free this man from all evil, and put to nought the work that Satan has done in him, to the honor of thy name and the strengthening of the faith of believers; through the same Jesus Christ, thy Son, our Lord, who liveth and reigneth with thee, world without end. Amen." Then, when you depart, lay your hands upon the man again and say, "These signs shall follow them that believe; they shall lay hands on the sick, and they shall recover."[13]

Do this three times, once on each of three successive days. Meanwhile let prayers be said from the chancel of the church, publicly, until God hears them.

In so far as we are able, we shall at the same time unite our faithful prayers and petitions to the Lord with yours.

Farewell. Other counsel than this I do not have.

I remain, etc.

The year 1545.   [Martin Luther.]

[10] John 16:23.   [11] John 16:24.   [12] Ps. 50:15.   [13] Mark 16:17, 18.

II

Consolation for the Bereaved

TO BARTHOLOMEW VON STAREMBERG.

September 1, 1524

A member of the Austrian nobility, Bartholomew von Staremberg (1460-1531) served for a while as regent for Emperor Maximilian I in Lower Austria and was sent on a mission to Spain in 1519 as a legate of the princes of the empire. He seems to have had Evangelical sympathies, and certainly his son was a supporter of the Reformation. In 1524, von Staremberg's wife, Magdalene, nee Losenstein, died, and her death was the occasion for the following letter of consolation. Furnished with a short preface by an unknown hand, it was printed in leaflet form the same year "as a comfort for those who are mourning for loved ones who have fallen asleep or died." [Text in German; WA, XVIII, 1-7.]

Grace and peace in Christ.

Honored Sir:

Moved by Christian concern and loyalty, Vincent Wernsdorfer[1] has urged me to write this letter to you. I ask at the outset that you receive it kindly. He told me that since the death of your dear wife, who departed this life in God, you have been trying hard to help her soul with services and good works, particularly with Masses and vigils. She was remarkable for her love and fidelity to you, he said, and richly deserved all you could do. He begged me to write you a letter on the subject, and I have not known how to refuse him. I have tried to consider your best interests and humbly pray that you will take this letter in good part.

First, let me remind you of what Job says: "The Lord gave, and the Lord hath taken away; as it seemed good to the Lord, so hath he done."[2] You should sing the same song to a dear and

---

[1] Not otherwise identifiable.   [2] Cf. Job 1:21.

53

faithful God who gave you a dear and faithful wife and has now taken her away. She was his before he gave her; she was his after he had given her; and she is still his (as we all are) now that he has taken her away. Although it hurts us when he takes his own from us, his good will should be a greater comfort to us than all his gifts, for God is immeasurably better than all his gifts. In this case his will should be esteemed more than the best wife. Although we cannot perceive God's will as well as we can perceive a wife, we can apprehend his will by faith. Accordingly you should cheerfully give God what is his and accept this just exchange and strange barter whereby instead of a dear, tender wife you have a dear, tender will of God— and, what is more, God himself. How blessed and rich we would be if we could engage in such an exchange with God! We could do so, in fact, if we knew how to, for God confronts us with the opportunity daily, but we cannot ask him.

Secondly, honored sir, I ask you to discontinue those Masses and vigils and daily prayers for her soul. It is enough to pray God once or twice for her, because he has said to us, "Whatsoever ye shall ask, if ye believe, ye shall receive."[3] If we keep on praying for the same thing, it is a sign that we do not believe, and we only annoy him with our unbelieving prayers. For what does it mean if I repeatedly pray for the same thing except that my earlier prayers were not answered and that I have prayed contrary to his will? It is true that we ought to pray at all times, but we should do so in faith, certain that we are heard, otherwise the prayer is vain. And we are never at a loss for something new to pray for.

More especially I ask you to leave off the Masses and vigils for her soul, for they are unchristian practices which greatly anger God. Anyone can see that there is neither earnestness nor faith in vigils, but only a useless mummery. We are to pray quite differently if we are to be heard by God. Such vigils are a mockery of God. Moreover, inasmuch as he instituted the Mass to be a sacrament for the living and not an offering for the dead, it is a shameful and terrible thing that men should be so bold as to change this and other institutions of God from a sacrament for the living into a good work and a sacrifice for the dead. Beware of this. Do not be a participant in this horrible error which priests and monks have invented for the sake of their bellies. A Christian should do nothing unless he knows that God has commanded it. The clergy have no such

3 Cf. John 14:12–14.

command concerning Masses and vigils; they are their own little invention to get money and property without helping either the dead or the living.

You may inquire further about this from the aforementioned Vincent Wernsdorfer, who wishes you well and therefore asked me to write to you. May it please you that I have done so, and may you not be led astray by those who oppose their own prattle and human notions to the Word of God. Christ enlighten and strengthen you in true faith and in love of your neighbor.

Your willing servant,

Saint Aegidius' (Giles') Day, 1524.   Martin Luther.

TO ELECTOR JOHN OF SAXONY. May 15, 1525

Elector Frederick the Wise of Saxony (1486-1525) played a prominent role in the early years of the Reformation as protector of Martin Luther. He was timid in his support, however, and avoided personal contact with the Reformer in order to escape involvement. During the Peasants' War he became gravely ill, and before his death in Lochau on May 5, 1525, he received the sacrament in both kinds. Frederick was unmarried and was succeeded by his brother John, who was a warm friend of the Evangelical cause. [Text in German; *WA, Br,* III, 496, 497.]

To the serene and highborn prince and lord, Duke John of Saxony, elector of the Roman Empire, landgrave in Thuringia, and margrave of Meissen, my gracious lord: grace and peace in Christ.

Serene, highborn Prince, gracious Lord:

I have ample reason to write to Your Grace (if only I could write as I ought) now that Almighty God has in these perilous and terrible times[4] taken away our leader, our gracious lord elector, Your Grace's brother, and has left us—especially Your Grace, on whom the burden of all this misfortune falls—in sorrow. Your Grace may well say, in the words of the Psalter, "Innumerable evils have compassed me about; they are more than the hairs of mine head: therefore my heart faileth me," etc.[5]

But God is faithful. He does not let his wrath outweigh his mercy in dealing with those who put their trust in him, but he gives them courage and strength to bear misfortune and in the end gives ways and means to escape it. Thus we can only say,

---

[4] The Peasants' War was in its last stages.   [5] Ps. 40:12.

again in words of the Psalter, "The Lord hath chastened me sore: but he hath not given me over unto death,"[6] and again, "Many are the afflictions of the righteous (that is, of the believer); but the Lord delivereth him out of them all."[7] Solomon also offers us the same comfort and says: "Whom the Lord loveth he correcteth; even as a father the son in whom he delighteth. My son, despise not the chastening of the Lord; neither be weary of his correction."[8] And Christ himself says, "In the world ye shall have tribulation, but in me ye shall have peace."[9]

This is the school in which God chastens us and teaches us to trust in him so that our faith may not always stay in our ears and hover on our lips but may have its true dwelling place in the depth of our hearts. Your Grace now is in this school. And without doubt God has taken away our leader in order that God may himself take the deceased man's place and draw nearer to Your Grace, and in order to teach Your Grace to give up and surrender your comforting and tender reliance upon that man and draw strength and comfort only from the goodness and power of Him who is far more comforting and tender.

I have written this hurriedly for Your Grace's consolation. I hope that Your Grace will graciously accept it and find yet more of joy in the Psalter and the Holy Scriptures, which are full of all kinds of comfort. Herewith I commit Your Grace to God's keeping.

Your Grace's humble servant,
Monday after Cantate, 1525.   Martin Luther.

TO QUEEN MARY OF HUNGARY. November 1, 1526

King Lewis of Hungary was a vigorous opponent of the Reformation while his consort, Queen Mary, sister of Ferdinand of Austria and of the wife of King Christian II of Denmark, was favorably inclined toward the Evangelical cause. Probably at the suggestion of the king and queen of Denmark, Luther undertook to write an exposition of four psalms and dedicate them to Queen Mary in order to encourage her in her Evangelical sentiments. Before this little book was completed, however, King Lewis was killed in the Battle of Mohács on August 29, 1526. While altering little in his treatment of the psalms, Luther now prefaced his book with a dedicatory epistle in which he attempted to comfort the queen in her bereavement. [Text in German; *WA*, XIX, 542-553.]

[6] Ps. 118:18.   [7] Ps. 34:19.   [8] Prov. 3:12, 11.   [9] Cf. John 16:33.

To the serene and highborn lady, Mary, by birth queen of Spain, etc., queen of Hungary and Bohemia, etc., my most gracious lady: grace and comfort from God our Father and from the Lord Jesus Christ.

Most gracious Queen:

At the suggestion of some pious people I decided to dedicate these four psalms to Your Majesty so that by this means I might exhort Your Majesty to continue cheerfully and confidently to further God's holy Word in Hungary, for I received the good news that Your Majesty is inclined to favor the gospel but that the godless bishops (who are powerful and are said to exercise almost the greatest influence in Hungary) have been greatly hindering and obstructing it, in some cases even shedding innocent blood[10] and raging horribly against the truth of God.

But seeing that in the meantime the matter has unhappily taken a turn through the power and providence of God, that the Turk has caused so much distress and misery, and that the noble young monarch, King Lewis, Your Majesty's beloved husband, has been slain, my original intention also had to be altered. If the bishops had given the gospel free course, all the world would now be crying out that this calamity has come upon Hungary because of the Lutheran heresy. What a scandal that would have been! Let them now find someone else to blame! As I understand it, God has seen to it that there is no ground for such an accusation.[11]

Be this as it may, inasmuch as Saint Paul writes to the Romans that the Holy Scriptures "were written for our learning, that we through patience and comfort of the Scriptures might have hope,"[12] I have adhered to my purpose and have published these same psalms to comfort Your Majesty (with such comfort as God enables me to give) in this great and sudden misfortune with which Almighty God has at this time visited you, not in anger or displeasure (as we have every reason to hope) but as a trial and chastisement in order that Your Majesty may learn to trust alone in the true Father who is in heaven and to be comforted by the true bridegroom,[13]

[10] George Buchführer was burned at the stake in Ofen and a monk was similarly burned at the stake in Prague.
[11] Luther was mistaken in his assumption that he and the Reformation would not be blamed for the disastrous defeat at the hands of the Turks at Mohàcs.   [12] Rom. 15:4.
[13] Cf. Mark 2:19, 20.

Jesus Christ, who is our brother and, indeed, our very flesh and blood, and in order that Your Majesty may find joy with your true friends and faithful companions, the dear angels, who ever surround and care for us.

For although it is (and properly should be) a grave and bitter trial for Your Majesty to be left a widow so soon and to be deprived of your dear husband, still much consolation is to be found in the Scriptures, and especially in the psalms, which abundantly point to the dear and gracious Father and Son in whom sure and everlasting life lies hidden. And certainly anyone to whom it is given to see in the Scriptures and to experience the Father's love toward us can easily endure all the misfortune that may come upon him on this earth. On the other hand, he who does not really experience this can never be truly joyful, although he may be reveling in all the world's pleasures and delights.

No such calamity can overtake any human being as once overtook the Father himself when his beloved Son was rewarded for all his miracles and benefactions by being maligned, cursed, and finally subjected to the most shameful of deaths on the cross. Everyone thinks that his own cross is the heaviest and takes it to heart more than the cross of Christ—even if he had endured ten crosses. This is so because we are not so patient as God is, and consequently a smaller cross is more painful to us than Christ's cross.

The Father of mercies and the God of all comfort[14] console Your Majesty in his Son Jesus Christ and with his Holy Spirit so that Your Majesty may soon forget this wretchedness or be enabled to bear it bravely. Amen.

Your Majesty's obedient servant,

The first of the winter month, 1526.   Martin Luther.

TO WIDOW MARGARET. December 15, 1528

The husband of the unidentified addressee of this letter had attempted suicide and died some time afterward. Of suicide Luther declared on another occasion: "I am not inclined to think that those who take their own lives are surely damned. My reason is that they do not do this of their own accord but are overcome by the power of the devil, like a man who is murdered by a robber in the woods."[15] [Text in German; *WA, Br*, IV, 624, 625.]

---

[14] Cf. II Cor. 1:3.   [15] *WA, TR,* I, No. 222.

Grace and peace in Christ.

Honored, virtuous Lady:

Your son N[16] has told me of the grief and misfortune that have befallen you in the death of your dear husband, and I am moved by Christian love to write you this letter of consolation.

It should comfort you to know that in the hard struggle in which your husband was engaged, Christ finally won the victory. Besides, it should console you to know that when your husband died he was in his right mind and had Christian confidence in our Lord, which I was exceedingly glad to hear. Christ himself struggled like this in the Garden, yet he won the victory at last and was raised from the dead.

That your husband inflicted injury upon himself may be explained by the devil's power over our members. He may have directed your husband's hand, even against his will. For if your husband had done what he did of his own free will, he would surely not have come to himself and turned to Christ with such a confession of faith. How often the devil breaks arms, legs, backs, and all members! He can be master of the body and its members against our will.

You ought therefore to be content with God's will and number yourself among those of whom Christ says, "Blessed are they that mourn: for they shall be comforted."[17] All the saints have to sing the psalm, "For thy sake are we killed all the day long; we are counted as sheep for the slaughter."[18] Suffering and misfortune must come if we are to be partakers of comfort.

Thank God, too, for this great blessing of his that your husband did not remain in his despair, as some do, but was lifted out of it by God's grace and in the end had faith in the Word of Christ. Of such it is said, "Blessed are the dead that die in the Lord,"[19] and Christ himself says, in John, ch. 11, "He that believeth on me, though he were dead, yet shall he live."[20] God the Father comfort and strengthen you in Christ Jesus. Amen.

Tuesday after Saint Lucy's, 1528.   Martin Luther.

TO CONRAD CORDATUS. April 2, 1530

On January 3, 1530, Luther had written to Conrad Cordatus, pastor in Zwickau, to congratulate him on the birth of a son.[21] As sponsor of

[16] Symbol for an undesignated name.   [17] Matt. 5:4.
[18] Ps. 44:22.   [19] Rev. 14:13.   [20] John 11:25.
[21] The letter in *WA, Br,* V, 215–217.

the child at baptism, Luther was especially interested in him and was
distressed to learn of his early death. In the letter of consolation which
follows Luther refers to the grief he himself experienced in a similar
situation when his second child, Elizabeth, died in 1528 at the age of
seven months.[22] [Text in Latin; *WA, Br,* V, 273, 274.]

Grace and peace in Christ.

My dear Cordatus:

May Christ comfort you in this sorrow and affliction of yours.
Who else can soothe such a grief? I can easily believe what you
write, for I too have had experience of such a calamity, which
comes to a father's heart sharper than a two-edged sword,
piercing even to the marrow, etc.[23] But you ought to remember
that it is not to be marveled at if he, who is more truly and
properly a father than you were, preferred for his own glory
that your son—nay, rather, *his* son—should be with him rather
than with you, for he is safer there than here.

But all this is vain, a story that falls on deaf ears,[24] when your
grief is so new. I therefore yield to your sorrow. Greater and
better men than we are have given way to grief and are not
blamed for it. Nevertheless, it is a good thing for you too to have
had this kind of trial and to have tasted the power of conscience
so that you may learn in your own experience what is that
power of the Word and of faith which is proved in these agonies.
You have not yet felt the thorn in the flesh and the buffeting of
Satan's messenger.[25] What you have so far suffered you have
suffered in glorious and trusting innocence—that is, with a good
conscience. Let this suffice.

I hear that you wish to hurry to the diet.[26] I advise against
it. First, because I was not called thither and will, for certain
reasons, go with the prince only on the journey through his
lands. Secondly, because the matter of the gospel will hardly be
dealt with, or at least only after long delay, for the princes are
not in a great hurry about the cause of religion, especially since
the discussion will rather have to do with the Turk. You will be
able to go there at the proper time.[27] Meanwhile, labor with
your Zwickauers and make them more tractable.[28] Greet the

---

[22] Cf. *WA, Br,* IV, 511.   [23] Cf. Heb. 4:12.
[24] Cf. Terence, *Heautontimorumenos,* II, 1, 10, and Erasmus, *Adagia,* I, 4, 87.
[25] Cf. II Cor. 12:7.   [26] The Diet of Augsburg. See Chapter V.
[27] In letters to Cordatus on June 19 and July 6 (*WA, Br,* V, 380, 381, 441,
    442), Luther reiterates that Cordatus might go to Augsburg with Luther
    if the latter goes.
[28] Concerning later difficulties of Cordatus in Zwickau, see Chapter X.

companion of your sorrow, and rejoice the while in the living Christ more than you grieve over your son who is dead—nay, who is alive but has been taken from you.

My Katie and our whole household send you greeting.
April 2, 1530.   Dr. Martin Luther.

TO MR. AND MRS. MATTHIAS KNUDSEN.

October 21, 1531

John Knudsen, "of the diocese of Schleswig" near the border of present-day Denmark, was matriculated in the university in Wittenberg on June 7, 1529, and was in all probability the student whose death a little more than two years later led Luther to write the following letter of consolation to the deceased boy's parents. Nothing is known about the circumstances of his death, but the letter suggests that it followed an illness of some duration. [Text in German; *WA, Br*, VI, 212, 213.]

Grace and peace in Christ, our Lord and Saviour.

Honored, dear, good Friends:

The preceptor[29] of your dear son of blessed memory has asked me to write you this letter to console you in the misfortune which, as parents, you have experienced in the death of your son.

It is quite inconceivable that you should not be mourning. In fact, it would not be encouraging to learn that a father and mother are not grieved over the death of their son. The wise man, Jesus Sirach, says this in ch. 22: "Weep for the dead, for light hath failed him; but do not mourn much, for he hath found rest."[30]

So you too, when you have mourned and wept moderately, should be comforted again. Indeed, you should joyfully thank God that your son had such a good end and that he has gone to sleep in Christ so peacefully that there can be no doubt that he is sleeping sweetly and softly in the eternal rest of Christ. For everyone marveled that he continued steadfast to the end in his prayers and in his confession of Christ. This great blessing should be more agreeable to you than if he had enjoyed all this world's goods and honors for a thousand years. He has taken with him the greatest treasure[31] he could obtain in this life.

Be of good cheer, therefore. He is well off in comparison with many thousands of others who perish miserably, and sometimes dishonorably, and even die in their sins. Accordingly it is very

[29] Paul Hockel.   [30] Cf. Ecclus. 22:11.   [31] Cf. Matt. 6:20.

much to be desired that you and all your loved ones, together with all of us, should by God's grace have such a death. Your son has cheated the world and the devil while we are still in danger of being overcome by them and are exposed to all the perils against which he is now secure. You sent him to the right school and invested your love and your means very well. God help us to depart in similar fashion. Amen.

The Lord and supreme Comforter Jesus Christ, who loved your son even more than you did and who, having first called him through his Word, afterward summoned him to himself and took him from you, comfort and strengthen you with his grace until the day when you will see your son again in eternal joy. Amen.

Saturday after Saint Luke, 1531.   Martin Luther, Doctor.

TO AMBROSE BERNDT. Early in 1532

There has been a great deal of uncertainty about the date of this letter because the tragedy referred to has sometimes been confused with a similar tragedy which overtook Ambrose Berndt later in his life. Here his first wife, Margaret, died in childbirth and her newborn son died with her. It appears that one or more of Berndt's other children died shortly after this letter was written. Berndt had studied in Wittenberg for some time and had received his master's degree there in 1528, and hence Luther knew the man to whom he addressed this consolation. [Text in Latin; *WA, Br*, VI, 279-281.]

Grace and peace.

My dear Ambrose:

I am not so inhuman that I cannot appreciate how deeply the death of Margaret distresses you. For the great and godly affection which binds a husband to his wife is so strong that it cannot easily be shaken off, and this feeling of sorrow is not so displeasing to God, if only it be held in check, since it is an expression of what God has assuredly implanted in you. Nor would I account you a man, to say nothing of a good husband, if you could at once throw off your grief.

Nevertheless, my dear Ambrose, I allow your mourning only in so far as it is not contrary to the will of God. For it is necessary to put a limit to one's sorrow and grief. Wherefore you ought to reflect in this manner: You are at first wretched in this world because your wife and son have been taken away. No hurt so painful as this can befall a man in his domestic life. It is especially so in your case because you had a wife who was furnished with such uncommon gifts, who was so accommodating to you in all respects, who was so modest and adorned with the best manners, and, what is most important, who was able in an unusual degree to delight your heart and move your soul with pleasant and Christian conversation. And I know for certain that nothing makes you more wretched than the realization that she was a gentle spirit who was well suited to your temperament.

On the other hand, you must also reflect on the fact that this very death of your wife ought to make you exceedingly happy before God inasmuch as she died in childbirth, that is, in the performance of her God-given duty and in the exercise of her proper calling. Moreover, she did this with a resolute spirit and a firm faith in Christ. Knowing that she was facing death, she confessed him again and again, called upon Christ alone, and, offering herself wholly to God, was resigned to his will. In addition, it is to be reckoned a singular blessing that she was graciously enabled by God, amid her great suffering, to bear you a son, John, who was baptized and then buried together with his mother.[32]

You should give careful thought to these two things. If you compare physical with spiritual gifts, you will certainly come to the conclusion that spiritual gifts are greater than physical ones. Occupy yourself with these thoughts unceasingly and control your grief as much as you can. Comfort yourself with the Word of God, the pre-eminent consolation. Learn too to thank God for the spiritual gifts which he gave your wife, Margaret. At the same time pray that our common Father may allow you and all of us to die in faith in Jesus Christ.

Yours,
Martin Luther.

TABLE TALK RECORDED BY JOHN SCHLAGINHAUFEN.[33] Spring, 1532

I know that God's mercy is greater than your tragedy. Of course, you have cause to mourn, but it is not so bad as you

[32] That is to say, it would have been a greater misfortune if the child had not been born and baptized.

[33] Macaronic text; *WA, TR,* II, No. 1361. In one version this table talk is entitled "Consolation to Master Ambrose Berndt on the death, within a week, of his wife, his children, and their mother." Cf. *WA, TR,* I, No. 987.

make it. There is sweet sugar mingled with the bitter vinegar. Your wife is well off. She is now with Christ. She has taken the leap. Would that I too had already done so! I should not long to be back here again. Do not look only at the vinegar; consider the sugar too. Behold the calamities which have befallen others —calamities that are all vinegar and no sugar, disastrous cases like those of Zwingli,[34] Münzer,[35] and others. Your sufferings are only earthly ones.

Your wife had a good death. She has left you the sweet memory of her walk and conversation here. Let this comfort you. Show by this affectionate memory of yours that you were a good husband and that you have not forgotten her.

You are a good dialectician. You teach this art to others. Put it to use now and make fine divisions, distinctions, conclusions. Learn to distinguish the spiritual from the earthly. Compare your tragedy with that of others, etc.

TO THOMAS ZINK. April 22, 1532

John Zink was matriculated as a student in Wittenberg in October, 1530, and was recorded as coming from Königsberg, in Franconia. He must have been quite young, for he sang soprano at the musical evenings in Luther's home. At the end of March, 1532, he took to his bed with a serious illness, and he died on April 20. Here Luther consoles the boy's father and mother.[36] [Text in German; WA, Br, VI, 300-302.]

Grace and peace in Christ, our Lord.

My dear Friend:

By this time I trust that you will have learned that your dear son, John Zink, whom you sent here to study, was overtaken by a grave illness and, although nothing was spared in the way of care, attention, and medicine, the disease got the upper hand and carried him off to heaven, to our Lord Jesus Christ. We were all very fond of the boy, who was especially dear to me because I had him in my home many an evening for singing. He was quiet, well-behaved, and diligent in his studies. Accordingly we are all deeply distressed by his death. If it had

---

34 Huldreich Zwingli died in battle on Oct. 11, 1531. Luther did not approve of his political activities.

35 A leader of the peasants in the Peasants' War, Thomas Münzer was captured and beheaded on May 27, 1525.

36 See also the account in *WA, TR*, I, No. 249.

been possible, we should have been glad to save and keep him. But God loved him even more and desired to have him.

It is only natural that your son's death and the report of it should distress and grieve you and your dear wife, his parents. I do not blame you for this, for all of us, and I in particular, are stricken with sorrow. Yet I admonish you that you should much rather thank God for giving you such a good, pious son and for deeming you worthy of all the pains and money you have so well invested in him. But let this be your best comfort, as it is ours, that he fell asleep (rather than departed) decently and softly with such a fine testimony of his faith on his lips that we all marveled. There can be as little doubt that he is with God, his true Father, in eternal blessedness, as there can be doubt that the Christian faith is true. Such a beautiful Christian end as his cannot fail to lead heavenward.

In addition, you should also consider how grateful you ought to be that, unlike many others, he did not have a perilous and pitiful death. Even if he had lived a long time, you could not, with your means, have helped him to anything higher than some sort of office or service. And now he is in a place which he would not exchange for all the world, even for a moment. Grieve in such a way, therefore, as to console yourselves. For you have not lost him, but have only sent him on ahead of you to be kept in everlasting blessedness. Saint Paul says that we should not mourn over the departed, over those who have fallen asleep, like the heathen.[37]

I shall see to it that Master Veit Dietrich, your son's preceptor, writes down for you some of the beautiful words which your son uttered before his death. They will please and comfort you.

I have not wished to omit writing these lines to you out of love for the godly boy in order that you may have a reliable report of what happened to him. Christ, our Lord and Comforter, allow me to commit you to his grace. Amen.

> Dr. Martin Luther, written with my own
> hand although I too am weak.

TO LAWRENCE ZOCH. November 3, 1532

Lawrence Zoch had been chancellor to the archbishop of Magdeburg. In 1527 he was accused of heresy on the ground that he sympathized with his wife's refusal to receive the Sacrament in one kind. When it

[37] Cf. I Thess. 4:13.

developed that he had been converted to Luther's views, he was imprisoned. Upon release he entered the service of the elector of Saxony and became professor of law in Wittenberg. His first wife, Clara, nee Preusser, died in 1532, and this death was the occasion for the letter of consolation that follows. Subsequently Zoch married a daughter of Jerome Schurf, Wittenberg jurist. [Text in German; *WA, Br,* VI, 382, 383.]

God's grace and peace in Christ be your comfort and strength. Amen.

My dear Doctor and special Friend:

It is with heartfelt sorrow that I learn of the great misfortune and grief that has come to you. As your letter indicates, God has taken your dear wife in such a way as to make it very hard to bear.

And yet God's Son had not only to endure the hatred and persecution of the devil and the evil world, but, as Isaiah says, he had also to be "smitten of God, and afflicted,"[38] and as Ps. 22 says, "I am a worm, and no man."[39] So it must be with us Christians too. What must distress us most is that God himself seems to be smiting us; yet it is from him that all our comfort is to come. On the other hand, the godless rise to such heights that it seems as if they were loved and exalted not only by this world, but by God himself. Consequently they can doubly boast, and we must doubly sorrow.

Thus it appears as if God himself has now attacked you, and your enemies can boast and say, "So fare these Christians; this is the reward of your new gospel." This is more than suffering and dying; it is being buried and descending into hell.

But, my dear doctor, be steadfast. This is the time for firmness. Remember that Christ also had this experience, and even worse. But God, who seemed to be assailing him, did not forsake him, but raised him up in honor. So God will also raise us up with him.

It is, indeed, a great comfort that your good wife died with all her senses and in such a Christian way, and that she is undoubtedly gone to Christ, her Master, whom she confessed here. But it is a far greater comfort that Christ has made you a type of himself and that you are suffering as he suffered—that is, punished and confounded not only at the devil's hands, but also as if by God himself, who is and wishes to be your comfort.

Therefore, although your flesh murmurs and cries out, as

[38] Isa. 53:4.   [39] Ps. 22:6.

Christ also cried out in his weakness,[40] your spirit ought to be ready and willing and ought to cry with groanings that cannot be uttered, "Abba, dear Father,"[41] that is to say, "Thy rod is sharp, but thou wilt always be Father; that I know very well."

Our dear Lord and Saviour, who is also the model of all our sufferings, comfort you and stamp himself upon your heart that you may offer him this sacrifice of a broken spirit[42] and give him your Isaac willingly.[43] Amen.

Sunday after All Saints', 1532.   Martin Luther, Doctor.

TO BENEDICT PAULI. June, 1533

An early print of this document bears the title "Consolation of Dr. Martin Luther Addressed to a Certain Distinguished Man on the Death of His Only Son in the Year 1533." In some editions of Luther's works it was taken to be a letter of consolation, but it is now clear that these words were delivered orally rather than in writing and were recorded by Veit Dietrich "as they fell from Luther's lips in the home of Dr. Benedict," as Dietrich himself wrote. The words were addressed to Benedict Pauli (1490-1552), a jurist and burgomaster in Wittenberg, on the death by accident of his first, and at the time only, son. [Macaronic text; WA, TR, I, No. 949.]

The Scriptures do not prohibit mourning and grieving over deceased children. On the contrary, we have many examples of godly patriarchs and kings who mournfully bewailed the death of their sons. Nevertheless, there ought to be a certain moderation in our grief.

Consequently you do well that you mourn for your son, but at the same time you ought to leave room for consolation. And this consolation is that the Lord gave you and now has taken away your son.[44] You cannot withstand him, and so you ought rather to imitate Job, who, when he lost his goods and his children, said, "Shall we receive good [at the hand of God, and shall we not receive evil]?"[45] He rightly contemplated both the good and the evil and made a comparison between the good things which he had received from the Lord and the evil things which had happened to him. You should do likewise, and you will discover that you have received and have more and much greater good things from the Lord than the evil you now experience. But at the present time your eyes are fixed only on the

40 Cf. Matt. 27:46.   41 Cf. Rom. 8:26, 15.   42 Cf. Ps. 51:17.
43 Cf. Gen. 22:1–14.   44 Cf. Job 1:21.   45 Job 2:10.

evil—that is, that your son died the kind of death he did when he plunged from the top of the house and was carried away lifeless—and accordingly you forget the great and most excellent goods and gifts of God, namely, that you have a knowledge of the Word, that you have Christ's favor, and that you have a good conscience. These things are in and of themselves such a great treasure that they deservedly surpass all the other evils that can have befallen you. No one who has not experienced it can believe how great a cross it is to have a bad conscience, which is death itself and hell. Since, therefore, you have a good conscience, why should you grieve so much over the death of your son?

We concede, of course, that the evil that has befallen you is a very grave one. However, it is not something new and it is not something that has happened to you alone. Many of your friends have experienced this evil. Abraham had more and greater grief from his son while he was living than you have from your son now that he is dead, for Abraham was commanded by the Lord to slay with his own hand that son of his in whose seed all peoples were to be blessed.[46] How do you think he felt when he grasped the sword to kill his son? Jacob suffered infinite grief when it was reported to him that his beloved son Joseph had been torn to pieces by wild beasts.[47] Finally, what father was ever more grieved than David was when he learned that his son Absalom, for whom he bore a unique love, would drive him out of his kingdom?[48] No doubt it seemed to him that his heart would melt like wax. If you reflect on these and similar examples, you will understand that your misfortune is not at all to be compared with even a part of the misfortune and grief of those men, and by this comparison your own grief will be greatly relieved and lightened.

But you will say, "Yes, but my only son is dead, and by what manner of death!" Why do you torment yourself so much about this? God is omnipotent. He who has given you one son can also give you more. And even if he were not to give you another son and, in addition, you were to lose your wife, your fortune, and all that you have, you ought nevertheless not to grieve so much, for you still have the favor of Christ, a Heavenly Father who is gracious to you through him, and many spiritual gifts which remain safe and everlasting even after we die.

"But," you will say, "he died such a horrible death!" As if every kind of death were not terrible because death is horrible

46 Gen., ch. 22.   47 Gen. 37:34.   48 II Sam, chs. 15;18.

to human nature, and especially to those who have no God. To us, however, who are children of God the tragic image of death should be pleasant because we have a God who consoles us by saying, "Because I live, ye shall live also."[49]

Are you afraid, then, that the Lord took your son in wrath? Such an opinion is not from God. But this would be hitting it right: Certainly it is the good will of God that your son should die, although human nature cries out against this and imagines that God is angry. It is characteristic of our human nature to think that what we wish is best and what God does is unsatisfactory to us. But it would not be good if our will were always done because we would then become too sure of ourselves. It is enough for us that we have a gracious God. Why he permits this or that evil to befall us should not trouble us at all.

TO JOHN REINECK. April 18, 1536

A boyhood schoolmate of Luther, John Reineck was superintendent of a foundry in Mansfeld, Thuringia, at the time of his wife's death. This loss was the occasion for the following letter of consolation. [Text in German; *WA, Br,* VII, 399, 400.]

Grace and peace in Christ, our Lord and Saviour.

Honored Sir and good Friend:

I have learned that our dear Lord and Father has afflicted you by taking your dear wife unto himself. It is natural that on account of your love this should grieve you sorely, and I am heartily sorry for you since I am favorably inclined to you for many reasons and have a friendly and good will toward you.

How should we conduct ourselves in such a situation? God has so ordered and limited our life here that we may learn and exercise the knowledge of his very good will so that we may test and discover whether we love and esteem his will more than ourselves and everything that he has given us to have and love on earth. And although the inscrutable goodness of the divine will is hidden (as is God himself) from the old Adam as something so great and profound that man finds no pleasure in it, but only grief and lamentation, we nevertheless have his holy and sure Word which reveals to us this hidden will of his and gladdens the heart of the believer. For it is written everywhere in the Scriptures that when he chastises his children, he does so out of pure grace and not wrath. So Saint James says that we

[49] John 14:19.

should count it all joy when we fall into divers tribulations,[50] for tribulation works patience, and patience, experience.[51] Since you have abundant knowledge of the Word of God, therefore, I hope that you will know how to put it into practice so that you will find more pleasure in God's grace and Fatherly will than you will have pain from your loss.

If we are sure of God's grace, everything will be well with us, even if, like Job, we lose all that we have. Although the old Adam is reluctant and unwilling to act like Job, the spirit is willing and praises God's will and activity in our sorrow and suffering. We must put up with and allow ourselves to be burdened by our old carcass until the last day, when we shall lay aside our carnal, rotten flesh and become entirely spiritual flesh.

I have wished to write this hasty note to you because you are one of my best friends, and I hope that our dear Lord Christ will be with you in his Holy Spirit and comfort you better than I can. For he has begun a good work in you and called you to his Word. He will not withdraw his blessing from you or forsake you.

It should also be a great comfort to you that your wife departed this vale of tears with so many graces and in so Christian and fine a way. Thereby God indicates in a tangible way that he deals with you in pure grace and not in wrath. An affectionate wife is the greatest treasure on earth, but a blessed end is a treasure above all treasures and an everlasting comfort.

God help us that we too may leave our sinful carcasses in like fashion and proceed from this wretchedness to our home and fatherland. The grace of Christ be with you forever. Amen.

Your willing servant,

Tuesday after Easter, 1536.   Martin Luther.

TO JOHN VON TAUBENHEIM. January 10, 1539

John von Taubenheim was chamberlain in Prussia, and on the death of his wife, Margaret, Luther wrote him the following letter of consolation. [Text in German; *WA, Br*, VIII, 352-354.]

To the gracious and esteemed John von Taubenheim, collector of revenues, my gracious, kind, dear sir and friend: grace and peace in Christ.

---

[50] Cf. James 1:2.   [51] Rom. 5:3,4. The quotation in Latin.

Gracious and dear Sir, kind and dear Friend:

It has come to my attention that our dear Lord God has again allowed his rod to fall upon you and has taken your dear wife unto himself. Truly, I am heartily sorry for you on account of your loss and grief. For I know that your sentiments are very different from those of the loose fellows who are happy to see their wives dead, and I think that I know you very well to be one who is not hostile to Christ, who loves his Word and Kingdom, and who dislikes all vice and dishonor, as I have had occasion to experience. In short, I esteem you a godly man about whom I am not mistaken, even as you consider me a godly man, and God grant that you are not mistaken. My situation is different from that of a man who deals with important matters in the world, and consequently I should sin more gravely if God were to withhold his help. Since I know that you are not God's enemy, he cannot be your enemy, for he has first enabled you not to be his enemy, and he has loved you before you have loved him,[52] which is the case with all of us.

Therefore, let the rod of your dear Father so smart that you find much greater comfort in his gracious and Fatherly will toward you. In the struggle with your grief let the peace of God, which passes all understanding,[53] keep the victory, even if the flesh gags and grumbles. I am aware that, instructed by God's Word without my counsel, you yourself know that the peace of God is not a matter of the five senses or of the understanding but goes beyond these and is a matter of faith. Our dear Lord Jesus Christ be with you.

God knows, and I hope that you have no doubt, that I am kindly disposed toward you and love you with all my heart. To be sure, I am nothing and am not worth anything at all now, yet Christ must have such a poor and rusty instrument and suffer me to occupy a corner of his Kingdom. God grant that I may be and remain such an instrument.

I pray too that you commend yourself to my dear friend the tax collector[54] and that, if he needs your favor and help, you will be kind to him, for I have not hitherto known him to be anything but a very upright man. But envy and hate offend God and crucify his Son. The world is not only the devil's but the devil himself. The prefect[55] has always been a great danger to us despite our good words. If I encounter him, he shall hear

[52] Cf. I John 4:19.   [53] Cf. Phil. 4:7.
[54] Wolfgang Schieferdecker, of Wittenberg.
[55] John Metzsch; see also Chapter IX.

this from my own lips. But it is reported that he has left.[56] Whether this is true or not, things cannot continue as they are.

My Katie sends cordial greetings, bitterly laments your misfortune, and says that if God did not love you so much or if you were a papist, he would not allow you to suffer such a loss. He torments his own here, but spares them in the world to come, as Saint Peter says.[57]

Herewith I commit you to God's keeping.

Friday after the Three Kings, 1539.   Martin Luther.

TO CATHERINE METZLER. July 3, 1539

John Metzler, a teacher in Breslau, had died on October 2, 1538, and about eight months later a son of his, Kilian, who had just matriculated in the university in Wittenberg in December, 1538, also died. According to Philip Melanchthon[58] the boy had been sick only nine days. "At first he had jaundice, which is not fatal, and the physicians and I had good hopes of his recovery. Then colic set in, and this in turn was followed by epilepsy, which he was not able to overcome since he was by nature very frail." In the following letter Luther consoled the widow, Catherine, nee Auer, on the death of her son. [Text in German; WA, Br, VIII, 484, 485.]

To the honorable and virtuous Mrs. Catherine Metzler, citizen in Breslau, my gracious and good friend: grace and peace in Christ.

Honored, virtuous, dear Lady:

I could not refrain from writing to you and, in so far as God enables me, sending you these lines of comfort since I can well imagine that the cross which God has now laid upon you through the death of your beloved son sorely oppresses and hurts you. It is natural and right that you should grieve, especially for one who is of your own flesh and blood. For God has not created us to be without feeling or to be like stones or sticks, but it is his will that we should mourn and bewail our dead. Otherwise it would appear that we had no love, particularly in the case of members of our own family.

However, our grief should be moderate, for our dear Father is testing us here to see whether we can fear and love him in sorrow as well as in joy and whether we can give back to him

---

[56] Early in 1539 he was removed to Kolditz.

[57] Cf. II Peter 2:9; 3:7.

[58] Melanchthon's letter to Catherine Metzler is reproduced in *WA, Br*, VIII, 486.

what he has given us in view of his intention to give us something more and better. I pray you, therefore, that you acknowledge the gracious and good will of God and that you patiently bear this cross for his sake, remembering in fervent faith what a cross it was that he himself bore for you and for all of us, a cross in comparison with which our crosses are light or as nothing.

This too should comfort you, that your son was a well-behaved and godly boy, a good Christian who had a blessed departure from this wretched world, and so it appears that God was well disposed toward him and perhaps wished to protect and save him from greater evil. For we are living in such perilous and evil times that all of us may well say with Elijah and Jonah, "It is better for me to die than to live."[59] Let those mourn whose children die a shameful death and go to the devil. That is heartache such as David suffered at the hands of his son Absalom. But your son is with the Lord Christ, in whom he fell asleep. Thank the God of grace for taking your child unto himself so graciously. This is better for him than occupying a high station in the court of an emperor or king. God, the Father of all comfort,[60] abundantly strengthen your faith with his Spirit. Amen.

Thursday after the Visitation of Mary, 1539.   Martin Luther.

TABLE TALK RECORDED BY ANTHONY LAUTERBACH.[61] July 16, 1539

On that day the very virtuous matron Dr. Bleikard's[62] wife died in childbirth. She arose from her husband's bed in good health at five o'clock in the morning, and at seven o'clock, after having given birth to a daughter, she was dead. Dr. Martin Luther went there to console the husband. Then when he had returned to his home he said that the physical separation of two married persons who dearly love each other is exceedingly sad. "Our God," he said, "is the greatest breaker of marriages.[63] He joins

---

[59] I Kings 19:4; Jonah 4:3.   [60] Cf. II Cor. 1:3.
[61] Macaronic text; WA, TR, IV, No. 4709.
[62] Bleikard Sindringer was a jurist.
[63] *Unser Herre Gott ist der gröste Ehebrecher.* Etymologically the word *Ehebrecher*, adulterer, means breaker of marriage(s). It appears that Luther sometimes liked to shock his table companions, as when he also referred to Jesus as an adulterer (in the estimation of contemporary opponents, WA, TR, II, No. 1472), or when he asserted that preachers are the greatest murderers (because they exhort magistrates to punish the wicked, WA, TR, III, No. 2911).

people together and then separates them. This morning she slept with her husband, and tonight she sleeps with our Lord God. How fleeting is our life! Alas, it must be painful for a loving couple to be separated in this way!"

TO MRS. JOHN CELLARIUS. May 8, 1542

John Cellarius, or Kellner (1496-1542), served as instructor in Hebrew at Heidelberg and Leipzig before he adopted the Evangelical faith as a result of the disputation in Leipzig between Luther and John Eck (1519). He was pastor in Frankfurt and Bautzen before he was made the first superintendent (or bishop) in Dresden on the eve of his death. He died there on April 21, 1542, and the following letter of consolation was addressed to his widow. [Text in German; WA, Br, X, 63, 64.]

Grace and peace in Christ.

Honorable, virtuous, dear Lady:

I have learned with sorrow that God, our dear Father, has chastised you (and us too) with his rod in that he has taken away from you (and from us) that dear man, your husband, John Cellarius. This is a cause of grief to all of us, although we know that he is now enjoying a good and blessed rest.

Let this be your comfort: Your sorrow is not the greatest experienced by the children of men. There are many who suffer and endure a hundred times as much. And even if all our sufferings on earth were heaped together, they still would be as nothing when compared with those which the innocent Son of God suffered for us and for our salvation: for no death can be compared with the death of our Lord and Saviour Jesus Christ, through whose death we are all saved from eternal death.

Be therefore comforted in the Lord, who died for you and for us all, and who is worth more than we, our husbands, our wives, our children, and all that we possess. For we are the Lord's, whether we live or die,[64] are rich or poor, or whatever our condition may be. And if we are his, then he is ours, with all that he is and has. Amen.

I commend you to his grace. My Katie implores that God's comfort and grace may be yours.

Monday after Cantate, 1542.   [Martin Luther.]

64 Cf. Rom. 14:8.

TO JUSTUS JONAS. December 26, 1542

Because of the intimate relationship that existed between the Luther family and the Jonas family, news of the death of Justus Jonas' wife, Catherine, nee Falk, came as a shock to the Reformer and his wife. This was especially so because the death came suddenly, presumably as a result of complications connected with childbirth. Jonas wrote to Philip Melanchthon that his wife's last words to him were, "I should like to have borne you a child, for I know that you love children." [Text in Latin; *WA, Br*, X, 226-228.]

To the distinguished and excellent gentleman, Justus Jonas, doctor of theology, ambassador of Christ in Halle, Saxony, dean in Wittenberg,[65] my venerable brother in Christ: grace and peace in Christ, who is our consolation and salvation.

Beloved Jonas:

I have been so completely prostrated by the unexpected calamity which has befallen you that I do not know what to write. We have all sustained a loss in the death of the dearest companion of your life. Not only was she dear to me in truth, but her cheerful disposition was always a great comfort, especially because we knew that she shared all our joys and sorrows as if they were her own. It is indeed a bitter parting, for I had hoped that after I was gone she would be, among all women, the chief and best comforter for those whom I might leave behind. I am overwhelmed by sorrow when I think of her sweet spirit, her quiet manner, her faithful heart. Grief over the loss of a woman so distinguished by piety, nobility, modesty, and friendliness causes me anguish.

How you feel I can easily imagine from the effect that her death has had on me. Consolation is not to be found in the flesh at such a time as this. One must find it in the spirit, in the realization that she has gone on before us to Him who has called us all and who in his good time will take us from the misery and wickedness of this world unto himself. Amen.

You have good cause to mourn. But I pray that when you mourn you will be mindful of our common Christian lot: that although parting is very bitter according to the flesh, yet in the life beyond we shall be reunited and gathered in sweetest communion with Him who so loved us that he secured eternal life

---

65 Jonas had been dean (*Probst*) and professor in Wittenberg before he moved to Halle.

for us with his own blood and death. "If we be dead with him, we shall also live with him," as Saint Paul says.[66] And it is well with us as long as we fall asleep with sure confidence in the Son of God. This means truly that God's goodness and mercy extend beyond this life. What a gulf separates the Turks, Jews, and (what is worse) the papists and cardinals, Heinz and Mayence,[67] from this glory! Would that they could weep now in order that they might be spared weeping hereafter!

After mourning for a season, we shall enter into joy unspeakable,[68] where your Cathy and my Magdalene,[69] together with many others, have preceded us and daily call, admonish, and beckon us to follow. For who is not weary of the abominations of our world?—if it ought to be called a world and not a very hell of evils with which those Sodomites torment our souls and eyes day and night. And (as we read happened to Noah)[70] they grieve the Holy Spirit[71] so that he is displeased with the whole creation which, together with us, groans for its and our redemption with groanings which cannot be uttered.[72] He who knows and understands our groanings will shortly hear them. Amen.

I have desired to write these things to you, for I have no doubt that you are overwhelmed with the greatest grief. Distressed as I am on your account, I cannot write more at this time. My Katie was beside herself [when she heard the news], for she and your wife were as intimately united as if they were one soul. We pray that God will comfort your flesh. For your spirit has cause to rejoice when you reflect that this good and pious woman has been snatched from your side to enjoy eternal life in heaven. This you cannot doubt, for she fell asleep on Jesus' bosom with so many godly and blessed expressions of faith in him. It was in this way that my daughter also fell asleep, and this is my great and only consolation.

May the Lord, who has suffered you to be humbled, comfort you again now and forever. Amen.

Yours,

Tuesday after the Nativity, 1542.   Martin Luther.

[66] II Tim. 2:11.
[67] *Heintz et Meintz*: a designation for opponents of the Reformation, which Luther used often. Cf. *WA*, LI, 579.
[68] I Peter 1:6, 8.
[69] Luther's daughter Magdalene had died in September, 1542.
[70] Gen. 6:5, 6.
[71] Eph. 4:30.
[72] Rom. 8:22, 26.

TO WOLF HEINZE. September 11, 1543

*During the pestilence which was raging in Halle and its environs at this
time, some six thousand people were reported to have died. Among them
was the wife of Wolf Heinze, organist in Halle, where Justus Jonas
was pastor. Since Jonas was visiting Wittenberg at this time, it is
probable that he learned of the death by courier and persuaded Luther to
write the following letter.* [Text in German; *WA, Br,* X, 394, 395.]

To the honorable and excellent Wolf Heinze, organist in Halle,
etc.: grace and peace in Christ.

My dear Wolf Heinze:

Dr. Jonas informed me within the last hour that he received
word from Halle to the effect that your beloved Eva has gone
to God, her Father.

I can well imagine how painful this parting is to you, and I
assure you that I am deeply grieved for your sake. You know
how truly and faithfully I love you. I know too that God loves
you. And because you love his Son, Jesus, your loss moves me
deeply.

What, then, should we do? There is so much wretchedness
and woe in this life in order that we may learn how much
greater than anything here is that eternal wretchedness from
which the Son of God has redeemed us. In him we have our
most precious treasure, and although everything temporal (including ourselves) must pass away, he will remain ours forever.
Our dear Lord Christ, whom you love and whose Word you
honor, will comfort you and will cause this trial to turn out in
your best interest and to his glory.

Your dear wife is better off where she is than she would be if
she were still with you. God help you and all of us to have a
blessed end, although this cannot and should not happen without mourning. But leave the weeping to that scoundrel in
Mayence[73] and to those who are of his kind; they are the people
who are really wretched.

Herewith I commit you to God's keeping. Amen.

Martin Luther, Doctor.

Tuesday after the Nativity of Mary, 1543.

TO MRS. GEORGE SCHULZ. October 8, 1544

*After completing his studies in the university in Wittenberg, where he
was matriculated in 1515, George Schulz remained in Wittenberg for*

[73] Cardinal Albert of Mayence.

*some time before moving to Freiberg, in Saxony, where he died. The
following is a letter of consolation to his widow.* [Text in German;
WA, Br, X, 663, 664.]

To the honorable and virtuous woman, Eva, Master George
Schulz's widow, my good and kind friend: grace and peace in
the Lord.

I am deeply grieved at your misfortune. I can well believe
that such parting is painful to you. In fact, it would not be well
if it were not so, for that would be a sign that your love is cold.

On the other hand, it should be a great comfort to you, first
of all, that your husband's departure was so Christian and
blessed, and, in the second place, that you know it to be the
will of God, our dear Father, who gave his Son for us. How
fitting it is, then, that we should sacrifice our own will to his, in
his service and according to his pleasure! This is not only our
duty, but great and eternal blessing will also come from it.
May he, our dear Lord Jesus Christ, abundantly comfort you
with his Spirit. Amen.

I thank you for the mining shares.[74] You really should not
have sent them. Inasmuch as I am inexperienced in such
matters, I shall consult some good friends for their advice.

Herewith I commit you to the keeping of the dear Lord.
Wednesday after Saint Francis.   Martin Luther, Doctor.

TO GEORGE HOESEL. December 13, 1544

*Three months before this letter was written, Jerome Hösel had enrolled
as a student in the university in Wittenberg. He was taken with a fever,
died on December 10, 1544, and was buried the following day. Luther
undertook the sad task of informing the young man's father, who was a
mine clerk in Marienberg.[75]* [Text in German; *WA, Br,* X, 698,
699.]

The grace and comfort of God through his only-begotten Son,
Jesus Christ, our Saviour, be with you.

Gracious, honored, prudent Sir:

Although I am reluctant to inform you of the sad news that
your dear son Jerome departed this life in accordance with
God's will, necessity requires that this be done. I pray that as

74 *Kuckus,* i.e., *Kuxen.*
75 A Latin superscription reads: "To George Hösel, mine clerk in Marienberg."

a Christian man you will consider what our Saviour, Jesus Christ, said: "Even so it is not the will of your Father which is in heaven, that one of these little ones should perish."[76] Inasmuch as Christ here clearly asserts that this young man, who had a knowledge of God and was in the Church, is acceptable to God and is not to perish, and inasmuch as Christ indicates that "in heaven their angels do always behold the face of my Father which is in heaven,"[77] you must have no doubt that your son is rejoicing with our Saviour, Christ, and with all the saints.

I too am a father, and I have lived to see several of my own children die.[78] I have also experienced other adversities which are worse than death. I know that these things are painful. However, we must resist these pains and comfort ourselves with the knowledge of eternal salvation. God wishes us to love our children and to mourn when they are taken from us. But our sorrow should be temperate and not too severe. Our faith in eternal salvation should be our comfort.

With respect to your son's illness you should know that he was laid low by a fever which caused the death of several others in recent times, including a competent young man from Lüneburg and another from Strasbourg.[79] This happened despite the fact that the physicians took excellent care of your son.

May the eternal Father of our Lord Jesus Christ help to comfort and strengthen you now and forever.

December 13, 1544.   Martin Luther.

TO CASPAR HEYDENREICH. April 24, 1545

Caspar Heydenreich, who had been a table companion in Luther's home shortly before this, was now chaplain at the court, in Freiberg, of Duchess Catherine of Saxony. While he was away from home a son was born to him and died almost immediately. Luther wrote to console him. [Text in Latin; WA, Br, XI, 75, 76.]

Grace and peace in the Lord.

My beloved Caspar:

I hear that you had a little son and that, while you were absent, he was not only born but also died. It is said that you

---

[76] Matt. 18:14.   [77] Matt. 18:10.   [78] See Chapter I above.
[79] An unidentified student from Lüneburg died at the end of July or August, and at the end of October, Theobald Fontanus, of Strasbourg, also died.

are deeply distressed by this because you did not even get to see the fruit of your flesh.

Lay aside your sorrowing. Rejoice, rather, because he was reborn in Christ[80] and because you will see him in glory whom you have not seen here in this wretched world. It is as the Wise Man said: "He was snatched away, lest wickedness should change his understanding. Being made perfect in a little while, he fulfilled long years."[81] But all these things are known to you, for you are obliged and are able to instruct others in them.

However, there is nothing disgraceful about your being moved somewhat by the natural, carnal affection of a father. The term "father" is in itself one of sweet affection. For we are not stones, nor ought we to be. But moderation is necessary in these things.[82]

Farewell in Christ.

The eighth day before the Kalends of May.   [Martin Luther.]

TO ANDREW OSIANDER. June 3, 1545

In 1537, the year in which his first wife died, Andrew Osiander (1498-1552) had remarried. His second wife, the former widow Helen Künhofer, died about the same time as a daughter of Osiander, and this double tragedy evoked the following letter of consolation from Luther. [Text in Latin; WA, Br, XI, 113, 114.]

To the illustrious gentleman, Dr. Andrew Osiander, faithful and true servant of God in the church at Nuremberg, my reverend brother and excellent sir: grace and peace in Christ, who is our consolation and is altogether ours, even as we are altogether his, for, as Saint Paul says, "Whether we live or die, we are the Lord's."[83]

Excellent and beloved Osiander:

We have heard that you have again been visited by a cross, and indeed a twofold cross, through the death of your wife and of your dearly loved daughter. I know from the death of my own dearest child[84] how great must be your grief. It may appear strange, but I am still mourning the death of my dear Magdalene, and I am not able to forget her. Yet I know surely that she is in heaven, that she has eternal life there, and that God has thereby given me a true token of his love in having, even

---

80 I.e., because he was baptized.   81 W. of Sol. 4:11, 13.
82 Cf. Horace, *Satires*, I, i, 106.   83 Rom. 14:8.
84 Magdalene Luther died September 20, 1542. See Chapter I.

while I live, taken my flesh and blood to his Fatherly heart. This love of which I speak is natural love,[85] which, although in itself good and human, must be crucified with us so that the good, acceptable, and perfect will of God may be done.[86] For God's Son, through whom and by whom all things were made,[87] gave his very life although this was neither deserved nor required of him.

I write this as a testimony, and I am sure that you share with me the belief that we are partakers together in your sufferings, even as God has made you a true and faithful participant in our faith and doctrine. Thus you must yield up your dear Isaac as a burnt offering[88] and for a sweet-smelling savor[89] to God—not your daughter or your wife, for these live and are blessed in the Lord, but that natural and strong affection which asserts itself too powerfully in us. While for the Lord this burnt offering is necessary, for us it is a consolation. But why should I try to explain these things to you when you understand them far better than I?

Farewell, and be assured that we love you.

Yours,

June 3, 1545.   Martin Luther.

[85] Written in Greek: *storge physike*.   [86] Cf. Rom. 12:2.
[87] Cf. John 1:3.   [88] Cf. Gen. 22:2.   [89] Cf. Eph. 5:2.

III

Cheer for the Anxious and Despondent

TO MRS. JOHN AGRICOLA. June 10, 1527

Probably on the same day as the following letter, Luther wrote to John Agricola (1494-1566), at the time head of the Latin school in Eisleben, to suggest that his wife return to Wittenberg for a visit for the sake of her health. "It seemed to us," Luther wrote, "that it would be good for your Elsa if she came here for a few days to breathe again the air to which she was accustomed. . . . We shall be glad to do for her whatever may in any way be of benefit to her."[1] [Text in German; *WA, Br,* IV, 210, 211.]

To the esteemed and virtuous Mrs. Elizabeth Agricola, wife of the schoolmaster in Eisleben, my dear friend: grace and peace.

My dear Elsa:

I intended to write you before, but Mr. Matthes[2] was gone before I got to it. I take it that by this time your schoolmaster is back home again and that, God willing, you feel better.

You must not be so fearful and downhearted. Remember that Christ is near and bears your ills, for he has not forsaken you, as your flesh and blood make you imagine. Only call upon him earnestly and sincerely and you will be certain that he hears you, for you know that it is his way to help, strengthen, and comfort all who ask him. So be of good cheer, and remember that he has suffered far more for you than you can ever suffer for his sake or your own. We too shall pray, and even now pray earnestly, that in his Son, Christ, God may be gracious to you and strengthen you in this your weakness of body and soul. Herewith I commit you to God's keeping. Amen.

[1] This letter in *WA, Br,* IV, 209, 210.
[2] The intended courier is not identifiable.

Greetings to your schoolmaster and your whole family from all of us.

Whitmonday, 1527. Martin Luther.

TO JOHN AGRICOLA. Beginning of July, 1527

John Agricola's wife accepted the invitation to Wittenberg (see above), and during her stay there Luther observed that her illness was more spiritual than physical in origin. [Text in Latin; *WA, Br*, IV, 219, 220.]

To John Agricola, servant of Christ in Eisleben, my friend in the Lord: grace and peace.

My dear Agricola:

I have been glad and willing to receive your Elsa here. Her illness is, as you see, more of the soul than of the body. I am comforting her as much as I know how to and can. You could have done the same thing except that in such circumstances a woman believes anybody else sooner than her own husband, for she thinks that everything her husband says is prompted by love rather than sound judgment.

In a word, her illness is not for the apothecaries (as they call them), nor is it to be treated with the salves of Hippocrates, but it requires the powerful plasters of the Scriptures and the Word of God. For what does conscience have to do with Hippocrates? Accordingly I should dissuade you from the use of medicine and recommend the power of God's Word. But such are our wives that they think the Word is not for them but only for us, their husbands, who are their guardians and protectors. Therefore, do not cease to impress it on her that when the Word of God is taught, whether you are present or absent, it has something to do with her. I have this same battle to fight all the time with my own Katie. Our wives must beware lest, when the time comes for using the Word, they may find to their sorrow that it fails them.

Otherwise everything is going well. Farewell in the Lord.

Martin Luther.

TO ELIZABETH VON CANITZ. August 22, 1527

One of the nine nuns who fled from the convent in Nimbschen in 1523,[3] Elizabeth von Canitz was visiting in Eicha, near Leipzig, when Luther

[3] See letter to George Spalatin, April 10, 1523, in Chapter VI.

wrote this letter to invite her to start a girls' school in Wittenberg. She refused, perhaps because she feared the plague which was rampant in Wittenberg at this time[4] or perhaps on account of the melancholy to which Luther referred here. [Text in German; *WA, Br,* IV, 236, 237.]

To the esteemed and virtuous Miss Elsa von Canitz, now in Eicha, my dear friend in Christ: grace and peace in Christ Jesus.

Honored, virtuous Miss Elsa:

I have written to your dear aunt, Hanna von Plausig, and asked her to send you to me for a time. I have in mind using you as a teacher for young girls and through you setting others an example in undertaking this work. You would live and board in my home, and thus you would run no risks and have nothing to worry about. I now ask you not to decline my invitation.

I hear too that the evil one is assailing you with melancholy. O my dear woman, do not let him terrify you, for whoever suffers from the devil here will not suffer from him yonder. It is a good sign. Christ also suffered all this, and so did many holy prophets and apostles, as the Psalter sufficiently shows. Be of good cheer, therefore, and willingly endure this rod of your Father. He will relieve you of it in his own good time. If you come, I shall talk to you further about the matter.

Herewith I commit you to God's keeping. Amen.

Thursday after Saint Agapitus, 1527.   [Martin Luther.]

TO JEROME WELLER. July, 1530

Turning from the study of law to the study of theology under Luther's influence, Jerome Weller (1499-1572) spent eight years, from 1527 to 1535, in almost daily contact with Luther, in whose home he lived and whose children he tutored. Later he was a teacher of theology in his native Freiberg, Saxony. His shyness and modesty made him particularly subject to fits of depression, and the following letter was addressed to him at such a time by Luther, who was absent from his home. [Text in Latin; *WA, Br,* V, 518-520.]

Grace and peace in Christ.

My dear Jerome:

You must believe that this temptation of yours is of the devil, who vexes you so because you believe in Christ. You see how

---

[4] See letter to George Spalatin, Aug. 19, 1527, in Chapter VIII.

contented and happy he permits the worst enemies of the gospel to be. Just think of Eck,[5] Zwingli,[6] and others. It is necessary for all of us who are Christians to have the devil as an adversary and enemy; as Saint Peter says, "Your adversary, the devil, walketh about."[7]

Excellent Jerome, you ought to rejoice in this temptation of the devil because it is a certain sign that God is propitious and merciful to you. You say that the temptation is heavier than you can bear, and that you fear that it will so break and beat you down as to drive you to despair and blasphemy. I know this wile of the devil. If he cannot break a person with his first attack, he tries by persevering to wear him out and weaken him until the person falls and confesses himself beaten. Whenever this temptation comes to you, avoid entering upon a disputation with the devil and do not allow yourself to dwell on those deadly thoughts, for to do so is nothing short of yielding to the devil and letting him have his way. Try as hard as you can to despise those thoughts which are induced by the devil. In this sort of temptation and struggle, contempt is the best and easiest method of winning over the devil. Laugh your adversary to scorn and ask who it is with whom you are talking. By all means flee solitude, for the devil watches and lies in wait for you most of all when you are alone. This devil is conquered by mocking and despising him, not by resisting and arguing with him. Therefore, Jerome, joke and play games with my wife and others. In this way you will drive out your diabolical thoughts and take courage.

This temptation is more necessary to you than food and drink. Let me remind you what happened to me when I was about your age. When I first entered the monastery it came to pass that I was sad and downcast, nor could I lay aside my melancholy. On this account I made confession to and took counsel with Dr. Staupitz (a man I gladly remember)[8] and opened to him what horrible and terrible thoughts I had. Then said he: "Don't you know, Martin, that this temptation is useful

[5] John Eck (1486–1543), a leading Catholic opponent of Luther.
[6] The Swiss Reformer, Huldreich Zwingli (1484–1531), had been locking horns with Luther over the interpretation of Holy Communion. See G. W. Bromiley, ed., *Zwingli and Bullinger* (Philadelphia, 1953), in The Library of Christian Classics.
[7] I Peter 5:8.
[8] Luther frequently referred with commendation to the help he received in the monastery from the Augustinian vicar-general John von Staupitz (d. 1524).

and necessary to you? God does not exercise you thus without reason. You will see that he intends to use you as his servant to accomplish great things." And so it turned out. I was made a great doctor (for I may with propriety say this of myself) although at the time when I suffered this temptation I never would have believed it possible. I have no doubt that this will happen to you too. You will become a great man. Just see to it that you are of good courage in the meantime, and be persuaded that such utterances, especially those which fall from the lips of learned and great men, are not without prophetic quality.

I remember that a certain man whom I once comforted on the loss of his son said to me, "Wait and see, Martin, you will become a great man."[9] I have often thought of these words, for, as I have said, such utterances have something of a prophetic quality. Be of good courage, therefore, and cast these dreadful thoughts out of your mind. Whenever the devil pesters you with these thoughts, at once seek out the company of men, drink more, joke and jest, or engage in some other form of merriment. Sometimes it is necessary to drink a little more, play, jest, or even commit some sin in defiance and contempt of the devil in order not to give him an opportunity to make us scrupulous about trifles. We shall be overcome if we worry too much about falling into some sin.

Accordingly if the devil should say, "Do not drink," you should reply to him, "On this very account, because you forbid it, I shall drink, and what is more, I shall drink a generous amount." Thus one must always do the opposite of that which Satan prohibits. What do you think is my reason for drinking wine undiluted, talking freely, and eating more often if it is not to torment and vex the devil who made up his mind to torment and vex me? Would that I could commit some token sin simply for the sake of mocking the devil, so that he might understand that I acknowledge no sin and am conscious of no sin. When the devil attacks and torments us, we must completely set aside the whole Decalogue.[10] When the devil throws our sins up to us and declares that we deserve death and hell, we ought to speak thus: "I admit that I deserve death and hell. What of it? Does this mean that I shall be sentenced to eternal damnation?

9 This story also appears in *WA*, *TR*, I, No. 223.
10 That is, turn from the Law to the Gospel. "The devil makes a law of the Gospel. The teachings of Law and Gospel are very necessary and are to be brought together, but with discrimination, lest men either despair or become complacent." *WA*, *TR*, III, No. 3799.

By no means. For I know One who suffered and made satisfaction in my behalf. His name is Jesus Christ, the Son of God. Where he is, there I shall be also."

Yours,

Martin Luther.

TABLE TALK RECORDED BY JOHN SCHLAGINHAUFEN.[11] December, 1531

Dr. Martin Luther said to Schlaginhaufen: "Our God is a God of the humble. He says, 'My strength is made perfect in weakness.'[12] If we were not weak, we should become too proud. He can manifest his power only in weakness. For the smoking flax he will not quench.[13] However, the devil desires not only that it burn with evil but that it be consumed altogether.

"God both loves and hates our afflictions. He loves them when they provoke us to prayer. He hates them when we are driven to despair by them. But it is written, 'Whoso offereth praise glorifieth me,[14] for the sacrifices of God are a broken spirit and a contrite heart.'[15] Therefore, if you are merry, sing psalms and praise God.[16] If you are sorrowful (that is, if temptations assail you), pray, for the Lord taketh pleasure in them that fear him and—this is the best of all!—in them that hope in his mercy.[17] The Lord helps those who are of low degree, for he says, 'The Lord's hand is not shortened, that it cannot save.'[18] There is a time of war and a time of peace,[19] a time of folly and a time of wisdom, a time of temptations and afflictions. And the Lord hears the gentle sighs of the afflicted."

I [Schlaginhaufen] held a Psalter in my hand and he [Luther] inquired whether I found pleasure in it. "Do you find joy or sorrow in it?" I replied, "I have often derived consolation from it, but then Satan comes and asks what the psalms have to do with me." He said, signing himself with the cross, " 'Whatsoever things were written aforetime were written for us that we through patience,'[20] etc. Abraham, Isaac, Jacob, the dear Joseph, Rebecca, and Leah have no idea whatsoever that we are today reading narratives about them. David does not know that we now have his psalms in Germany and that we

---

[11] Macaronic text; WA, TR, II, No. 1270. There is a parallel in WA, TR, I, No. 956.   [12] II Cor. 12:9.   [13] Cf. Isa. 42:3.
[14] Ps. 50:23.   [15] Ps. 51:17.   [16] Cf. James 5:13.
[17] Cf. Ps. 147:11.   [18] Isa. 59:1.   [19] Cf. Eccl. 3:8.
[20] Cf. Rom. 15:4.

find comfort in them even as he did long ago. The Lord helped David, who put his trust in God. So he will also aid us who hope in him, for his word is yea and amen."[21]

Dr. Martin said: "When you are assailed by a temptation, ask the devil, 'Devil, in what Commandment is this written?' And if he cannot show you, say, 'Begone, you wretch, and spare me your filthy talk.' "

He also said to me: "If these temptations do not let up, excommunicate them in the name of the Lord Jesus Christ and say: 'God has forbidden us to accept these coins of yours. They do not come from Hungary or Bohemia or Saxony but were struck by the devil.' Therefore, we are to refuse his coins and not accept them from him."

TABLE TALK RECORDED BY JOHN SCHLAGINHAUFEN.[22] Spring, 1532

Those who are assailed by doubts should be given plenty to eat and drink. Early this morning the devil was disputing with me concerning Zwingli,[23] and I discovered that a person who is well-fed is better fitted for disputation with the devil than a person who is fasting. Think, for example, of the bishop who, when his sister came to him troubled with such great thoughts that she could not free herself from them,[24] gave her plenty to eat and drink. Three days later he asked her how she felt.

"Very well," she replied.

"What has happened to the thoughts that before troubled you?"

"I have quite forgotten them," she answered.

Accordingly you should eat and drink and enjoy yourself. Those who are afflicted with spiritual temptations should be given plenty to eat and drink, but whoremongers and those assailed by lust should fast.

TO JONAS VON STOCKHAUSEN. November 27, 1532

In the early sixteenth century it was customary for a city or town to select a neighboring nobleman to serve as captain who, with his mounted

---

[21] Cf. II Cor. 1:20.　　　　[22] Macaronic text: *WA, TR*, II, No. 1299.
[23] The teachings of Huldreich Zwingli, who died in 1531.
[24] In using the same story on another occasion (*WA, TR*, II, No. 1349), Luther describes the bishop's sister as "being greatly afflicted with sadness of spirit."

knights, would police the community. Jonas von Stockhausen served the town of Nordhausen, in Thuringia, as such a captain between 1521 and 1532. In the latter year he asked to be relieved on account of illness. He was also afflicted with melancholy, and the letter that follows was written by Luther to offer advice. [Text in German; *WA, Br,* VI, 386-388.]

To the honorable and brave Jonas von Stockhausen, captain in Nordhausen, my kind lord and good friend: grace and peace in Christ.

Honored, brave, dear Lord and Friend:

Good friends have informed me that the evil one is tempting you severely with weariness of life and longing for death. My dear friend, it is high time that you cease relying on and pursuing your own thoughts. Listen to other people who are not subject to this temptation. Give the closest attention to what we say, and let our words penetrate to your heart. Thus God will strengthen and comfort you by means of our words.

At the outset you know that you should and must be obedient to God and carefully avoid disobedience to his will. Since you must be certain and must understand that God gives you life and does not now desire your death, your thoughts should yield to this divine will, be obedient to it, and not doubt that your thoughts, being in conflict with God's will, were forcibly inserted into your mind by the devil. Consequently you must resist them sternly and either suffer them or eradicate them with like force.

Our Lord Christ also found life to be unpleasant and burdensome, yet he was unwilling to die unless it was his Father's will. He fled from death, held onto life as long as he could, and said, "My time is not yet come."[25] Elijah, Jonah, and other prophets likewise found life unendurable, cried out in their agony for death, and even cursed the day on which they were born,[26] yet they had to fight against their weariness of life and continue to live until their hour had come. Such words and examples you must truly obey and imitate as words and admonitions from the Holy Ghost, and you must cast out and reject the thoughts that impel you to act otherwise.

And if it is hard for you to do this, imagine that you are held fast and bound by chains and that you must work and sweat yourself out of their strangle hold by powerful exertions. For the darts of the devil cannot be removed pleasantly and without effort when they are so deeply imbedded in your flesh. They

[25] John 7:6.   [26] Cf. I Kings 19:4; Jonah 4:3; Jer. 20:14.

must be torn out by force. Accordingly you must be resolute, bid yourself defiance, and say to yourself wrathfully: "Not so, good fellow. No matter how unwilling you are to live, you are going to live and like it! This is what God wants, and this is what I want too. Begone, you thoughts of the devil! To hell with dying and death! You will get nowhere with me," etc. Grit your teeth in the face of your thoughts, and for God's sake be more obstinate, headstrong, and willful than the most stubborn peasant or shrew—indeed, be harder than an anvil or piece of iron. If you impose such demands on yourself and fight against yourself in this way, God will assuredly help you. But if you do not resist and oppose, but rather give your thoughts free reign to torment you, the battle will soon be lost.

But the best counsel of all is this: Do not struggle against your thoughts at all, but ignore them and act as if you were not conscious of them. Think constantly of something else, and say: "Well, devil, do not trouble me. I have no time for your thoughts. I must eat, drink, ride, go, or do this or that." In like manner say: "I must now be cheerful. Come back tomorrow," etc. Undertake to do anything else that you are able—whether play or something else—just so that you free yourself from these thoughts, hold them in contempt, and dismiss them. If necessary, speak coarsely and disrespectfully, like this: "Dear devil, if you can't do better than that, kiss my toe, etc.[27] I have no time for you now." On this read the examples of the crackle of lice, the hissing of geese, and the like in Gerson's *De cogitationibus blasphemiae*.[28] This is the best counsel. In addition, our prayers and those of all godly Christians should and will also help you.

Herewith I commit you to the keeping of our dear Lord, the only Saviour and real Conqueror, Jesus Christ. May he keep his victory and triumph over the devil in your heart. May he cause all of us to rejoice in the help he gives you and the miracle he performs in you. We confidently hope and pray for this in accordance with his command and promise to us. Amen.

Martin Luther, Doctor.

Wednesday after Saint Catherine's, 1532.

TO MRS. JONAS VON STOCKHAUSEN.
November 27, 1532

In addition to the above letter to Jonas von Stockhausen, Luther wrote on the same day to the melancholy man's wife, indicating to her how she

[27] *Kanstu mir nicht neher [kommen], so lecke mich.*   [28] John Gerson (1363–1429).

might help her husband to get well. [Text in German; *WA, Br,* VI, 388, 389.]
To the honorable and virtuous Mrs. N. von Stockhausen, wife of the captain in Nordhausen, my kind and good friend: grace and peace in Christ.

Honored and virtuous Lady:
I have hastily written a note of consolation to your dear lord. The devil hates you both because you love Christ, his enemy. You must suffer for this, as he himself says: "Because I have chosen you, therefore the world and its prince hate you. But be of good cheer. Precious in the sight of the Lord are the sufferings of his saints."[29]

Since I am in great haste, I can write but little. Be very careful not to leave your husband alone for a single moment, and leave nothing lying about with which he might harm himself. Solitude is poison to him. For this reason the devil drives him to it. There is no harm in your reading or telling him stories, news, and curiosities, even if some of them are idle talk and gossip or fables about Turks, Tartars, and the like, as long as they excite him to laughter and jesting. Then quickly recite comforting verses from the Scriptures. Whatever you do, do not leave him alone, and be sure that his surroundings are not so quiet that he sinks into his own thoughts. It does not matter if he becomes angry about this. Act as if it were disagreeable to you and scold about it, but let it be done all the more.

This hasty note must suffice. Christ, who causes you such heartache, will help you, even as he has done recently. Only hold fast to him. You are the apple of his eye; whoever touches you touches him.[30] Amen.

Martin Luther, Doctor.
Wednesday after Saint Catherine's Day, 1532.

TO JOHN SCHLAGINHAUFEN. December 12, 1533

John Schlaginhaufen (d. 1560) was an Evangelical clergyman in the village of Werdau, near Zwickau in Saxony, for some years before he returned to Wittenberg to serve as assistant pastor. He was a frequent table companion in Luther's home and on many occasions complained of spiritual trials and temptations. He seems to have been a man of mercurial temperament, who fluctuated between depression and

29 Conflation, with variations, of John 15:19; 16:33, and Ps. 116:15.
30 Cf. Zech. 2:8.

cheerfulness. The following conversation concerns one of his periods of despondency. [Text in German; *WA, Br,* VI, 561.]

To the reverend gentleman in Christ, Mr. John Schlaginhaufen, pastor in Köthen, faithful minister of the Word, and my brother: grace and peace in Christ.

My dear Pastor:

Thank you for the medlars you sent me. I like these native fruits better than the ones imported from Italy. If they are somewhat harsh to the taste, at least they are ripe.

I am sorry to hear that you are still depressed at times. Christ is as near to you as you are to yourself, and he will not harm you, for he shed his blood for you. Dear friend, honor this good, faithful Man. Believe that he esteems and loves you more than does Dr. Luther or any other Christian. What you expect of us, expect even more of him. For what we do, we do at his command, but what he who commands us does, he does spontaneously and out of his own goodness.

Herewith I commit you and yours to God's keeping. Amen.

In haste,

The vigil of Saint Luke, 1533.   Martin Luther.

TO PRINCE JOACHIM OF ANHALT. May 23, 1534

Nicholas Hausmann, who had been warmly recommended by Luther to the prince of Anhalt two years before, was pastor in Dessau, where Prince Joachim was living. On a visit to Wittenberg, Hausmann informed Luther that his prince was afflicted with a fever and that his illness was aggravated by morbid depression. In counseling the prince, Luther gave clear expression to the quality of his own piety, which was free of the ascetic scrupulosity so often recommended in his day. [Text in German; *WA, Br,* VII, 65-67.]

Grace and peace in Christ.

Serene Prince, gracious Lord:

It has often occurred to me that almost all the members of Your Grace's family have been of a retiring, quiet, and sober nature,[31] and this has led me to conclude that Your Grace's illness may be caused by melancholy and dejection of spirit.

---

[31] Luther was probably thinking of Prince William of Anhalt, who became a begging friar in 1473 (cf. *WA, TR,* V, No. 6859), and of Prince Joachim's two paternal aunts, who became abbesses.

Therefore, I should like to encourage Your Grace, who are a young man, always to be joyful, to engage in riding and hunting, and to seek the company of others who may be able to rejoice with Your Grace in a godly and honorable way. For solitude and melancholy are poisonous and fatal to all people, and especially to a young man. Accordingly God has commanded us to be joyful in his presence; he does not desire a gloomy sacrifice. This is frequently asserted by Moses, and in Eccl., ch. 12, we read, "Rejoice, O young man, in thy youth; and let thy heart cheer thee."[32] No one realizes how much harm it does a young person to avoid pleasure and cultivate solitude and sadness.

Your Grace has Master Nicholas Hausmann and many others near at hand. Be merry with them; for gladness and good cheer, when decent and proper, are the best medicine for a young person—indeed, for all people. I myself, who have spent a good part of my life in sorrow and gloom, now seek and find pleasure wherever I can. Praise God, we now have sufficient understanding [of the Word of God] to be able to rejoice with a good conscience and to use God's gifts with thanksgiving, for he created them for this purpose and is pleased when we use them.

If I am mistaken in my judgment and have done Your Grace an injustice, I hope that Your Grace will be good enough to forgive me. But it is my opinion that Your Grace is reluctant to be merry, as if this were sinful. This has often been my case, and sometimes it still is. To be sure, to have pleasure in sins is of the devil, but participation in proper and honorable pleasures with good and God-fearing people is pleasing to God, even if one may at times carry playfulness too far.

Be merry, then, both inwardly in Christ himself and outwardly in his gifts and the good things of life. He will have it so. It is for this that he is with us. It is for this that he provides his gifts—that we may use them and be glad, and that we may praise, love, and thank him forever and ever.

Old age and other circumstances will in time render present depression and melancholy superfluous. Christ cares for us and will not forsake us. To his keeping I commit Your Grace forever. Amen.

Your Grace's willing [servant],

Martin Luther, Doctor.

The eve of Pentecost in the year 1534.

32 Eccl. 11:9.

TO PRINCE JOACHIM OF ANHALT. June 26, 1534

A month later Luther wrote again to Prince Joachim, whose condition had not changed for the better, and he promised to visit him when he had more leisure. [Text in German; *WA, Br*, VII, 78, 79.]

Grace and peace of mind, and also comfort and strength of body, from Christ Jesus, our dear Lord and comforting Saviour.

Gracious Prince and Lord:

Inasmuch as Master Francis[33] is again returning to Your Grace to entertain you, I have not wished to see him go without some word from me, even if I had nothing to write except "Good morning"[34] or "Good evening." I have every expectation that Your Grace's condition will improve, although improvement may be slow.

I am still offering up my poor prayers in behalf of Your Grace. Meanwhile I remember that when I was sick it sometimes took a longer time and sometimes a shorter time before I was helped, and that I received more help than I prayed for.

Of course, I am speaking of spiritual consolation, for earthly comfort is of no avail unless it is offered to awaken spiritual consolation. So Elisha was awakened by his minstrel,[35] and David himself declares in Ps. 57 that his harp was his pride and joy: "Awake up, my glory; awake, psaltery and harp."[36] And all the saints made themselves joyful with psalms and stringed instruments. Accordingly, I rejoice that Master Francis is returning to Your Grace, for he is a well-bred and decent man, who will be able to gladden Your Grace's heart with good and Christian conversation, singing, and other things.[37]

I offer Your Grace my best wishes and pray that Master Francis' services will help in the restoration of health and the rout of the tempter. Amen. Unless I die or am stricken beforehand, I too intend to visit Your Grace (this is certain) as soon as I can free myself from the hames, bridle, saddle, and spurs

---

33 Francis Burghard was a teacher of Greek in Wittenberg, who was made rector of the university in 1532. An intimate friend of Prince Joachim, he was later attracted to politics and in 1536 became vice-chancellor of Electoral Saxony.

34 This expression in Latin.

35 Cf. II Kings 3:15.

36 Ps. 57:8.

37 In his letter to Prince Joachim of June 12, 1534 (*WA, Br*, VII, 74), Luther refers to Francis Burkhard's skill as a chess player.

of the printers.[38] Herewith I commit Your Grace to God's keeping. Amen.

Friday after Saint John's Day, 1543. [Martin Luther.]

TABLE TALK RECORDED BY AN UNKNOWN HAND.[39]
1534

More and graver sins are committed in solitude than in the society of one's fellow men. The devil deceived Eve in paradise when she was alone. Murder, robbery, theft, fornication, and adultery are committed in solitude, for solitude provides the devil with occasion and opportunity. On the other hand, a person who is with others and in the society of his fellow men is either ashamed to commit a crime or does not have the occasion and opportunity to do so.

Christ promised, "Where two or three are gathered together in my name, there am I in the midst of them."[40]

Christ was alone when the devil tempted him. David was alone and idle when he slipped into adultery and murder. I too have discovered that I am never so likely to fall into sins as when I am by myself.

God created man for society and not for solitude. This may be supported by the argument that he created two sexes, male and female. Likewise God [founded the Christian Church, the communion of saints, and][41] instituted the Sacraments, preaching, and consolations in the Church.

Solitude produces melancholy. When we are alone the worst and saddest things come to mind. We reflect in detail upon all sorts of evils. And if we have encountered adversity in our lives, we dwell upon it as much as possible, magnify it, think that no one is so unhappy as we are, and imagine the worst possible consequences. In short, when we are alone, we think of one thing and another, we leap to conclusions, and we interpret everything in the worst light. On the other hand, we imagine that other people are very happy, and it distresses us that things go well with them and evil with us.

---

38 Luther was occupied with seeing the first edition of his translation of the complete Bible through the press; it appeared in this same year. Luther finally visited the prince with several friends from July 15 to July 19, and again from July 24 to July 28.

39 Macaronic text; WA, TR, IV, No. 4857 p. The date is uncertain.

40 Matt. 18:20.

41 Text in brackets from a variant version.

TO MATTHIAS WELLER. October 7, 1534

A brother of Jerome Weller, Matthias (1507-1563) was employed in the chancellery of Duke Henry of Saxony for many years. Contemporaries thought well of his musical gifts, and for a time he was organist in the cathedral church in Freiberg, Saxony. Luther therefore advised him to find solace in music when he suffered from a fit of melancholy. Luther also explained to him that the word of God comes to man in a variety of ways, among others through "the mutual conversation and consolation of brethren."[42] [Text in German; *WA, Br,* VII, 104-106.]

Grace and peace in Christ.

Honorable, kind, good Friend:

Your dear brother has informed me that you are deeply distressed and afflicted with melancholy. He will undoubtedly tell you what I have said to him.

Dear Matthias, do not dwell on your own thoughts, but listen to what other people have to say to you. For God has commanded men to comfort their brethren, and it is his will that the afflicted should receive such consolation as God's very own. Thus our Lord speaks through Saint Paul, "Comfort the fainthearted,"[43] and through Isaiah: "Comfort ye, comfort ye my people. Speak ye comfortably."[44] And elsewhere our Lord indicated that it is not his will that man should be downcast, but that he should rather serve the Lord with gladness[45] and not offer him the sacrifice of sorrow. All this Moses and the prophets declared often and in many places. Our Lord also commanded us not to be anxious,[46] but to cast our cares upon him, for he careth for us,[47] as Saint Peter taught from Ps. 55.[48]

Inasmuch, then, as God desires everyone to comfort his brother, and desires that such comfort be received with a believing heart, be done with your own thoughts. Know that the devil is tormenting you with them, and that they are not your thoughts but the cursed devil's, who cannot bear to see us have joyful thoughts.

Listen, then, to what we are saying to you in God's name: Rejoice in Christ, who is your gracious Lord and Redeemer. Let him bear your burdens, for he assuredly cares for you, even

---

[42] Cf. Luther's Smalcald Articles (1537), in Henry E. Jacobs, ed., *The Book of Concord,* 2 vols. (Philadelphia, 1883), I, 330.
[43] I Thess. 5:14. [44] Isa. 40:8, 9. [45] Cf. Deut. 28:47.
[46] Cf. Matt. 6:25. [47] Cf. I Peter 5:7. [48] Cf. Ps. 55:22.

if you do not yet have all that you would like. He still lives. Look to him for the best. This is the greatest sacrifice in his eyes, for as the Scriptures say,[49] no sacrifice is more pleasing and acceptable than a cheerful heart that rejoices in the Lord.

When you are sad, therefore, and when melancholy threatens to get the upper hand, say: "Arise! I must play a song unto the Lord on my regal[50] (be it the *Te Deum laudamus* or the *Benedictus*), for the Scriptures teach us that it pleases him to hear a joyful song and the music of stringed instruments." Then begin striking the keys and singing in accompaniment, as David and Elisha[51] did, until your sad thoughts vanish. If the devil returns and plants worries and sad thoughts in your mind, resist him manfully and say, "Begone, devil! I must now play and sing unto my Lord Christ."

In such fashion you must learn to oppose him and not permit him to put thoughts in your mind. If you allow one thought to enter, and you pay attention to it, he will force ten additional thoughts into your mind until at last he overpowers you. Therefore, the best thing you can do is to rap the devil on the nose at the very start. Act like that man who, whenever his wife began to nag and snap at him, drew out his flute from under his belt and played merrily until she was exhausted and let him alone. So you too must turn to your regal or gather some good companions about you and sing with them until you learn how to defy the devil.

If you are convinced that such thoughts come from the devil, you have already gained the victory. But since you are still weak in your faith, listen to us, who by God's grace know it, and lean on our staff until you learn to walk by yourself. And when good people comfort you, my dear Matthias, learn to believe that God is speaking to you through them. Pay heed to them and have no doubt that it is most certainly God's word, coming to you according to God's command through men, that comforts you.

May the same Lord who has told me these things, and whom I must obey, communicate all these things to you in your heart and enable you to believe them. Amen.

Martin Luther, Doctor.

Wednesday after Saint Francis, 1534.

[49] It is not apparent that Luther had any specific texts in mind.
[50] A portable organ, which in the sixteenth century consisted of a case enclosing reed pipes, with keys on one side and bellows on the other.
[51] Cf. II Kings 3:14, 15.

TO PRINCE JOACHIM OF ANHALT. December 25, 1535

The melancholy of Prince Joachim, which evoked two letters from Luther in 1534 (see above), was still not relieved. It appears from the following letter that the prince may also have been assailed by religious doubts. Luther begins this Christmas letter by reminding the prince of the comfort of the incarnation. [Text in German; *WA, Br*, VII, 335, 336.]

Our dear Lord Christ comfort Your Grace with his incarnation. He became incarnate to comfort and show his good will to all men, as the dear angels sing today, "Glory to God in the highest, and on earth peace, good will toward men."[52]

I trust that Your Grace will have no doubts or perplexities about the creed or the gospel inasmuch as Your Grace has now been well instructed in that which is the truth over against the lies of the devil and the pope. If we are satisfied with the creed and the doctrine, what does it matter even if hell and all the devils fall upon us? What can distress us—other, perhaps, than our sins and bad conscience? Yet Christ has taken these from us, even while we sin daily. Who can terrify us except the devil? But greater than the devil is He that is in us,[53] weak though our faith may be. Even if the devil were holy and sinless, *we* acknowledge that we are sinners. And even if the devil were so strong that he did not require Christ's help and strength, *we* need the dear Saviour. We must be weak, and are willing to be, in order that Christ's strength may dwell in us; as Saint Paul says, "Christ's strength is made perfect in weakness."[54]

Your Grace has not yet betrayed or crucified the dear Lord. Even if Your Grace had, Christ nevertheless remains gracious. He prayed even for those who crucified him. Therefore, be of good cheer. In the strength of Christ resist the evil spirit, who can do no more than trouble, terrify, or slay.

The dear Lord Jesus Christ, our friend and our consolation, be with Your Grace and leave not Your Grace comfortless.

[Martin Luther.]

TO CONRAD CORDATUS. May 21, 1537

Conrad Cordatus (1475-1546) had received a call to serve as pastor in Eisleben, Luther's birthplace, but could not make up his mind to accept.

---

52 Luke 2:14.   53 Cf. I John 4:14.
54 II Cor. 12:9.

Although Luther encouraged him to go, it appears that Cordatus remained in the village of Niemegk, near Wittenberg. In this letter Luther takes his friend to task for his hypochondria and points out that there is often a relationship between mental and physical illness. To imagine that one is sick may produce sickness. [Text in Latin; *WA, Br*, VIII, 79, 80.]

Grace and peace in Christ.

Dear Cordatus:

Your acceptance of the call to my native town of Eisleben would please me very much, for there you would be close at hand to oppose Witzel, whom you hate with a holy and righteous hatred.[55] However, you ought to go there first in order to inspect everything. Then, if it pleases you, you can leave your little spot in Niemegk without regret. God's will would be done and I should be happy about it. Perhaps you would also find that the air there is healthier for you than that of the swamps here, for there the air is purified day and night by many fires.[56]

I thank God that your health is being restored.[57] But I pray you to curb your suspicion that you are assailed by who knows how many diseases. You know the proverb, "Imagination produces misfortune."[58] Therefore, you ought to take the pains to divert rather than to entertain such notions. I too must do this. For our adversary, the devil, walks about, seeking not only to devour[59] our souls but also to weaken our bodies with thoughts of our souls in the hope that he might perhaps slay our bodies, for he knows that our physical health depends in large measure on the thoughts in our minds. This is in accord with the saying, "Good cheer is half the battle,"[60] and, "A merry heart doeth good like a medicine: but a broken spirit drieth the bones."[61] I

---

55 George Witzel, a Roman priest in St. Andrew's Church, Eisleben, from 1533 to 1538, was at this time engaged in a controversy with Lutherans. In 1534, Cordatus had written a preface to a book that Michael Cölius had written against Witzel. The latter's career is referred to in *WA, TR*, IV, No. 5029.
56 The reference is to smelting ovens connected with the mines near Eisleben.
57 Cordatus had written to Philip Melanchthon on April 17, 1537, of "another sign of apoplexy" (*C.R.*, III, 351).
58 *Imaginatio facit casum.*
59 Cf. I Peter 5:8.
60 The saying is in German, *Guter Mut, halber Leib.*
61 Prov. 17:22.

give you this advice although I confess that I do not take it myself, as Saint Paul says of the Jews in Rom., ch. 2.[62]
Farewell in the Lord.
Whitmonday, 1537.   Martin Luther.

TABLE TALK RECORDED BY ANTHONY LAUTERBACH.[63] March 29, 1538

Then came Dr. [Jerome] Weller, who was sorely tempted and discouraged. Luther comforted him by saying that he should be of good courage in the Lord and seek the company of men. He asked, "Are you angry with God, or with me, or with yourself?" Dr. Weller replied, "I confess that I am murmuring against God." Luther responded: "God does not give up anything. I myself often worship God thus. When I ought to offer him sweet-smelling incense, I offer him, instead, the stinking pitch and asafetida of my murmuring and impatience. If we did not have the article of the forgiveness of sins[64] which God has promised that he will surely keep, we should be in a bad way."

Weller said, "The devil is a master at finding the spot where it hurts most." Luther replied: "Yes, and he does not learn this from us. He is very clever at it. If he did not spare the patriarchs, the prophets, or even that prince of prophets, Christ, he will not exempt us. He can fashion the oddest syllogisms. For example, 'You have sinned; God is wrathful toward sinners; therefore, despair.' Here it is necessary that we proceed from the Law to the Gospel and lay hold of the article of the forgiveness of sins. You are not the only one who suffers such temptations, my brother, for Peter exhorts us not to be discouraged since the same afflictions are accomplished in our brethren.[65] Moses, David, and Isaiah suffered many and great afflictions. Think how great the trials of David must have been when he wrote that psalm, 'O Lord, rebuke me not in thine anger,' etc.[66] He would rather have died by the sword than experience that dread in the face of God and that wrath of God toward him. Therefore, I believe that such confessors greatly excel the martyrs, for the former behold daily idolatries, offenses, sins, and the prosperity and security of the wicked while the godly

---

[62] Cf. Rom. 2:21.
[63] Macaronic text; *WA, TR,* III, No. 3798.
[64] Summarized in the Apostles' Creed.   [65] Cf. I Peter 5:9.
[66] Ps. 6:1.

suffer distress, and they are accounted as sheep for the slaughter."[67]

TO BERNARD VON DOELEN. May 27, 1538

Since 1537, Bernard von Dölen had been an Evangelical clergyman in St. Peter's Church in Freiberg, Saxony. He seemed to be dissatisfied with his lot wherever he was. Before he went to Freiberg he was in Wittenberg and complained to Luther about his "arrogant auditors who scorned to read the catechism."[68] It is not clear what specific complaint he had now. Luther himself did not know, and his reply to von Dölen suggested that a personal interview would be more helpful than correspondence in uncovering his spiritual malady and applying an appropriate remedy. [Text in Latin; *WA, Br,* VIII, 231, 232.]

To my dearly beloved brother, Dr. Bernard von Dölen, disciple and faithful minister of the crucified Lord: grace and peace in the Lord.

Dear Bernard:

I have not been able to reply earlier to your last letter concerning your trials because the courier left when I was obliged to go to lecture. There is nothing that I can write now to comfort you unless it be this: if you desire my counsel, come to see me here as quickly as possible. Perhaps your temptation is too severe to be relieved by a brief letter; it can better be cured, God willing, by a personal encounter with me and my living voice.[69] Consider too that I do not know what sort of disturbance[70] this is from which you are suffering, what the cause of it is, whether it is a matter of conscience, whether it is due to weakness of faith, etc. Therefore, I can write nothing in particular except that, until you come to see me, you must believe that you are not the only one who suffers such things. Christ himself was tempted in all points,[71] and so he undoubtedly experienced this trial of yours, else he would not have been tempted in all things like as we are. But Christ was tempted in all respects in order that we may know and believe that all our temptations have been overcome by him, for he said, "Be of good cheer, I have overcome the world."[72]

---

[67] Cf. Ps. 44:22; Rom. 8:36. [68] *WA, TR,* III, No. 3573.
[69] *Viva voce.* The *viva vox evangelii* was prominent in Luther's pastoral counseling as it was in his theology.
[70] *Perturbatio.* [71] Cf. Heb. 4:15.
[72] John 16:33.

May God himself, the conqueror of sorrow, death, and hell, comfort and preserve your heart by his Holy Spirit. Amen.

Pray for me, who am also tempted, as I pray for you, who are tempted.

Yours,

Monday after Rogate, 1538.   Martin Luther.

TO MRS. M. January 11, 1543

Earlier editors of Luther's correspondence conjectured that M stood for Margaret and that the Margaret in question might have been Mrs. Margaret Eschat, or Eschaus. However, Mrs. Eschat is not known to have had a brother John, as the letter requires, nor is it known that her husband was ever a burgomaster anywhere. Although the identity of the recipient remains hidden, the letter makes it clear that she was a sensitive —not to say an overscrupulous and squeamish—woman who was troubled by some words that she had inadvertently uttered in a fit of anger. Luther advises her not to take her sin more seriously than the promise of forgiveness. [Text in German; WA, Br, X, 239, 240.]

God's grace and peace in the Lord.

My dear Mrs. M:

Your brother John informs me that the evil spirit is troubling you because these wicked words slipped from your lips: "I wish that all those who brought it about that my husband was made burgomaster would go to the devil!" Your brother tells me that the evil spirit is tormenting you and making you believe that on account of these words you must remain in the devil's power forever.

Now, dear M, since you believe and acknowledge that it is the evil spirit who elicited such words from you, and that it is a wicked suggestion of his that you must remain in his power forever, you may be sure that all these suggestions are lies. "He is a liar [and the father of lies]."[73] Certainly it was not Christ who put into your mind the notion that you belong to the devil, for Christ died in order that those who belong to the devil may be released from his power. Therefore, do this: Spit on the devil and say: "Have I sinned? Well, I *have* sinned, and I am sorry. [But I shall not despair, for] Christ has taken away the sins of the whole world, of all who confess their sins. So it is certain that this sin of mine has also been taken away. Begone, devil, for I am absolved. This I am bound to believe. And if I had

[73] John 8:44. The text in brackets, here and below in this letter, is from a somewhat fuller version published by George Rörer in 1554.

committed murder or adultery, or had even crucified Christ himself, this too would be forgiven if I repented and acknowledged the sin, as Christ said on the cross, 'Father, forgive them.' "[74]

Dear M, you must not believe your own thoughts, nor those of the devil. But believe what we preachers say, for God has commanded us to instruct and absolve souls, as Christ said, "Whosoever sins ye remit, they are remitted."[75] This you must believe [and by no means doubt]. Now, we preachers absolve and free you in Christ's name and at his command, not only from this one sin, but from all the sins which you have inherited from Adam. These are so many and so great that God does not let us understand them all, or understand them fully, in this life. Much less does he reckon them against us [if we have faith in him].

Therefore, be content and confident. Your sin is forgiven. Rely resolutely on this. [Do not revive your own notions.] Give heed to all that your pastor and preacher tell you [from the Word of God]. Do not despise their counsel and comfort, for it is God himself who speaks to you through them, as Christ said, "Whosoever sins ye remit, they are remitted," and, "He that heareth you heareth me, and he that despiseth you despiseth me."[76] Believe this, and the devil will stop bothering you.

Or [if you are still weak in your faith] say this: "I should like to be stronger in my faith, and I know very well that these things are true and to be believed. Although I do not believe them as I ought, yet I know that they are the [pure] truth." This is what it means to believe unto [righteousness and] salvation [as Christ says, "Blessed are they which do hunger and thirst after righteousness"[77]].

Our dear Lord Christ, who suffered for our sins and not for our righteousness [and who was raised again for our justification],[78] comfort and strengthen your heart in true faith. And do not be troubled any more about your sin.

Thursday after Epiphany, 1543.   Martin Luther, Doctor.

TO PRINCESS SIBYL OF SAXONY. March 30, 1544

The wife of Elector John Frederick of Saxony had written to Luther, probably on March 27, 1545,[79] to inquire about his health and that of

[74] Luke 23:34.   [75] John 20:23.   [76] Luke 10:16.
[77] Matt. 5:6.   [78] Rom. 4:25.
[79] The date of the extant letter is uncertain. See *WA, Br*, X, 546.

his family, but especially to complain that she sorely missed her absent husband, who was attending the diet at Spires. Luther's letter was written to cheer her in her loneliness. [Text in German; *WA, Br,* X, 548, 549.]

To the serene, highborn princess, Lady Sibyl, by birth duchess of Jülich, Cleve, etc., duchess of Saxony, spouse of the elector and the landgrave in Thuringia, the margrave of Meissen, and the burgrave of Magdeburg, my gracious lady: grace and peace in the Lord.

Serene, highborn, most gracious Lady:

I have received Your Grace's letter and humbly thank Your Grace for inquiring so particularly and carefully about my health and about my wife and children, and also for your good wishes. Thank God, we are well. God has been better to us than we deserve. That my head is sometimes weak[80] is not surprising, for it is old, and age brings with it senility, frigidity, deformity, sickness, and weakness. The pitcher goes to the well until it is broken. I have lived long enough. God grant me a blessed end before my sluggish, useless carcass is taken to its like under the earth to become a prey to worms. I think that I have seen the best days that I shall ever see on the earth. Things look as if they were going from bad to worse. May God help his own. Amen.

I can well understand that, as Your Grace writes, you feel sad and forlorn while your husband, our gracious lord, the elector, is absent. But since it is necessary, and his absence is for the good and advantage of Christendom and the German nation, you must bear it with patience according to the divine will. If the devil could keep peace, we too should have more peace and less to do, especially less to suffer. Be this as it may, we have the advantage of possessing the precious Word of God, which comforts and sustains us in this life and promises and gives us salvation in the world to come. Moreover, we have prayer, which (as Your Grace also writes) we know pleases God and will be heard in time. Two such unspeakable treasures neither the devil, nor the Turk, nor the pope, nor their followers can have, and they are consequently much poorer and more wretched than any beggar on earth.

Surely we should glory in these things and find comfort in them. We should also thank God, the Father of all mercies in Christ Jesus, his dear Son, our Lord, that he has given us such

[80] Luther had recently had an attack of what was thought to be apoplexy.

good and precious treasures and by his grace has called us, unworthy as we are, into such an inheritance. Accordingly we should not only patiently endure the ephemeral evils which we encounter, but we should also have compassion on those exalted heads of this dark and wretched world who have been deprived of this grace and have not been deemed worthy to participate in it. May God enlighten them in his good time so that they, as well as we, may acknowledge, understand, and desire it. Amen.

My Katie humbly offers her poor prayers for Your Grace and thanks you for thinking so kindly of her.

Herewith I commit Your Grace to the dear Lord God. Amen.

Your Grace's obedient [subject],

Judica, 1544.   Martin Luther, Doctor.

TO MRS. MARTIN LUTHER. February 7, 1546

As early as 1540, Luther had complained about the oppression of the counts of Mansfeld, who confiscated mines and forges of their subjects.[81] During the years since then the counts had had a falling out among themselves, and the same greed for wealth played a part in it. Count Albert of Mansfeld asked Luther in 1545 to act as mediator and arbitrator in the dispute among the noblemen. In response Luther journeyed to Mansfeld in October and again in December, 1545. The matter was not settled, however, and a third journey became necessary. Although sick and exhausted, Luther set out with his three sons and famulus on January 25, 1546, in the winter's worst weather. In Halle the party was joined by Justus Jonas (1493-1555). Luther faithfully reported his travel experiences to his wife, and she in turn wrote frequently to express her concern over his health. In the following letter Luther tenderly rebuked his wife for her worry. [Text in German; *WA, Br*, XI, 286, 287.]

To my dear wife, Catherine Luther, doctor's spouse in Wittenberg, keeper of the pig market,[82] and gracious wife whom I am bound to serve hand and foot: grace and peace in the Lord.

Dear Katie:

You should read the Gospel according to Saint John and the Small Catechism,[83] of which you once said, "Everything in this book has to do with me!" You are worrying in God's stead as

---

[81] See Chapter XI.
[82] Luther playfully refers to his wife's activity on the little farm in Zülsdorf which Luther had bought from Claus Bildenhauer in 1532.
[83] Luther's Small Catechism (1529).

if he were not almighty. He could create ten Dr. Martins if the old one were to drown in the Saale River,[84] or burn in a fire,[85] or be caught in Wolf's bird traps.[86] Do not plague me any longer with your worries. I have a better worrier than you and all the angels. He lies in a cradle and clings to a virgin's breast, and yet he is at the same time seated at the right hand of God the Father Almighty. Therefore, be satisfied. Amen.

I believe that all the devils have left hell and the rest of the world to concentrate on Eisleben, perhaps on my account, so deadlocked are the negotiations. Jews are also here, some fifty of them, as I have before written to you.[87] It is said that about four or five hundred Jews go in and out of Rissdorf, just outside of Eisleben, where I was sick on my arrival. Count Albert, who controls the whole region around Eisleben, has exposed the Jews in his territory to shame, but no one is willing to do anything about them. The countess of Mansfeld, Widow Solms,[88] is despised as a protector of Jews. I do not know if it is true. But I have expressed my opinion today, and roughly enough,[89] in the hope that it may help those who heed it.

Pray, pray, pray, and help our negotiations to succeed. Today I had a mind to have the wagon greased with my wrath [and start for home], but I was restrained by the wretchedness of my fatherland which I beheld.[90]

Let Master Philip[91] read this letter, for I have not had time to write to him. This[92] should comfort you with the knowledge that I love you very much, as you already know, and since he has a wife too he will certainly understand.

We are living well here. At every meal the councilor presents me with two quarts of Reinfal,[93] and it is very good. Sometimes I share it with my companions. The local wine is also good.

---

84 When Luther was in Halle, on his way to Eisleben, the Saale River was overflowing its banks and threatening to "rebaptize" him by immersion, as he playfully reported to his wife on January 25 (*WA, Br,* XI, 269).

85 See letter of Feb. 10, 1546, below.

86 *Oder auff Wolffes vogel herd.* Luther's famulus, Wolfgang Sieberger, called "Wolf" by Luther, was a bird trapper.

87 On Feb. 1, 1546 (*WA, Br,* XI, 275).

88 Countess Dorothy, nee Solms, widow of Count Ernest of Mansfeld.

89 The sermon which Luther preached on this day (*WA,* LI, 173–187) contains no attack on the Jews, but it is possible that this was deleted before publication.

90 Luther was a native of Eisleben, County of Mansfeld.

91 Philip Melanchthon.

92 That is, the fact that Luther wrote to his wife instead of to Melanchthon.

93 Wine imported from Rivoglio in Istria.

The Naumburg beer is excellent, except that I believe it fills my chest with phlegm. The devil has spoiled the beer everywhere with pitch, and he spoils your wine at home with sulphur. But here the wine is pure, although it is, of course, affected by soil and climate.

In order that you may not worry about it, you should know that all the letters which you have written have arrived here. The one you wrote last Friday reached me today together with Master Philip's letters.

Your loving husband,
Sunday after Saint Dorothy's Day, 1546. Martin Luther.

TO MRS. MARTIN LUTHER. February 10, 1546

The negotiations to reconcile the counts of Mansfeld (see above) were finally successful, but they contributed to the sapping of Luther's strength. On February 18, 1546, he died peacefully in the presence of some friends, including Justus Jonas, who had gone to Eisleben with him. The following letter, again admonishing his wife not to be anxious, was written a week before his death. It was one of the last he was to write. [Text in German; *WA, Br*, XI, 290-292.]

To the pious and anxious lady, Mrs. Catherine Luther, of Wittenberg, keeper of Zülsdorf,[94] my gracious and dear wife: grace and peace in Christ.

Most precious Spouse:

Thank you most heartily for your great anxiety which keeps you from sleeping, for while you have been worrying about us, we were almost consumed by a fire which broke out near the door to my room in the place where we are staying. And yesterday, doubtless as a consequence of your anxiety, a stone almost fell on our heads and might have crushed us like mice in a mousetrap. For several days little pieces of plaster were drifting down from overhead in our private quarters, and when we summoned help and the ceiling was examined, a stone fell down which was as long as a large pillow and more than a hand's breadth wide. Think of what might have happened as a result of your blessed worrying if the dear angels had not intervened!

I fear that if you do not stop worrying, the earth will swallow us up and all the elements will fall upon us. Is this the way in which you have learned the Catechism and understand faith?

94 See note 82 above.

I beg you to pray and leave the worrying to God. You are not commanded to worry about me or yourself. It is written, "Cast thy burden upon the Lord, and he shall sustain thee,"[95] and similarly in many other places.

Thank God, we are in good health and spirits. The negotiations do not distress us unduly. [Justus] Jonas has a sore leg because he bumped himself inadvertently against a chest; such is the envy common to humanity that he was unwilling that I should have a lame leg all by myself!

God keep you! We hope soon to be finished and on our way back home if God wills it. Amen.

Your Holiness' willing servant,

M. L[uther.]

[95] Ps. 55:22.

IV

Instructions to the Perplexed and Doubting

TO GEORGE SPENLEIN. April 8, 1516

For almost four years George Spenlein had been a friar in the Augustinian monastery in Wittenberg. Shortly before this letter was written he had transferred to the Augustinian monastery in Memmingen, and Luther undertook to dispose of some possessions that he had left behind. In 1520, Spenlein abandoned monastic life altogether and in time became an Evangelical clergyman. Years later Luther found it necessary to rebuke him[1] for his sharp tongue. Here Luther expounded his new understanding of the distinction between justification by works and justification by God's grace through faith. [Text in Latin; *WA, Br,* I, 33-36.]

To the godly and sincere Friar George Spenlein, Augustinian eremite in the monastery at Memmingen, my dear friend in the Lord: grace and peace to you from God the Father and from the Lord Jesus Christ.

My dear Brother George:

I wish you to know that I sold some of your things for two and a half gulden, namely, the coat of Brussels for one gulden, the larger work of the Eisenach theologian[2] for half a gulden, and the cowl and some other things for one gulden. Some things are left, such as the *Eclogues* of Baptista Mantuan[3] and your collections. These you must consider a loss, for hitherto we have not been able to dispose of them. The two and a half gulden which you owe to the reverend father vicar[4] we gave him in your name. The other half gulden which you still owe him you must either try to pay or get him to cancel. I felt that

---

[1] See letter to George von Harstall, Jan. 27, 1543, in Chapter XI.

[2] *Summulae totius logicae, quod opus maius appellitare libuit,* by Jodocus Trutvetter, of Eisenach (Erfurt, 1501).

[3] A Carmelite poet (1448–1518).　　　　[4] John Staupitz.

the reverend father was so well disposed toward you that he would not object to doing so.

Now I should like to know whether your soul, tired of its own righteousness, is learning to be revived by and to trust in the righteousness of Christ. For in our age the temptation to presumption besets many, especially those who try with all their might to be just and good without knowing the righteousness of God which is most bountifully and freely given us in Christ. They try to do good of themselves in order that they might stand before God clothed in their own virtues and merits. But this is impossible. Among us you were one who held this opinion, or rather, error. So was I, and I am still fighting against the error without having conquered it as yet.

Therefore, my dear brother, learn Christ and him crucified. Learn to pray to him and, despairing of yourself, say: "Thou, Lord Jesus, art my righteousness, but I am thy sin. Thou hast taken upon thyself what is mine and hast given to me what is thine. Thou has taken upon thyself what thou wast not and hast given to me what I was not." Beware of aspiring to such purity that you will not wish to be looked upon as a sinner, or to be one. For Christ dwells only in sinners. On this account he descended from heaven, where he dwelt among the righteous, to dwell among sinners. Meditate on this love of his and you will see his sweet consolation. For why was it necessary for him to die if we can obtain a good conscience by our works and afflictions? Accordingly you will find peace only in him and only when you despair of yourself and your own works. Besides, you will learn from him that just as he has received you, so he has made your sins his own and has made his righteousness yours.

If you firmly believe this as you ought (and he is damned who does not believe it), receive your untaught and hitherto erring brothers, patiently help them, make their sins yours, and, if you have any goodness, let it be theirs. Thus the apostle teaches: "Receive ye one another, as Christ also received us, to the glory of God."[5] And again: "Let this mind be in you, which was also in Christ Jesus: who, being in the form of God, thought it not robbery to be equal with God."[6] Even so, if you seem to yourself to be better than they are, do not count it as booty, as if it were yours alone, but humble yourself, forget what you are, and be as one of them in order that you may help them.

Cursed is the righteousness of the man who is unwilling to

5 Rom. 15:7.   6 Phil. 2:5, 6.

assist others on the ground that they are worse than he is and who thinks of fleeing from and forsaking those whom he ought now to be helping with patience, prayer, and example. This would be burying his lord's talent[7] and not paying what is due.[8] If you are a lily and a rose of Christ, therefore, know that you will live among thorns.[9] Only see to it that you will not become a thorn as a result of impatience, rash judgment, or secret pride. The rule of Christ is in the midst of his enemies,[10] as the psalm puts it. Why, then, do you imagine that you are among friends? Pray, therefore, for whatever you lack, kneeling before the face of Jesus Christ. He will teach you all things. Only keep your eyes fixed on that which he has done for you and for all men in order that you may learn what you should do for others. If he had desired to live only among good people and to die only for his friends, for whom, pray, would he have died and with whom would he ever have lived? Act accordingly, my dear brother, and pray for me. The Lord be with you. Farewell in the Lord.

Your brother,
Martin Luther, Augustinian.

Tuesday after Misericordias Domini, 1516.

TO GEORGE SPALATIN. January 18, 1518

George Spalatin was an early disciple of Luther and occupied an influential position as chaplain and secretary to the elector of Saxony. He put many practical and theological questions to Luther during the early years of the Reformation, and among these was a request for advice as to the best helps for a study of the Scriptures. [Text in Latin; *WA, Br,* II, 132-134.]

To my blameless friend, George Spalatin, in truth a disciple of Christ, a brother, etc.: greeting. Jesus.[11]

Excellent Spalatin:

You have hitherto asked me things that were within my power, or at least my daring, to answer, but now that you ask to be directed in those things which pertain to a thorough knowledge of the Scriptures, you demand something far beyond my abilities, especially as I have hitherto been able to find no guide for myself in this matter.

Different men think differently about this subject, even the most learned and most gifted. You have Erasmus, who plainly

---

7 Cf. Matt. 25:18.   8 Cf. Matt. 18:28.   9 Cf. S. of Sol. 2:1, 2.
10 Cf. Ps. 110:2.   11 Traditional invocation of the name of Jesus.

asserts that Saint Jerome is such a great theologian in the Church that he alone deserves to be considered. If I prefer Saint Augustine to Jerome, I shall seem to be an unjust and partial judge, not only because I am a member of the Augustinian order but also on account of the opinion which Erasmus has expressed and which has long been accepted, namely, that it would be most impudent to compare Augustine with Jerome. Still other men think differently. Among such judges I feel unable to decide anything concerning this matter on account of the limitations in my learning and gifts. But among those who either passionately hate or slothfully neglect good letters (that is, among all men), I always praise and defend Erasmus as much as I can, and I am very careful not to ventilate my disagreement with him lest perchance I should thus confirm them in their hatred of him. Yet, if I may speak as a theologian rather than as a grammarian, there are many things in Erasmus which seem to me to be far from the knowledge of Christ; otherwise there is no man more learned or ingenious than he, not even Jerome, whom he so much extols. But if you communicate this opinion of mine concerning Erasmus to others, you will violate the laws of friendship. I warn you to be prudent. There are many, as you know, who search out every occasion to slander sound learning. What I tell you is therefore a secret. Indeed, you should not believe it until you have proved it by your reading. If you extort from me the result of my studies, I shall conceal nothing from you, as my dearest friend, but only on condition that you will not follow me except by exercising your own judgment.

In the first place, it is most certain that one cannot enter into the Scriptures by study or skill alone. Therefore, you should begin by praying that, if it pleases the Lord to accomplish something through you for his glory, and not for your own glory or that of any other man, he may grant you a true understanding of his words. For there is no master of the Scriptures other than Him who is their author. Hence it is written, "They shall all be taught of God."[12] You must completely despair of your own industry and ability, therefore, and rely solely on the influx of the Spirit. Believe me, for I have experience in this matter.[13]

Then, having achieved this despairing humility, read the Scriptures in order from beginning to end so as to get the substance of the story in your mind (as I believe you have already done long since). Saint Jerome's epistles and commentaries will

12 John 6:45.   13 *Experto crede.*

be of great help in this. But for an understanding of Christ and the grace of God (that is, for the hidden knowledge of the Spirit) Augustine and Ambrose seem to me to be far better guides, especially because it appears to me that Jerome Origenizes[14] (that is, allegorizes) too much. I say this although it is contrary to the judgment of Erasmus. But you asked for my opinion and not for his.

You may begin, if you like my course of study, by reading Augustine on the spirit and the letter, which our Carlstadt, a man of incomparable zeal, has now edited and furnished with remarkable annotations.[15] Then take the book against Julian, and likewise the book against two epistles of the Pelagians. You might also add Saint Ambrose's work on the calling of all heathen; although this book appears from its style, contents, and chronology to have been written by someone other than Ambrose, it is nevertheless a very learned book. If these suggestions appeal to you, I shall send you more later on. Forgive my temerity that in so difficult a subject I should be so bold as to offer my opinions about such great men.

Finally, I am sending you the apology of Erasmus.[16] I am very sorry that such a fire should have been kindled between these great princes of letters. Erasmus, indeed, excels and speaks the better, even if the more bitterly, though in some things he acts as if he wished to preserve friendship.

Farewell, dear Spalatin.

Saint Prisca's Day, 1518.   Brother Martin Eleutherius.[17]

TO DUKE JOHN FREDERICK OF SAXONY.

March 31, 1521

Duke John Frederick, who became elector of Saxony on the death of his father in 1532, wrote to Luther to seek answers to a few questions which his reading of the Bible had suggested. The questions are of some interest in so far as they illustrate one type of problem which concerned a devout layman in the early years of the Reformation, and Luther's

---

14 Origen (c. 182–251) was notorious for his allegorization.

15 Andrew Carlstadt's commentary on Augustine's *De spiritu et litera.*

16 Desiderius Erasmus, *Apologia ad Iacobum Fabrum Stapulensem* (Antwerp, 1517). The French humanist Lefèvre d'Étaples (Faber Stapulensis) and Erasmus disagreed sharply over the proper interpretation of the Epistle to the Hebrews.

17 In the fashion of contemporary humanists Luther occasionally affected a Hellenization of his name; the Greek word *eleutheria* means freedom.

answers may be taken as fairly typical of his handling of similar questions. [Text in German; *WA, Br,* II, 294, 295.]

Serene, highborn Prince, gracious Lord:

Your Grace's letter concerning the good works of Christ and his sleeping was humbly received by me. It is true that there is only one reference in the Gospels to Christ's sleeping, and Your Grace cited this.[18] But if every instance of his sleeping had been recorded, what a large book would have been required! It is enough to have mentioned this once. And the natural, true manhood of Christ is reflected in it. He undoubtedly prayed, fasted, walked, and did wonders more often than the Gospels mention, as Saint John clearly asserts in his last chapter: "[Many other signs truly did Jesus in the presence of his disciples, which are not written in this book:] but these are written, that ye might believe that Jesus is the Christ."[19]

That he always and in all things pleased his Father is true. His eating, drinking, and sleeping pleased his Father as much as his greatest miracles, for the Father sees not the works but the intent in the works, as I have more than sufficiently taught in my book on good works.[20]

It is not necessary to believe that when Christ was hanging on the cross he prayed the entire psalm, "My God, my God, why hast thou forsaken me?"[21] word for word. On the other hand, it is not unchristian for those who wish to do so to believe that he did. Everyone is at perfect liberty to believe this or not, for the Scriptures say nothing about it.

Herewith I send Your Grace the first part of the Magnificat.[22] The fourth quaternion is on the press. I must allow it to be put off until I return. Your Grace will remember that I was ordered to drop everything and go to the diet.[23] If it is God's will that I return home, Your Grace will have the whole book promptly.

---

[18] Matt. 8:24.

[19] John 20:30, 31.

[20] "Von den guten Werken" (1520) in *WA,* VI, 196–276; English translation in *Works of Martin Luther,* Philadelphia ed., I, 173–285.

[21] Matt. 27:46. Quotation in Latin.

[22] "Das Magnificat verdeutscht und ausgelegt" (1521) in *WA,* VII, 538–604; English translation in *Works of Martin Luther,* Philadelphia ed., III, 117–200.

[23] This letter was written on the eve of Luther's departure for the Diet of Worms, to which he had been officially summoned by Emperor Charles V.

Herewith I say farewell and pray that God may be gracious to Your Grace.

Your Grace's humble chaplain,

Easter, 1521.   Dr. Martin Luther.

TO BARBARA LISSKIRCHEN. April 30, 1531

A sister of Jerome and Peter Weller, Barbara Weller married George Lisskirchen, of Freiberg, in Saxony, in 1525. The doctrine of predestination troubled her, and she allowed the question whether she was herself one of the elect to torment her. In counseling her, Luther referred to his own experience with the problem. [Text in German; WA, Br, VI, 86-88.]

Grace and peace in Christ.

Dear and virtuous Lady:

Your dear brother Jerome Weller has informed me that you are sorely troubled about eternal election. I am very sorry to hear this. May Christ our Lord deliver you from this temptation. Amen.

I know all about this affliction. I was myself brought to the brink of eternal death by it. In addition to my prayer in your behalf, I should gladly counsel and comfort you, but it is difficult to discuss such matters in writing. Nevertheless, if God will grant me the necessary grace, I shall do what I can. I shall show you how God helped me out of this trouble and by what means I now protect myself against it every day.

First, you must firmly fix in your mind the conviction that such thoughts as yours are assuredly the suggestions and fiery darts[24] of the wretched devil. The Scriptures declare in Prov., ch. 7, "He who searches out the lofty things of majesty will be cast down."[25] Now, such thoughts as yours are a vain searching into the majesty of God and a prying into his secret providence. Jesus the son of Sirach declares in the third chapter: "Search not out things that are above thy strength. The things that have been commanded thee, think thereupon."[26] It is of no profit to you to gape at that which you are not commanded. David also complained in Ps. 131 that he did not fare well when he inquired into matters that were too high for him.[27] Accordingly, it is certain that these notions of yours come, not from God, but from the devil, who torments us with them to make us hate God

24 Eph. 6:16.   25 Cf. Prov. 25:27.
26 Ecclus. 3:21, 22.   27 Cf. Ps. 131:1.

and despair. God has strictly forbidden this in the First Commandment. He desires that we love, trust, and praise him by whom we live.

Secondly, when such thoughts assail you, you should learn to ask yourself, "If you please, in which Commandment is it written that I should think about and deal with this matter?" When it appears that there is no such Commandment, learn to say: "Begone, wretched devil! You are trying to make me worry about myself. But God declares everywhere that I should let him care for me. He says, 'I am thy God.'[28] This means, 'I care for you; depend upon me, await my bidding, and let me take care of you.' " This is what Saint Peter taught, "Cast all thy care upon him, for he careth for you."[29] And David taught, "Cast thy burden upon the Lord, and he shall sustain thee."[30]

Thirdly, if these thoughts nevertheless continue (for the devil is reluctant to give up), you too must refuse to give up. You must always turn your mind away from them and say: "Don't you hear, devil? I will have nothing to do with such thoughts. Moreover, God has forbidden me to. Begone! I must now think of God's Commandments. Meanwhile I shall let him care for me. If you are so clever in these matters, go up to heaven and dispute with God himself; he can give you an adequate answer." In this way you must always put these thoughts away from you and turn your attention to God's Commandments.

Fourthly, the highest of all God's commands is this, that we hold up before our eyes the image of his dear Son, our Lord Jesus Christ. Every day he should be our excellent mirror wherein we behold how much God loves us and how well, in his infinite goodness, he has cared for us in that he gave his dear Son for us.

In this way, I say, and in no other, does one learn how to deal properly with the question of predestination. It will be manifest that you believe in Christ. If you believe, then you are called. And if you are called, then you are most certainly predestinated. Do not let this mirror and throne of grace be torn away from before your eyes. If such thoughts still come and bite like fiery serpents, pay no attention to the thoughts or serpents. Turn away from these notions and contemplate the brazen serpent, that is, Christ given for us. Then, God willing, you will feel better.

But, as I have said, it requires a struggle to shun such thoughts. If they enter your mind, cast them out again, just as

[28] Cf. Ex. 20:2.   [29] Cf. I Peter 5:7.   [30] Ps. 55:23.

you would immediately spit out any filth that fell into your mouth. God has helped me to do this in my own case. It is his urgent command that we keep before us the image of his Son, in whom he has abundantly revealed himself to be our God (as the First Commandment teaches) who helps and cares for us. Therefore, he will not suffer us to help or take care of ourselves. That would be to deny God, and to deny the First Commandment and Christ as well.

The wretched devil, who is the enemy of God and Christ, tries by such thoughts (which are contrary to the First Commandment) to tear us away from Christ and God and to make us think about ourselves and our own cares. If we do this, we take upon ourselves the function of God, which is to care for us and be our God. In paradise the devil desired to make Adam equal with God so that Adam might be his own god and care for himself, thus robbing God of his divine work of caring for him. The result was the terrible Fall of Adam.

For the present this is advice enough. I have also written to your brother Jerome Weller[31] that he warn and admonish you with all diligence until you learn to put away such thoughts and let the devil, from whom they come, plumb their depth. He knows very well what happened to him before in a similar situation: he fell from heaven into the abyss of hell. In short, what we are not commanded should not disturb or trouble us. The devil, and not God, is the instigator of such perplexity.

May our dear Lord Jesus Christ show you his hands and his side[32] and gladden your heart with his love, and may you behold and hear only him until you find your joy in him. Amen.

The last day of April, 1531.   Martin Luther.

TABLE TALK RECORDED BY CONRAD CORDATUS.[33]

Autumn, 1531

Those who are tempted by doubt and despair I should console in this fashion. First, by warning them to beware of solitude and to converse constantly with others about the Psalms and Scriptures. Then (although this is hard to do, it is a very present

---

[31] This letter is not extant.   [32] Cf. John 20:27.

[33] Macaronic text; *WA, TR*, II, No. 2268 b. This is one of several table talks that were conflated by Michael Stiefel with a letter to Wenzel Link dated July 14, 1528, and so published in most editions of Luther's letters. On this problem see *WA, Br*, IV, 495, 496.

remedy) let them persuade themselves if they can that such thoughts are really not theirs but Satan's, and that they should strive with all their might to turn their minds to other things and leave such thoughts to him.

Dwelling on these thoughts, wrestling with them, wishing to conquer them or wishing idly for them to come to an end will only make them more disturbing and strengthen them unto perdition without providing a remedy. The best thing is to let them vanish as they came and not to think much about them or dispute with them. I have no other counsel for him who neglects to do this. You must know, however, that it is hard to follow this advice. For when we are disturbed by such thoughts about God and eternal salvation, it is our nature to refuse to give up or despise them until we have reached the conclusion that it is impossible to achieve the certainty and victory we desire by dwelling upon and disputing with these thoughts. Our own powers and ideas are not sufficient to cope with such matters. Satan knows this very well. Therefore, he suggests such thoughts and makes them seem so important to us that we are unwilling to leave them or turn aside from them but wish to scrutinize them and think them through to the end. To do so is to surrender to Satan and let him reign.

But that those who are tempted may divert their thoughts, let them listen to the words of some good man as to the voice of God from heaven. So I have often been refreshed by the words which [John] Bugenhagen once spoke to me: "You ought not to despise my consolation because I am convinced that I speak words of God from heaven." Then those who are tempted will understand the text, "Thy word hath quickened me."[34] Christ suffered a like temptation when he said to Satan, "Thou shalt not tempt the Lord thy God."[35] With these words he conquered the devil and enabled us to conquer him too. Truly, thoughts of this kind are nothing but a tempting of God; although we do not think it while they are present but esteem them as important and very profitable to salvation, they tempt us to oppose God even if we do not dare in our hearts to despise him or say to him, "Thou art not God," and, "I do not wish thee to be my God." Nevertheless, it is necessary to speak thus in order to make you turn away from such thoughts and think of God in a different way. This can be done by believing the word of him who can comfort you and lead you back to God and by placing your reliance on that word. I have been diffuse, although I

34 Ps. 119:50.   35 Matt. 4:7.

have not said enough, because I know from experience what Satan can do with this kind of temptation.

Finally, let those who are so tempted pray and believe that God will help, for surely those who believe will be helped. Let them not struggle and suffer alone. All of us should aid them with our prayers and bear one another's burdens.[36]

In addition, if Satan should not let up, let them bear this patiently in the knowledge that what Satan cannot take suddenly by force and cunning, he tries to wear down by his relentless perseverance. It is as the psalmist sings, "Many a time have they afflicted me from my youth: yet they have not prevailed against me."[37] To behold this is a joy to God and the angels, and it will have a salutary and blessed end.

TO VALENTINE HAUSMANN. February 19, 1532

A younger brother of the clergyman Nicholas Hausmann (1479-1538), Valentine Hausmann was burgomaster in Freiberg, Saxony. He was assailed for some time by doubts, unbelief, and consequent terror. In the following letter, the date of which is uncertain, Luther warns him not to be too distressed. [Text in German; *WA, Br,* VI, 267.]

Grace and peace.

My dear Sir and Friend:

Your brother Nicholas has just been here. He told me that you are still assailed by terror and unbelief. As I have before written to you,[38] this is my faithful counsel: Accept this scourge as laid upon you by God for your own good, even as Saint Paul had to bear a thorn in the flesh,[39] and thank God that he deems you worthy of such unbelief and terror, for they will drive you all the more to pray and seek help and say, as it is written in the Gospel, "Lord, help thou mine unbelief."[40] How many there are who have less faith than you have! Yet they are not aware of it and remain in their unbelief. The fact that God makes you sensible of this is a good sign that he wishes to help you out of your condition. The more you are aware of it, the nearer you are to improvement. Cling calmly to God, and he will cause everything to turn out well.

Herewith I commit you to God's keeping. Amen.

Monday after Invocavit, 1532.   [Martin Luther.]

[36] Cf. Gal. 6:2.
[38] This letter is not extant.
[40] Mark 9:24.

[37] Ps. 129:2.
[39] Cf. II Cor. 12:7.

TABLE TALK RECORDED BY JOHN
SCHLAGINHAUFEN.[41] Spring, 1532

The papists and Anabaptists[42] teach that if you wish to know Christ, you must seek solitude, avoid association with men, and become a Nicolaitan.[43] This is manifestly diabolical advice which is in conflict with the First and Second Tables [of the Decalogue]. The First Table demands faith and fear of God. In the Second Commandment, God wishes that his name be proclaimed and praised before men and spoken of among men rather than that one should flee into a corner. Likewise, the Second Table teaches us to do good to our neighbors, and hence we must not be segregated from them but associate with them. This advice is also destructive of the family, economic life, and the state, and it is at odds with the life of Christ, who did not like to be alone and whose career was one of constant turmoil because people were always crowding about him. He was never alone except when he prayed. Have nothing to do, therefore, with those who say, " Seek solitude and your heart will become pure."

TO VALENTINE HAUSMANN. June 24, 1532

Valentine Hausmann continued to worry about his unbelief (see letter of February 19, 1532, above) and Luther gave him further instructions as to what he ought to do under the circumstances. [Text in German; WA, Br, VI, 322, 323.]

Grace and peace in Christ, our Lord.

My dear Valentine:

I have learned of the trouble you are having on account of your terror. You should not worry too much about it, for God deals with us in a wondrous way; it may appear to us that he means evil and harm, and yet what he does is for our benefit, even if we do not understand it. Who knows what worse things might have happened to you if he had not laid hold of you with his rod and held you with this fear of him. Consequently you

---

41 Macaronic text; WA, TR, II, No. 1329.
42 Both Catholic and Protestant mystics suggested the discipline of solitude as a means of attaining knowledge of Christ.
43 *Ein Niklos bruder.* The term was used by Luther to designate a libertine or a monk or both. Cf. also Rev. 2:14, 15.

should under no circumstances allow yourself to become impatient because you do not at once have strong faith. Saint Paul declares in Rom., chs. 14 and 15, that those who are weak in the faith are not cast off.[44] God is not the kind of father who casts off sick and erring children; if he were, he would have no children. Accordingly you should say: "Dear Father, if it pleases thee to chastise me so, I shall be glad to suffer it. Thy will be done.[45] Grant me the patience to bear it."

In the second place, although I do not know what attitude you take toward your terror, you should call upon God and pray, especially at the time when you become aware of the terror. You should fall upon your knees and cry out to heaven. Do not leave off even if the law is distasteful to you and you think your prayers are unavailing and cold. Make a brave effort. Pray all the harder when you think it is to no purpose. You must learn to struggle until the terror lets up of its own accord. Do not simply remain passive, look on, and suffer whatever happens to you, for then your condition will get worse as time passes. You must pray powerfully, cry out against your terror, and repeat the Lord's Prayer in a loud voice. Above all, you must take to heart that there is no doubt that your terror comes from the devil. God wants you to resist, and it is on this account that he allows this to happen. And you may be sure that he will hear fervent prayers and help.

In the third place, if you are unable to pray well, have something from the Psalms or the New Testament read to you in a clear voice, and listen attentively to the reading. For at such a time you must accustom yourself not to wrap yourself up in your misfortune and sink into your own thoughts, without the Word of God, as if you proposed to wait until the terror subsides. On the contrary, you must remember at that very time to hear nothing but prayers and the Word of God. To be sure, you should do this at other times too, and prayerfully resist the terror as much as you can. Then, if it please God, things will in time go better with you. Without the Word of God the enemy is too strong for us. But he cannot endure prayer and the Word of God.

Herewith I commit you to God's keeping. Amen.
The Day of John the Baptist, 1532.   Martin Luther.

---

[44] Cf. Rom. 14:1 and ch. 15:1.   [45] Matt. 6:10.

TABLE TALK RECORDED BY CONRAD CORDATUS.[46]
Autumn, 1532

He [Luther] spoke of predestination and said that when a man begins to dispute about it, it is like a fire that cannot be extinguished, and the more he disputes the more he despairs. Our Lord God is so hostile to such disputation that he instituted Baptism, the Word, and the Sacrament as signs to counteract it. We should rely on these and say: "I have been baptized. I believe in Jesus Christ. I have received the Sacrament.[47] What do I care if I have been predestined or not?" In Christ, God has furnished us with a foundation[48] on which to stand and from which we can go up to heaven. He is the only way and the only gate which leads to the Father.[49] If we despise this foundation and in the devil's name start building at the roof, we shall surely fall. If only we are able to believe that the promises have been spoken by God and see behind them the one who has spoken them, we shall magnify that Word. But because we hear it as it comes to us through the lips of a man, we are apt to pay as little attention to it as to the mooing of a cow.

TO GREGORY ROSSEKEN. March 28, 1533

After his unfortunate experience in Zwickau (see letter to Hausmann, May 19, 1531, in Chapter X), Nicholas Hausmann was for a time a guest in Luther's house and went to Dessau at the beginning of 1533. It was apparently at his suggestion that the following letter was written. The recipient of the letter was unknown to Luther and he has been identified with some difficulty as Gregory Rosseken, a Franciscan friar who was confessor in Dessau to Prince George of Anhalt. Here Luther instructs Rosseken how he might break with the authority of popes and councils. [Text in Latin; WA, Br, VI, 438, 439.]

To the reverend gentleman in the Lord, George N,[50] disciple of Christ, my sincere friend: grace and peace in Christ.

My dear Brother:

That good man Nicholas Hausmann has told me of your true

---

[46] Macaronic text; WA, TR, No. 2631 b.
[47] This sentence from a variant text.
[48] Cf. I Cor. 3:11.   [49] Cf. Matt. 7:14.
[50] Enders (IX, 278) conjectured that the addressee was an unknown George Funk. Presumably "George" was written for "Gregory" by mistake.

piety in the Lord, though he says that it is still weak and sticks firmly to the authority of pope and council. I do not wonder at that, for I too, after living almost twenty years as an Augustinian, was by long use and habit so thoroughly saturated and immersed in that notion in which you are held that unless God had plucked me out of it by force (as Mr. Hausmann will tell you) I could scarcely have been torn away from it by any words, however sure I may have been that they were all true. So difficult it was to put words into deeds and to dare to do the things I had taught! For this reason I wonder less that you feel as you do, for you have been accustomed for many years to this way of life, as I hear, and are not compelled, as I was, to urge the Word of God against it every day.

Do not despair, therefore, but do this: Pray with all your heart that the Lord Jesus may grant you to see that divine logic which teaches that Christ is other than Moses, pope, or all the world— indeed, that he is other and greater than our own conscience, which is above Moses and the pope. For if we must believe Moses and our conscience, which vexes us and convicts us by means of the law, how much more must we believe Christ, the Lord of all things, who says, "Believe,"[51] and again, "In vain do they worship me with the commandments of men."[52] Though there be popes and councils without end, what are they compared with Christ? They are as a candle to the sun. These things you will learn in time by prayer, for they are so great that they cannot be grasped at once by a mind long accustomed to thinking otherwise. I speak out of experience, and so I can easily believe you. Nevertheless, I urge you to strive after these things by prayer and practice, and the Lord will be with you. I wish to have Mr. Roseler[53] hear and read what I am saying and writing to you. Greet him with your own words and with my heart.

Farewell in Christ. May he make you stronger day by day. Amen.

Saturday after Laetare, 1533.   Dr. Martin Luther.

TABLE TALK RECORDED BY VEIT DIETRICH.[54]
About 1533

He [Luther] was asked how to counsel persons who are tempted by the thought that they are not numbered among those who

[51] Mark 11:24.   [52] Matt. 15:9.   [53] Unidentified.
[54] Text in Latin; WA, TR, I, No. 865.

are justified and to be saved because they do not experience that peace which the godly have according to the text in Rom., ch. 5, "Therefore being justified by faith, we have peace with God."[55]

He replied: "Such a person should first be admonished so that he might understand that the Christian life is to be lived amid sorrows, trials, afflictions, deaths, etc. Then those who are troubled and vexed by Satan with such disquieting thoughts are to be reminded that they are children of God and have a Father in heaven who accepts them in accordance with that verse in Heb., ch. 12, 'My son, despise not thou the chastening of the Lord,' etc.[56] If, then, those who are thus vexed by Satan are children of God, it follows that God cares for them and will in no wise despise or reject them. Even amid their tribulations, therefore, they ought to be joyful and sure concerning God's good will toward them."

"But what do you say about the text of Paul, 'We have peace with God'[55]?"

He replied: "It is true, they have peace in faith, but it is invisible and beyond our senses; so in death, although life is not felt, we should nevertheless hope that we have it. However, according to the flesh and the senses they suffer the greatest disquietude and disturbance. So David complains, 'There is no rest in my bones,'[57] and Christ did not experience peace on the cross. Besides, if Christians did not suffer temptations, what would be the purpose of the promises and consolations of the gospel and the preaching of grace? For example: 'The poor have the gospel preached to them'[58]; 'Fear not, little flock'[59]; 'Receive ye your brother who is weak'[60]; and 'Comfort one another.'[61] Because Christians always feel sorrows and afflictions, therefore, it is the prime precept of God that we encourage and console the afflicted who are in sorrow. And on the other hand, those who are thus tempted should allow themselves to be cheered and should put an end to their depression and fear."

TO PETER BESKENDORF. Early in 1535

An old friend of Luther asked for suggestions on the best way to pray. Luther's response took the form of an open letter, "How One Should Pray, for Master Peter the Barber," which was published early in 1535 under the title A Simple Way to Pray, for a Good Friend.

[55] Rom. 5:1.   [56] Heb. 12:5.   [57] Ps. 38:3.   [58] Matt. 11:5.
[59] Luke 12:32.   [60] Cf. Rom. 14:1.   [61] Cf. II Cor. 13:11.

The man here referred to as Peter the Barber, and elsewhere as a chirurgeon, was Peter Beskendorf. Shortly after the appearance of the booklet, and presumably while under the influence of alcohol, he stabbed his son-in-law, a soldier who had boasted that he could make himself impervious to wounds. The intercession of Luther saved Peter from the penalty of death, but he paid for his folly with exile and the loss of his property. [Text in German; *WA*, XXXVIII, 351-373.]

Dear Master Peter:

I shall tell you as well as I know how what I myself do when I pray. May our Lord God help you and others to do it better. Amen.

To begin with, when I feel that I have become cold and disinclined to pray on account of my preoccupation with other thoughts and matters (for the flesh and the devil always prevent and hinder prayer) I take my little Psalter, flee to my room, or, if it is during the day and there is occasion to do so, join the people in church, and begin to repeat to myself the Ten Commandments, the Creed, and, if I have time, some sayings of Christ or verses from Paul and the Psalms. This I do in all respects as children do.

It is a good thing to make prayer the first business of the morning and the last at night. Diligently beware of such false and deceptive thoughts as suggest: "Wait awhile. I shall pray in an hour or so. I must first take care of this or that." Such thoughts will lead away from prayer and will involve you in other affairs which will so occupy your attention that nothing will come of your prayers that day.

It is true that some tasks may confront you that are as good or better than prayer, especially if they are required by necessity. A saying is ascribed to Saint Jerome to the effect that every work of the faithful is prayer,[62] and a proverb declares, "He prays double who works faithfully."[63] This is undoubtedly said because the believer, when he is working, fears and honors God and remembers God's Commandments so that he does not deal unjustly with his neighbor, steal from him, take advantage of him, or misappropriate what belongs to him. Such thoughts and such faith undoubtedly make his work prayer and praise as well.

On the other hand, it is also true that an unbeliever's work

62 The reference is probably to Jerome's Commentary on Matthew, Book IV, under Matt. 25:11.
63 Cf. Ernst Thiele, *Luthers Sprichwörtersammlung* (Weimar, 1900), 51.

is nothing but cursing, and that he curses double who works unfaithfully, for the thoughts of his heart so permeate his work that he scorns God, transgresses God's Commandments, and intends to deal unjustly with his neighbor, steal from him, and misappropriate what belongs to him. What are such thoughts but a frivolous cursing of God and man by which a person's labor and work become a double curse, by which he is himself cursed, and by which he will remain a beggar and bungler? Of such constant prayer Christ says in Luke, ch. 11, "Pray without ceasing,"[64] for one should unceasingly beware of sins and wrong. This cannot happen unless one fears God and keeps God's Commandments in mind, as Ps. 1 states, "Blessed is he who meditates in his law day and night."[65]

Yet we must also see to it that we do not grow away from true prayer, go so far as to imagine that works are necessary that are not, and as a consequence at length become too careless and lazy and cold and listless to pray. The devil who hounds us is not lazy or careless, and our flesh is still all too active and eager to sin and inclined to oppose the spirit of prayer.

Now, when your heart is warmed by such meditation[66] and comes to itself, kneel down or stand with folded hands, lift up your eyes toward heaven, and speak or say to yourself as briefly as you can: "Dear God, Heavenly Father, I am a poor, unworthy sinner. I do not deserve to lift up my eyes or hands to thee in prayer. But inasmuch as thou hast commanded us all to pray, hast promised to hear us when we pray, and through thy dear Son, our Lord Jesus Christ, hast taught us both how and what to pray, at this thy command I come before thee obediently, rely on thy gracious promise, and in the name of my Lord Jesus Christ pray with all thy saints or Christians on earth as he hath taught us, 'Our Father which art in heaven,' " etc.,[67] continuing word for word to the end.

Afterward repeat a part, or as much as you wish. For example, repeat the first petition, "Hallowed be thy name," and say: "Yes, Lord God, dear Father, do thou hallow thy name both in us and in all the world. Root out and destroy the abominations, idolatry, and heresy of the Turk, the pope, and all false teachers or fanatics who take thy name in vain,[68] shamefully misuse it, and horribly blaspheme when they say and boast that they teach thy Word and the laws of the

[64] I Thess. 5:17; cf. Luke 11:8–13.   [65] Cf. Ps. 1:1, 2.
[66] *Durch solch mündlich gesprech.*   [67] Matt. 6:9.   [68] Cf. Ex. 20:7.

THE PERPLEXED AND DOUBTING

Church although what they teach is devilish lies and deception, and with these, under the cloak of thy name, they pitifully seduce many poor souls throughout the world and persecute, slay, and shed innocent blood in the belief that they are thereby rendering thee divine service. Dear Lord God, curb and convert. Convert those who are still to be converted in order that they with us and we with them may praise and hallow thy name with true and pure doctrine and with good and holy lives. On the other hand, curb those who are unwilling to be converted in order that they may be obliged to stop misusing, profaning, and dishonoring thy holy name and seducing the poor people. Amen." . . .[69]

You should observe that I do not propose that all these words be spoken in prayer, for in the end this would become mere babbling and empty prattle read out of a book, as laymen used to say the rosary and priests and monks used to read the prayers in their breviaries. My intention is simply to stir up and instruct your heart so that you may know what thoughts to lay hold of in the Lord's Prayer. When your heart is properly warmed and in a mood for prayer, you may express such thoughts with different words and perhaps with fewer words or more. I myself do not bind myself to such words and syllables, but use one form of words today and another tomorrow according to my ardor and disposition. However, I adhere as closely as I can to the same thoughts and sense. It sometimes happens that I lose myself in the rich thoughts of one part or petition and then I let the other six wait. When such rich and good thoughts come, one should let the other prayers go, make room for such thoughts, listen quietly, and by no means present an impediment, for the Holy Ghost himself is preaching here, and one word of his preaching is better than a thousand words of our praying. In this way I have often learned more in one prayer than I have been able to get out of much reading and reflection.

It is, therefore, of the greatest importance that our heart be free and in the mood for prayer. The preacher also suggests, "Let not thine heart be hasty to utter anything before God, lest thou tempt God."[70] What is it but tempting God to blabber with one's mouth and let one's mind wander? This is what the priest did who prayed: " 'Make haste, O God, to deliver me.'

---

[69] Luther's treatment of the remaining petitions of the Lord's Prayer is here omitted.
[70] Cf. Eccl. 5:2.

Boy, hitch up the horse. 'Make haste to help me, O Lord.'[71] Girl, go milk the cow. 'Glory be to the Father, and to the Son, and to the Holy Ghost.'[72] Run, boy, and may the fever take you!" In the time when I was under the papacy I heard and became aware of many prayers of this kind, and almost all the papists' prayers are like this. God is mocked by them. It would be better for the papists, if they are unable or unwilling to do better, to play instead. I myself have in my time often prayed such canonical hours, so that the psalm or hour was at an end before I was aware whether I had begun or was half through.

Although not all of them let themselves go orally as did the aforementioned priest who jumbled up business and prayer, yet they do this with the thoughts that run through their minds. They turn from one thought to another, and when they are done, they do not know what they have been about or what they have touched upon. They begin with "Praise God"[72] and at once their thoughts are far away. I reckon that no one will ever come upon a more ridiculous hocus-pocus than would be encountered in the thoughts that run helter-skelter through a cold, irreverent mind in prayer. But I am now aware, praise God, that it is not good praying if I forget what I have said. A person who prays properly will well remember all the words and thoughts of the prayer from beginning to end.

So a good and painstaking barber must be careful to keep his thoughts, his mind, and his eyes on the razor and the hairs, and he must not forget where he is stropping and shaving. If he insists on a great deal of chatter and lets his thoughts and his eyes wander while he is working, he may well cut somebody's mouth and nose, and perhaps even his throat. If a thing is to be done well, no matter what it is, it requires the full attention of our senses and members, as the proverb puts it, "He who is intent on many things is less perceptive in details,"[72] or, "He whose thoughts are scattered does not think, and he accomplishes no good." How much more does prayer require attentiveness, concentration, and singleness of heart if it is to be good prayer!

This, in short, is the way in which I am myself accustomed to use the Lord's Prayer and to pray. To this day I am still suckling on the Lord's Prayer like a child and am still eating and drinking of it like an old man without growing weary of it. I regard it as the best of prayers—superior even to the Psalter, which I am very fond of. Indeed, it turns out that it was com-

[71] Ps. 70:1. Quoted in Latin.   [72] In Latin.

posed and taught by the real Master. What a pity it is that such a prayer by such a Master should be babbled and gabbled so thoughtlessly throughout the world! Many people probably repeat the Lord's Prayer several thousand times a year, and if they pray like this for a thousand years, they will not have tasted or prayed a single jot or tittle[73] of it. In short, the Lord's Prayer (along with God's name and the Word of God) is the greatest martyr on earth, for everybody misuses and tortures it while few comfort and cheer it by proper use.

If I have time and opportunity to go beyond the Lord's Prayer, I deal similarly with the Ten Commandments, taking up one part after another until I am as ready as possible for prayer. Out of each Commandment I make a garland of four strands. First of all, I take each Commandment as a teaching, which is what it really is, and reflect on what our Lord God earnestly demands of me here. Secondly, I make a thanksgiving of it. Thirdly, a confession. Fourthly, a prayer. I do it with some such thoughts and words as these:

"I am the Lord thy God," etc. "Thou shalt have no other gods before me," etc.[74] Here I consider, first, that God demands and teaches that I should have sincere confidence in him under all circumstances, that it is his earnest purpose to be my God, and that I must take him to be this at the risk of eternal blessedness. My heart should rely and trust in nothing else, be it goods, honor, wisdom, power, or any creature. Secondly, I am thankful for his unfathomable mercy, that he has in so fatherly a fashion come down to me, a lost creature, and that, without any merit on my part, unasked and unbidden, he has offered himself to me to be my God, to accept me, and to be my comfort, refuge, help, and strength in every time of trouble —all this in spite of the fact that we poor, blind mortals have sought other gods and would continue to do so if he did not deign to speak to us so openly and offer in our own human speech to be our God. Who can ever thank him enough for this? Thirdly, I confess and lament my great sins and unthankfulness, that I have so shamefully despised this beautiful teaching and great gift all my life and that I have so horribly stirred up his wrath with countless idolatries. I repent of this and pray for forgiveness. Fourthly, I pray: "O my Lord and God, help me by thy grace, that I may learn to know and understand this thy Commandment better day by day and that I may live accordingly with more sincere trust. Watch

[73] Cf. Matt. 5:18.   [74] Ex. 20:2, 3.

over my heart that I may no longer be so negligent and unthankful and seek other gods or help on earth or in any creature, but rather cling wholly and alone to thee, my only God. Amen, dear Lord God and Father. Amen." . . .[75]

These are the Ten Commandments treated in a fourfold way —as a doctrinal book, hymnbook, confessional book, and prayer book. As a man uses it he should come to himself and his heart should be warmed to pray. But see to it that you do not use all of it or too much of it, lest your spirit become weary. A good prayer need not be long and should not be drawn out, but prayer should be frequent and ardent. It is sufficient if you can find a portion, even a small portion, from which you can strike a spark in your heart. The Holy Spirit must and will do this, and he will provide further instruction when your heart is brought into conformity with the Word of God and is freed from extraneous thoughts and concerns.

I shall not discuss the Creed or the Scriptures here, for that would be endless. Anyone who is practiced in it can take the Ten Commandments one day and a psalm or chapter of the Bible the next day and with such flint strike fire in his heart.[76]

TABLE TALK RECORDED BY ANTHONY LAUTERBACH.[77] June, 1539

He [Luther] also said something about the cause of the difference with respect to election. Why does God elect this man and not that man?

"This difference is to be ascribed to man, not to the will of God," he replied, "for the promises of God are universal. He will have all men to be saved.[78] Accordingly it is not the fault of our Lord God, who promises salvation, but it is our fault if we are unwilling to believe."

TABLE TALK RECORDED BY JOHN MATHESIUS.[79] June, 1540

"I," said Luther, "used to be troubled by these thoughts [about predestination], by what God intends to do with me, but I have turned those thoughts away and have thrown

---

[75] Luther's treatment of the other nine Commandments is here omitted.
[76] In later editions of the booklet Luther appended a section on the Creed here.   [77] Macaronic text; *WA, TR,* IV, No. 4665.
[78] Cf. I Tim. 2:4.   [79] Macaronic text; *WA, TR,* IV, No. 5070.

myself altogether on the revealed will of God. We are not able to get beyond that. The hidden will of God cannot be searched out by man. God conceals it in order to deceive that very cunning spirit, the devil; for the devil learned to know the revealed will from us, but the hidden will God has kept to himself. We have enough to learn in the humanity of Christ, in which the Father revealed himself. But we are proud; we disregard the Word and will of the Father which is revealed in Christ and inquire into the mysteries which ought only to be adored. Therefore, many break their necks on such thoughts."

TABLE TALK RECORDED BY CASPAR HEYDENREICH.[80] February 18, 1542

Speculations concerning predestination are now being spread abroad indiscriminately by epicureans who say: "I do not know whether I am predestined to salvation. If I am elected to eternal life, I shall be saved no matter what I do. On the other hand, if I am not elected, I shall be damned no matter what I do." Although these opinions are true, nevertheless the Passion of Christ and his Sacraments are thereby made of no effect, for it would follow either that it was very foolish of God to send his Son into the world, and so many prophets before him, or that we are surely quite mad. These are poisonous speculations and weapons of the devil. They deceived our first parents when the devil said to them, "Ye shall be as gods."[81] Yet it may be objected that it is necessary that I be saved because God has this intention (if it be God's will).

I reply: Well, are you to climb up to heaven and inquire into this opinion as if it were possible for you to investigate it? It would be most foolish of God to give us his Son and the Scriptures and the prophets if he wished us to be uncertain and to doubt concerning our salvation. It is the work of the devil to make us unbelieving and doubtful. People are assailed either by disdain or by despair when they think, "If I am to be saved, I shall be saved no matter what I do." It is not for you to inquire into the secret will of God without a word of revelation, nor should you imagine that God will fail to keep his promises to you. God is truthful, and he has given us assurances in the

---

[80] Macaronic text; *WA, TR,* V, No. 5658 a. One version bears the title "Dr. Martin Luther's Opinion Concerning Predestination, Written as It Fell from His Lips on Feb. 18, 1542."   [81] Gen. 3:5.

Scriptures in order that we may be certain. Otherwise it will come to pass that books, Bibles, and Sacraments will be cast aside and, like the Turks, we shall say, "Let me live, for tomorrow we die." Such an opinion leads to scorn or despair. I was once freed from this notion by Staupitz,[82] otherwise I should long since have been burning in hell.

For us this is an exceedingly necessary doctrine. A distinction must be made between knowledge of God and despair of God, and consideration must be given to the revealed God on the one hand and to knowledge of the unrevealed will of God on the other. Of the latter nothing at all is known to us. We must confess that what is beyond our comprehension is nothing for us to bother about. Nevertheless, Satan reproaches me with this impenetrable mystery. Apart from the Word of God I am not supposed to know whether I am predestined to salvation or not, and because reason seeks thus to inquire into God, it does not find him. We are not to know even if we break our heads over it. Moses was reproved when he asked, "Lord, show me thy face,"[83] and God replied, "Thou shalt see my back parts!"[84] God has disapproved of and forbidden knowledge of his hidden will. Christ says, "No man knoweth God or the Father save the Son."[85] Without the Word there is neither faith nor understanding. This is the invisible God. The path is blocked here. Such was the answer which the apostles received when they asked Christ when he would restore the kingdom to Israel, for Christ said, "It is not for you to know."[86] Here God desires to be inscrutable and to remain incomprehensible.

He says in effect: "Let me remain hidden. Otherwise you will fall into the abyss of hell, as it is written, 'He who inquires into the majesty of God shall be crushed by it.'[87] In this place leave me untouched. Carnal wisdom shall here have its limit. Here I wish to remain unrevealed. I shall reveal your election in another way. From the unrevealed God I shall become the revealed God. I shall incarnate my Son and shall give you one who will enable you to see whether you are elected. Do this: Give up your speculations which are apart from the Word of God, thoroughly root them out, and drive them to the devil in hell. 'This is my beloved Son. Hear ye him.'[88] Behold his

---

[82] John Staupitz was Luther's superior in the Augustinian monastery in Wittenberg who gave him important spiritual counsel in a crisis in his life.   [83] Cf. Ex. 33:18.   [84] Ex. 33:23.
[85] Cf. Matt. 11:27.   [86] Acts 1:7.   [87] Cf. Prov. 26:27.
[88] Matt. 17:5.

death, cross, and Passion. See him hanging on his mother's breast and on the cross. What he says and does you may be sure of. ' No man cometh unto the Father, but by me,'[89] says the Lord, and to Philip he said, 'He that hath seen me hath seen the Father.'[90] Here you have me and will see me."

Whosoever accepts the Son and is baptized and believes on his Word will be saved. I should indeed like to have it otherwise. But the Lord will not have it so. Begin at the bottom with the incarnate Son and with your terrible original sin. If you wish to escape from despair and hate, let your speculation go. There is no other way. Otherwise you must remain a doubter the rest of your life. God did not come down from heaven to make you uncertain about predestination or to cause you to despise the Sacraments. He instituted them to make you more certain and to drive such speculations out of your mind. Whoever doubts the revealed will of God will perish, for where there is doubt there is no salvation.

What more do you want him to do? He reveals himself to you so that you may touch and see him not only in your thoughts but also with your eyes. It is as Christ says, "He that hath seen me hath seen the Father."[90] Christ will lead you to the hidden God. You ought not to risk having the child Jesus snatched away from you. If you embrace him with true love of your heart and with true faith, you will know for sure that you are predestined to salvation. But the devil has a special fondness for making us most uncertain about predestination at the point at which we are most certain, namely, in the revelation of his Son.

A wretched woman who was troubled by such temptations of the devil once came to me and said, "I do not know if I am predestined or not."

I said to her: "Dear woman, you have been baptized. Do you believe what you hear in the preaching of the Word and do you accept it as the truth?"

"Yes," she replied, "I have no doubt that it is true, but I am unable to believe it."

I said: "To have faith in him is to accept these things as true without any doubting. God has revealed himself to you. If you believe this, then you are to be numbered among his elect. Hold to this firmly and with assurance, and if you accept the God who is revealed, the hidden God will be given to you at the same time. 'He that hath seen me hath seen the Father.'[90]

[89] John 14:6.   [90] John 14:9.

Cling to the revealed God, allow no one to take the child Jesus from you, hold fast to him, and you will not be lost. The Father desires you. The Son wishes to be your Saviour and Liberator. In so kind and friendly a fashion has God freed us from these terrible temptations. Otherwise our hearts are deprived of that certain trust and predestination. Those with terrified hearts will disagree, and those whose hearts are hardened will be filled with contempt. Christ said, 'Murmur not among yourselves. No man can come to the Father except the Father which hath sent me draw him.'[91] And [Jesus] Sirach said, 'Search not out things that are above thy strength.'[92] Do this, as I said to you at the beginning, and accept the incarnate Son."

This is the way in which [John] Staupitz comforted me when the devil was similarly vexing me: "Why do you trouble yourself with these speculations of yours? Accept the wounds of Christ and contemplate the blood which poured forth from his most holy body for our sins—for mine, for yours, for those of all men. 'My sheep hear my voice.'[93]"

There is a beautiful example in the lives of the Fathers, where it is written that a young man named Neophile ascended to heaven and, having placed one foot inside of heaven, drew it back in order to thrust his other foot in, and he fell and plunged headlong into hell. So those who try to climb into heaven without the revealed Christ, and think that they have both feet in heaven, tumble down to hell. We should accept the child Jesus and cling to him because the Father is in the Son and the Son is in the Father. This is the only way. You will find no other, and you will break your neck if you try. This means that God cannot deny himself.[94] If we cling to him, he will hold us fast, and he will tear us away from sin and death and will not let us fall. Besides, these speculations about predestination are of the devil. If they assail you, say: "I am a son of God. I have been baptized. I believe in Jesus Christ, who was crucified for me. Let me alone, devil." Then such thoughts will leave you.

There is an account of a nun who was troubled by the devil with such wretched thoughts. When he addressed her and attacked her with his fiery darts,[95] she said no more than this: "I am a Christian." The devil understood her very well, for it was as if she said: "I believe in the Son of God, who died on

91 John 6:43, 44.   92 Ecclus. 3:21.   93 John 10:27.
94 Cf. II Tim. 2:13.   95 Eph. 6:16.

the cross, who sits at the right hand of the Father, who cares for me, and who is accustomed to intercede in my behalf. Let me alone, you cursed devil! With his inscrutable seal God has given me assurance." At once the temptation ceased, and at once she had peace of conscience and love for God. He wishes his predestination to be more surely grounded on many certain arguments. He sent his Son to become man, and he gave us the Sacraments and his Word, which cannot be doubted. The words of that nun come to mind in time of temptation, for unless we flee to this Christ, we shall either despair of our salvation or become blasphemous epicureans who hide behind divine predestination as an excuse. These opinions are impious and wicked.

The fact that Isaac doubted cannot be adduced here as an example, for it is allowable to doubt with respect to man, as Isaac doubted whether he would have a good omen and a friendly reception. But God is not man. It is permissible to doubt man because we are commanded not to put our trust in princes.[96] If we rely on them and they fail us, or if one of them renders us a service, we call it fortuitous or a chance occurence. It is not so with the help of God, however, concerning whom we have many signs that he is not a God who deceives us and is to be doubted. This is demonstrated for us by spiritual and corporeal arguments in the incarnation of his Son and in the Sacraments, which are plainly from God and meet our carnal eyes and are administered with external ceremonies, under which external marks God manifests himself to us and distributes his benefits to us. Consequently one should say of a man, "I do not know if he is friend or foe." But not so of God. In this case I have no doubt that God is absolute and that your sins are forgiven. But we are such scoundrels that we prefer to put our constant reliance on man rather than on God.

Adam did this when God placed him in paradise and said, "Of every tree of the garden thou mayest freely eat, but of the tree of the knowledge of good and evil, thou shalt not eat of it."[97] What do you think drove Adam to eat of it? He wished to know what God's secret intention was with regard to this tree that he should not eat of it, and he thought, God certainly has something extraordinary on this tree. He was searching out God apart from the Word. Then the devil came and urged on Adam [and Eve] by saying: "Ye shall be as gods if ye eat of it. Your eyes shall be opened so that ye shall see everything as

96 Cf. Ps. 146:3.   97 Gen. 2:16, 17.

God sees it."[98] So they wished to be God and to eat of the tree which God had forbidden them to eat of when he said, "Ye shall not eat of it, neither shall ye know what I have on the tree."[99] Thereupon Adam said, "Truly, I must know!" He ate of it, and at once he knew what he had done and he saw that he was naked. That is, his eyes were opened.

We do the same thing in our relation to God. We wish to know what he has not commanded us to know. We should eat of every tree that he allows us to eat of, and we should rejoice to do so, but none of the fruit tastes so good to us as that of the tree we are forbidden to touch and on account of which he closed paradise and heaven to us so that we may know nothing of him except what he has revealed to us in his Word. If you wish to know what God's secret intention is, his dear Son will show it to you. We must have a God who is hidden from us, but we should not investigate into him, else we shall break our necks. It is God's will that we should be agreeable sons of his because we believe in his Son. There is no wrath here. Be satisfied with this.

TO GEORGE SPALATIN. February 12, 1544

For many years Luther had been concerned with problems connected with economic life and attempted to discuss them in ethical terms. As early as 1520 he had written A Treatise on Usury,[1] *and again in 1524 he had written* On Trading and Usury.[2] *The subject came up frequently in conversations at his table and played a part in his correspondence (see Chapter VIII). The following letter, written in answer to questions raised by George Spalatin (1484-1545), deals only with the fixing of fair prices for grain.* [Text in Latin; *WA, Br,* X, 532.]

To the venerable gentleman in the Lord, Master George Spalatin, bishop and pastor of the churches in Altenburg and Meissen, my beloved brother: grace and peace in the Lord.

My dear Spalatin:

I was sure that I had replied to your questions about usury, for I am conscious of having thought about the matter and of

---

98 Cf. Gen. 3:5.   99 Cf. Gen. 3:3.
1 *WA*, VI, 33–60; English translation in *Works of Martin Luther*, Philadelphia ed., IV, 37–69.
2 *WA*, XV, 279–322; English translation in *Works of Martin Luther*, Philadelphia ed., IV, 7–36.

intending to answer. This is happening to me daily in other cases as well, so occupied am I with a multitude of tasks and wretched affairs.

But to the point. Your questions concerning usury with grain cannot be settled by any certain rule on account of the great variations in times, places, persons, circumstances, and cases. Therefore, the matter must be left to individual conscience; every man, confronted by the natural law, must ask, Would you that others should do to you what you do to them? "For this is the law and the prophets,"[3] says Christ. At the same time a good conscience will observe what is written in Proverbs, "He that withholdeth corn, the people shall curse him: but blessing shall be upon the head of him that selleth it,"[4] and also what Amos said of the avaricious, that they make the ephah small and the shekel large.[5] This last, however, does not touch upon your questions since you have not written about avaricious but good men. Accordingly they must provide their own answers in such uncertain matters which cannot be regulated by laws.

Farewell in the Lord.

Yours,

Tuesday after Saint Scholastica, 1544.   Martin Luther.

TO AN UNKNOWN PERSON. August 8, 1545

It is not known to whom the following letter was addressed. It is clear, however, that it was intended for a person who was troubled about his or her election to salvation. [Text in German; *WA, Br*, XI, 165, 166.]

My dear friend N has informed me that you are at times troubled by the question of God's eternal election, and he has requested me to write you this brief letter, etc.

To be sure, it is a serious thing to be so troubled. But you should know that we are forbidden to concern and worry ourselves about this question, for we ought to be willing to remain in ignorance about things which God chooses to keep hidden. This is the apple of which Adam and Eve and all their descendants ate to their destruction, for they wished to know what they were not supposed to know. Just as murder, theft, and cursing are sins, so it is also a sin to trouble oneself about this question. And like all other sins, it is the work of the devil.

To counteract this, God has given us his Son, Jesus Christ. We should think of him daily and follow him. In him we shall

[3] Matt. 7:12.   [4] Prov. 11:26.   [5] Cf. Amos 8:5.

find our election to be sure and pleasant, for without Christ everything is peril, death, and the devil, while in Christ is pure peace and joy. Nothing but anxiety can be gained from forever tormenting oneself with the question of election. Therefore, avoid and flee from such thoughts, as from the temptation of the serpent in paradise, and direct your attention to Christ.

God keep you!

August 8, 1545.   Martin Luther, Doctor.

V

Admonitions to Steadfastness and Courage

TO ELECTOR FREDERICK OF SAXONY.

February 24, 1522

After the Diet of Worms (1521) Luther was taken for his own protection to the Wartburg Castle, where he translated the New Testament into German. During Luther's absence from Wittenberg his impetuous colleague, Andrew Carlstadt (1480-1541), and three self-styled prophets from the neighboring village of Zwickau introduced reforms in Church life which were more radical than Luther's conservative friends thought expedient. The reforms caused disturbances and violence, which naturally troubled the elector of Saxony. Luther served notice of his intention to return to Wittenberg to set things right, but for the time being he wrote especially to strengthen the elector's resolution and dispel his fears. [Text in German; WA, Br, II, 448, 449.]

To my very gracious lord, Duke Frederick, elector of Saxony, into whose hands this is to be delivered: grace and joy from God the Father on the acquisition of a new relic!

My gracious Lord:

I put this greeting in place of my assurances of respect. For many years Your Grace has been acquiring relics in every land,[1] but God has now heard Your Grace's request and has sent Your Grace, without cost or trouble, a whole cross together with nails, spears, and scourges. I say again: grace and joy from God on the acquisition of a new relic!

Only do not be terrified by it but stretch out your arms confidently and let the nails go deep. Be glad and thankful, for thus it must and will be with those who desire God's Word. Not only

---

[1] Because the elector of Saxony had formerly been an avid collector of relics, Luther referred to the disturbance in Wittenberg as a new cross (and a whole cross rather than just a piece of a cross) which the elector would have to bear.

must Annas and Caiaphas rage, but Judas must be among the apostles and Satan among the children of God. Only be wise and prudent, and do not judge according to reason or outward appearances. Do not be downhearted, for things have not yet come to such a pass as Satan wishes.

Have a little confidence in me, fool though I am, for I know these and other like tricks of Satan. I do not fear him because I know that this hurts him. Yet all of this is only a beginning. Let the world cry out and pass its judgments. Let those fall away who will—even a Saint Peter or persons like the apostles. They will come back on the third day, when Christ rises from the dead. This word in II Cor., ch. 6, must be fulfilled in us: "Let us approve ourselves in tumults," etc.[2]

I hope that Your Grace will take this letter in good part. I am in such haste that my pen has had to gallop, and I have no time for more. God willing, I shall soon be there, but Your Grace must not assume responsibility in my behalf.

Your Grace's humble servant,

Martin Luther.

TO ELECTOR JOHN OF SAXONY. May 20, 1530

When on January 21, 1530, he summoned the imperial diet to meet in Augsburg, Emperor Charles V had expressed the hope that "in the matter of errors and divisions concerning the holy faith . . . schisms may be allayed, antipathies set aside, . . . and every care taken to give a charitable hearing to every man's opinion . . . so that one true religion may be accepted and held by all."[3] In preparation for the diet, therefore, Elector John of Saxony asked his theologians in Wittenberg to prepare a statement setting forth the reforms introduced in the church in Saxony. Armed with this and other statements, the elector's party set out for Augsburg. Since he was still under imperial ban, Luther accompanied the party only as far as Coburg, where he remained during the sessions of the diet. Philip Melanchthon headed the Evangelical theologians who went on to Augsburg, where the party arrived on May 2. Great responsibility for the future of the Evangelical movement now rested on Elector John, and Luther wrote the following letter to encourage him to stand fast. [Text in German; *WA, Br,* V, 324-328.]

To the serene, highborn prince and lord, John, duke of Saxony, elector of the Holy Roman Empire, etc., landgrave in Thur-

---

2 Cf. II Cor. 6:4, 5.
3 M. Reu, *The Augsburg Confession* (Chicago, 1930), *69–72.

ingia, and margrave of Meissen, my gracious lord: grace and peace in Christ, our Lord and Saviour. Amen.

Serene, highborn Prince, gracious Lord:

I have for some time delayed answering Your Grace's first letter from Augsburg,[4] which was so graciously sent to me with all its news and admonitions in order that time might not hang heavily on my hands here. It was not necessary for Your Grace to be anxious and to think about me, but it is our duty to remember, be concerned about, and pray for Your Grace, and this we do, and do faithfully. I do not find the days to be long. We live like lords, and these last weeks passed so quickly that they seem like no more than three days.[5]

On the other hand, Your Grace is now obliged to be in a tiresome situation. May our dear Lord in heaven help with his grace, which he gives us so abundantly, that Your Grace may remain steadfast and patient. It is certain that Your Grace must endure all this trouble, expense, danger, and tedium solely for God's sake inasmuch as none of the raging princes and opponents can find any fault with Your Grace except on account of the pure, tender, living Word of God, for they know Your Grace to be a blameless, peaceful, pious, and faithful prince. Since this is certain, it may be taken as a sign that God loves Your Grace dearly, seeing that he so abundantly grants his holy Word and considers Your Grace worthy to suffer so much shame and enmity on its account. All of this should be a source of comfort, for God's friendship is more precious than that of the whole world. On the other hand, we see that God does not consider the angry and wrathful princes worthy of knowing and possessing his Word. Indeed, they are obliged in their blindness and callousness to revile and persecute it, and this senseless raging of theirs is a terrible sign of God's disfavor and wrath toward them. This ought to terrify them in their consciences and cause them to despair, and it will ultimately be so.

The merciful God is also giving a sign of his graciousness by making his Word so powerful and fruitful in Your Grace's land. For surely Your Grace's land has more excellent pastors and preachers than any other land in the whole world, and their

---

4 Elector John had written to Luther under date of May 11 (*WA, Br,* V, 310–312).
5 Luther had been in Coburg almost four weeks. In his letter the elector had expressed the hope that time would not pass too slowly for Luther.

faithful, pure teaching helps to preserve peace. As a consequence the tender youth, both boys and girls, are so well instructed in the Catechism and the Scriptures that I am deeply
moved when I see that young boys and girls can pray, believe,
and speak more of God and Christ than they ever could in the
monasteries, foundations, and schools of bygone days, or even
of our day.[6]

Truly Your Grace's land is a beautiful paradise for such
young people. There is no other place like it in all the world.
God has erected this paradise in Your Grace's land as a special
token of his grace and favor. It is as if he would say, "To you,
dear Duke John, I entrust my most precious treasure, my pleasant
paradise, and ask you to preside over it as father. I place it
under your protection and government and do you the honor
of making you my gardener and caretaker." For the Lord God,
who has set Your Grace over this land to be its father and
helper, feeds all the people through Your Grace's office and
service, for they must all eat of Your Grace's bread. This is as
if God himself were Your Grace's daily guest and ward inasmuch as his Word and those children of his who have his Word
are Your Grace's daily guests and wards.

Behold, how the fury of other princes harms the dear youth!
They turn this paradise of God into sinful, corrupt, and ruinous
mudholes of the devil, they spoil everything, and they have none
but devils as their daily guests at table. For in God's sight they
are not deserving of the honor of giving even a cup of cold
water[7] out of their great wealth. On the contrary, they have
nothing better to give the Saviour on the cross than vinegar,
myrrh, and gall.[8] Nevertheless, many godly people live in their
lands in secret, and they yearn eagerly for Your Grace's paradise and blessed land[9] and help to pray earnestly for it.

There is evidence that God dwells so richly in Your Grace's
land in the fact that he graciously allows his Word to have free
course there, the fact that Your Grace places all offices, property, and goods in his blessed service and use, the fact that

---

[6] In his "Sermon on Keeping Children in School," 1530 (*WA*, XXX[ii],
546, 547; English translation in *Works of Martin Luther*, IV, 154), Luther
wrote, "Even women and children can now learn more about God and
Christ from German books and sermons (I am telling the truth) than all
the universities, foundations, monasteries, the whole papacy, and all the
world used to know."

[7] Cf. Matt. 10:42.   [8] Cf. Matt. 27:34.

[9] See also the letter to the Evangelicals in Leipzig, Oct. 4, 1532, in
Chapter VII.

Your Grace ceaselessly offers up everything as daily alms and sacrifices in honor of the holy Word of God, and the fact that Your Grace is endowed with a peaceful disposition and is not bloodthirsty and cruel, as Your Grace's opponents are and must be. Consequently Your Grace has ample cause to rejoice in God and find comfort in these notable marks of his grace. For it is a great and glorious honor to be chosen, consecrated, and deemed worthy by God to place one's life and possessions, land and people, and all that one has in the service of God so that the divine Word is not only not persecuted but also preserved and cultivated. It matters not that some among us cause Your Grace difficulties, for in spite of this Your Grace's service and protection have the effect of preserving the Word.

Your Grace is also supported by the earnest and faithful prayers of all Christians, especially in Your Grace's lands, and we know that our prayers are effectual and our cause is just. Therefore, we are also certain that our prayers please God and are heard. Indeed, the young people will lift up their innocent voices and call to heaven and faithfully commend Your Grace to the merciful God as their dear father. On the other hand, we know that our opponents have an unjust cause, that they are unable to pray, that they employ clever devices to gain their ends, and that they rely on their own wit and power, as is manifest. In short, they are building on sand.[10]

May Your Grace receive this letter in good part, for God knows that I speak the truth and do not dissemble. I am sorry that Satan is trying to disturb and trouble Your Grace. I know him very well and am aware that he likes to involve me in the situation. He is a doleful, disagreeable spirit who cannot bear to see anyone happy or at peace, especially with God. How much less will he suffer Your Grace to be of good courage since he knows very well how much we depend on Your Grace! And not we alone, but almost the whole world and, I should almost say, heaven itself, because a large part of the Kingdom of Christ is constantly being edified by the saving Word in Your Grace's land. The devil knows this and is displeased by it. We are accordingly under obligation faithfully to support Your Grace with our prayers, help, love, and every other possible means at our disposal. For when Your Grace is happy, we live, but when Your Grace is sorrowful, we are sick.

Our dear Lord and faithful Saviour, Jesus Christ, whom the Father of all mercies has so abundantly revealed and given to

10 Cf. Matt. 7:26.

us, grant unto Your Grace, beyond all my asking, his Holy Spirit, the true and eternal Comforter, and may he ever preserve, strengthen, and keep Your Grace against all the cunning, poisonous, and fiery darts[11] of the disagreeable, grievous, and wicked spirit. Amen, dear God, and amen.

Your Grace's obedient servant,

May 20, 1530.   Martin Luther.

Dr. Apel[12] has also requested me to ask Your Grace to excuse him for taking leave at this time and departing to Prussia. He desired to mention this long ago, but because Your Grace was always so burdened with other duties, he was reluctant and timid about disturbing my gracious lord. I assume that Dr. Apel will himself report to Your Grace at greater length. Your Grace will know how to deal graciously with this matter. Herewith I commit Your Grace to God's keeping.

TO SON JOHN LUTHER. June 19, 1530

John (or Hans) Luther, the Reformer's oldest child, had just passed his fourth birthday. He had already begun his schooling under the tutorship of Jerome Weller, who had written to Luther (at the time away from home in Coburg) that his son was making progress. This playful letter was intended to give the boy an incentive to industry and piety, and it reveals the ability of the Reformer to address a child in terms that a child would understand. It is the more remarkable when it is recalled that the letter was written when Luther was anxious about the outcome of the Diet of Augsburg. [Text in German; *WA, Br,* V, 379, 380.]

To my beloved son Hans Luther in Wittenberg: grace and peace in Christ.

My beloved Son:

I am pleased to learn that you are doing well in your studies and that you are praying diligently. Continue to do so, my son, and when I return home I shall bring you a present from the fair.

I know of a pretty, gay, and beautiful garden where there are

---

11 Cf. Eph. 6:16.

12 John Apel, the messenger who delivered the exchange of letters between Elector John and Luther, had on Luther's recommendation been called by Duke Albert of Prussia to serve as chancellor. Apel was reluctant to inform the elector of his intended departure since the elector had just selected him for his own court five months earlier.

many children wearing golden robes. They pick up fine apples, pears, cherries, and plums under the trees, and they sing, jump, and are happy all the time. They also have nice ponies with golden reins and silver saddles. I asked the owner of the garden who the children were. He replied: "These are the children who love to pray, learn their lessons, and be good." Then I said: "Dear sir, I also have a son. His name is Hans Luther. May he too enter the garden, eat of the fine apples and pears, ride on these pretty ponies, and play with the other children?" The man answered: "If he likes to pray and study and is good, he may enter the garden, and also Lippus and Jost.[13] And when they are all together there, they shall get whistles, drums, lutes, and other musical instruments, and they shall dance and shoot with little crossbows." And he showed me a lovely lawn in the garden, all ready for dancing, and many gold whistles and drums and fine silver crossbows were hanging there. But it was still so early in the morning that the children had not yet eaten, and so I could not wait for the dancing. I said to the man: "Dear sir, I must hurry away and write about all this to my dear little son Hans and tell him to pray, study, and be good in order that he may get into this garden. He has an Aunt Lena,[14] and he must bring her along." "By all means," said the man, "go and write him accordingly."

Therefore, dear Hans, continue to learn your lessons and pray, and tell Lippus and Jost to pray too, so that all of you may get into the garden together.

Herewith I commit you to the dear Lord's keeping. Greet Aunt Lena, and give her a kiss from me.

Your loving father,

Martin Luther.

TO PHILIP MELANCHTHON. June 27, 1530

Shortly after his arrival in Augsburg, Philip Melanchthon read the "Four Hundred and Four Theses" by the Catholic theologian John Eck (1486-1543), which was on sale in Augsburg. The Theses bracketed Lutherans with Anabaptists and others and tried to demonstrate that all of these represented revivals of ancient heresies which had long since been condemned. The conciliatory Melanchthon was alarmed by the Theses and by the hostility he encountered in following weeks. In this

[13] Philip, son of Philip Melanchthon, and Justus, son of Justus Jonas, both of roughly the same age as Luther's son.
[14] Magdalene von Bora, aunt of Luther's wife; on her death see Chapter I.

atmosphere, with the help of the documents which the elector had brought with him to Augsburg, Melanchthon labored on a temperate statement of Evangelical faith and practice. Meanwhile Luther complained that he received no news in Coburg. Observing at the same time that the timid Melanchthon was assailed by fear and uncertainty, Luther tried to expose the source of his worries and cheer him up. [Text in Latin; WA, Br, V, 398-400.]

To Philip Melanchthon, beloved disciple of Christ and bearer of Christ:[15] grace and peace in Christ—in Christ, I say, and not in the world. Amen.

My dear Philip:

I shall write again about the apology which has been offered for your silence.[16] This courier has come unexpectedly and suddenly, and since he wished to depart he could hardly wait for the accompanying letters which came from Wittenberg and which he is to take along to Nuremberg for forwarding to you. Hence I must wait for another courier, to write more fully.

With all my heart I hate those cares by which you state that you are consumed. They rule your heart, not on account of the greatness of the cause but by reason of the greatness of your unbelief. The same cause existed in the time of John Hus[17] and many others, and they had a harder time of it than we do. Great though our cause is, its Author and Champion is also great, for the cause is not ours. Why, then, are you constantly tormenting yourself? If our cause is false, let us recant. But if it is true, why should we make Him a liar who has given us such great promises and who commands us to be confident and undismayed? "Cast thy burden upon the Lord," he says.[18] "The Lord is nigh unto all them that call upon him."[19] Does he speak like this for nothing, or to beasts?

I too am sometimes downcast, but not all the time. It is your philosophy that is tormenting you, not your theology, and the same is true of your friend Joachim,[20] who seems to be troubled by similar anxiety. What good do you expect to accomplish by these vain worries of yours? What can the devil do more than

---

15 *Christophoro.*

16 In his letter to Luther of June 12 (*WA, Br, V,* 355–361), Jonas suggested that Melanchthon had not been heard from because the couriers had not delivered his letters.

17 On John Hus see Matthew Spinka, ed., *Advocates of Reform from Wyclif to Erasmus* (Philadelphia, 1953), in The Library of Christian Classics.

18 Ps. 55:22.   19 Ps. 145:18.

20 Joachim Camerarius.

slay us?[21] Yes, what? I beg you, who are so pugnacious in everything else, fight against yourself, your own worst enemy, for you furnish Satan with too many weapons against yourself. Christ died once for our sins. He will not die again for truth and justice, but will live and reign. If this be true, and if he reigns, why should you be afraid for the truth? Perhaps you are afraid that it will be destroyed by God's wrath. Even if we should ourselves be destroyed, let it not be by our own hands. He who is our Father will also be the Father of our children.

I pray for you very earnestly, and I am deeply pained that you keep sucking up cares like a leech and thus rendering my prayers vain. Christ knows whether it comes from stupidity or the Spirit, but I for my part am not very much troubled about our cause. Indeed, I am more hopeful than I expected to be. God, who is able to raise the dead, is also able to uphold his cause when it is falling, or to raise it up again when it has fallen, or to move it forward when it is standing. If we are not worthy instruments to accomplish his purpose, he will find others. If we are not strengthened by his promises, where in all the world are the people to whom these promises apply? But more of this another time. After all, my writing this is like pouring water into the sea.

You should know that I forwarded your letters to Wittenberg yesterday, both the one written before and the one written after the arrival of the emperor.[22] For those who are at home are also troubled by your silence, as you will learn from the letter of Pomeranus,[23] though the fault of their not hearing from you is not, as Jonas suggests, the messenger's, but it is yours, and yours alone.

May Christ comfort all of you by his Spirit and strengthen and instruct you. Amen. If I should hear that things are not going well with you, or that the cause is in danger, I shall hardly be able to keep from hurrying to Augsburg in order to see what the Scriptures call "Satan's formidable teeth round about."[24] I shall write again soon. Meanwhile give my greetings to all my friends.

Yours,

Monday after Saint John's Day, 1530.   Martin Luther.

21 This sentence in German.
22 The emperor reached Augsburg on June 15.
23 John Bugenhagen, of Pomerania.   24 Cf. Job 41:15.

TO PHILIP MELANCHTHON. June 29, 1530

The Augsburg Confession, on which Philip Melanchthon had long been working, was read before the diet in Augsburg on June 25, 1530. Luther had now received a copy of it in virtually the form in which it had been read, and he was, on the whole, pleased with it. At the same time he was troubled by Melanchthon's readiness to make further concessions and tried in this letter to counteract his friend's misgivings and stiffen his back. [Text in Latin; WA, Br, V, 405-408.]

Grace and peace in Christ.

My dear Philip:

I have read the extravagant rhetoric with which you excuse yourself for your silence.[25] Meanwhile I have sent you two letters in which I have offered an adequate explanation of my silence—at least in the last letter which the courier who was sent to the elector by our tax collector[26] is delivering. Today your most recent letters, containing news as well as apology, were delivered. In these you remind me of your labors, perils, and tears in such a manner as to suggest that I have by my silence shamefully heaped sorrow upon sorrow[27]—as if I did not know this or were sitting here among roses without sharing your cares with you. Would that my concerns were of such a kind as to permit me to weep.[28] I swear that if your earlier letters reporting the emperor's arrival[29] had not come in the evening I was resolved to send a courier to you the next day at my own expense to find out whether you were alive or dead. Master Veit[30] will bear witness to this. Yet I believe that all your letters were delivered to us,[31] for the letters about the emperor's arrival and entry came tardily and at about the same time. Or if this was caused by Ate[32] or some devil, let them take the consequences.

I have received your Apology[33] and wonder what you have

---

[25] In Melanchthon's letter to Luther, June 25, 1530, in WA, Br, V, 386–388.

[26] Probably Valentine Förster, of Wittenberg.   [27] Cf. Phil. 2:27.

[28] In his letter of June 25, as elsewhere, Melanchthon referred to his tears.

[29] Melanchthon to Luther, June 13, and Jonas to Luther, June 12 and 13, in WA, Br, V, 355–366.

[30] Veit Dietrich, who was with Luther in Coburg.

[31] Justus Jonas had suggested in his letter of June 12 that some of the letters from Augsburg might have been lost on the way.

[32] An ancient Greek goddess or avenging spirit in Greek tragedies.

[33] The Augsburg Confession, not to be confused with the later Apology of the Augsburg Confession.

in mind when you ask what and how much should be conceded to the papists. As far as the elector is concerned, it is quite another matter to ask what he might concede in the event that danger threatens him. But as far as I am personally concerned, more than enough has been conceded in this Apology. If they reject it, I know of nothing more that I could yield, unless I should see in their arguments from reason and the Scriptures more than I have hitherto seen. I am occupied day and night with this matter. I think about it, ponder over it, weigh it, and search through all the Scriptures. Certainty[34] concerning this teaching of ours grows upon me increasingly, and I am more and more resolved that, God willing, I shall give up nothing more, come what may.

According to your request I have written to the young prince,[35] but I tore up the letter again for fear that I might put ideas into his head and later hear excuses that I do not wish to hear.

I am quite well, for that evil spirit who had before buffeted me[36] seems to have let up because he was beaten off by your prayers and those of the other brethren. However, I suspect that another has come in his place to vex my body. Yet I prefer to suffer this tormentor of the flesh rather than that other tormentor of the spirit. And I hope that He who overcomes the father of lies in me may also overcome this murderer.[37] I am well aware that he has sworn to kill me and will not rest until he devours me. But if he does so, he will swallow a purgative, God willing, that will burst his belly.[38] What does it matter? Whoever will have Christ must suffer. It would be easy for us to triumph if we were willing to deny Christ and reproach him. It is written, "Through much tribulation."[39] These are not simply words; they have become a reality, and we must govern ourselves accordingly. Yet He is present who puts an end to the tribulation of the faithful.[40]

It displeases me that you write in your letter that you have followed my authority in this cause. I do not wish to be or be called the author of this cause. Even if it might be interpreted properly, I dislike the term. If it is not at the same time and equally your cause, I do not wish it to be called my cause as if

---

[34] Greek: *plerophoria*.   [35] John Frederick, son of the elector of Saxony.
[36] Cf. II Cor. 12:7.   [37] Cf. John 8:44.
[38] *So soll er ein Purgation fressen, die ihm Bauch und Ars zu enge machen soll.* The preceding and following sentences, as well as this one, in German.
[39] Acts 14:22.   [40] Cf. I Cor. 10:13.

it were imposed on you. If it is mine alone, I shall plead my
own cause.

I believe that all your letters have been delivered which you
sent by Dr. Jonas' courier. None of the later ones which you
have sent up to now were delivered, except those which reported the emperor's arrival and entry. From this you should
know that I have the pictures of Vienna.[41] But during the time
between the arrival of Jonas' courier and the report of the
emperor's entry you have sufficiently crucified us with your
silence.

I have tried in my last letter to comfort you, and I pray that
the letter may have conveyed life rather than death to you.
What can I do in addition? You are torturing yourself about
the end and outcome of the cause because you cannot comprehend them. If you could comprehend them, I should not like to
be a participant, much less the author, of this cause. God has
put it in a certain commonplace[42] which you do not have in
your rhetoric or in your philosophy. This is faith. And in this
faith are comprehended all the things that are not seen and
do not appear.[43] If somebody tries to make this visible, apparent, and comprehensible, as you do, he may reap anxiety
and tears as the fruit of his labor, as you do, while all of us
vainly cry out against it. "The Lord said that he would dwell
in the thick darkness,"[44] and "he made darkness his secret
place."[45] Let him who will do otherwise. If Moses had insisted
on knowing the outcome when he wished to escape from
Pharaoh's army, Israel would perhaps still be in Egypt today.

May the Lord increase your faith and the faith of all of us.
If we have faith, what can Satan accomplish even with the
whole world? But if we do not have faith, why do we not at
least strengthen ourselves with the faith of others? For there are
bound to be others who have faith in our stead unless there is
no longer a Church in the world and unless Christ has ceased
to be with us before the end of the world.[46] If Christ is not with
us, where, pray, is he in all the world? If we are not the Church
or a part of it, where is the Church? Are the dukes of Bavaria,
Ferdinand,[47] the pope, the Turk, and others like them the

---

[41] Woodcut views of Vienna, done by Nicholas Meldemann, of Nuremberg,
sent by Melanchthon with his letter of May 22.

[42] *Locum quendam communem*, an article or locus of theology.

[43] In Greek from Heb. 11:1, 3.   [44] I Kings 8:12.

[45] Ps. 18:11.   [46] Cf. Matt. 28:20.

[47] King of Hungary and Bohemia and, like the dukes of Bavaria, a
vigorous opponent of the Reformation.

Church? If we do not have the Word of God, who has it? If, then, God be for us, who can be against us?[48] We are sinners and ingrates, but this does not make him a liar. Nor can we be sinners in this holy cause of God even if we be wicked in our way of life. But Satan so discourages and weakens you that you do not hear my words. I pray earnestly and without ceasing that Christ may heal you. Amen.

I wish that I might have an opportunity to visit you. I desire to go although I have neither command nor call to do so. This letter should have gone to Brenz[49] and Dr. Caspar[50] with the last letter, but the courier left without it. Greet everybody, for I cannot write again to each one. The grace of God be with you and all the rest of our friends. Amen.

Saint Peter's and Saint Paul's Day, 1530.   Martin Luther.

After closing the letter it occurred to me that it may perhaps appear to you that I have not sufficiently replied to your question: How much and to what extent should concessions be made to the adversaries? But your question was not full enough. You have not indicated what, or what sort of thing, you think will be demanded of us. As I have always written, I am ready to concede everything to them, provided only the gospel is permitted to have free course among us. However, I can make no concessions that conflict with the gospel. What, beyond this, can I reply?

TO ELECTOR JOHN OF SAXONY. June 30, 1530

After the public reading of the Augsburg Confession on June 25, 1530, the Evangelicals in Augsburg were given the impression that their statement of faith was too extreme to be acceptable to the Catholic party. It was reported to Luther that Duke George of Albertine Saxony was especially active in threatening violence and treachery. In the following letter to the elector Luther therefore counseled calm patience and resolute strength. [Text in German; *WA, Br,* V, 421, 422.]

To the serene, highborn prince and lord, Duke John of Saxony, elector, landgrave in Thuringia, and margrave of Meissen, my gracious lord: grace and peace in Christ Jesus.

48 Rom. 8:31.
49 John Brenz (1499–1570), whose greetings had been conveyed to Luther in Melanchthon's letter of June 25.
50 Caspar Lindemann, a physician.

Serene, highborn Prince, gracious Lord:

It is now manifest to Your Grace what kind of lord the devil is, that he takes wise and great people captive in his service, and that he carries out all his designs swiftly and with cunning tricks. Although I know that Your Grace is, thank God, well prepared to resist and has the capacity to understand and judge the devil's great art and counsels, yet in my concern I have wished to write and humbly admonish Your Grace not to worry about the wicked and poisonous onslaughts of your nearest blood relation.[51] For when the devil is powerless to do more, he tries at least to upset and bother us with his almost intolerable schemes.

Psalm 37 is an excellent remedy for this. It exposes the malice of Satan's emissaries, who try unceasingly to provoke us and elicit from us some impatient word, act, or gesture on account of which he might brand us with disobedience and sedition. But it is written, "If God be for us, who can be against us?"[52] We must learn to absorb the knavery of wicked people. As Saint Paul says in Rom., ch. 12, we must overcome evil with good.[53]

No doubt the emperor is a pious man, worthy of all dignity and honor, whose person cannot be held in too high esteem. But what in the world can one man do against so many devils unless God gives him powerful help? I am myself grieved that Your Grace's blood relation behaves so rashly and arrogantly, but I must have patience, else I should be wishing him all manner of evil. I can easily imagine how much more it must grieve and hurt Your Grace. But Your Grace will have patience for God's sake and will also pray with us for the miserable creatures who have not yet achieved anything by their defiance. If I err in supposing that Your Grace has been grieved by the malice of relatives, I rejoice. Forgive me, for my intentions are good. I sit here and think that here is something that will gnaw at this or that man's heart and make him unhappy, for I always attribute all wickedness to the devil.

Herewith I commit Your Grace to God's keeping. Amen.

Your Grace's humble servant,

The last day of June, 1530.   Dr. Martin Luther.

TO JUSTUS JONAS. July 13, 1530

Justus Jonas (1493-1555), at this time dean of the theological faculty in Wittenberg, was one of the advisers whom the elector of Saxony had

51 Duke George of Albertine Saxony.   52 Rom. 8:31.   53 Rom. 12:21.

*taken with him to Augsburg. There he assisted Philip Melanchthon in
the preparation of the Augsburg Confession and in the subsequent negotiations with Catholic theologians. Here Luther suggested how the
Catholic proposal to solve the religious problem by simply restoring
former conditions might be met.* [Text in Latin; *WA, Br, V*, 471,
472.]

To the honorable gentleman in Christ, Justus Jonas, confessor
of Christ in Augsburg, my superior in the Lord: grace and
peace in Christ.

My dear Jonas:

Here I sit thinking of you and anxious for you. I suppose that
our cause has reached a critical stage and I hope that it may
have a favorable outcome. Keep up your courage. The more
arrogant your opponents become, the less willing you must be
to yield. I believe they are confident that you will concede
everything in discouragement when they propose or command
something through the emperor. Who does not see that the
emperor is doing nothing here of himself but that he is being led
and is acted upon? If you stand firm and yield nothing, you
will compel them to think differently and alter their plans. If
this happens, our cause will more likely suffer from force and
threats than from those satanic stratagems which I have hitherto
feared most.

They may indeed press for a restoration of former conditions.[54] If they do, we should press for a restoration of Leonard
Keyser[55] and many others who have been wickedly killed, a
restoration of the many souls who have been lost on account of
their ungodly doctrine, a restoration of the great sums that have
been spent on their fallacious indulgences and other frauds, a
restoration of God's glory which has been injured by their many
blasphemies, and a restoration of the purity of the Church
which has been so horribly defiled in personnel and practice.
Who can enumerate all the things? Then we too shall deal in
terms of restoration.

Nevertheless, it has greatly pleased me that God has permitted them to begin to act so madly that they have not been
ashamed to put forward such an argument. God, who so blinds
and confounds them that they take these absurdities to be good
and convincing arguments, will go even farther. May this be

---

[54] Luther wrote in similar vein to Archbishop Albert of Mayence on July
6, 1530 (*WA*, XXXii, 410).
[55] See letter to Leonard Käser (or Keyser), May 20, 1527, in Chapter VII.

the beginning and a sign of God's hand, indicating that he intends to help us. This is my consolation. But by this time the proposals will be old and you will have received new ones.

I hope that my letters are delivered, for I have already written five times, and as many times to Philip.[56] May the Lord Jesus, our life and our salvation, our love and our hope, be with you. This I hope and pray. Amen. Greet Master Eisleben[57] and all the others.

Yours,

Martin Luther.

TO PHILIP MELANCHTHON. July 31, 1530

Philip Melanchthon was still engaged in almost daily conversations with Catholic theologians who were at work on a revision of their Confutation of the Augsburg Confession, which was to be read before the diet on August 3, 1530. Luther here sent Melanchthon a quiet letter of encouragement. [Text in Latin; *WA, Br,* V, 516, 517.]

To Master Philip Melanchthon, confessor of Christ, true martyr, my beloved brother: grace and peace in our Lord.

My dear Philip:

Although I have nothing to write, I did not wish the courier —or, rather, the man who brought the game—to return without letters.

I believe that you have wrestled manfully with the demons this past week, and I presume that this is the reason why Weller[58] and the tax collector's[59] courier have not yet returned from you. I am with you in faith and spirit as much as I am able. But I believe that the frail Christ is with you even more. So at least I pray with sighs and with words which he commanded and gave us.[60] God grant that you may be steadfast in the cause. Do not descend to mutual reproaches, for I believe that our adversaries, who are not so sure of their cause, would like this to happen. How will the matter end if you begin to cover up the pope's abominations against God and the State? But by God's grace you will know best how to avert this.

Do not be anxious about my health. To be sure, I do not know what is the matter. But because I feel that I am not suffering from any natural disease, I bear my condition more easily and scoff at the messenger of Satan who buffets my flesh.[61] If I cannot read and write, I can still meditate and pray

[56] Philip Melanchthon.   [57] John Agricola, of Eisleben.
[58] Peter Weller.   [59] Probably Valentine Förster, of Wittenberg.
[60] Cf. Matt. 18:19, 20; 28:20.   [61] Cf. II Cor. 12:7.

and in this way contend with the devil, and I can also sleep, loaf, play, and sing.

Only see to it, dear Philip, that you do not worry about a cause that is not in your hands but in the hands of Him who is greater than the prince of this world and from whose hands no one can pluck us.[62] Let us not permit him to say in vain, "He will give it to his beloved while they are asleep."[63] Cast thy burden upon the Lord,[64] who raises the dead, comforts the poor in spirit, and heals the broken in heart. The God of all comfort,[65] into whose arms and bosom I commit all of you, has called and accepted you to confess his glory. [I write] from the castle that is full of demons but where Christ reigns in the midst of his enemies.

Yours,

The last day of July, 1530.   Martin Luther.

TO GREGORY BRUECK. August 5, 1530

Gregory Brück, chancellor of the elector of Saxony and the man who publicly read the Augsburg Confession to the diet, was also assailed by doubts and uncertainty in Augsburg, as Philip Melanchthon reported to Luther.[66] That the following exhortation to faith and steadfastness was highly prized by the Evangelicals in Augsburg is suggested by John Brenz's letter to Anthony Hofmeister of September 2: "Herewith I send you several copies of the letter that Luther wrote to the elector of Saxony and his chancellor. Please read the letter and keep it so that it may not be lost."[67] [Text in German; *WA, Br*, V, 530-532.]

To the honorable and learned gentleman, Gregory Brück, doctor of laws, chancellor and councilor of the elector of Saxony, my gracious lord and dear friend: grace and peace in Christ.

Honored, learned, dear Lord and Friend:

I have now written several times[68] to my gracious lord and to our friends, and I think that I may have overdone it and given the impression that I had doubts as to whether His Grace has more encouragement and help from God than I have. But

---

[62] Cf. John 10:29.   [63] Luther's version of Ps. 126:1.
[64] Ps. 55:22.   [65] II Cor. 1:3.
[66] In his letter of June 27, 1530, in *WA, Br*, V, 402, 403.
[67] Theodor Pressel, *Anecdota Brentiana* (Tübingen, 1868), 96.
[68] Luther had written to Elector John on May 20, June 30, and July 9.

I did it at the urging of our friends, some of whom are so discouraged and worried that they think God has forgotten us, although he cannot forget us without forgetting himself, unless it be that our cause is not his cause and our Word is not his Word. But if we are sure and do not doubt that it is his cause and Word, it is certain that our prayer will be heard, that the decision to help us has already been made, that the help has been made ready, and that it cannot fail. For the Lord says: "Can a woman forget her sucking child, that she should not have compassion on the son of her womb? Yea, they may forget, yet will I not forget thee."[69]

I have recently seen two miracles. The first was this: When I looked out of my window, I saw the stars in the sky and the whole beautiful vault of heaven, but I saw no pillars on which the Master rested it all. Yet the sky did not fall, and the vault of heaven still stands fast. But there are some who look for the pillars and would like to touch and feel them. And when they are unable to do so, they become alarmed and tremble for fear that the sky will fall down for no other reason than that they cannot feel and see the pillars under it. If only they could do this, they would be satisfied that the sky is secure.

The second miracle was this: I saw great, thick clouds roll over us, so heavy that they looked like the waves of a great sea. I saw no ground on which they could rest, nor any tubs to hold them, and yet they did not fall on us but merely threatened us and drifted on. When the clouds had passed by, I beheld a rainbow—the roof and the floor, as it were, that held them up. It was such a weak, thin, little floor and roof that it was lost in the clouds. It looked more like a ray shining through a stained-glass window than a strong floor, and so it was as difficult to believe it was there as to believe that the weight of the clouds was suspended there. Yet it actually happened that this seemingly frail ray held up the weight of water and protected us. Some people look at the thickness of the clouds and the weight of the water more than they consider the thinness and lightness of the ray, and they are therefore afraid. They would like to feel the strength of the rainbow, and when they cannot do so they fear that the clouds will bring on a deluge.

I take the liberty of engaging in such pleasantries with Your Honor, and yet I write with more than pleasantries in mind, for I found special pleasure in learning that Your Honor, above all others, has been of good courage and stout heart in this

69 Isa. 49:15.

trial of ours. I had hoped that we might at least have peace in a political sense,[70] but God's thoughts are above our thoughts.[71] And this is as it should be, for God, as Saint Paul says, hears and does exceeding abundantly above all that we ask or think.[72] As we read in Rom., ch. 8, we know not what we should pray for as we ought.[73] If God should hear our prayers according to our request—namely, that the emperor grant us peace—perhaps it would turn out to be less rather than more than we think and the emperor would get the glory instead of God.

Now God himself desires to give us peace so that the glory might be his alone, as is fitting. Not that we should therefore despise the emperor, for it is our hope and prayer that he may do nothing against God and imperial law. If, however, he does this (which God forbid!), as faithful subjects we ought to believe that it is not the emperor himself who is doing this, but tyrannical advisers who speak in his name, and so we must distinguish between the acts of His Majesty and those of tyrants, even as we distinguish between God's name and the use that heretics and liars make of it, and honor God's name but pay no heed to lies. Under no circumstances should we or can we approve or accept the designs of the tyrants which appear under the cloak of His Majesty's name, but we are bound to defend His Majesty's name, guard his honor, and neither permit nor approve such abuses against God and imperial law, in order that we may not become participants in guilt and heap such alien sins, abuses, and dishonor of His Majesty's name on our consciences. For soverign rulers must be honored, not dishonored.

By his Spirit, God will bless and further this work which he has graciously given us to do, and he will find the fitting time, place, and method to help us. He will neither forget nor forsake us. Those men of blood have not yet accomplished what they are now undertaking, nor have they all achieved security or whatever it is that they desire. Our rainbow is frail and their clouds are mighty, but it will appear in the end to whose tune we shall dance.[74]

May Your Honor think well of these rambling words of mine and encourage Master Philip and the others. May Christ also strengthen and keep our gracious lord.[75] To God be praise and

[70] *Pax politica.*
[72] Eph. 3:20.
[74] *In fine videbitur cuius toni.*

[71] Cf. Isa. 55:9.
[73] Rom. 8:26.
[75] The elector of Saxony.

thanks forever. Amen. To his grace I also faithfully commend
Your Honor.
August 5, 1530.   Dr. Martin Luther.

TO PHILIP MELANCHTHON. September 15, 1530

*The negotiations in Augsburg were about at an end. Luther was awaiting
the return of Philip Melanchthon and addressed to him a final letter of
encouragement in a quieter vein.* [Text in Latin; *WA, Br,* V, 621,
622.]

To the honorable brother in Christ, Master Philip Melanchthon, my dear friend in the Lord: grace and peace in Christ.

Our younger prince[76] came today with Count Albert[77] as
quite unlooked for and unexpected guests. I was glad to see that
they had fled from that crowd. Would that I might shortly see
you too—as a runaway if your dismissal is too much to expect!
You have done enough and more than enough. Now it is time
to leave the rest to God, and he will accomplish it. Only be a
man and hope in God.

I am at once indignant and comforted by the empty cavil
with which [John] Eck and our opponents are raising an ob-
struction, namely, that if we assert that both kinds are necessary
in the Sacrament we are condemning the whole Church and
the emperor himself. The wretches have this last pretext to harp
on before the emperor while he is still there. Pray, let them go
on abusing the emperor with trifles of this sort. With these they
provoke Him who hath stretched his bow in the heavens and
prepared the instruments of death.[78] In like fashion the Turks
argue that it is not to be presumed that so great a people as
they are will be damned. If we admit the validity of this argument—that is, if articles of faith depend on majorities—what
article of faith is there that we can confess and retain?

But why should I write a letter about this? Do not forget
that you are one of those who are called Lot in Sodom, whose
soul those men vex day and night with their unlawful deeds.
But the Scriptures go on: "The Lord knoweth how to deliver
the godly out of temptation."[79] You have confessed Christ, you
have offered peace, you have obeyed the emperor, you have
borne injustice, you have been sated with blasphemies, and you
have not rendered evil for evil. In a word, you have done God's

76 John Frederick, son of the elector of Saxony.
77 Count of Mansfeld.   78 Cf. Ps. 7:12, 13.   79 Cf. II Peter 2:7-10.

holy work in a worthy fashion, as becomes a saint. "Be glad in the Lord, and rejoice, ye righteous."[80] Long enough have you had tribulation in this world. "Look up, and lift up your head, for your redemption draweth nigh."[81] I shall canonize you as a faithful member of Christ. What greater glory do you seek? Or is it not enough that you have rendered faithful service to Christ and acted as a worthy member of his? Far be it from you that you should think the grace of Christ to be such a small thing! But more of this when I see you.

My head has been quite well these last few days. I suspect that the winds which are now beating against the castle have before been in my head, and although they are now howling outside, they will come back into my head again some time. It seems to me that they take turns.

The prince gave me a golden ring. But to show that I was not born to wear gold, it at once fell off my thumb and onto the ground, for it was a little loose and too large for my finger. I said to myself: "You are a worm and no man.[82] He ought to have given it to Faber or Eck.[83] Lead would have suited you better, or a cord, or even a rope around your neck." He also wished to give me a chance to go home and offered to take me with him, but I asked him to let me stay here so that I might receive you when you come back and wipe away your sweat after the bath you have had.

I hope and pray that you may be strong and of good courage and undisturbed by the outward face and appearance of things present, for you know how fully everything is in the hand of God, who in a single moment can cover the heavens with clouds and clear them again. Indeed, he not only does this, but it pleases him to do it.

To his love I, a sinner, commend you, a sinner, for you confess your sins and do not defend them. Greet all our brethren in the Lord. May he soon release you there. Amen.

Yours,

Martin Luther.

Do not believe any stories about the plague in Wittenberg. All is well there, as you learned from my last letter. The fifth day after the autumnal equinox, 1530.

[80] Ps. 32:11. [81] Luke 21:28. [82] Ps. 21:7.
[83] John Fabri and John Eck, Roman theologians who were in Augsburg.

TO JOHN RIEDESEL. September 7, 1532

Elector John the Steadfast of Saxony died of apoplexy on August 16, 1532. As his chamberlain and confidant, John Riedesel had the honor of walking behind the coffin at the elector's funeral. Shortly thereafter he fell under the displeasure of the new elector, John Frederick, and was deeply distressed by his sudden change of fortune. [Text in German; *WA, Br,* VI, 353, 354.]

To the honorable and gracious John Riedesel, chamberlain to the elector of Saxony at the new market, my gracious lord and dear friend: grace and peace in Christ.

My dear Lord and Friend:

I was really afraid that after the death of our gracious lord you would grow bitter and, as your letter shows, regret the faithful services you rendered to His Grace, but I beg you for God's sake to be a man now and not take the matter so to heart. I should be sorry if you were overwhelmed by such grief. It is not always evening. There are still twelve hours in the day,[84] and it cannot always be cloudy and raining. We must learn to suffer somewhat and be patient, for it would not be good if we were to receive the reward of all our faithful services here on earth. If we were to receive all our recompenses on earth, what rewards would God have left for us in heaven?[85]

Thank God, things have not come to such an evil pass with you that they are worth talking about and worrying over. And it does no good to make your enemies happy with the sight of your grief. God is trying you a little. Be steadfast and you will learn what kind of God God is and how he reigns.

In truth, if I knew how to relieve your sadness I should gladly do it, for, please God, I shall not forget all the friendship you have shown me, nor shall I be unthankful for it. Although I have nothing to offer but my poor prayer and a word of comfort, all the knowledge and ability that I, a poor theologian, possess are altogether at your service. I commend you and your dear ones to the grace and goodness of God. Amen.

Please give my greetings to Mr. Wolf Calixtus[86] also.

Your willing doctor,

September 7, 1532.   Martin Luther.

---

[84] Cf. John 11:9.   [85] Cf. Matt. 6:1, 2.
[86] Wolfgang Callistus (or Chalikus), an Evangelical clergyman.

TO ANDREW OSIANDER. September 19, 1532

The combative nature of Andrew Osiander (1498-1552) kept him continually at odds with his fellow clergymen. The immediate cause of his dissatisfaction at this time is not clear, but a few months before this he had had a dispute with his Nuremberg colleagues in the ministry on the subject of conditional Baptism[87] and the next year he was engaged in a new and rather violent controversy with his colleagues over the retention of private confession. [Text in Latin; *WA, Br*, VI, 364, 365.]

Grace and peace in Christ.

My dear Andrew:

"Yield not to ills; press on the bolder."[88] This is the answer which, despite my illness, I would make to the letter in which you say that you are disgusted with your Nineveh.[89] I too am sick at the sight of it. Pray God, Christ may not be sick of it also. But there are twelve hours in the day,[90] and our eyes cannot discern the future. It is thus that God tries you. And even if everything goes wrong, the present state of affairs cannot last three years, for things are coming to a climax and the face of things must change for better or worse. If the change shall be for the worse, we shall gain nothing by running away; if for the better, we shall have everything to gain by staying. I see clearly that if peace shall come, wise men will be at a premium and, as Isaiah says, they will be more precious than fine gold.[91] Every day preachers are sought, but none are available. If your Ninevites are unwilling, you will be called and compelled to go whither they do not think, and they will seek the tip of your finger in your place and will not find it.[92]

Comrades, before this we have known evils harder to bear than these. God will put an end to them. Hold out, and save yourselves for prosperous days to come.[93]

Things cannot stay as they are.[94] Evil manners produce good laws.[95] "It will pass," said the fox; "the bird must molt to get his pretty feathers back."[96]

---

[87] Cf. Luther's letter to W. Link, Jan. 3, 1532 (*WA, Br*, VI, 245–247).
[88] Vergil, *Aeneid*, VI, 95.
[89] Cf. Jonah 4:1. The reference is to Nuremberg in particular and to the world in general.   [90] Cf. John 11:9.   [91] Cf. Isa. 13:12.
[92] Cf. Luke 16:24.
[93] These three sentences are an adaptation of Vergil, *Aeneid*, I, 199, 207.
[94] This sentence in German.   [95] Cf. Macrobius, *Satires*, III, 17, 10.
[96] This sentence in German.

Take this in the candid and faithful spirit in which I am writing. I too am very often troubled by the same thoughts that you express, and then I console myself as I am now consoling you. Greet all our people. I cannot and will not write more; my head is too weak. Christ be with you and all of yours, dear brother in Christ. Pray for me, and whether I live or die, let our ministry be held in high esteem.

Yours,

Friday after Saint Lambert's, 1532.   Martin Luther.

TO PRINCE GEORGE OF ANHALT. March 28, 1533

On the death in 1516 of Prince Ernest of Anhalt, his consort Princess Margaret assumed the regency for her three sons together with Elector Joachim of Brandenburg, Archbishop Albert of Magdeburg, and Duke George of Saxony. These Catholic princes tried to prevent the sons from adopting the Evangelical faith and introducing the Reformation in their land. In December, 1532, the Catholic theologian John Cochlaeus wrote to Prince George to warn him against Lutheranism,[97] and it appears that this letter came to Luther's attention and evoked the following communication. [Text in Latin; WA, Br, VI, 440, 441.]

To the reverend lord in Christ and illustrious prince, Lord George, set over the church in Magdeburg, prince of Anhalt, count of Ascania, and lord of Bernburg; above all, my clement lord: grace and peace in Christ.

Excellent and noble Lord:

I shall with propriety call you both reverend bishop (not to mention the title of overseer) and very distinguished prince because I observe that, alone in the whole empire, especially among those in such a position and estate, you love the Word of Christ sincerely and further it faithfully. It has often appeared to me, when I have reflected on it, to be a marvelous thing, and I am compelled to acknowledge it as a singular gift of God, that you have of your own accord undertaken to urge this teaching upon the people who are your subjects. God knows that I am not fawning and flattering when I say this, but I am praising and glorifying the grace of Christ which is so wonderfully breaking forth and shining in you.

At the same time I pray and hope with all my heart that He

[97] Cf. Otto Clemen, *Briefe von Hieronymus Emser, Johann Cochläus, Johann Mensing und Petrus Rauch. . . an die Fürsten von Anhalt* (Münster i.W., 1907), 47–50.

who has begun so great a work in you may also perfect it,[98] even if weakness occasionally appears in this work and it is greatly hindered and opposed by the various stratagems of Satan, the world, and the flesh. Christ says, "Be of good cheer; I have overcome the world."[99] If the world is overcome, the prince of the world is also overcome, just as a king is overcome when his kingdom is conquered. Since the prince of the world is overcome, the raging, wrath, sin, conscience, death, hell, and all things on which that strong man[1] relies for weapons are also overcome. Thanks be to God, therefore, who has given us this victory.[2] With great yearning of heart I pray and implore our Father in heaven that Your Grace may live and glory in this victory until that day. To his keeping I commit Your Grace as diligently as I can.

I trust that Your Grace will take in good part this boldness of mine in writing, for I could not but write this brief letter to thank God and to express my joy at the gift of God which, I have learned, has taken root in the heart of so great a prince.

Your Grace's devoted

Friday after Laetare, 1533.   Martin Luther, Doctor.

TO PRINCE JOHN OF ANHALT. March 28, 1533

Like his brother George (see above), Prince John of Anhalt was warned against embracing the Evangelical faith by Duke George of Saxony, Elector Joachim of Brandenburg, and Archbishop Albert of Magdeburg. The Catholic Duke George protested the call of Nicholas Hausmann, "one of the first and oldest Lutherans," as chaplain to the prince. John Cochlaeus also wrote to Prince John to remind him that he would have "to give an account before God for the many souls of his subjects."[3] Luther confronts the prince with the necessity of making a choice and taking a stand. [Text in German; *WA, Br*, VI, 441, 442.]

To the serene, highborn lord, John, prince of Anhalt, count of Ascania, lord of Bernburg, my gracious lord: grace and peace in Christ.

Most serene, highborn Prince:

Your Grace's chaplain, Master Nicholas Hausmann, has told me of Your Grace's heartfelt leanings toward the gospel and yet of your hesitation to embrace it, perhaps not only because of what you had formerly been accustomed to but also on

98 Cf. Phil. 1:6.   99 John 16:33.   1 Cf. Mark 3:27.
2 Cf. I Cor. 15:57.   3 Otto Clemen, *op. cit.*, 44–46.

account of what several powerful princes have written to dissuade Your Grace.

It is undoubtedly true that two such things as these—the force of old habits and the dissuasion of great people—have profoundly influenced stronger Christians than Your Grace may be. But we must learn in the course of time, if we cannot do so quickly and all at once, that Christ is more than all these things and that God the Father desires that Christ be heard above all others.[4] A council or pope may have the Holy Spirit and by his inspiration accomplish something, etc. But Christ does not have a devil either (John, ch. 8),[5] to say nothing of the fact that the Spirit descended upon him without measure (John, ch. 1),[6] while the holy apostles, prophets, Church, and councils have only a portion and the first fruits of the Spirit (Rom., ch. 8; I Cor., ch. 12).[7] If the prophets, apostles, Church, or councils decree something that is contrary to Christ, then Christ, as the one who possesses the Spirit without measure, and indeed bestows the Holy Spirit on them,[8] must be heeded rather than the saints who, quite unlike him, do not bestow the Holy Spirit but in some measure receive him.

So I pray the God of all mercies[9] that he teach Your Grace this one thing, that Christ and his Word are more, higher, greater, and more trustworthy than a hundred thousand holy fathers, councils, churches, popes, etc., for the Scriptures call all of these sinners and lost sheep.[10] Be bold, therefore, and do not fear the rulers of the earth. Christ is greater than all devils and more to be feared than princes.

To him and to his grace and mercy I commend Your Grace. Amen.

Your Grace's obedient servant,
Martin Luther.

TO ANTHONY LAUTERBACH. March 10, 1542

Anthony Lauterbach (1502-1569), earlier one of Luther's table companions in Wittenberg, was made superintendent (or bishop) in Pirna, near Dresden, in 1539 and remained in this office until his death. He encountered difficulties and opposition in Pirna, and his discouragement was further aggravated when his mother, Ursula, who had lived for a while with her son, returned to the Catholic town of Stolpe and to the

---

[4] Cf. Matt. 17:5.   [5] John 8:49.   [6] John 1:32.
[7] Rom. 8:23; I Cor. 12:4-13.   [8] Cf. John 20:22.
[9] Cf. II Cor. 1:3.   [10] Cf. Ps. 119:176.

Roman Church on the death of her husband. [Text in Latin; *WA, Br*, X, 2-4.]

To the venerable gentleman in the Lord, Anthony Lauterbach, pastor of the church in Pirna and bishop of that district, my beloved brother in Christ: grace and peace.

My dear Anthony:

Wait upon the Lord! Be of good cheer![11] Were there no such thing as tribulation to try Christian faith, what would become of secure, indolent, self-indulgent Christians? Surely, the same as has befallen the papacy! Inasmuch as tribulation serves the same purpose as rhubarb, myrrh, aloes, or an antidote against all the worms, poison, decay, and dung of this body of death, it ought not to be despised. We must not willfully seek or select afflictions, but we must accept those which God sees fit to visit upon us, for he knows which are suitable and salutary for us and how many and how heavy they should be.

Therefore, be steadfast! If we have to endure trials at all—and we must—surely it is better to endure those which are meted out to us rather than risk being visited with worse and severer ones. Suffer and bear whatever the nobles[12] and papists plot. Yet do not cease working upon, writing to, and pleading with the prince. Try to do everything that is necessary. Who knows when our hour will come! Let us not then be found weary and succumbing to that tireless foe the devil. It will be too late, when that hour comes, to repent and regret our softness.

Do not worry because your mother (to the scandal of the gospel) prefers to live under papal rule in Stolpe rather than in Pirna. Pray for her without ceasing and you will have done enough. Surely it would not be good if all the things we desire and seek were to be accomplished at once. God takes better care of us, for he sees how foolish are the things that we seek after now.

We have heard no news about the Turks or about an expedition [against them] by our side. The emperor has published an edict in Belgium forbidding the persecution of Lutherans. During two years of peace in France, the gospel was gradually introduced into that country by means of imported books. When this was discovered by the monks, the sophists, and the parliament, they were so furious that they put fifty to the flames; but the people were so indignant at this that the king, fearing a disturbance and uprising in Paris, was obliged to

[11] Ps. 27:14.   [12] *Centauri.*

intervene and curb the ferocity. The bishop of Cologne is beginning to correct abuses in his diocese. Blessed be God, who glorifies his gospel! When our countrymen, like those in Bethsaida, Chorazin, and Nazareth, do not accept a prophet in their own country,[13] they will be left in their shame while the Samaritans, the Canaanite woman, etc., receive him. Let us continue to preach, to pray, to bear. Our work will be rewarded. We shall not labor in vain.[14]

In haste, farewell in the Lord.

Pray for me too, that I may fall asleep at some favorable time. In so far as God has enabled me, I have fought a good fight, I have finished my course, I have kept the faith.[15]

Greet your Agnes and Elizabeth.[16] My Lord Katie greets you, as do all in our household.

Yours,

Friday after Reminiscere, 1541.   Martin Luther.

TO SON JOHN LUTHER. December 27, 1542

The Reformer's sixteen-year-old son John (or Hans) had been sent to Torgau to study grammar and music. He was homesick,[17] and perhaps he was also grieving over the loss of his sister Magdalene, who had died three months before. In any case, what he needed was not pity but encouragement to do his duty. His father could supply this better than his mother. [Text in Latin; WA, Br, X, 229.]

To my very dear son John Luther, at Torgau: grace and peace in the Lord.

Dear Son John:

Your mother and I and all the household are well. See to it that you conquer your tears manfully lest you add to your mother's distress and concern, for she is only too prone to worry and imagine things.[18] Be obedient to God, who, through us, commands you to work where you now are. Thus you will easily overcome your weakness. Your mother was unable to write, nor did she think it necessary. She wishes to explain that what she told you before (that you may come home if things do not go well with you) was intended to apply in case of illness.

---

13 Cf. Matt. 13:57.   14 Cf. Isa. 49:4.
15 II Tim. 4:7.   16 Daughters of Lauterbach.
17 See Luther's letters to Mark Crodel, Aug. 26 and Dec. 26, 1542, in *WA, Br*, X, 132–135, 228.
18 On Catherine Luther's worrying see letters of Feb. 7 and 10, 1546, in Chapter III.

Should you become ill, let us know at once. Otherwise she hopes that you will stop your lamentation and go on cheerfully and quietly with your studies.

Herewith a fond farewell in the Lord.

Your father,

On the day of John the Evangelist, 1542.   Martin Luther.

TO NICHOLAS AMSDORF. July 14, 1543

For some time Luther had been promising to visit his old friend Nicholas Amsdorf (1483-1565), Evangelical bishop of Naumburg, and his letters to Amsdorf refer again and again to the physical weakness and the pressure of duties which caused the visit to be postponed. Amsdorf, in turn, wrote frequently to ask Luther for advice or to express discouragement in the work of his office. Here Luther wrote that Amsdorf should take heart in the knowledge that he was doing God's will. [Text in Latin; WA, Br, X, 344, 345.]

To the reverend gentleman in the Lord, etc., Nicholas Amsdorf, true bishop, my esteemed brother in Christ: grace and peace in the Lord.

My dear and reverend Bishop:

To this day I have not ceased planning for a time when I might visit you. During the winter it was impossible. After Pentecost I had absolutely and certainly decided to go and had made all preparations for departure, but my health was so uncertain that I did not venture to undertake the journey. And today—indeed, yesterday too—I almost sank into unconsciousness, so that I must daily expect the hour of my death. Would to God that I might be taken from this satanic kingdom of the world at some good time very soon!

I can very well believe, even without your testimony, that the episcopal office is burdensome to you. But it is, and has been, the will of God, of whom we say, "Thy will be done."[19] According to his will we must live, be cheerful, and endure whatever may befall. Even if what we endure and suffer pleases no one else, it is enough that this is well-pleasing to him. In his good time God will requite us for submitting to his gracious will, although we may not be able to recognize and understand his will. You are living in misery, but because in your servitude you are serving God's will and not your own, your misery is connected with eternal glory and God's good pleasure. At the

[19] Matt. 6:10.

same time you are an impediment to the devil and his adherents, preventing them from doing evil.

Far be it from you that you should be a bishop like those bellies who find their consolation in this world and their shame and punishment in the world to come. For they do not participate in our sufferings, nor are they plagued like other men.[20] Be comforted, therefore, and be strong in the Lord, for you know that you are included with all the saints in this Beatitude, "Blessed are they that mourn: for they shall be comforted."[21]

Pray for me that I may either die quickly in the Lord or that, if I should recover my health, I may visit you soon. Amen.

Yours,

Saturday after Saint Margaret's Day, 1543. M. Luther, Doctor.

TO ANTHONY LAUTERBACH. September 30, 1543

The situation in which Anthony Lauterbach found himself in Pirna continued to be discouraging (see letter of March 10, 1542, above) and Luther again wrote to encourage him. [Text in Latin; *WA, Br,* X, 401, 402.]

To the illustrious gentleman, Master Anthony Lauterbach, true and faithful bishop of the church in Pirna, my beloved brother in Christ: grace and peace in Christ.

My dear Anthony:

Let your heart be strengthened! Be of good courage! Wait on the Lord![22] Let the godless boast and celebrate; their glory is in their shame.[23] How often have those inflated water bags[24] been puffed up, only to travail with iniquity and bring forth falsehood,[25] as Ps. 7 says, or, as Isaiah puts it, "Ye shall conceive chaff, ye shall bring forth stubble."[26] Someday the heavens will collapse and will be burned together with the earth, and yet even then we shall not be undone and we shall not lose God.

This is not the first time that your Meisseners[27] are showing me their true colors. I have long since been aware that they are the sort of persons who look for an opportunity to manifest their hypocrisy, which they have not managed to conceal. The only thing that need concern us is that we be sure of the Word and diligently teach it. We must cast all our care upon the Lord, for he careth for us.[28] "Cast thy burden upon the Lord!"[29]

20 Cf. Ps. 73:5.   21 Matt. 5:4.   22 Cf. Ps. 27:14.
23 Cf. Phil. 3:19.   24 *Bullae et vesicae aquatiles.*   25 Cf. Ps. 7:14.
26 Isa. 33:11.   27 Adherents of the bishop of Meissen.
28 Cf. I Peter 5:7.   29 Ps. 55:23.

Sufficiently frightful things are reported about the Turks. But the emperor will not yet accomplish what the papists boast of. He takes too much into his mouth all at once.[30] But let us teach, believe, pray, work, and suffer what we must, and let the dead bury their dead.[31] For what have we to do with those who are without?[32]

Farewell in the Lord, and pray for me. My Katie respectfully greets you and your household.

Yours,

The last of September, 1543.   Martin Luther.

TO CONRAD CORDATUS. December 3, 1544

Since 1540, Conrad Cordatus (1475-1546) had been chief pastor or dean in Stendal and vicinity, in Brandenburg. His station was difficult because many of the clergymen under him still had Roman leanings and some of the canons of St. Nicholas in Stendal were still living in concubinage. Ill-health may have been caused by these difficulties; certainly it aggravated them. Cordatus was thoroughly discouraged and on the point of despair when Luther wrote to him. [Text in Latin; WA, Br, X, 644, 645.]

Grace and peace in the Lord.

My dear Cordatus:

I hardly know what to write to you. I should very much like to write something pleasant and cheerful inasmuch as you are not the least among my best friends and because I have learned, and know for certain, that you have always been very faithful and a lover of our doctrine—that is, of that Word who is the Son of God and of the Virgin. Him you have always faithfully acknowledged, and of him you have always testified purely— not, to be sure, without encountering a good deal of evil slander and hostility, which is our reward in this world. It is as Christ said, "Ye shall be hated of all men for my sake."[33] But the same Word of the Father also says, "Rejoice, and be exceeding glad: for great is your reward in heaven."[34] This fruit, this reward, this glory is sufficient. Indeed, we receive too much in return for the brief labor which we perform in his behalf. What is the world, what is the raging of the world, and what, indeed, is the prince of this world, but mere vapor and an insignificant water

---

[30] This saying is quoted in German.   [31] Luke 9:60.
[32] Cf. I Cor. 5:12.   [33] Luke 21:17.   [34] Matt. 5:12.

blister in comparison with that Lord who is with us, whom we serve, who (that is to say) works in us.[35] But you can express this better than I.

I am also sorry that your strength is failing you. I pray the Lord that he may sustain and strengthen you.

I can well believe that your patience is sorely tested there in Brandenburg, for you wish that the land (which follows its own inclinations) be served as well as possible, even at the cost of your life and your health. But let us rejoice in tribulations, no matter what happens. It is our glory, and also yours, that we let the unclouded sun of our doctrine rise on the godless and ungrateful world in accordance with the example of our Father, who makes this his sun to rise on the evil and on the good.[36] And since the sun of our doctrine is his, there is no wonder that those of the household who hate the master of the house also hate our doctrine.[37]

Outwardly we are living in the kingdom of the devil, and so we should not expect to see and hear good things on the outside.[38] But inwardly we are living in the Kingdom of Christ, where we may behold the riches of God's glory and grace. This is what it means to "rule in the midst of thine enemies."[39] Because it is a kingdom, there is glory there; and because it is in the midst of enemies, there is offense there. But we shall make our way through glory and shame, through good report and evil report,[40] through hate and love, through friends and foes, until we arrive where there are none but friends, in the Kingdom of the Father. Amen.

Farewell in the Lord.

Yours,

December 3, 1544.   Martin Luther.

---

[35] Cf. Phil. 2:13.   [36] Cf. Matt. 5:45.   [37] Cf. Matt. 10:25.
[38] Most of this sentence is in German.   [39] Cf. Ps. 110:2.
[40] Cf. II Cor. 6:8.

VI

Intercessions for Those in Trouble or Need

TO GEORGE SPALATIN. June 7, 1522

George Spalatin (1484-1545) was a secretary and trusted confidant of Elector Frederick the Wise of Saxony until the latter's death in 1525. During the early years of the Reformation, Spalatin was an influential buffer for Luther at the court of his prince, and Luther frequently approached the elector through his friend. Here the Reformer employed the services of Spalatin to intercede in behalf of a fisherman who had wittingly or unwittingly invaded waters reserved for the use of the prince. [Text in German; *WA, Br*, II, 556.]

To the worthy gentleman, Master George Spalatin, preacher and chaplain to the elector, my especially gracious friend: grace and peace in Christ. Amen. Jesus.[1]

My dear Master Spalatin:

A poor fisherman made a mistake and on only one occasion fished too close to the waters of my gracious lord. I interceded in his behalf with the tax collector, and I am now informed that the tax collector transferred responsibility for the case to my gracious lord. I beg you, therefore, to intercede in my name with my gracious lord in order that the penalty may be changed. I understand that a fine of 120 silver gulden has been imposed on him. I do not ask that he go unpunished, for there must always be respect for the power of government, but I ask that his punishment should not deprive him of his living. I should suggest that he be put in prison for several days or be made to live on bread and water for a week in order that it may be manifest that the purpose is to reform and not destroy the man.

---

[1] A traditional invocation of the name of Jesus at the beginning of letters and other documents.

Moreover, it appears to me that this would be a just penalty for a poor man; the rich, on the other hand, may properly have their purses plucked. I hope that you will take care of this.

Herewith I commit you to God's keeping.

Eve of Pentecost, 1522.   M. Luther.

TO GEORGE SPALATIN. April 10, 1523

On the night of April 4-5, 1523, twelve nuns left the Cistercian convent in Nimbschen, Saxony. From nearby Grimma, a town that had become Evangelical earlier, Luther's teachings had been introduced into the convent and some of the nuns were influenced by these teachings to wish to abandon their cloistered life. Failing to secure help from their relatives, they appealed to Martin Luther, and the latter made arrangements with Leonard Koppe, of Torgau, to assist them in their escape. This was accomplished quietly. Three of the twelve nuns were at once taken up by their families, and the remaining nine were conveyed to Wittenberg, where Luther became responsible for them. Here Luther asked his friend to intercede at court in behalf of the support of the nuns. [Text in Latin; *WA, Br*, III, 54-57.]

Grace and peace.

Nine apostate nuns, a wretched group, have been brought to me by honest citizens of Torgau (that is, by Leonard Koppe and his nephew and Wolf Dommitzsch)[2] and there is no reason to suspect hostile action. I feel very sorry for them, but most of all for the many others who are perishing everywhere in their cursed and impure celibacy. This sex, which is so very weak by itself and which is joined by nature, or rather by God, to the other sex, perishes when so cruelly separated. O tyrants! O cruel parents and kinsmen in Germany! O pope and bishops, who can curse you as you deserve? Who can sufficiently execrate the blindness and madness which caused you to teach and enforce such things? But this is not the place to do it.

You ask what I shall do with the nuns. First I shall inform their relatives and ask them to take in the girls. If they are unwilling, then I shall have the girls provided for elsewhere. Some families have already promised to take them. For some I

---

[2] Leonard Koppe was a retired merchant in Torgau who had supplied the convent with fish, beer, etc. He had a nephew or cousin named Erasmus, later burgomaster in Torgau, and a cousin named John, who was a tailor. Wolf von Dommitzsch also appears to have been a cousin of Leonard Koppe.

shall get husbands if I can. These are their names: Magdalene von Staupitz,[3] Elsa von Canitz,[4] Avę Gross,[5] Ave von Schönfeld and her sister Margaret,[6] Laneta von Goltz,[7] Margaret and Catherine Zeschau, and Catherine von Bora.[8] Here they are, and how truly deserving of pity! Whoever helps them serves Christ. They escaped from the cloister in a miraculous way.

I pray that you also do a charitable work and beg some money for me from your rich courtiers in order that I might support the girls for a week or two until it is convenient for me to turn them over to their kinsmen or those who have promised to provide for them. For my Capernaites have made such progress as a result of the abundant and daily preaching of the Word that a short time ago I was unable to borrow ten gulden for a poor citizen.[9] The poor, who would willingly give, have nothing, and the rich either refuse to give or give so reluctantly that they lose credit for the gift in God's sight and rob me of my time. But this is not unexpected in the world and among those who are of a worldly spirit. I receive only 540 gulden[10] as my annual salary, and beyond this not a penny has been given me or my brothers by the town. But I ask them for nothing in order that I might emulate the boast of Saint Paul that he despoiled other churches to serve his Corinthians free of charge.[11]

There is also another matter about which I have often wished to write to you and just as often forgot. I wonder why our prince, since he knows that the administrators at the court of his brother, Duke John,[12] are of such character that property is daily going to ruin there, does not employ Sebastian von Kötteritzsch,[13] a man who is uncommonly skillful in administering affairs, as he daily demonstrates by what he does. Of course,

---

[3] The oldest among the fugitive nuns, probably a sister of John von Staupitz; see Luther's letter to Elector John Frederick of Saxony, March 27, 1545, below.
[4] See Luther's letter to Elizabeth von Canitz of Aug. 22, 1527, in Chapter III.   [5] Later married to John Marx.
[6] The former later married the physician Basil Axt, and the latter (Veronica instead of Margaret) was married to a man in Brunswick.
[7] Later married to a clergyman, Henry Kind.
[8] Married June 13, 1525, to Martin Luther.
[9] An ironical reference to the Wittenbergers; cf. Matt. 11:23.
[10] *9 antiguas sexagenas.* See Jacob and Wilhelm Grimm, *Deutsches Wörterbuch,* IX (Leipzig, 1899), 1433.   [11] Cf. II Cor. 11:7 f.
[12] Brother of Elector Frederick and his successor (1525–1532).
[13] Kötteritzsch, who was unemployed at this time, later participated in the visitations of parishes in Saxony (1528–1530) and accompanied the elector of Saxony to the Diet of Augsburg (1530).

I wish that Kötteritzsch might be helped, but I am more concerned about the electoral court, especially that the excellent young prince, John Frederick, the future ruler,[14] might be instructed by some excellent example to take care of the property and have a better understanding of the deceitful character of men. For I have a mean opinion of those who are now in power since they grow rich at the prince's expense. I beg you to mention this to the prince in my name, for I am eager to see the place filled by a man who is at once godly and able. Farewell and pray for me.

Friday after Easter, 1523.   Martin Luther.

TO ARCHBISHOP ALBERT OF MAYENCE.
July 21, 1525

In 1524 and 1525 the peasants of Central Europe rose up in armed revolt against their lords. Their grievances, expressed most compendiously in the Twelve Articles, were substantially approved by Luther, but when the peasants tried to improve their hard lot by resort to arms rather than by peaceful means, he denounced them roundly and urged the lords to suppress the uprising. This they did with almost unbelievable brutality. One of the victims is referred to in the following letter, and Luther intercedes in his behalf with a spiritual prince.[15] [Text in German; WA, Br, III, 547, 548.]

To the serene, highborn prince and lord, Archbishop Albert of Mayence and Magdeburg, etc., elector, margrave of Brandenburg, etc., my gracious lord: grace and peace in Christ Jesus.

Very reverend Father in God, serene, highborn Prince, gracious Lord:

I am informed that a certain Asmus Günthel, the son of a citizen of Eisleben, was arrested by Your Grace on the charge of having helped to storm a barricade. His father is sore distressed and tells me that he did not take part in the storming but only ate and drank there at the time. Since the father begged me piteously to intercede with Your Grace for his son's life, I could not refuse him. I humbly pray Your Grace to consider that this insurrection has been put down, not by the hand or counsel of man, but by the grace of God, who has had

[14] John Frederick became elector of Saxony on the death of his father in 1532.
[15] For the Twelve Articles and translations of Luther's tracts on the Peasants' War see *Works of Martin Luther*, Philadelphia ed., IV.

pity on us all, and especially on those in authority. Accordingly
I pray that Your Grace may treat the poor people mercifully
and graciously, as becomes a spiritual lord even more than a
temporal one, in order that the grace of God may thus be
thankfully acknowledged and all the world may have a proof
that personal gain was neither sought nor desired.

Unfortunately there are all too many who treat the people
horribly and who act unthankfully toward God, as if they would
recklessly awaken and invite the wrath of God and the people
once again and provoke a new and worse rebellion. God has
decreed that those who show no mercy should also perish
without mercy.[16]

It is not good for a lord to incite his subjects to displeasure,
ill will, and hostility, and it is also foolish to do so. It is right to
show sternness when the people are seditious or when they are
unmanageable and stubborn in the performance of their duties,
but now that they are beaten down, they are a different people
and deserve mercy along with punishment. Putting too much
in a bag bursts it. Moderation is good in all things, and, as
Saint James says, "mercy rejoiceth against judgment."[17]

I hope that Your Grace will act as a Christian in this matter.
Herewith I commit Your Grace to God's keeping. Amen.

Your Grace's obedient servant,
Friday, Saint Praxedes' Day, 1525.   Martin Luther.

TO ELECTOR JOHN OF SAXONY. February 21, 1526

*Among the many monasteries that were deserted as a result of the
Reformation was the Gray Cloister of the Franciscans in Wittenberg.
At the beginning of 1526 only five friars were left in this monastery, and
these were so advanced in years that they could not adapt themselves to
secular life. Luther appealed to his prince in their behalf and suggested
that provision be made for their support. [Text in German; WA,
Br, IV, 34, 35.]*

To be delivered into the hands of my gracious lord, Duke John,
elector, etc.: grace and peace in Christ.

Serene, highborn Prince, gracious Lord:

As Your Grace will learn from their petition, the poor friars
of the Cloister of the Barefooted are complaining. It is quite
right that others should derive benefit from their monastery,
even as some have already received considerable property from

16 Cf. James 2:13.   17 James 2:13.

it, but it would not be right to drive the remaining friars out into the cold world penniless and in their old age, for this would cause great offense and bring Your Grace, all of us, and the gospel itself into bad repute. I know very well that this is not Your Grace's intention. But the poor friars are not able to come forward in their own behalf, and others have not befriended them in the Christian spirit of fairness one might expect, as Your Grace has already been sufficiently informed. Accordingly I beg Your Grace to command that the poor friars be supported from the monastic property as long as it lasts. Who knows how long the remaining friars will live, and among them may be one who will sit in judgment over us all on the last day. Herewith I commit Your Grace to God's keeping. Amen.

Wednesday after Invocavit, 1526.   Martin Luther.

TO WENZEL LINK. May 21, 1529

The following letter was probably written in behalf of Magnus Person, who was a merchant and town councilman in Wittenberg when he died in 1561. At the time of his death he was described as having left his homeland in Scotland (probably Edinburgh) while a young man "on account of his hatred of idolatry" and as having lived in Wittenberg for almost thirty-three years. [Text in Latin; WA, Br, V, 74, 75.]

To the honorable gentleman, Mr. Wenzel Link, preacher in Nuremberg, my revered friend: grace and peace in Christ.

My dear Wenzel:

I commend to you the bearer of this note, a Scotsman who was driven from his homeland and exiled on account of the Word. Wishing to visit you, he asked me to write these lines to you in the hope that he might somehow be able to secure help. It appears that he comes from an honorable background among his countrymen and that he has a good, and even excellent, knowledge of scholastic theology. If he were able to speak in our language, it would be easy to make use of his gifts. Do for him, therefore, what it behooves us to do. Despite our poverty we would have kept him here, but he had reasons for suggesting something else.

In order that I might not be idle, we translated the Book of Wisdom[18] although Philip was away and I was sick. It is now set in type, and the text has been checked with Philip's help.

18 The Wisdom of Solomon.

It is remarkable that the translation by Leo Jud, of Zurich, done perhaps at Zwingli's instigation,[19] is so poor. Farewell in the Lord and pray for me.

Yours,

May 21, 1529. Martin Luther.

TO KING FREDERICK I OF DENMARK.
September 28, 1532

During the reign of Frederick I of Denmark (1524-1533) the former king, Christian II, who had been driven from his throne in protest against his arbitrary rule, sought to regain the crown. He failed and was taken prisoner. Not only did Luther write to Christian II to comfort him in his imprisonment (see Chapter VII), but he also wrote to his successor and cousin, Frederick I, to ask him to have compassion on his political prisoner. This plea was fruitless, for Christian spent the remainder of his life (until 1559) in prison, but he was not put to death. [Text in German; *WA, Br,* VI, 368-370.]

To the mighty, serene prince and lord, Frederick, king of Denmark and Sweden and duke of Holstein, etc., my gracious lord: grace and peace in Christ our Lord, who died for our sins and rose again from the dead to give us life.

Serene, mighty King, gracious Lord:

Your Majesty understands and perceives that God is a just and gracious judge, for Your Majesty always desired to have peace with your cousin, King Christian, and God has given you a glorious victory. Although I realize that Your Majesty understands this very well and knows how to thank God for it, and also that Your Majesty will, in fear of God, make a Christian and humble use of the said victory over this aforementioned cousin, I am nevertheless moved by the wretchedness (or, rather, the grief) of my gracious lord, King Christian, and by my concern lest Your Majesty might be incited by some people to proceed against the imprisoned man and act without the fear of God.

On this account I make bold to write this humble and (as I hope) unnecessary letter to request and admonish Your Majesty in all humility to have compassion on your imprisoned cousin. I beg Your Majesty to follow the example of Christ, who died for us, his enemies. We need not die for our enemies,

[19] A translation of the Prophets "by the preachers of Zurich" and of the Apocrypha by Leo Jud (1482–1542) was published in Zurich in 1529.

but we should have pity on them. If Your Majesty's cousin were to have come to you not as a friend but as an enemy in bonds, Your Majesty would undoubtedly have treated him in cousinly fashion. How much the more will Your Majesty treat him so inasmuch as he has renounced everything and (as I hear) has submitted to Your Majesty as a lost son submits to his father! Since this is a great humiliation, and since we ourselves require grace to stand before God, Your Majesty would certainly make a noble sacrifice and render a glorious service to God by showing paternal grace and fatherly faithfulness toward this poor prisoner. Besides, this benefaction would be a great comfort on Your Majesty's deathbed, it would be a source of especial joy in heaven, and it would meanwhile contribute to Your Majesty's reputation and honor here on earth. For it would be a great work, done for a great man in a great cause and among great people. Accordingly it would shed a bright light both here on earth, as an example to all the world, and there in heaven, as a cause for rejoicing to all saints and angels and as a joy and a pleasure to the divine majesty.

Therefore, my gracious Lord, let this work be a fruit of faith, a glorious thank offering to God, a comfort and refreshment to the prisoner, and a pleasure and delight to us all. Ultimately Your Majesty will be glad and will be thankful to yourself and all who gave such counsel, and Your Majesty will at length confess that you would have been heartily sorry if you had acted otherwise.

Christ, our Lord and Helper, grant to Your Majesty his abundant Spirit in order that the will of God may be done in this and all other situations. Amen.

May Your Majesty think graciously and well of this audacious letter of mine, for God himself bids us to do as I have done and to be concerned about our fellow man.

Your Royal Majesty's willing servant,

Vigil of Saint Michael, 1532.   Martin Luther, Doctor.

TO ELECTOR JOHN FREDERICK OF SAXONY.
October 17, 1532

Unfortunately neither the names of the persons referred to in the following letter nor their offense are known. As pastor in Altenburg, George Spalatin was concerned about the stiff (and, he believed, unjust) sentence imposed on a girl, her parents, and her relatives. Apparently Luther's appeal for relief was fruitless, for he wrote to George Spalatin on

July 10, 1533[20]*: "That exiled girl whose aged father and mother were seized in their home in Altenburg was here to complain to me and implore help and counsel. God alone knows what I may be able to accomplish in a case that has already been decided as this one has."* [Text in German; *WA, Br*, VI, 377, 378.]

Grace and peace in Christ.

Serene, highborn Prince, gracious Lord:

Master Spalatin has written to me in great distress of the severe sentence that has been passed upon a young woman of Altenburg and her parents and relatives. I cannot yet bring myself to believe that at the very beginning of Your Grace's reign,[21] Your Grace would have dealt so summarily with old and honorable people, driving them out of house and home, confiscating all their goods, throwing them into prison, and so on. I am obliged to think that D. C.[22] has secured this sentence or is acting on his own responsibility. However that may be, I join my humble petition to that of Master Spalatin, who is greatly disturbed over this hasty action, that Your Grace may mitigate the sentence. The matter at issue is not so important that the sentence should be so severe and distress so many people. Moreover, the law that is in D.C.'s books, or in his head, is not the only law there is, still less is it the eternal law, and there are beams enough to pull out to make it unnecessary for him to exercise his drastic laws (if I may so characterize them) on poor little motes.[23]

Doubtless Your Grace will know how to deal with this matter graciously. God be with Your Grace at all times. Amen.

Your Grace's humble servant,

Thursday after Saint Gallus, 1532.   Martin Luther.

TO ELECTOR JOHN FREDERICK OF SAXONY.
August 27, 1533

Among those who were driven out of Oschatz by the Catholic Duke George of Albertine Saxony on account of their Evangelical faith and profession (see letter of January 20, 1533, in Chapter VII) were Francis von der Dahme and his wife Anna. On June 15, 1533, Luther had appealed to his own prince, Elector John Frederick, for help in behalf of this couple, but nothing had been done. Perhaps as a result of

[20] In *WA, Br*, VI, 501.   [21] John Frederick succeeded his father in 1532.
[22] Presumably Dr. Christian Baier, chancellor of the elector.
[23] Cf. Matt. 7:1–5.

Luther's reiterated intercession, von der Dahme was finally given the post of manager of a farm, formerly connected with a monastery, just before Christmas. In all probability this position was similar to the one that he had held in Oschatz. [Text in German; *WA, Br,* VI, 515.]

To the serene, highborn prince and lord, John Frederick, duke and elector of Saxony, landgrave in Thuringia, margrave of Meissen, my gracious lord: grace and peace.

Serene, highborn Prince, gracious Lord:

I venture humbly to inform Your Grace concerning the two good people, Mr. and Mrs. von der Dahme, in whose behalf I interceded before Your Grace in Wittenberg and on whose account Your Grace was good enough to send the sequestrator a note to the effect that they should be given a modest office in Zwickau. Although the von der Dahmes were given assurances, nothing has come of them. I am not in a position to know what it is that may stand in the way. But I do know that the poor people are worried now that winter will soon be upon us and they have no place to go. Accordingly I beg Your Grace to do something to help the poor exiles in keeping with the assurances on which they have so far been placing their hope. Your Grace will, I am sure, look with favor on their distress and their hopes.

Herewith I commit Your Grace to God's keeping. Amen.

Your Grace's humble servant,

Martin Luther, Doctor.

Wednesday after Saint Bartholomew, 1533.

TO DOROTHY JOERGER. April 27, 1534

Dorothy Jörger, a widow whom Luther had interested in the needs of poor students, had sent 500 gulden to provide scholarships for students of theology in Wittenberg. Luther proposed that part of the money might profitably be invested and the interest used for the support of two students annually. Here Luther gives an accounting of what had so far been done with the money.[24] [Text in German; *WA, Br,* VII, 60, 61.]

Grace and peace in Christ.

Honored, virtuous Lady:

I wish you to know that your charitable gifts have, praise God, been very well spent and have helped, and continue to help, many poor [students]. I have no doubt that God, who

[24] Cf. *WA, Br,* VI, 273–275, 407–410, 461, 462, 546, 547.

prompted you to do this excellent thing, openly shows that he is well pleased with your thank offering, by means of which you confess and praise the grace which he has manifested to you in his dear Son, Jesus Christ. May God strengthen you in stead-fast faith and perform the good work he has begun in you until the day of Jesus Christ.[25] Amen.

I myself did not know and would not have believed that in this little town and poor university there are so many godly and gifted students who live all year on bread and water, enduring frost and cold, in order that they might study the Holy Scrip-tures and the Word of God. Your charitable gifts have been a great boon and refreshment to them. I have already distributed about half of the money, and I have receipts in the form of letters and seals to show that the money was given to upright young men and not to unworthy scoundrels. I wish to inform you of this that you might know what is happening to your money. I have given more to Andrew[26] than to the others; he received ten gulden, and later another ten, while the others received two, three, and four gulden. This was done with advice from good friends, and all are delighted and thankful. As a token of appreciation they send you the accompanying bound book at the hands of Michael Stiefel,[27] to whom, because he is at present without a parish, I have given ten gulden. He extends to you his best greeting.

Christ be with you and all yours. Amen.

Monday after Jubilate, 1534.   Dr. Martin Luther.

TO ELECTOR JOHN FREDERICK OF SAXONY.
June 5, 1534

In an attempt to counteract the spread of the Reformation, Cardinal Archbishop Albert of Mayence in 1533 forbade the people of Halle to attend Evangelical services in neighboring towns. The edict remained ineffective. During the Easter season of 1534, Evangelicals in Halle, including seventeen members of the town council, refused to receive Communion in one kind according to Roman belief and practice. For their stubborn adherence to Evangelical opinions they were compelled to sell their property by Pentecost and go into exile. Many of the exiles settled in Köthen, near Dessau, and when Luther visited Prince Joachim

[25] Cf. Phil. 1:6.   [26] Probably Andrew Hügel, of Salzburg.
[27] See Luther's letter to Michael Stiefel, June 24, 1533, in Chapter X. Stiefel was for a time without a parish on account of his Adventist opinions.

of Anhalt to comfort him in his illness,[28] *they asked him to persuade the elector of Saxony to intercede in their behalf with the archbishop.* [Text in German ; *WA, Br,* VII, 68-70.]

To the serene, highborn prince and lord, John Frederick, duke of Saxony, elector and marshal of the Holy Roman Empire, landgrave in Thuringia, and margrave of Meissen, my gracious lord: grace and peace in Christ.

Serene, highborn Prince, very gracious Lord:

The pious people who were exiled from Halle requested me so earnestly to write to Your Grace that I could not refuse them. That treacherous man, a typical cardinal, is wretchedly tormenting the pious people, as Your Grace will learn from their petition. The innocent blood of Master George,[29] which the cardinal spilled and devoured, has been stirred up and aroused and is moving the cardinal to pronounce judgment on himself. If Your Grace is in a position to help the good people by addressing that bloodhound orally or in writing, Your Grace must acknowledge that it is a necessary, Christian, charitable, and good work to do so. And I humbly request Your Grace for God's sake to do something for these people and not to be annoyed by their petition.

Would to God that that timid and soft man might again[30] be so terrified as to recognize the gravity of his conduct. Then his malice would surely vanish. May Christ soon give him the reward of an enemy. Amen.

Herewith I commit Your Grace to God's keeping. Amen.

Your Grace's obedient [servant],

Friday after Trinity, 1534.   Martin Luther, Doctor.

TO FRANCIS BURKHARD. August 22, 1536

Nothing specific is known about the mentally ill woman who is the subject of this letter beyond the information that the letter itself contains. Presumably she had been arrested for some act that she had committed in her derangement. Luther here intercedes for her, and especially for her daughter, who was a victim of her mother's condition. [Text in Latin; *WA, Br,* VII, 508, 509.]

---

[28] See letters to Joachim of Anhalt, May 23 and June 26, 1534, in Chapter III.

[29] George Winkler, Evangelical pastor in Halle since 1523, was murdered on April 23, 1527. See "Tröstung an die Christen zu Halle" in *WA,* XXIII, 390–434.

[30] See letter of Dec. 1, 1521, in *WA, Br,* II, 405.

To the distinguished gentleman, Lord Francis Burkhard, vice-chancellor of Saxony, my special friend in the Lord: grace and peace in Christ.

My dear Vice-Chancellor Francis:

I beg of you to find out whether I can intercede profitably in behalf of that old insane woman, Mrs. Kreuzbinder. Her daughter here has been weeping pitifully. It is nothing new for the old woman; she is accustomed to rage, as Licentiate Blanck,[31] her neighbor, can also testify. We often laughed at him because he quarreled with her over the hedge that separates their houses until they became angry with each other and she put him to flight with a long spear.

It is not laudatory for the prince to punish this insane old woman severely, especially because she is a widow and because all the townspeople here regard her as insane. You may tell my gracious lord, on the strength of my word, that she is mad. When she has been sufficiently punished, my gracious lord will do well to release her. After all, punishment will not improve her or make her more rational.[32]

Some consideration must also be given to her unmarried daughter, who has already suffered harm enough on account of her mother's madness. Since she now is a fully grown girl, and altogether sensible, I myself wish that she might have a worthy husband. But these misfortunes which have befallen the girl as well as her mother are more and more alienating those men who might perhaps be interested in marrying her. Here is a case where mortals are bound to each other by a chain of misery. But mercy ought to break the fetters.

Tell me, therefore, if this is a propitious time for me to intercede in her behalf. If so, I shall do that, for I feel sorry, not so much for the mother or the son-in-law, but for the daughter, who needs mercy.

Farewell in the Lord.

Tuesday after Saint Agapitus, 1536.   Martin Luther, Doctor.

TO GEORGE SPALATIN. September 28, 1536

On March 29, 1533, Luther had written to George Spalatin that Elizabeth von Reinsberg, a former nun, had appealed to him for help. She had lost her position as a teacher in a girls' school in Altenburg and lacked the wherewithal to support herself. It appears from the following

31 Christopher Blanck, a lawyer.
32 The last three sentences in German.

letter that she was still in want three years later. [Text in Latin; *WA, Br*, VII, 551.]

To the distinguished gentleman, Master George Spalatin, pastor and bishop of the churches in Altenburg, my very dear friend in the Lord: grace and peace in Christ.

My very dear Spalatin:

I beg of you that, as soon as Master Brisger[33] returns, you may do what you can to collaborate faithfully with him in helping to care for that wretched woman, Elsie von Reinsberg. See to it that she is somehow supplied with food among you, and let no one treat her unkindly. Who knows in what poor mendicant we may have the opportunity of honoring Christ!

Everywhere I see things that trouble me, and I fear that we shall soon be deprived of the Word of grace on account of our incredible ingratitude and our contempt for it. Almost all the churches are thinking, "Let us free ourselves from the burden of the poor and send them to Wittenberg." We have daily experience of this sentiment. No one is any longer willing to do good and help the poor.[34] Meanwhile we pursue our own interests to the point of frenzy. Very well, then,[35] the world is rushing headlong to its fate. Farewell, and pray for us.

Yours,

Sunday after Saint Matthew's, 1536.   Martin Luther, Doctor.

TO ELECTOR JOHN FREDERICK OF SAXONY.
May 29, 1537

A wool merchant in Zwickau, Wolf Schalreuter, was accused in 1535 of counterfeiting. He was discovered to be passing bad Bohemian pennies, and although he claimed that he was not guilty of deliberate fraud, he was arrested and sentenced to life imprisonment. At the request of the prisoner's relatives (a brother of his was choir director in the church in Zwickau), Luther interceded with the elector of Saxony in behalf of Schalreuter. He was not released, however, until four years later. [Text in German; *WA, Br*, VIII, 85-87.]

To the serene, highborn prince and lord, John Frederick, duke of Saxony, marshal and elector of the Holy Roman Empire,

---

[33] Eberhard Brisger was a pastor in Altenburg.
[34] This sentence in German.   [35] This phrase in German.

landgrave in Thuringia, and margrave of Meissen, my gracious lord: grace and peace, etc., and my poor prayers.

Serene, highborn Prince, gracious Lord:

The good people who are relatives, etc., of the imprisoned Wolf Schalreuter have requested me to write to Your Grace (as they have themselves already written in all earnestness to my gracious lord, Duke John)[36] that Your Grace may mercifully commute the sentence of life imprisonment which has been imposed on him at great risk, as they report in their letter.[37] I am sure that Your Grace will be good enough to acknowledge and weigh the reasons reported and will act accordingly. If the danger is as urgent as they represent, there are special circumstances that require consideration.

Although my experience with criminal cases has taught me to hesitate to make requests, yet I am unwilling to refuse my services, where possible, to poor people.

I commit the matter to Your Grace's merciful consideration. May God's grace and spirit govern and preserve Your Grace unto salvation. Amen.

Your Grace's humble subject,

Tuesday after Trinity, 1537.   Martin Luther, Doctor.

TO ALL GODLY CHRISTIANS AND FRIENDS.
May 24, 1538

Wittenberg attracted students, visitors, and beggars from far and near. Among other foreigners from a distance was the subject of this letter. In earlier editions of Luther's correspondence he was referred to vaguely as a Moor. It appears probable, however, that he was a Greek named Francis Megara, to whom there are contemporary references in writings of Philip Melanchthon and others. [Text in German; WA, Br, VIII, 228, 229.]

To all godly Christians and friends in Christ: grace and peace in the Lord.

I recommend this good man, Mr. Francis, who has come to Germany from a distant land, to any and all whom he may visit, and I pray that you may be helpful to him. We here in Wittenberg are already overburdened, beyond what our poverty will bear, with many good people who are refugees or

---

[36] *An m. gnedigen herrn Hertzog Johans Ernsten gethan.*

[37] Because this letter is not extant it is not known to what risk or danger the relatives of Schalreuter refer.

who desire to study. They visit us in the hope of securing help, and they fail to find here as much as the reputation of Wittenberg led them to expect. It is only fair that others in neighboring towns, who have been spared such a daily burden, should also help and contribute. Who knows whether God may be testing us and visiting us! And who knows what he intends to make of these people?

Some foreigners found refuge among the people of Israel too, and they turned out better than many an Israelite—for example, the tenth leper in the Gospel of Luke[38] and the centurion in Capernaum.[39] From this we ought to conclude that we should assist such people for Christ's sake. We should do so even if, as sometimes happens, our gifts are lost on wicked people, for we should not make godly people suffer on account of the wicked.

Let everyone do as his conscience prompts.

Herewith I commit all to God's keeping. Amen.

Friday after Cantate, 1538.   Martin Luther, Doctor

TO DUKE MAURICE OF SAXONY. September 17, 1541

About the year 1520 a youth named Luke Pittig had entered the Augustinian monastery in Dresden, Saxony, and had transferred his patrimony to the monastery. Sometime before 1539 he had withdrawn from the monastery, whose property was now sequestered by the duke of Albertine Saxony. Luther here requests Duke Maurice to return Pittig's inheritance, or a part of it, to enable the man to live. [Text in German; *WA, Br,* IX, 516, 517.]

To the serene, highborn prince and lord, Maurice, duke of Saxony, landgrave in Thuringia, margrave of Meissen, my gracious lord: grace and peace in Christ.

Serene, highborn Prince, gracious Lord:

Luke Pittig, a poor man who is now a village sexton, was formerly an Augustinian friar in Dresden. In his youth, before he knew better, he was persuaded to become a monk. This was about the time when the gospel was beginning its free course,[40] and shortly afterward he transferred his father's property to the monastery. When, as Your Grace knows, Duke George[41]

---

[38] Luke 17:15.   [39] Luke 7:9.
[40] I.e., at the beginning of the Reformation movement.
[41] An opponent of the Reformation, Duke George of Albertine Saxony had died in 1539.

was raging fiercely [against the gospel], Pittig was forced to flee secretly from the monastery, but he left his father's lands, etc., behind. Because he has nothing in reserve and is suffering want, he now humbly requests that Your Grace, acknowledging that he was talked out of his father's property and defrauded, may graciously grant him a fair portion of the monastery's property to help him maintain his poor home.

Inasmuch as Your Grace will understand that the request is a just one, and also that the man needs such charity because of his poverty, I hope that Your Grace will allow him to have that for which I am interceding. I believe that this will not impose a burden on Your Grace, for it involves a single grant and not frequent payments or repeated requests. If it were otherwise, I should gladly have spared Your Grace. But under the circumstances I am glad to make this request in his behalf, knowing as I do that Your Grace is already sufficiently occupied[42] with weighty matters of length and breadth, of height and depth, of eternal and temporal concern.

Herewith I commit Your Grace to God's keeping. Amen.

Your Grace's willing [servant],

Saturday, Saint Lambert's Day, 1541.   Martin Luther.

TO JEROME BAUMGAERTNER. October 3, 1541

An unidentified Englishman, armed with a recommendation from Andrew Osiander, a relative by marriage of Archbishop Thomas Cranmer in England, arrived in Wittenberg with a child who was presumably his son. The man departed suddenly and unceremoniously, leaving the boy behind him in Luther's home. In this letter Luther asks that the boy be admitted to a foundling home in Nuremberg, which was done.[43] [Text in German; WA, Br, IX, 527-529.]

To the distinguished gentleman, Dr. Jerome Baumgärtner, patrician and town councilman in Nuremberg, my very dear friend in the Lord: grace and peace and my poor prayers.

Honorable, excellent, dear Sir and good Friend:

Such confidence do I have in you that I am sending along a boy from England who was knavishly and deceitfully left on my hands. He was brought to me with a recommendation from Dr. Osiander, who was likewise deceived. Since you know how

---

42 Duke Maurice had just entered upon his reign on Aug. 18.

43 For more details see Philip Melanchthon's letters in *C.R.*, IV, 661, 662, 696.

overrun with beggars our town is, and inasmuch as the boy still requires the attention of a maid to wait upon him, wash him, etc. (which I cannot afford), I pray that you may do me the great favor of persuading the gentlemen in Nuremberg to receive the boy in your home for foundlings. Apart from this case, we here in Wittenberg—and I in particular—are sufficiently burdened. Indeed, we are burdened quite beyond our ability to bear.

God protect me that I may not be deceived like this again.[44] Do what you can, I pray, to relieve me of this burden which was treacherously heaped upon me.

She who was once your flame,[45] and who now bears you a new love on account of your admirable virtues and wishes you well with all her heart, respectfully greets you. Farewell in the Lord.

Yours,

October 3, 1541.   Martin Luther.

TO ELECTOR JOHN FREDERICK OF SAXONY.
March 27, 1545

On March 26, 1545, a widowed relative of John Staupitz had written a letter (referred to here as "the enclosed letter") to Luther in which she complained of her poverty and of having been deprived by her relatives of her rightful share in a paternal inheritance. Upon Luther's intercession in her behalf the elector had his councilors investigate the matter. The extant correspondence on the case does not suggest that a decision favorable to the widow was reached. The letter is of added interest on account of its reference to Luther's indebtedness to Staupitz, who had helped him in his early understanding of the gospel. [Text in German; WA, Br, XI, 63-67.]

To the serene, highborn Prince and Lord, John Frederick duke of Saxony, imperial marshal and elector, landgrave in Thuringia, margrave of Meissen, and burgrave of Magdeburg, my gracious lord: grace and peace in Christ and my poor prayers. Amen.

Serene, highborn Prince, gracious Lord:

The good, aged matron Margaret von Staupitz sent me the enclosed letter, from which Your Grace will learn what is

---

44 Here Luther turns from German to Latin.

45 *Ignis olim tuus.* The reference is to Luther's wife. Luther had once, when she first left the convent, hoped that she might be married off to Baumgärtner.

happening to this forsaken, aged widow. Inasmuch as she earnestly appeals to me through Dr. Staupitz, whom (if I do not wish to be a cursed and ungrateful papal ass) I acknowledge as my spiritual father in Christ and as the man who first suggested to me the teachings I now embrace, I am in duty bound to be of service to all those whom he, if he were still living, might ask me to help. Accordingly I humbly pray Your Grace to be gracious to this good matron for Dr. Staupitz' and my sake. It is unkind of her relatives to treat her as she claims they do, for poor widows ought to be helped and not neglected. Your Grace will know what means may be employed to assist her.

Herewith I commit the matter to our dear Lord. Amen.

Your Grace's obedient servant,

Martin Luther, Doctor.

March 27, 1545, the day of our Lord's resurrection according to the course of the sun.

VII

Encouragement to the Persecuted and Imprisoned

TO JOHN SCHWANHAUSEN. March 7, 1523

An early graduate of the university in Wittenberg, John Schwanhausen had been appointed preacher in St. Gangolf's in Bamberg, Bavaria. By 1520 he had embraced Evangelical views, and he was reproached for these by his Catholic bishop in the spring of 1523. A year later he was removed from his office and fled to Nuremberg. He died on September 1, 1528. It is likely that Luther learned of Schwanhausen's views and activities from Joachim Camerarius, who had visited his native Bamberg, on his mother's death, several months before this letter was written. [Text in Latin; *WA, Br*, III, 40, 41.]

To the preacher at St. Gangolf's in Bamberg, excellent and learned gentleman: grace and peace in Christ.

Dear Sir:

Although I am unknown to you and you to me, He[1] whom you preach (as the Bambergers testify) is by God's grace known to both of us. This impels me at least to seek your acquaintance by letter and to send you a greeting so that, as Saint Paul modestly puts it, we may comfort each other with our common faith.[2] Advance boldly, dear brother. Be of good courage, let your heart be strengthened, and wait on the Lord.[3] "The servant is not greater than his lord. If they have persecuted me, they will also persecute you. Be of good cheer, for I have overcome the world. In the world ye shall have tribulation, but in me ye shall have peace."[4] But why should I comfort one who is stronger than I am? Only this one thing shall I ask of you, that you pray God for us and that you commend me in your prayers to our Lord. In him may you fare well. Amen.

Martin Luther.

1 Jesus Christ. Cf. I Cor. 1:23.
3 Cf. Ps. 27:14.
2 Cf. Rom. 1:12.
4 John 15:20; 16:33.

TO THREE COURT LADIES. June 18, 1523

Because they had been found to be reading some of Luther's writings, the Catholic Duke George of Albertine Saxony dismissed three of his wife's ladies in waiting at the ducal court in Freiberg. Luther assumed that the duke's chancellor, Wolfgang Stählin, was responsible for the dismissal. Luther's friend Nicholas von Amsdorf asked him to write a letter of consolation to the young ladies, and he did so in the following. [Text in German; WA, Br, III, 92-94.]

To the honorable and virtuous young ladies, Hannah von Draschwitz, Milia von Oelsnitz, and Ursula von Feilitzsch, my special friends in the Lord: grace and peace in Christ.

Honored, virtuous, and dear young Ladies:

Mr. Nicholas von Amsdorf has acquainted me with your distress and with the opprobrium that you have experienced at the court in Freiberg on account of my books, and he has at the same time asked me to write you a letter of consolation. Although I am confident that you do not require comfort from me and am disinclined to write to persons unknown to me, I do not know how to refuse him.

It is my earnest and friendly request that you set your hearts at rest and neither do nor wish evil to those who are responsible for the situation in which you find yourselves. You should rather act as Saint Paul teaches and says, "Being reviled, we bless."[5] Christ also says, in Matt., ch. 6, "Bless them that curse you, do good to them that hate you, and pray for them which despitefully use you and persecute you."[6] Act thus because you are enlightened by the grace of God, while they are blind and impenitent. Moreover, they do more injury to their own souls than all the world can do to them. Unhappily, you are only too well revenged on them for treating you unjustly and raging and horribly rebelling against God. Accordingly it is fitting that you should have pity on them, seeing that they are mad, unthinking men who do not realize how deplorably they are ruining themselves when they think to do you an injury. Wait on Christ, and let him act. He will richly recompense you for the wrong done you and will lift you up higher than your fondest hope, if only you will not interfere and will leave everything to him.

Even if you should feel in your conscience that you have given

5 I Cor. 4:12.   6 Matt. 5:44.

cause for the treatment you have received, have no fear on this account, for it is a good and gracious sign that Christ has called you directly to repentance. You should also remember that if you tried to do anything against your persecutors, you could effect nothing, for it is a divine cause for which you suffer, and God will allow no one but himself to judge or avenge it, as he says by the prophet, "He that toucheth you, toucheth the apple of his eye."[7] I can well believe that that blind wretch, Dr. Wolf Stählin, is the instigator. But he is held under another judgment than he supposes, and unfortunately it will be very hard for him.

Act in this way, my dear sisters, and urge your friends to do likewise. Then God's grace and peace will be with you. Amen. Take my letter in good part.

Thursday after Saint Vitus, 1523.   Martin Luther.

TO THE CHRISTIANS IN THE NETHERLANDS.
August, 1523

On October 6, 1522, Margaret, regent of Emperor Charles V in the Low Countries, had all the inmates in the Augustinian monastery in Antwerp arrested on suspicion of Evangelical sentiments. Most of them were quickly exonerated and others succeeded in escaping, but three were held in custody: Henry Vos, John van den Esschen, and Lambert Thorn. They were asked to recant, were finally taken to Brussels, and there they were tried for heresy. The first two Augustinians remained firm in their faith, were condemned, turned over to the state, and burned at the stake on July 1, 1523. The third, Lambert Thorn, was given more time for reflection. Vos and Esschen were the first Protestant martyrs, and their execution caused a considerable stir. Luther addressed the following letter to the Evangelicals in the Netherlands, and it was sent as a printed leaflet. [Text in German; WA, XII, 73-80.]

To all my dear brethren in Christ living in Holland, Brabant, and Flanders, together with all believers in Christ: grace and peace from God our Father and from our Lord Jesus Christ.

Praise and thanks be to the Father of all mercy, who now again permits us to see his wonderful light, hitherto hidden on account of our sins while we were compelled to submit to the terrible powers of darkness and serve such disgraceful errors and the Antichrist. But now the time is come when the voice of the turtle is heard and flowers appear on the earth.[8]

7 Zech. 2:8.   8 S. of Sol. 2:12.

My dear friends, you have not been the only participants in this joy, but you have become the foremost among those who have given us such joy and pleasure. For it has been your privilege before all others in the world not only to hear the gospel and know Christ but also to be the first to suffer shame and injury, anxiety and distress, imprisonment and death, for Christ's sake. You have now become so strong and productive that you have watered and strengthened the cause with your very blood, for among you those two precious jewels of Christ, Henry and John, have held their lives of no account in Brussels in order that Christ and his Word might be glorified. O how contemptuously were those two souls condemned, but how gloriously and with what eternal joy will they return with Christ to judge justly those by whom they were here unjustly condemned! What a little thing it is to be put to shame and to be slain by the world when those who are so treated know that their blood is precious and their death dear in God's sight, as the psalms say![9] What is the world in comparison with God? With what gladness and joy all the angels must have looked upon these two souls! How welcome must that fire have been which hurried them from this sinful life to eternal life yonder, from this ignominy to everlasting glory! God be praised and blessed forever that we who have known and worshiped so many false saints have lived to see and hear real saints and true martyrs. We up here in Germany have not yet been sufficiently deserving to become so precious and worthy an offering to Christ, though many of our members have not been, and still are not, without persecution.

Therefore, my dearly beloved, be of good cheer and rejoice in Christ, and let us thank him for the great signs and wonders that he has begun to do among us. He has given us a new and fresh illustration of his own life, and now it is time that the Kingdom of God should be not in word but in power.[10] Here we learn what is meant by the saying, "Be joyful in tribulation."[11] "For a small moment," says Isaiah, "have I forsaken thee, but with great mercies will I gather thee,"[12] and in Ps. 90 God says, "I will be with him in trouble; I will deliver him, and honor him because he hath known my name."[13] Because, then, we see our present tribulation and have such strong and comforting promises, let us renew our hearts and be of good courage and joyfully allow the Lord to slay us. He has said (and he will not lie), "The very hairs of your head are all numbered."[14] And although our adversaries will cry out that these saints were Hussites, Wycliffites, and Lutherans, let us not be startled but rather strengthened by this, for the cross of Christ must have its slanderers. Our Judge is not far off, and he will pass a different judgment. This we know for certain.

Pray for us and for one another, dear brethren, that we may uphold one another with faithful hands and all of us may cling in unity of spirit to our Head, Jesus Christ. May he strengthen and perfect you with his grace to the honor of his holy name. To him be praise and thanks among you and all creatures forever. Amen.[15]

Martin Luther, preacher in Wittenberg.[16]

TO THE CHRISTIANS IN RIGA, TALLINN, AND TARTU. August, 1523

As a result of the circulation of Luther's writings there was evidence of the beginning of an Evangelical movement in Livonia (the present Latvia and Estonia) at least as early as 1521. It had the support of many noblemen and knights, who prevented the local prelates from employing effective measures against the movement. In August, 1522, John Lohmüller, secretary of the town council in Riga, wrote to Luther to report that there were two Evangelical clergymen there and to ask for a letter of greeting and encouragement.[17] Luther responded in the following open letter which was addressed not only to the Evangelicals in Riga (Latvia) but also to those in Tallinn (Estonia) and Tartu (Estonia). It offers a summary of Reformation teaching in contrast to that of the Medieval Church. [Text in German; WA, XII, 143-150.]

To the dear friends and elect of God, to all Christians in Riga, Tallinn, and Tartu in Livonia, my dear sirs and brethren in Christ: grace and peace in the Lord.

My dear Sirs and Brethren:

I have learned from letters and by word of mouth that God, the Father of our Lord and Saviour Jesus Christ, has begun to work wonders among you too, has visited your hearts with the gracious light of his truth, and has so highly blessed you that

14 Matt. 10:30.
15 Here followed, in the printed leaflet, "The Articles to Explain Why the Two Christian Augustinian Friars Were Burned in Brussels."
16 *E.W.*, i.e., *Ecclesiastes Witebergensis.*
17 See letter of Aug. 20, 1522, in *WA, Br,* II, 590–593.

you receive it with joyful hearts as a true Word of God, which indeed it is. Most of us here will neither listen to it nor endure it, but the richer and the greater is the grace which God offers us here, the more madly do the princes, the bishops, and all the big scales of behemoth strive against it, slander it, condemn it, and persecute it. They have gone so far as to put many people in prison, and recently they have burned two,[18] and so in our day new martyrs are being sent to Christ in heaven. Therefore, I rejoice to call you blessed who are at the ends of the world because, like the Gentiles in Acts, ch. 14, you receive with all gladness the saving Word,[19] which our Jews in this Jerusalem—nay, this Babylon—not only despise but prevent others from hearing. "The wrath of God," says Saint Paul, "is come upon them to the uttermost."[20] But you are ruled by grace.

Therefore, my beloved, be thankful for God's grace and know the time of your visitation, that ye receive not the grace of God in vain.[21] And, first of all, be careful not to become like the Galatians who made such a glorious beginning and became such fine, pure, and good Christians but were soon led away by deceivers on the erring path of works and were perverted.[22] Beyond all doubt wolves will come among you too, especially if the good shepherds whom God has now sent you go astray, speak ill of the right way, and lead you back again into Egypt, where you will become false worshipers who serve the devil instead of God. This is the very thing from which Christ by his heavenly light has freed you, and continues to free you daily, so that you may come to the knowledge of him and be sure that he, alone and always, is our Lord, Priest, Teacher, Bishop, Father, Saviour, Helper, Comforter, and Protector in all sins, in death, in necessity, and in every need, whether temporal or eternal.

You have heard and learned that if anyone believes that Jesus Christ has by his blood, without any merit on our part and in accord with God the Father's will and mercy, become our Saviour and the Bishop of our souls, then his faith, without any works, assuredly makes Christ his own and gives as he believes; for the blood of Christ is certainly not mine or yours so that we may fast or say Mass, but in order that we may believe, as Paul says in Rom., ch. 4, "We conclude that a man is

---

[18] On the martyrdom of Henry Vos and John van den Esschen see the letter to the Christians in the Netherlands, above.
[19] Cf. Acts 14:27.   [20] I Thess. 2:16.
[21] Cf. II Cor. 6:1.   [22] Cf. Gal. 3:1.

justified by faith, without the deeds of the law."[23] This faith makes us joyful and at peace with God and it must make us love him because we see that it is God's will and the gracious attitude of his favor toward us that causes Christ thus to deal with us. This means, then, that we come to the Father and are drawn to the Father through Christ, have peace with God, and unconcernedly and gladly await death and all misfortune. Where such faith is wanting there is blindness, there are no Christians, there is not even a spark of God's work and favor.

From this you have gone on and learned that all the doctrines that have been proposed to us hitherto in order to make us righteous and save us by works, by the laying aside of sin and the doing of penance (such, for example, as the appointed fasts, prayers, pilgrimages, Masses, vigils, charitable endowments, monkery, nunnery, priestcraft)[24]—all such things are devilish doctrine and blasphemy because they pretend to do for us what only the blood of Christ can do through faith. Thus they ascribe to man's doctrines and works what belongs only to the Word and works of God. But the light of faith clearly reveals that all this is nothing but thick and terrible darkness, is without God's grace in Christ, and lets go the merits Christ has with God. This is the way to heaven and the chief thing in the Christian life.

Afterward you heard that such a man is obliged to do nothing except love his neighbor, as Saint Paul says in Rom., ch. 13, and Christ says in John, ch. 16, "This is my commandment, that ye love one another."[25] For Christ's disciples can do nothing for themselves, for their own sins, or for their own salvation, but Christ's blood has already done everything and accomplished everything, and because he has loved them they no longer need to love themselves or seek or wish anything good for themselves, but what they might do and seek for themselves they must now turn to their neighbor's good and do for others the good works which they do not require for themselves. They are to do for others what Christ has done for us; he gave and poured out his blood for us, not for himself. This is the sign too by which true Christians are known, as Christ says, "By this shall men know that ye are my disciples, if ye love one another."[26] And this is the second chief thing in the Christian life.

These things teach and do, my beloved, and let no other wind

23 Rom. 3:28.
24 *Moncherey, nonnerey, pfafferey.*
25 Cf. Rom. 13:9; John 15:12.
26 John 13:35.

of doctrine move you,[27] whether it blow from Rome or from Jerusalem. Everything depends on faith in Christ and love to one's neighbor. Avoid, as you would deadly poison, indulgences, the worship of saints, and all other works that are applied to ourselves and the good of our souls. But if you hold to this pure doctrine and abide in it, you will not escape cross and persecution, for the evil spirit cannot endure it that his holiness, which he has established by works with the help of priests throughout the world, should thus be put to shame and brought to nought. But be steadfast, and remember that you have no right to fare better than your Lord and Bishop, Christ, who also suffered on account of this doctrine when he rebuked the work righteousness of the Pharisees. Such a cross is necessary and profitable for you, for it brings you a firm and assured hope, so that you hate this life and wait cheerfully for the life to come. Thus you will be prepared and perfected in these three things—faith, love, and hope.[28]

Your preachers will tell you enough of what is to be said about the Sacraments and external things, about eating and drinking, dress and conduct. If the aforementioned three things are right, all these external things will take care of themselves in Christian freedom. May our Lord Jesus Christ make you perfect, strengthen, and stablish you[29] for his eternal Kingdom with all the fullness of his wisdom and knowledge. To him be praise and thanks forever. Amen.

I hope that you will accept this exhortation from me, dear brethren, for although you know these things already and do not need to hear them from me, I am yet in duty bound to care for and serve you even in unnecessary things. I commend you to your preachers. Pray for us too. God's grace be with you. Amen.

Martin Luther, preacher in Wittenberg.

TO LAMBERT THORN. January 19, 1524

At the time when two Augustinian friars, Henry Vos and John van den Esschen, were burned at the stake in Brussels for their stubborn adherence to the Evangelical faith (see above), a third Augustinian, Lambert Thorn, was arrested for similar reasons. He died in prison five years later, in 1528, without recanting. The following letter of encouragement was sent to this prisoner by Luther. [Text in Latin; WA, Br, III, 237-239.]

[27] Cf. Eph. 4:14.   [28] Cf. I Cor. 13:13.   [29] Cf. I Peter 5:10.

To Brother Lambert Thorn, disciple of Christ, who is bound in
chains on account of the gospel, my beloved friend in Christ:
grace and peace in the Lord.

Dear Brother Lambert:

Christ, who is in you, has given me abundant testimony that
you do not need my words, for he himself suffers in you and is
glorified in you. He is taken captive in you and reigns in you.
He is oppressed in you and triumphs in you. He has given you
that holy knowledge of himself which is hidden from the world.[30]
Not only this, but he strengthens you inwardly by his Spirit in
these outward tribulations and consoles you with the double
example of John and Henry.[31] Thus both they and you are to
me a great consolation and strength, to the whole world a
sweet savor,[32] and to the gospel of Christ a special glory. There
is little need, therefore, to burden you with my consolation.
Who knows why the Lord was unwilling to have you die with
the other two? Perhaps you were saved for another miracle.

Therefore, I rejoice with you and congratulate you with my
whole heart, giving thanks to the faithful Saviour, our Lord
Jesus Christ, who has given me not only to know his Word and
his Spirit but also to see in you the rich and splendid increase
of his grace. Alas, though I am the first to teach these things, I
am the last to share your chains and fires, and perhaps I shall
never be found worthy to share them. Nevertheless, I shall
avenge myself for this unhappiness of mine and console myself
with the thought that your chains and prisons and fires are all
my own, as indeed they are so long as I confess and preach
these doctrines and sympathize with you and rejoice with you.
But may the Lord Jesus, who has begun his glory in you, perfect
it until his day.[33]

And so, my brother, pray for me as I do for you, mindful that
you are not suffering alone but that He is with you who says,
"I will be with him in trouble; because he hath set his love
upon me, therefore will I deliver him: I will set him on high
because he hath known my name."[34] But all of us too are with
you, as the Lord is, and neither he nor we will desert you. Be
of good courage and he will strengthen your heart; wait on the
Lord.[35] He has said: "In the world ye shall have tribulation:
but be of good cheer; I have overcome the world."[36] Do not
argue with Satan but fix your eyes on the Lord, relying in

[30] Cf. Matt. 11:25.   [31] John van den Esschen and Henry Vos.
[32] Cf. Ex. 29:18.   [33] Cf. Phil. 1:6.   [34] Ps. 91:14, 15.
[35] Cf. Ps. 27:14.   [36] John 16:33.

simple faith on Jesus Christ, and know that by his blood we are saved. Just as our works and human laws cannot be the blood of Christ, so they can neither take away our sins nor justify us, can neither condemn us nor accuse us.

Here in the duchy of our elector there is peace, but the duke of Bavaria[37] and the bishop of Treves are killing and driving out and persecuting many.[38] Other bishops and princes are indeed abstaining from blood but not from violence and threats, and everywhere Christ has again become a reproach of men and despised of the people.[39] You have become a member of him by the holy calling of our Father. May he perfect his calling in you to the glory of his name and of his Word. Amen.

Farewell in Christ, my brother. All our friends and our whole church send you greetings.

Tuesday after Saint Anthony's, 1524.   Martin Luther.

TO THE CHRISTIANS OF MILTENBERG.
February 14, 1524

John Drach was called as the first Evangelical clergyman in Miltenberg, a small town in the jurisdiction of Elector Albert of Mayence, in the spring of 1522. By his popular preaching he quickly won the support of many of the people and members of the town council. But he also encountered opposition from the local priests, who charged that Drach held heretical opinions about fasting, celibacy, holy days, private confession, the reception of Communion in one kind, etc. Summoned to appear for a hearing before his ecclesiastical superiors, he was excommunicated in the fall of 1523 and fled from Miltenberg. Consequent dissatisfaction among the people was greatly increased when some of Drach's adherents were beheaded and the Evangelical movement was forcibly suppressed. It was under such circumstances that Luther wrote the following letter, which was sent out as a printed document. The reason for this he explained in a letter to the elector, Archbishop Albert of Mayence: "Since the poor people are also forbidden to receive letters I cannot refrain from publishing an open letter of consolation in order that Christ may not say to me on the last day, 'I was in prison and ye visited me not.' "[40] [Text in German; WA, XV, 54-78.]

[37] Duke William of Bavaria.
[38] A man was beheaded in Munich for mocking the Virgin Mary, and two men were burned at the stake in Ingolstadt for circulating a tract about the martyrs in Brussels.   [39] Ps. 22:6.
[40] Cf. Matt. 25:35–39. Luther's letter to Albert of Mayence, Feb. 14, 1524, in WA, Br, III, 244.

To all dear friends of Christ in Miltenberg: grace and peace from God the Father and the Lord Jesus Christ.

The holy apostle Saint Paul, when he wished to comfort his Corinthians, began as follows: "Blessed be the God and Father of our Lord Jesus Christ, the Father of mercies and the God of all comfort, who comforteth us in all our tribulation, that we may be able to comfort them that are in tribulation with the comfort wherewith we ourselves are comforted of God."[41] In these words he teaches us by his own example that we are to comfort those who are in trouble, but in such wise that the comfort be not of men, but of God. He purposely adds this in order that we may avoid the false and shameful comfort which the world, the flesh, and the devil also seek and give, by which all the profit and benefit of suffering and the cross are hindered and destroyed.

What this comfort is that comes from God he shows in Rom., ch. 15: "What has been written was written for our learning, that we through patience and comfort of the Scriptures might have hope."[42] He says, "Have hope," but hope is for that which we neither see nor feel.[43] This world's comfort tries to see and feel what the afflicted desire to have and will have nothing to do with patience; but here we are told that patience is to abide and that the comfort of the Scriptures is in hope. This is, in fact, what Saint Paul does to the Corinthians. For when he has told them of God's comfort he comes at last to praising them, telling them that they are a letter of Christ prepared by the preaching of the gospel and written by the living Spirit. Then he begins a psalm of praise to the gospel, and when a carnal man reads it he may well think: Is the man drunk? He wishes to comfort the Corinthians but only praises himself and his preaching and boasts of the gospel. But he who regards it rightly perceives that good Saint Paul draws God's true and rich comfort out of the Scriptures and strengthens the Corinthians and makes them glad by means of the gospel.

Accordingly I too have undertaken to comfort your hearts in your tribulation with the comfort that I have from God. For I have had full information from your exiled pastor, Dr. John Carlstadt [Drach], and from others as to how the enemies of the gospel and murderers of souls have treated you because of God's Word, which with their outrageous blasphemy they call Lutheran doctrine so that they may have the appearance of

41 II Cor. 1:3, 4.   42 Rom. 15:4.
43 Cf. Rom. 8:24, 25.

doing God a service by persecuting human doctrine. So the Jews did to the apostles, as Christ prophesied they would.[44]

It would be a worldly consolation and altogether profitless—nay, hurtful—to your souls and to the cause if I were to console you, or we were to console ourselves, with the thought that by scolding and complaining we would avenge ourselves on those blasphemers for their outrages and wickedness. Even if we were to kill them all or drive them all out by force, or if we were to rejoice in the punishment that someone else would mete out to them because of our sufferings, that would do no good. For that would be a worldly consolation and a worldly revenge that is unworthy of us. It is rather worthy of our enemies, for you see that they have cooled their rage on you and taken their revenge, and they are pleased about this and feel much better. But what sort of consolation is this? Is there any hope in it? Is there any patience in it? Is there any Scripture in it? In place of God they have put violence; in place of patience they have shown vengefulness; in place of hope they plainly give vent to their own will and they feel that they have got what they wanted. Whence comes such consolation as this? It is not of God. So it must certainly be of the devil, and that is the truth. But what will the devil's consolation lead to? Paul tells us, "Their glory will have a shameful end."[45]

Now, see what a rich, proud comfort you may have in this tribulation. You are certain that you suffer these outrages and ignominies for the sake of God's Word. What does it matter that they call it heresy? You are sure that it is God's Word, and they cannot be sure that it is heresy, for they will not listen to it. They have not proved, nor can they prove, that it is heresy. And yet on this uncertain ground they go on to blaspheme and persecute that which they do not know, as Saint Peter says[46]; therefore, they cannot have a clear conscience in the matter. But you have the sure and certain knowledge that you suffer for God's sake.

Who can or will reckon what a proud and blessed consolation it is when one is certain that one is suffering for God's sake? For who is it that suffers? Whose concern is it? Who will avenge our suffering for God's sake? Saint Peter says, "Blessed are ye, if ye suffer for righteousness' sake."[47] If a man were emperor of all the world, he ought not only willingly to give up his empire to have such suffering but even count his empire as dung in comparison with such a treasure of consolation.

[44] Cf. John 16:2.   [45] Phil. 3:19.   [46] Cf. II Peter 2:12.   [47] I Peter 3:14.

Therefore, dear friends, you have no reason at all to desire revenge or to wish evil to your enemies. You ought to pity them from the bottom of your hearts. For your revenge upon them— save for that which will come to them at the end—is already too great. They have already been hurt enough. And they have brought you nothing but good since their raging has given you God's consolation. They have done themselves an injury from which they will hardly, and many of them will never, recover.

For what does it matter that they have injured you for a time in body and goods? That must have an end. And what does it matter that they rejoice for a little while in their tyranny? It will not last long. Rather compare your salvation and their misery. You have a good, quiet conscience and a righteous cause; they have a bad and uncertain conscience and a blind cause, and they themselves do not yet know how unrighteous it is. You have the consolation of God with patience and hope out of the Scriptures; they have the devil's consolation in revenge and visible tyranny. If you had the power to choose between their lot and your own, ought you not flee from theirs as from the devil himself, even though it were a kingdom of heaven that they had, and hasten to choose your own lot, even though it were a hell? For heaven cannot be glad if the devil reigns there, and hell cannot be sad if God reigns there.

Therefore, dear friends, if you would comfort yourselves and revenge yourselves proudly and completely, not only on your human persecutors but rather on the devil who rides them, treat him thus: Be glad and thank God that you have been counted worthy to hear and learn his Word and suffer for it, and be satisfied with the certainty that your cause is God's Word and your consolation is from God. Pity your enemies because they do not have a good conscience in their own cause and have only the sad and wretched consolation of the devil that comes from their outrages, their impatience, their vengefulness, and their temporary tyranny. Be sure that with such gladness of spirit, praise, and thanksgiving you will hurt their god, the devil, more than if you killed a thousand of your enemies. For he did not bring this to pass in order to comfort them and do you bodily harm, but what he wished to do was to make you sad and sorrowful, as people for whom God has no use. Be all the more glad, therefore, and mock him so that his attempt may fail and he may be vexed.

I shall show you another way to tickle him. It is the thing he fears most. He knows very well that there is a little verse in the

Psalter that says, "Thou hast laid a strong foundation by the mouths of babes and sucklings, that thou mayest make an end of the enemy and the avenger."[48] This threatens him not only with sorrow and misery, but with destruction; and that not by great power, which would be an honor, but by weak sucklings, who have no strength. It hurts and cuts this proud and mighty spirit that his great power, his fearful raging, his wild revenge shall be cast down without the use of force, by the weakness of children, without his being able to prevent it. Let us help in all earnestness to bring this about. We are the babes and sucklings if we are weak, if we allow our enemies to be strong and mighty over us and do and say what they will for their cause. But we must keep silent about our cause and suffer as though we could neither do nor say anything, while they act like mighty heroes and giants. Meanwhile through our words God speaks his Word, which praises his grace. It is a rock and a sure foundation, against which the gates of hell can do nothing.[49] If the Word remains and has free course, it will at length happen that some of our enemies will be converted. They are the devil's scales, and when these scales are stripped off the devil by the Word of God, he is naked and becomes weak. Thus it comes to pass, as this verse says, that the Word makes an end of the enemy and the avenger. This is a joyful victory and conquest, won without sword and fist and therefore painful to the devil. For he is pleased only if by his servants he can move us to wrath, vengefulness, impatience, and sadness, but if the result is joy and praise of God and glory for his Word, that is the devil's true hell.

"But," someone will say, "it is forbidden to mention the Word of God on pain of death and confiscation." Well and good! If a man is strong, let him defy this command, for they have no right to make such a prohibition. God's Word ought not, must not, and will not be bound. But if anyone is too timid and weak, I shall give him other counsel: Let him be joyful in secret, thank God, and praise his Word, as has been said above, and let him pray God for strength to speak of it also in public that the enemy and the avenger may be destroyed. To this end I shall present you with a German translation of Ps. 119, together with a brief explanation of it, that you may see how God comforts you with his Scriptures and how you are to pray against the false blasphemers and raging persecutors.

Following is the psalm and its exposition.

Psalm 119 [120]

[48] Ps. 8:3.   [49] Cf. Matt. 16:18.

"In my distress I cried unto the Lord, and he heard me.

"Deliver my soul, O Lord, from lying lips, and from a deceitful tongue.

"What shall be given unto thee? or what shall be done unto thee, thou false tongue?

"Sharp arrows of the mighty, with coals of juniper.

"Woe is me, that I sojourn in Mesech, that I dwell in the tents of Kedar!

"My soul hath long dwelt with him that hateth peace

"I am for peace: but when I speak, they are for war."

The first verse teaches us where we should turn when misfortune comes upon us—not to the emperor, not to the sword, not to our own devices and wisdom, but to the Lord, who is our only real help in time of need. "I cried unto the Lord in my distress," he says. That we should do this confidently, cheerfully, and without fail he makes clear when he says, "And he heard me." It is as if he would say, "The Lord is pleased to have us turn to him in our distress and is glad to hear and help us."

The second verse sets forth the request and expresses what the distress is—not as if God did not know this beforehand but in order that we may be moved and driven to pray more diligently. And the distress is that very trouble that confronts you in Miltenberg, and others like you in various German lands, namely, that lying lips and deceitful tongues are unwilling to suffer the Word of God, that they wish to uphold their human notions and lies, and that they command us to be silent in order that nothing may be preached save only their wicked, false, and poisonous doctrine.

The third verse weighs what may be done under the circumstances. For timid men desire and would gladly have help and protection in the world. Many are ready to compromise, as this verse shows with its proposals, but the Spirit rejects all this and will have nothing to do with such help, as we see in what follows.

The fourth verse mentions the true help, namely, "sharp arrows of the mighty." This means that help comes from God when he sends strong preachers who boldly proclaim his Word. They are the arrows of God, and they are sharp when they pierce, when they do not spare but shoot and wound everything that is a fabric of human opinions. In this way lying lips are overcome and transformed into good and Christian lips.

"Coals of juniper" are true Christians who bear witness to

the Word of God (suggested by the sharp arrows) in their lives, who manifest their faith in their works, and who kindle the flame of ardent love (for it is said that coals of juniper keep fires glowing). So this verse calls for excellent preachers who proclaim the Word of God powerfully and with faith, who beat down whatever is of the devil, and who are fired to do works of love and let their faith shine forth. There are many preachers of the Word today, but many of them have no power and do not act forcefully. Even if they do, they do not pierce, for they spare those who ought not to be spared—the bigwigs—and, besides, their love is so cold and their manner of life is so coarse that they offend more than they reform, and so they make the arrows of God dull and ineffective.

The fifth verse laments and shows what happens to those preachers who have little faith in the gospel and who beat the air with their words. This offends the Spirit, who desires that everybody receive the Word with joy. Therefore he says: "Woe is me! I regret that I must sojourn here so long as a stranger, for I do not find the Kingdom of God among them. Nor do they wish to enter it. They preach at great length but without helping anybody. The people remain as they were, and I am obliged to live and dwell among them in the tents of Kedar." *Kedar* is the Hebrew word for Arabia, and in German it means "sorrowful" or "dark" and is applied to those who are in trouble. The Arabs are a rude, wild, insolent, uncivilized people, and so he here calls those who are disobedient to the gospel, who will not be corrected by the gospel, "Kedar."

The sixth verse shows that he is not only despised but also persecuted, and yet he must dwell among them. They hate peace, he says—that is, godly peace, the possession of inward peace and a good conscience before God and outward peace with all men, harming nobody and doing good to everybody. They hate peace because they persecute the Word, which teaches and brings about such peace, and because they defend their own doctrine and unbelieving works, which result in a bad conscience before God and create sects and divisions in many classes of society.

The seventh verse is a defense and answer against the false charge which the godless prefer against true Christians when they say that their Christian doctrine is seditious and introduces dissension in the world. To this he responds: "It is not my fault. I kept the peace and did no one any harm. But when I taught what true peace is, they could not suffer it, began to fight, and persecuted me." In similar fashion Elijah was once charged by King Ahab with troubling Israel although, as Elijah answered, it was the king and not Elijah who was troubling Israel.[50]

So you see, dear friends, your situation is described here and you are experiencing what is written in this psalm. You must suffer yourselves to be called seditious although you have done nothing except hear and speak the Word of God. For this cause the temple servants and soul chasers of Mayence[51] started a controversy and hated and persecuted the peace which you taught, and you must continue to dwell and sojourn among such enemies of peace for God's sake and must be unwelcome strangers in the tents of Kedar.

What are you to do? You cannot revenge yourselves, and even if you could, it would not help. To wish your enemies evil will not do either, for Christ says: "Bless them that curse you. Pray for them which despitefully use you and persecute you."[52] What, then, are you to do? You can do no better than to turn your eyes away from those who harm you and see how you may get revenge and cool your rage on that scoundrel who possesses and drives them. But he has neither flesh nor blood. He is a spirit. Consequently, as Saint Paul says, you must wrestle not against flesh and blood but against spiritual scoundrels in high places, against the rulers of this dark and blind world.[53] What else could those wretched whoremongers and fat bellies of Mayence do? They have to do what their god, the devil, impels them to do. They are not on their own. For this reason they are heartily to be pitied. They claim to uphold Christian doctrine while they live more disgracefully than whores and knaves. As if the Holy Spirit could do something for God's glory with such diabolical vessels! And yet he does, without their knowing or willing it, as he once did through Judas, Caiaphas, and Pilate.

There is only one thing left to do. As Ps. 120 suggests, turn to the Lord in your distress, cry unto him about those lying lips, pray earnestly and with all your heart for good marksmen who might shoot sharp arrows at the devil so as to hit and not miss him, and pray also for fiery coals of juniper in order that the blind people who have been misled may be warmed by your ardor and have their path lighted by your good life to the

50 Cf. I Kings 18:17, 18.
51 The clergy in Miltenberg under Archbishop Albert of Mayence.
52 Matt. 5:44.   53 Cf. Eph. 6:12.

praise and glory of God's name. If you do this you will shortly
see that you are so abundantly revenged on the devil and his
imps that your heart will rejoice. Only see to it that you pray
with all confidence and without doubting that God, on account
of whose Word you are suffering, will hear you and send his
arrows and coals in large numbers so that for every place, such
as Miltenberg, in which the Word is suppressed, it will be given
free course in ten others, and the more they blow on the fire
the more it will burn.

That the Word of God has not yet spread as it ought and as
we desire (though our adversaries think it has spread too far)
can be blamed only on the fact that we are too lazy to pray for
sharp arrows and hot coals. Our Lord has commanded us to
pray that his Kingdom come and his name be hallowed[54]—
that is, that his Word be extended and Christians increase. But
because we allow things to go their own way and do not pray
earnestly, progress is slow, our arrows are dull and flabby, our
coals are cold and unrefined, and the devil is no longer afraid
of us. So let us be up and about. The time is here. The devil is
playing evil tricks on us everywhere. Let us for once do something to vex him and revenge ourselves on him. In other words,
let us pray God without ceasing until he sends us enough instruments, marksmen, sharp arrows, and coals.

You see now, dear sirs and friends, that I have undertaken
to write you this letter of consolation although another might
have done it better and with greater reason, but because my
name is involved and you are persecuted as Lutherans, I think
it was right of me to take this duty upon myself. To be sure, I
do not like doctrines and people to be called Lutheran. I am
obliged to suffer my adversaries to slander God's Word by
giving it my name. Nevertheless, they will not overthrow
Luther and Lutheran doctrine and Lutheran people and prevent them from coming to honor, just as they and their doctrine
will be destroyed and put to shame even though the world
regret it and all the devils be angry. If we live, they will not
have peace in our presence. If we die, they will have peace even
less. In a word, they will not be rid of us unless they submit
and surrender to us of their own accord, and their wrath and
their raging will not help them, for we know whose Word it is
that we preach and they will not take it from us. This is my
prophecy, and it will not fail. God have mercy on them.

May God in his grace and mercy keep you, dear friends.

[54] Cf. Matt. 6:9, 10.

Pray to God for me, a poor sinner. I commend you to your preachers who preach Christ and not the pope or temple servants of Mayence. The grace of God be with you. Amen.

Martin Luther, preacher in Wittenberg.

TO THE CHRISTIANS IN BREMEN. March, 1525

An early graduate of the university in Wittenberg and a fellow Augustinian of Luther there, the Dutchman Henry of Zutphen (1488-1524) was a popular preacher of Evangelical doctrine while he was prior of the Augustinian monastery in Antwerp. When charges of heresy were preferred against him in 1522, he fled before the Inquisition to Bremen. There he was persuaded to remain as preacher under the protection of the town council. In November, 1524, he was called to Meldorf, in Dithmarschen, south of Denmark. There he was at once attacked by Dominican and Franciscan friars, and on December 10 was burned at the stake. Luther received news of his death from James Probst, a fellow preacher in Bremen who had also been made to suffer for his Evangelical faith. Probst requested Luther to address a letter to the people of Bremen, and Luther did so in the following communication which, together with a short exposition of Ps. 10 and an account of the martyr's life and death, was printed in several editions. [Text in German; WA, XVIII, 215-229.]

To my dear friends in Christ and elect of God in Bremen: grace and peace from God our Father and from our Lord Jesus Christ.

Dearly Beloved in Christ:

I have not wished that the story of the life and martyrdom of your evangelist, the sainted Brother Henry of Zutphen, part of which I know from personal experience and part of which I have assembled from the trustworthy testimony of godly people, should remain hidden in obscurity and uncertainty. I thought that it should be made known for the praise and honor of divine grace, which is so abundantly given to us in our time although we are unworthy, lost, and condemned creatures. Not only do we have, hear, and read the pure Word of God and see it rise in many places like the bright sun, but we also feel the accompanying Spirit of God and experience the great and mighty deeds by which he has furthered, demonstrated, and confirmed his Word from the beginning. Especially is this manifest in the free and courageous men he has called. He has daily increased the number of his saints, both preachers and hearers, in many places. Some of these have poured out their blood, some have suffered imprisonment, some have been driven into exile, and all of them bear the reproach of the cross of Christ. The quality of true Christian life has been restored, and the world may see horrible examples of the suffering and persecution it brings with it. But these are precious and pleasing in God's sight; as the Psalter puts it: "Precious in the sight of the Lord is the death of his saints"[55]; and, "Precious shall their blood be in his sight."[56]

The one who shines brightest among all these is your Henry of Zutphen, who suffered such a shameful death in Dithmarschen for the sake of God's Word and who so effectively sealed the gospel with his blood. The first martyrs, who also became two fine lights, were John and Henry in Brussels[57]; the beautiful deaths they were made to suffer were sweet-smelling sacrifices to God. To be included among these martyrs are also Caspar Tauber,[58] burned to death in Vienna, and George Buchführer,[59] who was put to death in Hungary. More recently, as I am informed, a man was put to death by fire in Prague, Bohemia, for abandoning the impure chastity of his order and entering the holy estate of matrimony, the order of pure chastity. These and others like them will drown the papacy and its god, the devil, in their blood. They will also preserve the Word of God in its purity against the impure profaners of the Word, the new false prophets,[60] who are now springing up and spreading everywhere. No doubt God in his grace is allowing them to die and spill their blood at this time in which so many errors and sects are appearing in order to warn us and to show us through them that the doctrine which they have believed and taught and for which they have died and suffered martyrdom is the true doctrine which brings the right Spirit with it. It was even thus that the holy martyrs died for the sake of the

---

[55] Ps. 116:15.   [56] Ps. 72:14.

[57] John van den Esschen and Henry Vos were burned at the stake in Brussels on July 1, 1523. See letter to the Christians in the Netherlands, above.

[58] Caspar Tauber was beheaded and his corpse was burned in Vienna on Sept. 17, 1524.   [59] Cf. *WA, Br,* III, 374.

[60] Radical prophets were appearing in northern Germany and the Low Countries at this time. In his "Sendschreiben an die Christen zu Antwerpen" (1525) Luther referred to some of them: "This man will have nothing to do with Baptism, another rejects the Sacrament, still another teaches that there will be another world between this one and the Last Judgment, some assert that Christ is not divine, etc." (*WA,* XVIII, 547).

gospel in olden times and with their blood sealed and certified the same.

Since the merciful God has so graciously visited you in Bremen, has been so near to you, and has also (so manifestly that you can grasp them) revealed his Spirit and his power among you in the person of this Henry, I have thought it well to write and send you an account of his suffering, in order that I may admonish you in Christ not to grieve and not to defame his murderers in Dithmarschen but rather to rejoice and thank and praise God for making you worthy to behold and possess such divine wonders and graces. Since his murderers have already received much more than they merited by soiling their hands so deplorably with innocent blood and so horribly offending God, they need to be wept over and bewailed more than the sainted Henry. It is necessary to pray for them that they may be converted and come to a knowledge of the truth—and not they alone, but the whole land of Dithmarschen as well. It is confidently to be hoped that such may be the outcome of this suffering of Henry, especially because there are already many in that land who are eager for the gospel and regret that such a murder was committed among them. For God, who allowed the sainted Henry to suffer there, probably intends not only to punish the godless who are not converted but also to use that murder for the benefit of many in the land who may thereby be led to eternal life. Accordingly I suggest and recommend that in these circumstances you sing and read Ps. 10, which is very appropriate here, so that you may not be discouraged on account of the martyrs but joyfully praise God for the fruits which he produces on earth by means of their martyrdom. I do not mind taking the trouble of singing through the psalm with you, who are present with me in spirit, and of expounding it briefly.[61]

You see, my dear sirs and friends, how this psalm comforts us and bids us hope that God will accomplish much good and benefit by means of Henry's precious blood. Be comforted, therefore, with such divine comfort and pray with the help of this psalm that God's name may be hallowed and his Kingdom extended. Amen.

I beg you for God's sake to take the people of Dithmarschen to your hearts and comfort and help them in friendly fashion that they may join us. For I hear that many of the people regret

61 Here follows "A Short Exposition of Psalm 10 Concerning the Martyrs of Christ."

that such a tragedy was brought about by the monks in their land. This is a good spark kindled by God. It will grow into a great fire if you act with a friendly spirit so that it may not be extinguished. Commit yourselves to James Probst, your preacher, and to the others.[62] May God strengthen them and all of you, and grant you the grace to persevere in the doctrine which is sealed by Henry's blood and to follow cheerfully wherever God leads you. Amen. All our brethren greet you in Christ. Pray for us. God's grace be with you. Amen.[63]

Martin Luther, preacher in Wittenberg.

TO CONRAD CORDATUS. November 28, 1526

A native of Austria, Conrad Cordatus (1475-1546) studied in Vienna and Ferrara and later (1523-1525) also in Wittenberg. He went to Hungary to preach the gospel as he had learned to understand it from Luther. He was soon arrested on account of his Evangelical sentiments and was cast into a dark dungeon. Released after nine months by a sympathetic guard, he returned to Wittenberg. In September, 1526, he was sent to Liegnitz, in Silesia, where he encountered difficulties at the hands of Schwenckfelders and Catholics. He was thoroughly discouraged when Luther wrote the following letter. [Text in Latin; WA, Br, IV, 138-140.]

Grace and peace be with you in the Lord.

My dear Cordatus:

You write strange things about your Liegnitz when you report that both spirit and flesh are so mighty in the same place at the same time. Some[64] boast of nothing but the spirit while others[65] live in nothing but the flesh. Although this is a common plague throughout the world—that is, scorn of the Word—you must nevertheless persevere in trying. Who knows whether God may not be intending something novel and unusual in your community so that, whereas elsewhere zeal for the gospel is at first hot and then grows cold, there it may first be cold and later grow hot. God grant that the people may be like the son who at first refused to go into the vineyard but later repented and went and who was therefore preferred above the other son who at first promised to go and went not.[66]

---

[62] John Timann, of Amsterdam, was also an Evangelical preacher in Bremen.
[63] Here follows an extensive "History of Brother Henry of Zutphen."
[64] Followers of Caspar Schwenckfeld (1490–1561), native of Liegnitz.
[65] Roman Catholics.   [66] Cf. Matt. 21:28–31.

Carry on with courage, therefore, and the Lord will be with you. Fear not those who claim to be spiritually most spiritual. What they imagine is folly in God's sight. But Christ be with you. And write to us as often as you can. Your letters please us both because they are testimonies of your faith (which mean much to your people as well as ours) and because they are filled with accounts of deeds (which we are eager to read and find refreshing).[67] Farewell in the Lord.

Yours,

November 28, 1526.   Martin Luther.

TO THE TOWN COUNCIL OF CROSSEN. April 13, 1527

Between 1524 and 1527, Evangelical clergymen appeared in the small duchy of Crossen, which was subject to Elector Joachim I of Brandenburg. In 1527 the elector ordered these heretical preachers to be driven out, and several had to flee. This raised the question as to whether the people, who had now become accustomed to the celebration of Holy Communion in both kinds, should revert to the Catholic practice, and it also raised the question as to whether the burgomaster and town council should resist the elector on the religious issue. [Text in German; WA, Br, IV, 192-194.]

To the honorable and wise burgomaster and town council of Crossen, my gracious sirs and good friends: grace and peace in Christ our Lord.

Honored, wise, dear Sirs:

Your burgomaster, Francis Neumann, wrote to me secretly in your behalf as well as his own to ask for advice as to what you ought to do in view of the fact that your prince has ordered the old practice of the Mass to be restored and observed. My dutiful reply to this question is that the honorable council should address the prince and declare that it is not the function of the council but that of the ministers to regulate ceremonies as they would be answerable for them, and that the honorable council, as a secular authority, is unwilling to interfere in spiritual matters.

The councilmen must tolerate the godless behavior of the priests without consenting in their hearts and without participating with their actions. If this is not deemed sufficient, and if the honorable council is pressed to assist in the restoration of this spiritual abomination, there is no escape in such an

[67] The reading *recreant* is preferred to *terreant*.

extremity from making a bold confession. Each man for himself or the whole council as a body (but it would be preferable for every man to speak for himself in order that the action might be sure and certain, for no one can rely with assurance on another's faith) should assert that this is unjust, should refuse to do what is demanded, and should be ready to suffer or flee as a consequence.

You will find support for this if you read II Kings, ch. 5, where the prophet Elisha agreed to go into the temple of the false god with Prince Naaman and agreed to stand there and look on, but refused to worship the idol, etc.[68] Saint Paul also says in I Cor., ch. 10, that it is not perilous to the conscience of a Christian to enter a heathen house or eat there, etc.[69] So, likewise, there is no danger in our presence at a godless act in a godless community, so long as we do not participate. But when the attempt is made to allure or compel us to participate, it is time to say no. Then we may no longer remain silent or hidden.

The same is to be said about confession, the Sacrament, fasting, and holy days. You may continue, as before, to oppose these in secret. This is good and without peril. But if you are asked about these things and they are dragged out into the light of day, you must come out clearly and confess what and how you believe and not leave Christ in the lurch, come what may. So I have written more fully to the burgomaster.[70]

May God, who has led and called you to a knowledge of the truth, strengthen and preserve you to his praise and glory. To him and to his grace I commend you. Amen.

Saturday after Judica, 1527.   Martin Luther.

TO LEONARD KAESER. May 20, 1527

A native of Raab, in Bavaria, Leonard Käser (or Keyser) adopted Evangelical sentiments while serving as clergyman in a village parish near his birthplace. Reported to the authorities, he was asked to recant in the fall of 1524. Instead, he went to Wittenberg to study, and from there he sent "wickedly seditious letters and books back to Bavaria" which were not calculated to improve his standing at home. Upon receiving news of his father's grave illness, he hurried home, helped bury his father, remained with his mother in Raab for five more weeks, and while there preached openly about his new convictions. As a

---

[68] Cf. II Kings 5:18, 19.   [69] Cf. I Cor. 10:27-31.
[70] This letter is not extant.

consequence he was arrested in March, 1527, investigated, given a hearing, and finally burned at the stake on August 16, 1527. After his death Luther published a documentary account of Käser's martyrdom.[71] *The following letter was written to comfort Käser during his imprisonment.* [Text in Latin; *WA, Br,* IV, 204-206.]

To the esteemed brother in Christ, Leonard Käser, faithful servant and beloved prisoner of Christ, my friend in the Lord: grace, strength, and peace in Christ.

My dear Leonard:

That your old man[72] should be a prisoner is in accord with the will and calling of Christ, your Saviour, and for you and your sins he also offered up his new man[73] into the hands of the godless so that he might redeem you with his blood and make you his brother and joint heir of eternal life.[74]

We are grieved on your account, and we are taking steps[75] and praying earnestly that you may be set free, not simply for your sake but, if it be his will, for the benefit of others and the glory of God. But if it be the will of heaven that you should not be free, you are nevertheless free in spirit. Only see to it that you remain strong, constantly overcoming the weakness of the flesh, or at least that you patiently endure what you must with the strength that Christ gives you. He who is with you in your cell will stand by you in all your afflictions, even as he has faithfully and pleasantly promised when he said, "I will be with him in trouble."[76]

It is therefore necessary that you cry out to him confidently in your prayers and that you cheer and sustain yourself with comforting psalms amid these ragings of Satan so that you may be strengthened in the Lord and not speak too timidly or softly in the teeth of behemoth,[77] as if you were overcome by him and feared the arrogance of Satan. Call upon Christ, who is everywhere present and powerful. Defy and ridicule the raging and arrogance of Satan in the certainty that he cannot harm you and that the more he rages, the less he can do to you. It is as Saint Paul said, "If God be for us, who can be against us?"[78] All things are put under his feet.[79] In that he

---

[71] In *WA,* XXIII, 452 ff.   [72] Cf. Rom. 6:6.
[73] Cf. Eph. 4:24; Rom. 5:15.   [74] Cf. Rom. 8:17.
[75] Luther interceded in Käser's behalf with the elector of Saxony and Margrave Casimir of Brandenburg, both of whom appealed to the Bavarian authorities.   [76] Ps. 91:15.
[77] Cf. Job., ch. 40.   [78] Rom. 8:31.   [79] Cf. Ps. 8:6.

suffered himself to be tempted in all things, he is able to succor them that are tempted.[80]

Therefore, my dear brother, be strong in the Lord, and in the power of his might[81] so that, whether or not you are set free, you may with a good heart acknowledge, bear, love, and praise the Fatherly will of God. The Father of our Lord Jesus Christ, who is the Father of all mercies and the God of all comfort,[82] enable you according to his riches in grace and glory[83] to do this to the honor of his gospel. Amen. Fare well in him, and pray for us too.

Monday after Cantate, 1527.   Martin Luther.

TO CASPAR LOENER AND NICHOLAS MEDLER.
June 7, 1531

Caspar Löner, an Evangelical clergyman who distinguished himself as a hymn writer and liturgical reformer, entered upon a second pastorate in Hof, Brandenburg, in 1527 or 1528. He had a loyal associate in Nicholas Medler, who had charge of the town school and collaborated with his superior in introducing Evangelical forms of worship. Opposition was aroused by their activity and they asked Luther whether they ought to leave Hof. The question was soon settled for them when the margrave's representative, Christopher von Beulwitz, who had Roman sympathies, drove them out on July 13, 1531. [Text in Latin; WA, Br, VI, 118, 119.]

To the honorable brethren in Christ, Caspar Löner, minister of the Word, and Nicholas Medler, schoolmaster, faithful colleagues in the town of Hof: grace and peace in Christ.

Dear Brothers:

I have read your letter in which you ask my counsel as to whether you ought to yield to those cunning enemies of the gospel who are in your neighborhood and who pretend to be your friends.

It is my opinion that you should under no circumstances withdraw lest you give the appearance that you are hirelings who forsake your sheep.[84] Therefore, continue in the office—both of you—which you have assumed and which your Church has committed to you. Suffer whatever you are made to suffer until you are forcibly ejected or until you are driven out

[80] Cf. Heb. 2:18; ch. 4:15.
[82] II Cor. 1:3.
[84] Cf. John 10:12, 13.

[81] Eph. 6:10.
[83] Cf. Phil. 4:19.

by command of the prince.[85] Otherwise you must not give in to the fury of Satan.

You are not the only ones who are suffering thus. Persecution at the hands of false brethren is the lot of all of us, even if we live under the best princes. We here are now free from external persecution, but since it is characteristic of the gospel that it cannot exist, to say nothing of spreading, without persecution, we should be willing to endure such persecution as those in our own household heap upon us. It must be borne, whether it comes from within or without.[86]

Be strong, therefore, and bear this cross of yours as you follow Christ, for so you will find rest unto your soul.[87] May Christ, who is our Lord and Comforter, keep you and uphold you with his free spirit.[88] Amen.

June 7, 1531.   Martin Luther.

TO KING CHRISTIAN II OF DENMARK.
September 28, 1532

During the reign (1513-1523) of King Christian II the first tentative steps were taken to introduce reforms in Denmark. The king was driven from his throne in protest against his arbitrary rule, and during his exile in Saxony he was influenced by Evangelical teaching. In the reign of his successor, Frederick I (1524-1533), the Reformation movement continued to gain ground in Denmark, especially under the leadership of Hans Tausen. Catholic bishops and noblemen resisted the extension of Lutheran teaching, however, and in this tense situation supporters of the exiled Christian II (who had returned to the Roman Church in 1530) tried to put him back on the throne. The attempt was unsuccessful and at the end of July, 1532, Christian II was imprisoned in Sonderburg Castle on the island of Alsen. [Text in German; WA, Br, VI, 366-368.]

Grace and peace in the consolation of our dear Lord and Saviour Jesus Christ.

Serene, mighty King, gracious Lord:

Requested by Your Majesty's sister, wife of my gracious margrave and elector,[89] that I write, and moved by the obligation and compulsion of Christian love, I cannot forbear

[85] Margrave George of Brandenburg.
[86] The first half of the sentence is in German.
[87] Cf. Matt. 11:29.   [88] Cf. Ps. 51:12.
[89] Elizabeth, wife of the elector of Brandenburg.

to address this letter of comfort to Your Majesty. I regret, my gracious Lord and King, that Your Majesty is in such difficult straits. That it is deplorable everyone will agree. But I beg Your Majesty to seek earnestly and with patient faith for God's will in this state, for surely the same gracious God is by this chastisement indicating that he has not and will not forsake Your Majesty. It is as it is written, "He scourgeth every son whom he receiveth,"[90] and again, "As many as I love, I rebuke and chasten."[91]

It would also be well to consider that Your Majesty is better off in God's sight than most other kings and princes whom God in his wrath allows to go on unpunished, to live in sacrilege and all manner of arrogance and blindness, and finally to die in their sins, without believing, as rejected, undisciplined, and uncorrected children. But by being humbled and chastened Your Majesty is protected against such arrogance and sins and is admonished to turn to God. Accordingly Your Majesty ought (if wishing could accomplish it) to prefer a thousand times to be such a chastened and punished king rather than be the most glorious king who remains in his sins unpunished, unadmonished, and damned.

After all, life here on earth is but momentary, and we hope for a better life to come. Yet all kings, whether good or bad, must leave their crowns behind them. Wicked kings who die unpunished cannot have the hope that Your Majesty certainly possesses by patiently and faithfully acknowledging and accepting this rod of God. For God cannot do otherwise. He must be a God of the afflicted, as he has everywhere allowed himself to be called.[92] And it is characteristic of him to humble the proud and exalt those of low degree.[93] Accordingly, my gracious lord and king, look at the situation in which Your Majesty is in terms of the gracious and Fatherly will of God, who humbles Your Majesty for a time here on earth in order that he might exalt Your Majesty eternally in heaven. After all, if we would but believe, what does that amount to which we lose and forego here on earth in comparison with that which we are to find and keep in heaven?

Christ, our only consolation and treasure, strengthen and comfort Your Majesty with his Word and Spirit in all the fullness of his consolation and, according to the measure of his power, make this painful and sharp rod sweet and dear to Your Majesty, even as he makes all things out of nothing and

[90] Heb. 12:6. [91] Rev. 3:19. [92] E.g., Matt. 11:28. [93] Cf. Luke 1:52.

without doubt can turn tribulation into consolation, chastisement into pleasure, and wretchedness into joy. Whatever I may be able to accomplish with my poor prayers I am happy to place at Your Majesty's service with all diligence.

Graciously accept this comfort of mine as coming from God himself in heaven, for he has commanded us to comfort one another. Consequently our comfort is assuredly God's comfort, commanded by him. Amen.

Your Majesty's willing servant and doctor,
Vigil of Saint Michael, 1532.   Martin Luther.

TO THE EVANGELICALS IN LEIPZIG.
October 4, 1532

People in Leipzig who embraced the Evangelical faith had for some time been crossing the border into Electoral Saxony to attend Evangelical services and receive the Sacrament in both kinds. Duke George of Albertine Saxony ordered the mayor of Leipzig to post watchmen, and these listed the names of those who were observed to cross the border on Sundays and holy days. At the end of August and beginning of September, 1532, the persons listed were given a hearing before the town council. Duke George ordered that those should be exiled who were found to adhere obstinately to Evangelical teaching and practice. The people who were thus condemned to exile petitioned for letters of recommendation, and the town council supported the petition on the ground that they were good and respectable citizens despite their departure from the Catholic religion. But Duke George refused to grant the request. [Text in German; WA, Br, VI, 370-372.]

To my dear sirs and friends in Christ, N and N,[94] who are now, one and all, to be driven from Leipzig for Christ's sake: grace and peace in Christ.

My dear Sirs and Friends in Christ:

Peace is not to be found anywhere until the Lord comes and overthrows the enemy of peace.

Wolf Bräunlein[95] has showed me the petition which you have addressed to your gracious lord. I am well pleased with it, and I am delighted that you have lighted two torches to the devil, for this will be of great advantage to you, even as it

94 Symbols for unnamed persons.
95 A dealer in books, formerly in Leipzig, now in Augsburg.

will heap great confusion and disadvantage on that headstrong man.[96]

If you can get nowhere with that willful man, and if you cannot secure a certificate of your upright walk from him, still you have achieved more than enough, seeing that both God and the world, and even Duke George's own adherents, testify that you do and suffer all this in a Christian spirit and solely for Christ's sake. For the whole world knows that you are being persecuted by Duke George for no other reason, especially at this time, than that the emperor has granted peace to the Lutherans,[97] which is a great grief to the wretched fellow. But be steadfast. Christ is beginning his reign. He will put an end to the whole business.

Here in our principality there is no problem.[98] No one will reproach you for anything here or place impediments in your way, for our gracious lord adheres to the Confession[99] that was published. Accordingly I pray that you speak only gentle words to that fool and that you concede nothing. You do this very well in your petition. If it helps, good. If not, it will do no harm, but rather further your cause in God's sight, who will soon make short work of the devil and his followers. It is written that the Lord "hath respect unto the lowly, but the proud he knoweth afar off."[1]

So be of good cheer, dear friends. Bitter experiences must precede good fortune. Only he can appreciate what is sweet who has tasted what is bitter. Before honor, the heart of man is humbled.[2]

May God the Father strengthen you through his abundant Spirit in Christ Jesus, and not in Duke George. For Christ lives, while Duke George dies. This is certain, and it will soon be proved. Amen.

On Saint Francis' Day, 1532.　　　　Martin Luther, Doctor.

TO EBERHARD BRISGER. December 12, 1532

Eberhard Brisger, of Altenburg, had embraced the Evangelical faith although his father and mother, who lived in Mühlheim, near Coblenz,

[96] Duke George of Saxony.

[97] The reference is to the Religious Peace of Nuremberg, which was confirmed by Emperor Charles V in Regensburg on Aug. 2, 1532.

[98] Luther suggests that the exiles settle in the Electorate of Saxony, where they need not fear persecution.

[99] The Augsburg Confession had been presented at the Diet of Augsburg on June 25, 1530.　　　　[1] Ps. 138:6.

[2] Cf. Prov. 18:12. This and the preceding sentence in Latin.

remained Catholics. Now that his father had died, his mother refused to let Brisger have his paternal inheritance unless he returned to the Roman Church. [Text in Latin; *WA, Br,* VI, 394, 395.]

Grace and peace in the Lord.

My dear Eberhard:

I seldom write to you, not only because I am prevented by the constant demand upon me for other writing, but also because you do not need my letters when everything goes well with you. But now that you tell me of your grief over the death of your father, the conduct of your mother, and the loss of your inheritance, you ought, like Job,[3] to compare the blessings you have received with the evils you are made to suffer. Your condition is not such (nor is it your desire) that you prefer to have the favor of your father and mother without Christ rather than your mother's hatred in and with Christ. Commend your parents to the judgment of God, therefore, and sing with Joseph, "The Lord hath made me to forget my father and my father's house in a strange land."[4]

How do you know for what purpose your father died, or what the Lord's intention was for him?[5] As for your mother, she still has twelve hours,[6] and who knows what the gospel can do in a short time? The papists are lamenting that even the emperor has become a Lutheran because he is unwilling to rage in order to exalt their wickedness. But even if everything turns out differently, congratulate yourself that you have been plucked as a brand from the burning[7] and as a piece of an ear from the mouth of the wolf.[8] Lot had to leave his own wife in Sodom, David was separated from his beloved Absalom, Christ lost the synagogue, and Saint Paul lost the Children of Israel, his brethren, etc. You are not the only one who has evils to endure; others have suffered, and are now suffering, greater and worse things. In some cases the saying must be fulfilled, "I am come to set a man at variance against his father,"[9] and there are many other passages in the Bible that can comfort you. Christ is enough for us, even if we have lost everything.

The Lord be with you and all of yours.

Yours,

December 12, 1532.   Martin Luther.

[3] Cf. Job 2:10.   [4] Cf. Gen. 41:51.
[5] Luther suggests that the father may have died to test the son's faith, or that he may even have been converted to the Evangelical faith on his deathbed.   [6] A reference to John 11:9.   [7] Cf. Amos 4:11 and Zech. 3:2.
[8] Cf. Amos 3:12.   [9] Matt. 10:35.

TO THE EVANGELICALS EXILED FROM OSCHATZ.
January 20, 1533

Some people in Oschatz, in Albertine Saxony, who had embraced the teachings of the Reformation occasionally crossed the border to attend Evangelical services in nearby towns and receive Holy Communion in both kinds. When he learned of this, Catholic Duke George ordered the dissenters out of his realm, and some of these were driven into exile during the Christmas season in 1532. Among those who fled to the Electorate of Saxony was the von der Dahme family, a member of which is mentioned in the following letter of consolation and encouragement. [Text in German; *WA, Br,* VI, 421-423.]

To the honorable and prudent citizens[10] of Oschatz who have been exiled for Christ's sake, my dear sirs and friends in Christ: grace, consolation, and peace in Christ.

Honored, prudent, dear Friends:

Mrs. von der Dahme[11] has informed me of the wretched situation in which Duke George has placed you and that you have been obliged to flee. Well, you have ventured and done a big thing. Christ, our Lord, for whose sake you are suffering, comfort, strengthen, and preserve your hearts that you may see it through and not become weary and remiss. For the devil will not stop at this. Because you have set yourself against him, he will continue to fight against you, and if he is not able to do anything else, he will incite our people here in this principality[12] to cause you harm and disfavor. For he is the host in this world, and the world is his home. Consequently no matter where one goes, this dreadful host is present.

Therefore, be firm and steadfast in the power of Jesus Christ. See to it that you are certain, and do not doubt, that your flight and wretchedness are well pleasing to God in heaven. And even if people belittle what you have done, and perhaps even you in your own minds estimate it as a small thing, you must nevertheless be certain that in the sight of God and his angels it is a great thing. To be sure, you have not done what you did in order that people might praise and marvel at you, but you have done it for the praise and honor of God. Whether people praise or blame, it matters not. It is enough that God

---

10 *Den . . . Bürgern und Bürgerin,* both male and female.
11 Francis and Anna von der Dahme appear to have been in Wittenberg at this time.   12 I.e., in the Electorate of Saxony.

and his angels praise what you have done and are pleased by it.

Accordingly you should sing with King David, who was also plunged into adversity, in Ps. 56, "Thou tellest my wanderings: put thou my tears into thy bottle: are they not in thy book?"[13] It is as if he would say: "Even if no man cares about my distress, thou, O Lord, lookest so closely upon it that thou countest every step that I take in my flight, no matter how far I am driven and must flee, and thou dost not forget any of the tears I shed. I know that thou dost record all of them in thy register and wilt not forget them."

Behold, how this king comforted himself with the assurance that his flight was reckoned, all his tears were counted, every painful stride and step he took was recorded, and all his tears were collected in God's bottle so that not a single drop might spill or be forgotten. It is as Christ also said in Matt., ch. 10, "The very hairs of your head are all numbered," and not one of them shall be lost.[14] Christ grant that such words of his may be a source of strength and power in your hearts and that you may be sure of them and have no doubt, even as he is himself worthy of trust and not of doubt. Amen.

Whatever Duke George does with his subjects, he has his judge and his sentence. Perhaps he does not realize this now, but he will and must experience it shortly. The verse in Ecclus., ch. 35, will be fulfilled in him: "The tears of the afflicted run down their cheeks, and these are their cries against him that has driven them out."[15] Amen and Amen.

This short and hasty letter of mine must suffice for the present. Let us pray with and for one another, for our prayers are certainly heard. And even if the answer is delayed, it will come and cannot fail, for God cannot lie or deceive us. To him be glory and thanks forever through our dear Lord Jesus Christ. Amen.

January 20, 1533.   Martin Luther, Doctor.

TABLE TALK RECORDED BY CONRAD CORDATUS.[16]
Probably 1533

The Christian wife of a certain citizen[17] of Oschatz was compelled to leave the town because she had received the Sacrament in both kinds and freely confessed it. She allowed

---

13 Ps. 56:8.   14 Cf. Matt. 10:30.   15 Cf. Ecclus. 35:15.
16 Text macaronic; *WA, TR*, III, No. 3464.   17 Francis König.

her husband, who is a pious and good man, to stay behind in that town. The question was asked, "What ought the husband to do in these circumstances?"

Luther replied: "The two are one flesh. Therefore, they ought to bear their cross together. Nevertheless, this suggestion might be made to him, that he send his wife to her relatives in our principality[18] for half a year and meanwhile hope for an end of the tyrants.[19] So he should allow his wife to go abroad in Christ's name."

TO THE EVANGELICALS IN LEIPZIG. April 11, 1533

Stephen Steinber, a goldsmith and stonecutter who had recently moved to Leipzig from Nuremberg, was asked by another Leipzig goldsmith, named Holtz, to write to Christian Döring, goldsmith in Wittenberg, to secure from Luther his counsel as to whether the Evangelicals in Leipzig might with good conscience continue to receive Holy Communion in one kind in order to avoid persecution at the hands of the Catholic town council and Duke George of Albertine Saxony. In response to this request Luther wrote the following letter, which within two weeks was discovered by the town council to be circulating in several copies. [Text in German; *WA, Br,* VI, 448-450.]

To the honorable sirs, my good friends in Leipzig who are now being exiled by Duke George, an enemy of the gospel: grace and peace in Christ, who suffers and is put to death among you,[20] but who will certainly rise again and reign.

Dear Friends:

I have learned that some of you wish to know whether you may with good conscience receive the Sacrament in one kind while giving the appearance that you are receiving it in both kinds[21] in order that your governing authorities may thus be satisfied.

Although I am not acquainted with any of you and do not know the condition of your hearts and minds, this is the best counsel I can give you: Whoever is convinced that it is in

---

[18] The Electorate of Saxony.   [19] Duke George and his officials.

[20] Since this letter was written on Good Friday, Luther here alludes to Christ's suffering and death and to the Easter hope.

[21] That is, in the form of bread and wine rather than of bread alone. Exactly what is meant by "while giving the appearance," *unter dem schein,* is not clear. It has been suggested (by Enders, IX, 291) that the Evangelicals in Leipzig were allowed, in addition to receiving the bread, to drink the wine that was used to cleanse the cup.

accord with God's Word and institution that the Sacrament be administered in both kinds should under no circumstances do anything contrary to his conscience since this would be tantamount to acting against God himself. Now that Duke George has undertaken to search out the secrets of men's consciences, he deserves, as an apostle of the devil, to be deceived. This can well be done, for he has no right to make such an inquiry but sins against God and the Holy Ghost. And yet, since we must not be governed by what other evil men do, be they murderers or robbers, but rather by what is proper for us to do and leave undone, under the circumstances it would probably be best to confront the murderer and robber and say to his face: "I shall not do what you command. If on this account you take my body and goods, you will be taking them from somebody other than me, and will have to pay him dearly. It is as Peter says, 'Jesus Christ is ready to judge the quick and the dead.'[22] Wherefore, dear robber, go ahead. I shall not go along with your wish. But what I wish, God will also wish one of these days, and you will soon find it out." One must smite the devil in his face with the cross and not whistle to his tune or flatter him. He must be made to know with whom he has to do.

May Christ our Lord strengthen you and be with you. Amen. Good Friday, 1533. Dr. Martin Luther, with his own hand.[23]

TO ANTHONY LAUTERBACH. June 27, 1535

In the town of Mittweida, in Albertine Saxony, 217 persons refused to receive Holy Communion according to Roman belief and practice during the Easter season in 1535, and 130 of these insisted on waiting until Communion was administered in both kinds. The response of Duke George was to order these protestants to leave the country before Pentecost. On May 9 they petitioned the duke for an extension, and although this was granted, their fate was uncertain when Lauterbach requested Luther to send them an open letter of consolation and encouragement. This Luther was reluctant to do for the reason expressed in the following letter. [Text in German; WA, Br, VII, 200-202.]

To the worthy Mr. Anthony Lauterbach, preacher in Leisnig, my good and gracious friend and dear brother: grace and peace in Christ.

[22] Cf. Acts 10:42. The sentence is in Latin.
[23] The original letter was dictated to Veit Dietrich, but signed by Luther himself, in Latin.

My dear Anthony:

What shall I write to comfort the good people of Mittweida in view of the fact that my letter to the exiles from Leipzig caused more harm than good?[24] The same thing might happen to the people of Mittweida if it should become known that I have written to them, and letters addressed to a number of people easily come to public notice.

Comfort the people orally as well as you can, and let them know that this is my desire too. I deplore the suffering and persecution of the innocent people. May my dear Lord Jesus Christ, for whose sake they are suffering, comfort and strengthen them for his glory and their salvation. The tribulations of those who confess Christ, as Saint Paul says, are a manifest token of their own salvation and of the punishment of the tyrants.[25] Although these tribulations are painful to flesh and blood, they are easy to bear in proportion to the certainty of our faith and hope that we are called to that life on whose account we suffer persecution and have compassion on those who suffer.

You see what that prelate is doing in Halle.[26] God has put it into his mind to do what he and others like him are doing. Meanwhile it is incumbent on us to be cheerful in the hope that God will make haste and put an end to the matter. Amen.

Tell the good people that I am praying for them, and express to them my faithful, heartfelt compassion. But please do not let this letter circulate, lest the good people have more trouble and others be drawn into their difficulties. I would not hesitate on my own account to write worse things about Duke George; he knows that I am not afraid of him, and if he wishes to take me to task, he knows where to find me.

Herewith I commit you to God's keeping. Amen.

Sunday after John the Baptist, 1535.   Martin Luther.

TO SIBYL BAUMGAERTNER. July 8, 1544

Because of his Lutheran leanings Mrs. Baumgärtner's father, Bernard Tichtel, had been interned in Munich in 1524, and he was not released until he had recanted and paid a fine of 2,000 gulden. Now her husband,

---

24 Letter to the Evangelicals in Leipzig, of Oct. 4, 1532, above.
25 Cf. II Thess. 1:5, 6.
26 During Holy Week, 1535, Archbishop Albert of Mayence ordered all citizens of Halle to make confession in preparation for the reception of Communion according to Roman belief and practice. Those who did not comply were threatened with severe punishment.

Jerome Baumgärtner, was also suffering unjust imprisonment. On his return from the Diet of Spires, Baumgärtner was attacked and captured on May 31, 1544, by a Franconian knight who was involved in a local feud. Baumgärtner was held in a secret place until August 21, 1545. Luther wrote to console the distraught wife of the prisoner. [Text in German; *WA, Br,* X, 604-607.]

To the honorable and virtuous lady, Sibyl, wife of Mr. Jerome Baumgärtner, of Nuremberg, my kind and good friend: grace and peace in our dear Saviour and Lord Jesus Christ.

Honorable, virtuous, and dear Lady:

God, who sees and hears my sighs, knows how deeply I am distressed by your sorrow and misfortune. Indeed, everybody is heartily sorry for the dear and godly man who has fallen so wickedly into the hands of the enemy. May God hear our prayer and that of all pious people! For it is certain that pious people everywhere pray anxiously for him, and assuredly such prayers will be acceptable and pleasing to God.

Meanwhile we must comfort ourselves with the divine promise that God will not forsake or forget those who are his, as the Psalter testifies throughout. We know that your husband is an upright man and that he has faith in Christ, which faith he has vigorously confessed and which has been adorned with many fine fruits. Accordingly it is impossible that God should have cast him off. Just as God has called him through his holy Word and received him into his gracious bosom, so God still keeps him in his bosom and will continue to do so forever. It is the same God who before this misfortune preserved him as his dear Christian and as a child of life. And he will remain the same God to him, though he may appear otherwise for a short time in order to try our faith and patience a little. He has said, "Ye shall weep and lament, but your sorrow shall be turned into joy, and your joy no man taketh from you."[27] This his promise he will keep without fail.

Besides, our suffering is not so great and severe as was that of his dear Son and our Lord's dear mother. This should comfort and strengthen us in our sorrows, as Saint Peter teaches us, "for Christ also hath once suffered for sins, the just for the unjust."[28] Although the devil and his adherents may rejoice in our misfortune, they will have to make up for this with horrible lamentations, and their brief joy shall become a long mourning. On the other hand, we have the great and glorious advantage

27 John 16:20, 22.   28 I Peter 3:18.

that God is merciful and gracious to us together with all angels and creatures. Therefore no misfortune of this life can injure our soul. On the contrary, misfortune must serve our interests; as Saint Paul says, "We know that all things work together for good to them that love God," etc.[29] In our bodies we suffer woe, and it must be so, for we should not be true Christians if we did not suffer with Christ and were wanting in sympathy for those who suffer.

Therefore, my dear lady, suffer and be patient. You do not suffer alone, for there are many excellent, faithful, godly people who have great sympathy for you and who always keep the saying, "I was in prison, and ye came unto me."[30] Indeed, great crowds of us visit the dear, godly Baumgärtner in his prison—that is, we visit the Lord Christ himself, imprisoned in the person of a true member, and we pray and call upon him to free our brother and thus gladden your heart and the hearts of all of us.

May the same Lord Jesus, who calls upon us to comfort one another, and who himself comforts us with his holy Word, comfort and strengthen your heart in steadfast patience by his Spirit until the happy end of this and all misfortune. To him, with the Father and the Holy Ghost, be honor and praise forever. Amen.

Martin Luther, Doctor.

Tuesday after the Visitation of Mary, 1544.

[29] Rom. 8:28.　　　　　[30] Matt. 25:36.

VIII

Advice in Time of Epidemic and Famine

TO GEORGE SPALATIN. August 19, 1527

Although its severity was minimized by Luther, the plague hit Witten-
berg so hard in the year 1527 that the university was temporarily
removed to Jena. On August 2, Luther wrote to Philip Melanchthon
to report his own recovery from illness and added: "We are persuaded
that the plague is really here, but we hope that it will be mild and light
. . . Hans Luft has been ill nine days. Yesterday he seemed to be out
of his mind, but it is hoped that he will recover . . . . Keep us in your
prayers as dead men who live."[1] [Text in Latin; *WA, Br,* IV,
232, 233.]

Grace and peace be with you in Christ Jesus.

I rejoice that you are restored to health and give thanks to
Christ our Lord. Pray for me, I beseech you, that I too may
fully recover,[2] if it be the will of God our Saviour. Do not let
rumors about the visitation disturb you too, for yesterday the
elector sent me the visitation articles that I might see them and
decide whether they are worth publishing.[3] They are all
excellent, if only they shall be carried out as determined upon.
You will then see how good they are. Let our opponents glory
in lies,[4] as is their wont, since they cannot console themselves
with the truth.

A pestilence has broken out here, but it is rather mild. Still

---

[1] *WA, Br,* IV, 227.
[2] On Spalatin's and Luther's illness see letter to Spalatin, July 10, 1527, in
Chapter I.
[3] Articles prepared to guide the clergymen and lawyers who were to visit
and inspect the parishes of Saxony. See *WA,* XXVI, 173-240.
[4] Desiderius Erasmus charged, for example, that the Evangelicals were
giving up their reforms. See *WA,* XXVI, 183.

the fear of men and their flight before it are remarkable. I have never before seen such a marvel of satanic power, so greatly is he terrifying everybody. Indeed, he is glad that he can so frighten men's hearts and thus scatter and destroy this one university[5] which he hates above all others, and not without reason. Nevertheless, during the whole time of the plague, up to today, there have not been more than eighteen deaths, counting all those who have died within the town—little girls, infants, and all taken together. In the fishermen's quarter[6] it has raged more cruelly, but in our quarter there has not been a single death so far, though all those who die are buried here. Today we buried the wife of Tilo Dene,[7] who died yesterday almost in my very arms, and this was the first death in the center of town. The eighteen burials have been conducted right around me here at the Elster gate.[8] Among them was Barbara, the sister of your Eberhard's wife,[9] and you will please report this to Master Eberhard. The daughter of John Grunenberg[10] has also died. Hans Luft[11] is up again and has conquered the plague. Many others are also recovering if they use medicine, but many are so ignorant that they spurn medicine and so die needlessly. Justus Jonas' little son John has also died. He and his family have gone to his birthplace.[12] I am staying here, and it is necessary that I do so because of the terrible fear among the common people. And so John Bugenhagen and I are here alone with the deacons,[13] but Christ is present too, that we may not be alone, and he will triumph in us over that old serpent,[14] murderer, and author of sin,[15] however much he may bruise Christ's heel.[16] Pray for us, and farewell.

Greet Master Eberhard and all our friends and commend us to them. The fanatics have written against me,[17] but I do not have their books as yet. I wanted to send you Zwingli's

[5] The university was moved to Jena on account of the pestilence.
[6] *In suburbano piscatorum*: beyond the town walls to the south.
[7] Dene, or Dhene, was for many years burgomaster in Wittenberg.
[8] This phrase in German.
[9] The sister of Eberhard Brisger's wife; Brisger was Spalatin's associate in Altenburg at this time.
[10] Grunenberg was a printer.
[11] The printer of many of Luther's books.   [12] Nordhausen.
[13] John Mantel and George Rörer.   [14] Cf. Rev. 12:9; 20:2.
[15] Cf. John 8:44.   [16] Cf. Gen. 3:15.
[17] The reference is to Huldreich Zwingli's *Das dise wort Jesu Christi, Das ist min Lychnam der für üch hinggeben wirt, ewigklich den alten eynigen sinn haben werded* (1527) and John Oecolampadius' *Das der missuerstand D. Martin Luthers, vff die ewigbstendige wort, Das ist mein leib, nit beston meg* (1527).

second letter[18] to me, which was fiercer than the first, but it was not at hand.

Yours,

Monday after the Assumption of Mary, 1527. Martin Luther.

TO JOHN HESS. November, 1527

Breslau, in Silesia, was hard hit by the plague during the late summer and fall of 1527, and the Evangelical clergymen there asked Luther, through John Hess, whether it is proper for Christians to flee in the face of such danger. After some delay and a repeated request Luther responded, and because the plague was also raging in Wittenberg at the time, he thought it well to publish his reply as an open letter. It was reprinted again and again in time of epidemic elsewhere. On account of his leadership in the introduction of the Reformation there, John Hess (1490-1547) is commonly called the reformer of Silesia. [Text in German; WA, XXIII, 323-386.]

To the esteemed Dr. John Hess, pastor in Breslau, and to his fellow ministers in the gospel of Christ: grace and peace from God our Father and from the Lord Jesus Christ.

I have long since received the question (whether it is proper for a Christian to flee when in danger of death) that you sent to me here in Wittenberg, and it should long since have been answered if Almighty God had not been scourging and chastising me so hard that I was unable to do much reading or writing.[19] Besides, I thought that, inasmuch as God the Father has so richly endowed you with all manner of understanding and truth in Christ, you would yourself be able, with the aid of his Spirit and grace and without my help, to decide and answer such a question as this, and greater ones too.

Since you have not stopped insisting and have so humbly desired to know my opinion in this matter in order, as Saint Paul teaches again and again, that we may all be found to have the same mind and judgment,[20] I am here expressing my opinion in so far as God has enabled me and I may have understanding. I am offering this opinion in all humility in order that, as is proper, it may be weighed and judged by your insight and that of all godly Christians. Because there are rumors of fatal disease here among us and in many other places, I have

---

[18] This letter is not extant.   [19] See letter above.
[20] Phil. 2:2; I Cor. 1:10; II Cor. 13:11.

had it printed in case others may also desire or use such instruction.

Some insist that one may not and should not flee under peril of death. They say that because death is a punishment which God has sent upon us on account of our sin, we should remain and patiently await God's punishment with true and firm faith. They regard flight as wrong and nothing short of unbelief in God. Others, however, hold that one may flee, especially if one is not encumbered with responsibilities.

I am unable to criticize the opinion of the first group, for they emphasize a good thing—strong faith—and are to be praised for desiring that all Christians have a strong, firm faith. It takes more than milk-fed[21] faith to await death, which terrified almost all the saints, and still does so. Who would not praise those who are sincerely of a mind to despise death and willingly submit to the scourge of God in so far as this may be done without tempting God, as I shall mention below?

However, since there are few strong Christians and many weak ones, all cannot be expected to bear the same thing. One who is strong in faith can drink poison without suffering harm, as we read in the last chapter of Mark,[22] but one who is weak in faith will die of it. Because he was strong in faith Peter could walk on the sea, but when he doubted and was weak in faith he sank and almost drowned.[23] When a strong man walks with a weak man he must be careful not to walk to the limit of his strength lest he walk the weak man to death. Christ does not wish his weak members to be cast away, as Saint Paul teaches in Rom., ch. 15, and I Cor., ch. 12.[24]

To put the matter briefly and precisely, there are two ways of dying and fleeing death. The first is to act contrary to God's Word and command, as when somebody who has been imprisoned for the sake of God's Word denies or recants God's Word in order to escape death. In such a case everyone has a clear order and command from Christ not to flee but rather to die, for he says, "Whosoever shall deny me before men, him will I also deny before my Father which is in heaven."[25] And in Luke, ch. 12, "Be not afraid of them that kill the body and after that have no more that they can do."[26]

In like fashion those who are in the ministry, such as preachers and pastors, are also obliged to stay and remain when there is peril of death, for there is a clear command of Christ, "The

[21] Cf. I Cor. 3:2.   [22] Mark 16:18.   [23] Matt. 14:29, 30.
[24] Rom. 15:1; I Cor. 12:22.   [25] Matt. 10:33.   [26] Luke 12:4.

good shepherd giveth his life for the sheep, but he that is a hireling seeth the wolf coming and fleeth."[27] In time of death one is especially in need of the ministry which can strengthen and comfort one's conscience with God's Word and Sacrament in order to overcome death with faith. However, where enough preachers are available and they come to an agreement among themselves that some of their number should move away because there is no necessity for their remaining in such danger, I do not count it a sin because an adequate ministry is provided and, if need be, these would be ready and willing to stay. So we read that Saint Athanasius fled from his church to save his life because there were many others there to perform the duties of the office.[28] In Damascus, Saint Paul's disciples let him down by the wall in a basket so that he escaped (Acts, ch. 9)[29] and it is written in Acts, ch. 19, that his disciples suffered him not to face danger in the market place because it was not necessary.[30]

Similarly all those who hold secular offices, such as burgomasters, judges, and the like, are obliged to remain. Here again there is a Word of God by which secular government was instituted and commanded in order to rule, protect, and preserve cities and lands. So Saint Paul says in Rom., ch. 13, "Government is God's minister to keep the peace," etc.[31] It would be a great sin for somebody who has been commanded to take care of a whole community to leave it without head and government in time of danger (such as fire, murder, rebellion, and other calamities which the devil might prepare) because there is no order there. Saint Paul says, "If any provide not for his own, he hath denied the faith, and is worse than an infidel."[32] If out of great weakness they flee, they must (as I have said above) see to it that a sufficient number of administrators are put in their places in order that the community may be well cared for and preserved, and they must also diligently inquire and insist that everything is done.

What I have now said about these two offices must be understood to apply to all other persons who are bound to others by duties and responsibilities. So a servant should not flee from his master, nor a maid from her mistress, unless it be with the knowledge and consent of the master or mistress. On the other hand, a master should not forsake his servant nor a mistress her maid unless these are sufficiently provided for in some other way or place. In all these cases it is God's command that

[27] John 10:11, 12.   [28] Augustine in Migne, *P.L.*, XXX, 1017.
[29] Acts 9:25.   [30] Acts 19:30.   [31] Cf. Rom. 13:6.   [32] I Tim. 5:8.

servants and maids are bound to serve, and should be obedient, while masters and mistresses must care for their servants. Fathers and mothers are similarly bound by God's command to serve and help their children, while children are bound to serve and help their parents. Nor may the common people who are hired for wages or pay (such as a town physician, town official, mercenary soldier, or whatever they may be) flee unless they put in their places enough other able persons who are acceptable to their superiors.

Where there are no parents, guardians and close relatives are obliged to take in those who are related to them, or at least be careful to see to it that others are provided in their places to care for their sick relatives. In fact, no one may flee from his neighbor unless there is somebody to take his place in waiting upon and nursing the sick. In all such cases these words of Christ are to be feared: "I was sick and ye visited me not."[33] These words of Christ bind each of us to the other. No one may forsake his neighbor when he is in trouble. Everybody is under obligation to help and support his neighbor as he would himself like to be helped.[34]

When no such need exists, when there are enough other people to do the nursing and helping (whether because it is their own duty or desire or whether because they have been commissioned by arrangement of those who are weak in faith), and when the sick do not want them to stay but rather object to this, I believe that they are free either to flee or to remain. Let him who is bold and strong in faith stay in God's name; he does not sin by doing so. On the other hand, let him who is weak and fearful flee in God's name so long as he does so without prejudice to his duty to his neighbor and after providing and arranging for adequate substitutes. The instinct to flee death and save one's life is implanted by God and is not forbidden, provided it is not opposed to God and neighbor. It is as Saint Paul says in Eph., ch. 4, "No man ever yet hated his own flesh; but nourisheth and cherisheth it."[35] Indeed, we are commanded to preserve our bodies and lives as well as we can and not neglect them. Saint Paul says in I Cor., ch. 12, that God has provided our bodies with members that one member may always have care and work for the other.[36]

It is not forbidden but rather commanded that we seek our daily bread, clothing, and all the necessities of life in the sweat

[33] Matt. 25:43.   [34] Cf. Matt. 7:12.
[35] Eph. 5:29.   [36] Cf. I Cor. 12:21–26.

of our face[37] and avoid harm and trouble where we can, provided this can be done without prejudice or injury to the love we are to bear and the duty we are to perform toward our neighbor. How proper it is, then, to try to preserve life and escape death where this can be done without disadvantage to neighbor! For behold, body and life are more than meat and raiment, as Christ himself says in Matt., ch. 5.[38] If anyone is so strong in faith that he can willingly endure nakedness, hunger, and want without tempting God and without attempting to extricate himself from the situation in which he finds himself, let him do so without condemning those who do not or cannot do likewise.

There are plenty of examples in the Scriptures to prove that fleeing from death is not wrong in itself. Abraham was a great saint, yet he feared death and fled from it when he gave his wife Sarah out to be his sister,[39] but because he did this without harming or neglecting his neighbor it was not reckoned against him as sin. His son Isaac did likewise.[40] Jacob also fled from his brother Esau to escape being killed.[41] David also fled before Saul and Absalom,[42] and the prophet Urijah fled into Egypt before King Jehoiakim.[43] The thirsty prophet Elijah too, when Queen Jezebel threatened him after he had slain the prophets of Baal in his great faith, was afraid and fled into the wilderness.[44] And before him Moses, when the king of Egypt sought him, fled into the land of Midian.[45] There are many other examples. All of these fled from death as they were able in order to save their lives, but without thereby depriving their neighbors of anything and only after first fulfilling their obligations.

"Yes," you will say, "but these are not examples of dying in pestilence but of being killed as a result of persecution." Answer: Death is death, no matter by what means it comes. So God refers in the Scriptures to the four plagues or punishments as the pestilence, the famine, the sword, and the noisome beast.[46] If one may with good conscience and God's permission flee from one or several of these, why not from all four? The above examples show how the dear patriarchs fled from the sword, and it is clear enough that Abraham, Isaac, Jacob, and his sons fled from the second plague—that is, from famine or hunger—when they fled into Egypt on account of the famine,

[37] Cf. Gen. 3:19.   [38] Cf. Matt. 6:25.   [39] Cf. Gen. 12:13.
[40] Cf. Gen. 26:7.   [41] Cf. Gen. 27:43–45.
[42] Cf. I Sam. 19:10–17; II Sam. 15:14.   [43] Jer. 26:21.
[44] Cf. I Kings 19:3.   [45] Cf. Ex. 2:15.   [46] Ezek. 14:21.

as we read in Genesis.[47] Why, then, should one not flee from the noisome beasts? Am I to suppose that if a war or the Turk comes, no one should flee from a village or town but must await God's punishment there at the hand of the sword? Very well. Let him who is so strong in faith stay, but let him not condemn those who flee.

Am I to suppose that if a house is on fire, no one must run out of it and no one must attempt to rescue those inside because fire is a punishment of God? or that if somebody falls into a lake, he should not swim out but allow himself to drown as a punishment from God? Well, if you are able, do so without tempting God, but let others do what they are able to do. Again, if a person breaks a leg or is wounded or bitten, must he avoid medical aid and say, "It is God's punishment, and so I shall endure it until it heals itself"? Cold and frost are also God's punishment, and one could die of them. Why do you run to a fire or into the house when it is cold? Be strong and stay out in the cold until it becomes warm again. According to this opinion there would be no need for apothecary shops, medicine, and physicians, for all sicknesses are punishments of God. Hunger and thirst are also great punishments and forms of martyrdom. Why, then, do you eat and drink and not allow yourself to be punished by these until they stop of their own accord? This notion will finally carry us so far that we will abolish the Lord's Prayer and cease praying: "Deliver us from evil, Amen,"[48] inasmuch as all kinds of evil are God's punishments and we could henceforth no longer pray to be delivered from hell and could not avoid it because it too is God's punishment. What would this lead to?

From all this we can conclude that we should pray against all manner of evil and should also defend ourselves against evil in so far as we are able, provided that in doing so we do not act against God, as I have said above. If God desires that we suffer evil and be overcome by it, our defense will not help us. Accordingly let everyone be guided by this. If anyone is bound to remain in peril of death in order to serve his neighbor, let him commit himself to God's keeping and say: "Lord, I am in thy hands. Thou has obligated me to serve here. Thy will be done,[49] for I am thy poor creature. Thou canst slay or preserve me here as well as if I were in duty bound to suffer fire, water, thirst, or some other danger." On the other hand, if anyone is not bound to serve his neighbor and is in a position to

47 Gen., chs. 40–47.   48 Luke 11:4.   49 Luke 11:2.

flee, let him also commit himself to God's keeping and say: "Dear God, I am weak and afraid; I am therefore fleeing from this evil and am doing all that I can to defend myself against it. Nevertheless, I am in thy hands, whether in this or some other evil which may befall me. Thy will be done. My flight will not save me, for evils and misfortunes will assail me everywhere and the devil, who is a murderer from the beginning and tries to commit murder and cause misfortune everywhere, does not sleep or take a holiday."

In like fashion we are obliged to treat our neighbor in all other troubles and perils too. If his house is on fire, love requires that I run there and help put out the fire. If there are enough other people there to extinguish the flames, I may either go home or stay. If he falls into a pit or into water, I must not go away but must hurry to his side as well as I can to help him. But if others are there who are rescuing him, I am free to depart. If I see that he is hungry or thirsty, I must not forsake him but give him to eat and drink without regard to the danger that I might thereby become poorer. If we are not to help and support our neighbor unless we can do so without danger and harm to our bodies and goods, we shall never help our neighbor, for it will always appear as if this will involve us in interruption, peril, loss, or neglect of our interests. We would rather take the risk of having the fire or other misfortune spread from our neighbor's house and destroy us, our bodies, goods, wife, child, and all that we have.

Anyone who refuses to help his neighbor, who allows him to remain in need, and who flees from him is a murderer in God's sight, as Saint John says in his epistle, "He that loveth not his brother is a murderer," and again, "Whoso hath this world's good and seeth his brother have need, how dwelleth the love of God in him?"[50] This was one of the sins that God reckoned to the account of the city of Sodom when he said through the prophet Ezekiel, "Behold, this was the iniquity of thy sister Sodom: pride and fullness of bread, yet she did not strengthen the hand of the poor and needy."[51] On the last day Christ will damn them as murderers and will say, "I was sick and ye visited me not."[52] If those who do not go to the poor and sick and offer help are to be judged so, what will happen to those who run away and let them die like dogs and pigs? Yes, what will happen to those who go beyond this, take from them what they have, and add to their troubles?—as the tyrants are now

50 Cf. I John 3:14, 15, 17.   51 Ezek. 16:49.   52 Cf. Matt. 25:43.

doing to the poor people who are accepting the gospel.[53] But let them go. They will have their reward.[54]

To be sure, it would be good, praiseworthy, and Christian for towns and lands that can do so to make provision for the maintenance of community houses and hospitals and for people to minister in them so that all the sick can be gathered from all homes and committed there. This is what our forefathers desired and intended when they established so many foundations, hospitals, and infirmaries in order that every citizen would not have to maintain a hospital in his own home. Where these exist it is altogether proper that everyone should help and contribute liberally to their support, especially the government. But where there are no such institutions (and there are few of them), each of us must be his neighbor's nurse and hospital director in time of need at the risk of losing salvation and God's favor. Here we have a word and commandment of God: "Love thy neighbor as thyself,"[55] and Matt., ch. 7, "All things whatsoever ye would that men should do to you, do ye even so to them."[56]

When people are beginning to die [in a time of pestilence], we should stay with them, make preparations to counteract the disease, and assure ourselves, especially those of us who have such responsibilities toward others (as I mentioned above), that we cannot leave or flee. We should be comforted by our certainty that it is God's punishment sent upon us not only to punish sin but also to test our faith and love—our faith in order that we may see and know what our attitude is toward God, and our love in order that we may see what our attitude is toward our neighbor. Although I believe that every pestilence, like other plagues, is spread among the people by evil spirits who poison the air or somehow exhale a noisome breath and inject deadly poison into men's bodies, nevertheless it is also God's will and punishment. Accordingly we should submit to it patiently and risk our lives in the service of our neighbor, as Saint John teaches: "Because Christ laid down his life for us, we ought to lay down our lives for the brethren."[57]

If the sick strike fear and terror into anyone's heart, let such a person be of good courage and so strengthen and comfort himself that he has no doubt that it is the devil who is responsible for this fear, terror, and horror. The devil is so very evil that he not only tries constantly to kill and murder but also gives vent to his spleen by making us fearful, afraid, and timid

---

[53] Cf. Chapter VII, above. [54] Cf. Matt. 6:2. [55] Matt. 22:39.
[56] Matt. 7:12. [57] I John 3:16.

about death in order that death might appear to us to be the worst possible thing, that we might have neither rest nor peace in this life, and that we might despair of our life. In this way he tries to bring it about that we despair of God, become unwilling and unprepared to die, become so enveloped in the dark clouds of fear and worry that we forget and lose sight of Christ, our light and life, forsake our neighbor in his need, and so sin against God and man. This is the devil's desire and purpose. Because we know that such fear and terror are the devil's game, we should be the more unwilling to be affected by it, gather up our courage in defiance of him and to vex him, and throw off his terror and cast it back at him. We should defend ourselves with such weapons and say:

"Away with you and your fears, devil! Because it will vex you, I shall defy you by going at once to my sick neighbor to help him. I shall pay no attention to you but shall attack you on two points. The first is that I know for certain that this work is pleasing to God and all angels when I do it in obedience to his will and as a divine service. It must indeed be especially pleasing to God because it displeases you so much and you so vigorously oppose it. How willingly and gladly I would do it if it pleased only one angel and he watched me and rejoiced over what I did! However, since it pleases my Lord Jesus Christ and all the heavenly host, and is at the same time the will and command of God my Father, why should I be so influenced by your terror as to prevent such joy in heaven, obstruct the desire of my Lord, and provide you and your demons in hell with an occasion to be gay, to laugh, and to mock me? Not so! You are not to have your way. If Christ shed his blood for me and died in my behalf, why should I not place myself in a little danger for his sake and face the effects of a powerless pestilence? If you can terrify, my Christ can strengthen. If you can slay, Christ can give life. If you have poison on your breath, Christ has more potent medicine. If my dear Christ with his command, his benefaction, and all his comfort would not mean more to my spirit than you, cursed devil, can do to my frail flesh with your false terrors, God would surely be displeased. Get thee behind me, Satan![58] Christ is here, and I am his servant in this work. He shall prevail. Amen."

The other point on which to attack the devil is the sure promise of God with which he comforts all those who consider the poor and needy. He says in Ps. 41: "Blessed is he that con-

[58] Cf. Matt. 16:23.

sidereth the poor: the Lord will deliver him in time of trouble. The Lord will preserve him, and keep him alive; and he shall be blessed upon the earth: and thou wilt not deliver him unto the will of his enemies. The Lord will strengthen him upon the bed of languishing: thou wilt transform his whole bed in his sickness."[59] Are not these great and glorious promises of God, showered in abundance on those who consider the poor and needy? What is there that can frighten us or move us to act contrary to this great comfort of God? To be sure, the service that we may render to those in need is a small thing in comparison with these promises and rewards of God. Saint Paul does well to say to Timothy, "Godliness is profitable unto all things, having promise of the life that now is, and of that which is to come."[60] Godliness is nothing but divine service,[61] and divine service is service to one's neighbor. Experience teaches us that those who minister to the sick with love, devotion, and earnestness are generally preserved. Even if they too should be infected, it does not matter, for this psalm says, "Thou wilt transform his whole bed in his sickness," that is, God will turn his sickbed into a bed for the well. But it is not surprising if one who nurses a sick person for the sake of greed or inheritance, seeking his own good in what he does, is finally infected and defiled and afterward dies before he comes into possession of the property or inheritance.

Whoever ministers to the sick on the strength of these comforting promises (even if, needing them, he accepts fairly large wages for his services inasmuch as the laborer is worthy of his hire)[62] has another great comfort, namely, that he will be ministered unto. God himself will nurse him, and will be his physician as well. What a nurse God is! What a physician he is! Or rather, what are all physicians, apothecaries, and nurses in comparison with God? Should not this give a person the courage to go to the sick and minister to their needs—even if they have as many pestilential boils as they have hairs on their whole bodies and they cough up enough pestilential poison to infect a hundred people? What are all pestilences and devils in comparison with God, who here promises to be your nurse and physician? Shame on you, and again I say, shame on you, O cursed unbelief, that you should despise such rich comfort and allow a small boil and uncertain danger to frighten you more than these certain, faithful promises of God strengthen you. What would it help if all physicians were there and all the

[59] Ps. 41:1–3.   [60] I Tim. 4:8.   [61] *Gotts dienst.*   [62] Luke 10:7.

world were attending you if God were not present? On the other hand, what harm would it do if all the world forsook you and no physician stayed with you as long as God remained with you with his promises? Do you not realize that you would be surrounded by thousands of angels who would help you to trample the pestilence underfoot? It is written in Ps. 91, "He shall give his angels charge over thee, to keep thee in all thy ways. They shall bear thee up in their hands, lest thou dash thy foot against a stone. Thou shalt tread upon the lion and adder: the young lion and the dragon shalt thou trample underfeet."[63]

Therefore, dear friends, let us not be so fearful as to forsake those to whom we have obligations and shamefully flee before the devil's terror, whereby we would give him pleasure and occasion to mock us while God and all his angels would undoubtedly be displeased and disgusted. It is certainly true that anyone who despises the abundant promises and commands of God and leaves his neighbors in the lurch will be guilty of breaking all the divine Commandments and will be regarded as a murderer of his forsaken neighbors. Then, I fear, the promises will be turned about and transformed into terrible threats, so that the psalm will be directed against such a person: "Cursed is he that considereth not the poor but fleeth and forsaketh them. The Lord will not deliver him in time of trouble, but will also flee from him and forsake him. The Lord will not preserve him and keep him alive, nor will he bless him upon the earth, but will deliver him into the hands of his enemies. The Lord will not strengthen him upon the bed of languishing, nor transform his bed in his sickness."[64] "For with what measure ye mete, it shall be measured to you again."[65] It cannot be otherwise. This is terrible to hear, more terrible to expect, most terrible to experience. If God takes away his hand and flees, what can you expect other than sheer devilishness and all evil? It cannot be otherwise if neighbors are forsaken contrary to God's Word and command. This will most assuredly happen to each and every one unless he honestly repents what he has done.

I know very well that if Christ himself or his mother were now ill, everybody would be so devoted as to wish to help and serve. Everybody would try to be bold and brave. No one would want to run away. Everybody would come running. Yet they do not hear what he himself says: "Inasmuch as ye have done it unto one of the least of these my brethren, ye have done it unto me."[66] And when he spoke of the first commandment he added, "The

---

[63] Ps. 91:11–13.   [64] Cf. Ps. 41:1–3.   [65] Matt. 7:2.   [66] Matt. 25:40.

second is like unto it, Thou shalt love thy neighbor as thyself."[67] Here you hear that the command to love your neighbor is like unto the first commandment, that we should love God. And what you do or omit doing to your neighbor means as much as that you have done or failed to do it to God himself. If, then, you would minister to and wait upon Christ, behold, you have a sick neighbor before you. Go to him and minister to him and you will assuredly find Christ in him, not according to the person, but in his Word. If you are unwilling to minister to your neighbor, you may be sure that if Christ himself were there, you would do the same thing—run away, and let him lie there. You would have nothing but false notions (which leave you in unprofitable ignorance) as to how you would minister to Christ if he were there. They are nothing but lies, for anyone who would minister to Christ in the body would also minister to his neighbor's needs. Let this be said as a warning and admonition against shameful flight and the terror with which the devil tempts us to act against God's Word and command with respect to our neighbor and to sin too much on the left hand.

On the other hand, some sin too much on the right hand and are too daring and foolhardy. They tempt God, neglect all the things with which they ought to protect themselves against pestilence or death, scorn the use of medicine, and do not avoid the places where there has been pestilence and the persons who have had it. On the contrary, they drink and play with such persons, try in this way to demonstrate their good cheer, and say: "It is God's punishment. If he wishes to protect me from it, he will do so without medicine and any effort on my part." This is not trusting in God but tempting God, for God created medicine and gave us our reason in order that we may so manage and care for our bodies as to be well and live. Whoever does not use medicine when he has it and can make use of it without injury to his neighbor neglects his body and runs the risk of being a suicide in God's sight. One might in similar fashion neglect food and drink and clothing and shelter, be foolhardy in one's faith, and say, "If God wishes to protect me from hunger and cold, he will do so without food and clothing." Such a man would really be a suicide. As a matter of fact, it would be worse for him to neglect his body in this way and not to employ such protection against the pestilence as is available because he might infect and defile others, who would have remained alive if he had taken care of his body as he ought. So

[67] Matt. 22:39.

he would be responsible for his neighbor's death and would be a murderer many times over in God's sight. Indeed, such a person would be like a man who, when a house is on fire in a town, will not help put it out but lets it burn until the whole town is on fire, and says, "If God wishes, he can preserve the town without water and without quenching the flames."

Not so, my dear friend. That would not be well done. Use medicine. Take whatever may be helpful to you. Fumigate your house, yard, and street. Avoid persons and places where you are not needed or where your neighbor has recovered. Act as one who would like to help put out a general fire. What is the pestilence, after all, but a fire which consumes body and life instead of wood and straw. Meanwhile think thus: "With God's permission the enemy has sent poison and deadly dung among us, and so I will pray to God that he may be gracious and preserve us. Then I will fumigate to purify the air, give and take medicine, and avoid places and persons where I am not needed in order that I may not abuse myself and that through me others may not be infected and inflamed with the result that I become the cause of their death through my negligence. If God wishes to take me, he will be able to find me. At least I have done what he gave me to do and am responsible neither for my own death nor for the death of others. But if my neighbor needs me, I shall avoid neither person nor place but feel free to visit and help him," as has already been said. Behold, this is a true and God-fearing faith which is neither foolhardy nor rash and does not tempt God.

Whoever has succumbed to the pestilence and has recovered should likewise avoid people and be reluctant to have them near without necessity. Although he is to be helped and not forsaken in his need, as has been said, when he has recovered from his illness he must so conduct himself in his relations with others that no one is unnecessarily endangered on his account and dies because of him. "He that loveth danger," says the wise man, "shall perish therein."[68] If the people in a town so conducted themselves that they were bold in their faith when the need of neighbors required it, careful when there was no need, and helpful to one another in counteracting the poison wherever possible, death would indeed be light in such a town. But when it happens that some of the people are too fearful and flee from their neighbors in time of need, while others are so foolhardy that they do not help to counteract the disease but

[68] Ecclus. 3:26.

rather spread it, the devil will take advantage of the situation and the mortality will certainly be high. Both are very injurious to God and man, the former by fearfulness and the latter by tempting God. So the devil chases the people who flee and restrains the people who stay, and no one escapes his clutches.

Some people are even worse. When they contract the pestilential disease they keep it secret, go out among other people, and think that if they can infect and defile others with the sickness they will themselves get rid of it and become well. With this notion they frequent streets and houses in the hope of saddling others or their children and servants with the pestilence and thus saving themselves. I can well believe that the devil obliges and helps to further this notion so that it actually comes to pass. I am also told that some individuals are so desperately wicked that they carry the pestilence among the people and into houses for no other reason than that they regret that the disease has not struck there, and so they spread the pestilence as if this were a great joke, like slyly putting lice in somebody's clothes or gnats in somebody's room. I do not know whether I should believe this or not. If it is true, I do not know whether we Germans are human beings or devils. To be sure, there are immoderately coarse and wicked people, and the devil is not inactive. If such people are found, it would be my suggestion that the judge should seize them by the hair and turn them over to the hangman[69] as real, malicious murderers and scoundrels. What are they but assassins in a town? They are like assassins who plunge a knife into a person so stealthily that it cannot be determined who did it. So these people infect a child here and a woman there and nobody knows how it happened. Meanwhile they go away laughing, as if they had done a good deed. It would be better to live among wild beasts than among such murderers. I do not know how to counsel these murderers, for they pay no attention. I commend them to the government, which must take care of them with the help and counsel not of physicians, but of the hangman. God himself commanded in the Old Testament that lepers be removed from a community and be required to live outside of a town in order to prevent infection.[70] We have even more reason to do this in the present dangerous sickness. Whoever gets it should at once remove himself or be removed from contact with other people and should quickly seek help in the form of medicine. He should be aided and not forsaken in his need, as I have made sufficiently

[69] *Uberantwortet sie Meister Hansen.*   [70] Lev., chs. 13; 14.

clear above, in order that the infection might in time be checked, for the benefit not only of the individual but of the whole community, which would become infected if the disease were allowed to break out and spread.

Our present pestilence here in Wittenberg had its origin in nothing else than such contagion. Thank God, the air is still fresh and pure. It is only through foolhardiness and neglect that some few have been infected. However, the devil has had his fun in spreading terror among us and causing flight. May God hold him in check. Amen.

This, then, is my understanding and opinion about fleeing when in peril of death. If you have another opinion, may God disclose it to you. Amen.[71]

Martin Luther.

TO NICHOLAS HAUSMANN. August 27, 1529

An epidemic of what was called the "engelische Schwyssucht," or English sweating sickness, swept through some parts of Germany in the summer of 1529. It appeared in Magdeburg during the middle weeks of August. It was reported that in Zwickau a hundred people became ill in one night, and on one day (August 14) nineteen were buried. Luther here suggests that fear of the disease was often as disastrous as the disease itself, and he shows an awareness of the effect of the mind on the body. [Text in Latin; *WA, Br*, V, 138-140.]

Grace and peace in Christ.

My dear Nicholas:

Although I had nothing of importance to write, I did not wish this messenger to go to Zwickau without a letter from me. The English plague is said to be epidemic among you and in Zerbst. Many think that it is epidemic here among us too, but I do not believe it. Our prefect[72] has made himself ill with his own imagination; he had no other symptons of illness except his own ideas. For if these are the real beginnings of that disease I should have had it often during these last three years or more. Even last night I broke out in a sweat and awoke in distress, and my thoughts began to trouble me. If I had given way to them,

---

[71] Omitted here is a section (*WA*, XXIII, 371-379) later appended by Luther in which he provides instruction on the preparation of the soul for death and on burial.

[72] John Metzsch, on whom see Chapter IX.

I should have taken to my bed, as others who make martyrs of themselves have done.

I write this so that you may join me in telling the people not to be afraid and not to allow their thoughts to bring down upon them an illness which they do not yet have. We have aroused, almost by force, many who had already taken to their beds with the sweating—Aurogallus,[73] Bleikard,[74] Dr. Brück,[75] Master Christian,[76] and others. They now laugh about it and say that they would perhaps still be in bed if they had not been aroused. Not that I think the disease should be made light of, but it is necessary to distinguish carefully because we see that more people contract the sickness from imagination and fear than from actual contagion. Imagination brings on the attack, and the state of mind affects the body.

But pray for me, a sinner, and if your guest[77] is still there, greet him in my name. Christ the Lord be with you. Amen.

Yours,

August 27, 1529. Martin Luther.

TO ELECTOR JOHN FREDERICK. July 9, 1535

Through Chancellor Gregory Brück, the elector had advised Luther to leave Wittenberg on account of the pestilence, which had showed signs of increasing since the beginning of summer. Two days after Luther had written the following letter in reply, plans were made by the elector and university officials once again to move the whole university temporarily from Wittenberg to Jena. A week later the students were informed of the plan, and by the end of the month lectures were begun in Jena, where monastery buildings were utilized for the purpose. When he wrote this letter Luther felt that reports of the pestilence were exaggerated. He remained in Wittenberg when his colleagues moved to Jena. [Text in German; *WA, Br,* VII, 200-208.]

To the serene, highborn prince and lord, John Frederick, duke of Saxony, elector and marshal of the Holy Roman Empire, landgrave in Thuringia, margrave of Meissen, my gracious lord: grace and peace in Christ and my poor prayers.

Serene, highborn Prince, most gracious Lord:

Your Grace's chancellor, Dr. Brück, has informed me of

---

[73] Matthew Aurogallus (1490–1543), professor of Hebrew.
[74] Bleikard Sindringer, professor of law.
[75] The Saxon chancellor, Gregory Brück.
[76] It is not clear just who is meant.   [77] John Cellarius (1490–1542).

Your Grace's kind suggestion in case the number of deaths here continues. I am very thankful to Your Grace for such kind consideration, and if necessary I shall obediently comply with Your Grace's proposal. But my reliable weather vane has been the prefect John Metzsch,[78] who has hitherto had a very trustworthy and sharp nose for the pestilence, which he would be able to smell even if it were five ells under the ground. As long as he remains here I cannot believe that there is a pestilence. It is true that a house or two have been touched by the disease, but the air is not infected as yet. Since Tuesday no case of illness or death has been reported.

However, since the dog days are at hand and the young students are terrified, I have allowed them to take walks in order that their fears may be allayed until we see how things turn out. Meanwhile I have observed that many of the young students have rejoiced over rumors of a pestilence, for some of them have developed sores from carrying their schoolbags, some have acquired colic from their books, some have developed scabs on the fingers with which they write, some have picked up goutiness from their papers, and many have found their ink to be getting moldy. In addition, many have devoured letters from their mothers, and these have made them heartsick and homesick. There may well be more weaknesses of this kind than I know.

In any case, there is danger in all this. Unless parents and rulers take serious measures to prevent such sickness[79] with various kinds of remedies, the contagion may spread through the whole country. Then neither preachers nor pastors nor schoolmasters will be available, and ultimately production will be reduced to the raising of pigs and dogs, a condition which the papists are eager to bring about.

May Christ our Lord continue to be gracious and merciful, as he has been hitherto, to Your Grace and to all godly and Christian rulers, and may he provide effective remedies and medicines to counteract this disease, to the honor and praise of God and to the vexation of Satan, who is hostile to learning and order. Amen.

Herewith I commit Your Grace to God's keeping. Amen.

Your Grace's humble servant,

Friday after the Visitation of Mary, 1535.   Martin Luther.

[78] See note 72 above.

[79] I.e., fear of pestilence, which causes people to leave their work and students to drop their studies, and such weaknesses as homesickness.

SERMON REPORTED BY ANTHONY LAUTERBACH.[80]
December 1, 1538

Although the pestilence was raging for about half a year among our neighbors on every side, this town was miraculously preserved by God. Now at last, in this cold, wintry weather, the disease invaded two houses. And since there were many rumors and great fear, Luther delivered an exhortation in his public sermon, a brief summary of which follows.

First he sharply reproved those who were spreading rumors concerning a pestilence, for by God's grace there was none. Then, on the ground that they had obligations to perform, he dissuaded the townspeople from fleeing. He declared that it would be most impious for them to leave their brethren, for it often happens at such a time that more people die from hunger and thirst than from the pestilence. Accordingly he exhorted the people to bear the chastenings of God: "If we are unwilling to suffer these light chastisements (for of all plagues the pestilence is lightest), how are we going to endure famine and war, when everything is destroyed? Moreover, the pestilence is only a purgation in this world [attended by no external inhumanity],[81] and godly people fall asleep[82] gently and quickly.

"Do not allow yourselves to be terrified by the rumor of pestilence in one house. Do not do the devil the favor of fleeing even if the pestilence invades your houses, beds, cradles, and tables. We can defy the devil with this assurance: that Christ is risen, who is even at the right hand of God, who also maketh intercession for us.[83] Since Christ is our mediator and we now hear his teaching of life, why should we be any more afraid than we were under the papacy? Then we had courage even though we still lived in darkness. Is this any more serious than if the devil were to poison a few people? He has the means to do it.

"I exhort you who are members of the town council that you keep the town supplied with public servants, physicians, surgeons, barbers, and nurses. Compel those who are fitted for service to the poor in hospitals to engage in this service or exile them from the town. Then I say to you townspeople who are planning to flee and leave your brethren behind: I shall not forsake the poor in their need. I shall have your wood hauled in

---

[80] Macaronic text; WA, TR, IV, No. 4789. A brief notice of a similar sermon is ascribed to Oct. 21, 1538, in WA, TR, IV, No. 4313.
[81] Text in brackets from variant version in EA, XLIV, 314–316.
[82] Obdormiscunt, i.e., die.   [83] Rom. 8:34.

from the woodland in order that it may serve as fuel, and I shall take into my hands and distribute among the poor your supplies of grain [and beer and whatever else may be used to sustain life]. Let this be a warning of what I shall do. It is not necessary that you flee but that you do what Christ says in Matt., ch. 25, 'I was an hungered, etc.;' 'I was sick, and ye visited me not.'[84]

"Besides, you know that I have never fled in time of pestilence, but that I have remained at home with my family and household. After all, I am as noble as you are and could have fled [with a good conscience], especially since the elector commanded me to do so. But I would not.

"Let everyone who has an obligation to a wife, brother, child, sister, or neighbor stay here to help [and minister in the common peril]. Each one of us owes it to his neighbor to be ready to lay down his own life. Even so, as your pastor and substitute preacher,[85] I am bound to remain in my pulpit. A hundred pestilences will not drive me from it. Moreover, together with my deacons I am ready to visit the sick. If we die while engaged in this work of love, it will be well with us, for the hour of death will be sweeter to us than a hundred thousand years of life. On the other hand, if you flee with a bad conscience, the time will come when you would a thousand times rather have died.

"Therefore, be of good cheer. Do not be so afraid, and do not flee when you are tried by the Lord for this short space of time. After all, you must eventually die; and in such dangerous times as these, amid such hopeless evils as are brought upon us by men (whether peasants, burghers, or nobles), no one ought to desire long life. The pestilence is such a good purgation [in the world] that I can hardly pray that we should be delivered from it, for if it were not for the pestilence no one would be able or willing to punish evildoers. May God visit and empty their money chests so that the greedy boors may acknowledge, whether they make their living by fair means or foul, that they are all called to repentance.

"Therefore, let those of us who have responsibilities not awaken God's wrath, lest he visit a greater punishment upon us. Let us rather suffer his chastisement, if it comes, one bearing another's burden. If we die now, we shall not have to be afraid of death in the years that lie ahead. [It is better to be prepared and not to be afraid of death when God comes. We are unwilling to go when God calls us, but we must go because he

[84] Matt. 25:42, 43.
[85] Substitute for John Bugenhagen, absent from Wittenberg.

wills it. Therefore, let us die, if this be his will, rather than desire to live as long as we wish. Nevertheless, I do not wish that anyone should be so bold as to tempt God or invite danger without just cause and apart from the duties of his office.] I say this in order that no one may, by despising the physicians, wish to despise God and place himself in danger. [On the other hand, those who have obligations should face the greatest danger in keeping with the law of love and the duties of their office, for it is a blessed thing to die while performing the duties that God has enjoined and commanded.

"[Twice have I been tested in a time of pestilence when I might have fled. Although the pestilence is let loose by the raging devil, yet nothing can happen to the godly which is contrary to God's will. I fulfilled the duties of my office by preaching, yet I was preserved together with my whole family. Although I was allowed to flee, I did not evade my responsibility to the Church. I wish that I might not have to endure greater temptations than fear of pestilence!]

"I am not saying these things to students who have come here from other places, who have been sent here by their parents to study [and who have no political or domestic obligations here]. They are our guests; we cannot close the gates to lock them in. [But the matter is different in the case of those students who have obligations here. Do you think that it is right for them to enjoy the freedom of the city in times of health, peace, and prosperity and then to flee from it in evil times and forsake neighbors who have often and in many ways ministered to their need?]

"Nevertheless, since by God's grace there is no pestilence among you as yet, I exhort you students not to flee, lest by your untimely flight you disperse this university of ours."

TABLE TALK RECORDED BY ANTHONY LAUTERBACH.[86] December 6, 1538

On December 6, after the contagion of the pestilence had entered two houses,[87] Luther was asked by the deacons what they should do and whether some special arrangement should be made, for they were reluctant to have Peter Hess,[88] who had

86 Macaronic text; *WA, TR*, IV, No. 4179.
87 At the end of November, 1538, it was reported that "in these days three persons died in two houses in Wittenberg" (*WA, TR*, IV, No. 4157).
88 Peter Hess was one of the *diaconi*, or assistant pastors, in Wittenberg.

visited those who were sick, appear in public. He replied: "Would to God that this were the only thing I had to worry about. Then I would have no trouble. Peter should not be forbidden in the future. We shall all go, if necessary, and leave the consequences in God's hands. God generally protects the ministers of his Word. There is no problem about hearing confession as long as one does not do so in lodgings and at bedsides, for we are the bearers of the Word of life."

Then he marveled at the fear of the people at a time when the gospel has free course, whereas the people were not so afraid before under the papacy. And this is the reason, he said: "Under the papacy we placed our confidence in the merits of monks and others; now everybody is thrown upon his own and must take his chance on what he believes."

TO THE TOWN COUNCIL OF WITTENBERG.
March, 1539[89]

A shortage of grain produced a serious food crisis in Wittenberg during the spring of 1539, and there were reports of a similar shortage in Leipzig, Torgau, and elsewhere. Bakers put such a high price on bread that poor people could no longer afford to buy it, and university students began to leave for their homes. One thing that Luther did in this situation was to help the victims of famine and to appeal to others for help. The following note was written in behalf of one of the victims, a student whose name is unknown. [Text in German; WA, Br, VIII, 399.]

Dear Sirs:

This poor fellow[90] must also leave on account of hunger. Like the others, he has nothing to eat and must travel far. Since he is a pious and learned man, he deserves to be helped.

You know that I am already called upon to give so much and so often that it is all beyond my means. Accordingly I beg you to give him thirty gulden. If this amount is not available, give him twenty gulden and I shall give him ten. If not, then give him half, or fifteen, and I shall give the other half. God will repay what you give.

Martin Luther.

---

[89] The date of this letter is uncertain, but it was probably written at the end of March or beginning of April.

[90] Presumably the needy student was the bearer of the note.

TABLE TALK REPORTED BY ANTHONY
LAUTERBACH. April 7, 1539

In addition to appealing for help in behalf of individual victims of the current food shortage, Luther made inquiries concerning the cause of the shortage. He was convinced that some noblemen had bought up grain from the farmers, were withholding it from the market, and were thus producing an artificial shortage. He appealed to the town council for a vigorous program of relief and threatened personal intervention. [Macaronic text; *WA, TR,* IV, No. 4472.]

In the evening he [Martin Luther] gave Dr. Cruciger[91] a note in which he admonished the town council to see to it that bakers supply the poor people lest they die of hunger. For such was the shortage in these days that the poor were unable to buy flour or bread with money. So he indirectly reproached the town council with negligence.

In the evening one of the councilmen, Lucas Cranach, came to him and excused the council by saying that shipments of grain had been held up beyond the town borders.

Dr. Martin Luther replied: "Would that our prince were not now outside the country![92] Great is the perfidy of the noblemen who are buying up all the grain from their farmers, taking it away, storing it up, and mischievously bringing about a shortage that is not caused by an act of God.[93] The situation requires a prince who will tell the noblemen whether they have the power to keep grain from the common market. It is nothing but wickedness on the part of these men. What would happen if an act of God caused famine? Dear Lord God, if the world is so wicked, I shall be glad to die of hunger in order to get out of it."

But then he said to the councilman: "The fault is the prefect's,[94] who exported grain on some ships from various parts of our sandy soil. He once said that if the townspeople did not make good beer and sell it cheap, he would raise the price of grain before they had time to wipe their mouths. This statement of his makes me especially suspicious of him. God has

---

[91] Caspar Cruciger (1504–1548).
[92] The elector of Saxony was in Frankfurt at the time.
[93] *Und noch keine Gottstraff.* A year earlier the destruction of crops in the fields by mice had threatened famine. Cf. *WA, TR,* IV, Nos. 4046, 4079.
[94] The *Landvogt* was John Metzsch, whom Luther had had occasion to criticize earlier for immoral conduct. See note 72, above.

marvelously blessed us on this sandy soil of ours,[95] more than he has blessed the Thuringians with their rich soil. Let us pray for our daily bread.

"I tried to persuade the tax collector to give me several bushels [of grain] for the poor. At the time of the pestilence[96] I complained to the elector that there was a shortage in our town because nothing was imported, with the result that we suffered from three plagues: pestilence, hunger, and cold. I told [wrote to] him, 'I shall have to pitch in and help the townspeople to distribute [Your Grace's] grain and wood.' The elector replied graciously, 'By all means help me to do so.' On the strength of these words of the elector I shall now venture to help the poor."

TO ELECTOR JOHN FREDERICK OF SAXONY.
April 9, 1539

The food crisis continued in Wittenberg, and Luther was thoroughly aroused. More was required, he felt, than measures of relief. Those who were manipulating the grain market had to be restrained. Since this demanded a higher authority than that of the town council, he addressed a letter to Elector John Frederick in which he proposed that something be done about the situation by the state government. [Text in German; *WA, Br,* VIII, 403-405.]

Grace and peace in Christ, and my poor prayers.

Serene, highborn Prince, gracious Lord:

A sudden shortage and unforeseen famine have overtaken us here. There is no wonder, therefore, that we feel compelled to call upon Your Grace, as the lord and father of our country, for help and counsel. Your Grace is undoubtedly in a position to reckon how large our store of food is here in Wittenberg. The villages of Kemberg and Schmiedeberg must now be supplied with baked bread from Wittenberg, with the result (the town council informs me)[97] that more bread is sent out into the country than is consumed here in the town. Meanwhile some believe that the shortage is not a result of actual scarcity, but that it is rather a result of the greed and wickedness of rich noblemen. All sorts of strange rumors are abroad, and I do not

[95] Cf. H. Boehmer, *Road to Reformation* (Philadelphia, 1946), 47–49.

[96] The reference is probably to the pestilence in 1527 which continued into the winter.

[97] Lucas Cranach gave Luther the point of view of the town council of Wittenberg. *WA, TR,* IV, No. 4472.

know how to reply to them. For example, it is reported that N.N.[98] declared that he would not sell a single kernel of grain until a bushel is worth a gulden, or many times the normal price. Meanwhile matters are made worse by the export of grain. And the Elbe River is contributing its share toward preventing milling and baking, for floods have brought the castle mill to a standstill.

Unless Your Grace provides help and counsel, the present trouble will become more serious. Accordingly, all of us pray that Your Grace may not only afford immediate relief in our want, but may also intervene with the power of government to prevent noblemen from selfishly buying up and exporting grain for purposes of shameless usury, which is ruinous to Your Grace's land and people. The noblemen are rich enough as it is without starving poor people to death in order to satisfy their greed. Your Grace will know what further steps need to be taken in the matter by the authority of government.

Herewith I commit Your Grace to the dear Lord Christ. Amen.

Wednesday after Easter, 1539. [Martin Luther.]

SERMON REPORTED BY ANTHONY LAUTERBACH.
April 13, 1539

After discussing at table the food crisis, and writing to the town council of Wittenberg and the elector of Saxony, Luther also introduced the subject into the pulpit. [Macaronic text; *WA, TR,* IV, No. 4496.]

On April 13 he [Martin Luther] delivered a sermon in which he sharply reproved the avarice of usurers. He declared that they deserve to be cursed by all men, for they are the greatest enemies of the country. With their devouring greed and usury they cause many to die. He treated admirably that verse in Solomon, "He that hath pity upon the poor lendeth unto the Lord."[99]

---

[98] It is probable that the assessor Frederick Brandt was in Luther's mind here. Cf. *WA, TR,* IV, No. 4749.
[99] Prov. 19:17.

TABLE TALK RECORDED BY ANTHONY
LAUTERBACH.[1] June 14, 1542

On June 14, Mr. James Probst,[2] pastor in Bremen, [former][3] colleague of Luther [in the monastery], distinguished Scotist,[4] and a learned, pious, and upright man, came to see his father [Luther]. There they had a remarkable discussion about many things. At first the usury which is rife in Flanders, etc., was mentioned. Luther replied that the whole world is overrun with usury. "Usurers," he said, "are so forward that they seize whatever they can. Therefore, those who practice usury should be convicted and punished."

He added: "We are willing to allow five or six per cent interest, provided that there is security and that the agreement is kept whereby the capital is not to be recalled by the lender— for example, the man who puts one hundred florins out at interest—but redeemed by the borrower. And so we allow six per cent interest because the cost of goods has risen and this amount may be necessary. The lender, however, should take the risk in case, let us say, the house should burn or the soil should wash away. It is this risk, and not the repayment of the capital, that makes it a just contract. How happy we would be if we could persuade people that this is so! But devilish usury and rapid conversion are devouring everything. The emperor himself is permitting twelve per cent in his own country. What a shame!"

He was asked, "If a poor man is in need of money and has no security, should he not borrow money on the strength of his trustworthiness and ability to work?"

Luther replied: "Let him live in his poverty and not sin. For money is a sterile thing.[5] We should not borrow on our ability to work and earn, for this is uncertain. The people should be encouraged to work with their hands, and the rich should be exhorted to do works of mercy. We do not oppose those who engage in trade so long as they come to just agreements among themselves without greed and fraud. But, alas! we see that the world is incapable of reforming itself and that it is proud of and glories in wickedness. Leipzig is like that, so submerged in

[1] Macaronic text; *WA*, *TR*, IV. No. 4805.
[2] James Probst, 1486–1562, was superintendent in Bremen.
[3] Text in brackets from a variant version.
[4] Adherent of the Scholastic Duns Scotus (d. 1308).
[5] A favorite expression of medieval Scholastics.

avarice that it has become a marsh! In short, the world is the devil's and full of devils.[6] Let us pray."

TABLE TALK RECORDED BY CASPAR HEYDENREICH.[7] October, 1542

When someone reported that two preachers had died of the pestilence in Nuremberg, the question was asked whether clergymen who had been employed for preaching alone could refuse to minister to sick people in time of pestilence.

He [Luther] replied: "No, by no means! Preachers should not be too ready to flee lest they frighten the people. When it is sometimes said that parsons and preachers should be spared and not overburdened in time of pestilence, this is intended to mean that if the pestilence should take some of the chaplains,[8] others should be available to visit the sick. It also means that people are not to shun the clergymen, as now happens when no one is willing to go to them and everybody flees before them. Consequently it would be a good thing if everyone were not burdened with it,[9] but only one or two, and let these take the risk.

"If it fell to my lot, I should not be afraid. I have now been exposed to three pestilences,[10] and I have visited some people who suffered from the pestilence—like Schadewald,[11] who had two attacks. I understand the danger very well, but it did not harm me, thank God. When I returned home that time I embraced my daughter Margaret, who was still a baby,[12] and touched her lips with my unwashed hands. I had forgotten the danger altogether, else I should not have done this, for it is tempting God.

"It pleases me that the Jews ascribe the psalm *Qui habitat*[13] to the pestilence. I should also like to have it interpreted with reference to the pestilence, but I am concerned about the superstitious who might afterward use the psalm to ward off pestilence, as the Gospel according to Saint John is considered

---

6 *Mundus est Diaboli genitivi casus et Diaboli nominativi pluralis.* Cf. letter to John Rühel, June 29, 1534, in Chapter I.

7 Text macaronic; *WA, TR,* V, No. 5503.

8 Deacons or assistants.   9 That is, burdened with visitation of the sick.

10 There were epidemics in Wittenberg in 1527, 1535, and 1539.

11 Bartholomew Schadewald, town councilman in Wittenberg.

12 Margaret was born in 1534, a year before the epidemic of 1535.

13 Ps. 90, whose opening lines are, "Lord, thou hast been our dwelling place in all generations."

a protection against thunder. At the conclusion of Mass the priest used to read Saint John's Gospel in a loud voice, and those who heard the reading were thought to be safe. Then a fable was introduced into the pulpit to confirm this lie. Three men were riding together when a storm broke. A voice was heard to say, 'Strike!' and one of the men was struck down. Again the voice said, 'Strike!' and the second man was felled. When the voice was heard to say, 'Strike!' a third time, another voice cried, 'Strike not, for he heard the reading of Saint John's Gospel today.' This man's life was saved. Such is the legend that is preached to confirm their idolatry.

"Here is a story of something that happened not far from here.[14] A man who intended to marry the wife of the painter Lucas[15] was sitting with a tailor in his castle and was having some fine clothes made for the wedding. Looking out of the window the tailor became aware of an approaching storm and said, 'I shall go fetch some palms and throw them in the fire, for I have not heard the Gospel of Saint John read today.' He went out and did accordingly. The young fellow said: 'What is this? Do you think the priest is the only one who can read the Gospel? I can do it just as well as he.' So he opened the window and began to read, '*In principio*,' etc.[16] Thereupon the thunder struck into the house and neatly stripped off the hose from the legs of the young, handsome, and rich fellow, and shortly afterward he collapsed and died. The tailor was struck on the soles of his feet, but he did not die. This most certainly happened.

"Even better was that peasant who, when a storm arose and there was thunder, made the sign of the cross four times and said, 'The four Evangelists, Matthew, Mark, Pilate, and Herod, help me!' It was remarkable under the papacy! Young people today know nothing of it."

Then someone said that in a certain town not far from Nuremberg a parish clergyman died of the pestilence, and likewise the schoolmaster, etc. The people there now died like beasts without the Sacrament, for they had been unwilling to support a deacon even before the pestilence began to spread. To this the doctor said: "It serves them right. They thought that they did not need a preacher and chaplain and that they

[14] In Gotha, according to a variant.
[15] The artist Lucas Cranach the Elder married Barbara Brengbier, daughter of the burgomaster of Gotha.
[16] John 1:1, "In the beginning."

could get along without them. The citizens of Zahna[17] were once unwilling to support a pastor, and I said to the judge there: 'How is it that you are unwilling to maintain a pastor or clergyman while you keep a herder of sheep? You must give your shepherd whatever he wants.' The judge replied, 'Yes, dear doctor, we cannot well get along without him.' You see what they were concerned about: only their bellies! They love whatever produces something for their bellies and nothing else."

[17] A village near Wittenberg.

IX

Counsel in Questions of Marriage and Sex

TO JOHN LUTHER. November 21, 1521

As Luther wrote to his friend Nicholas Gerbel on November 1, 1521, he was troubled by daily reports of the monstrous consequences of enforced celibacy which were coming to his attention.[1] And when monks in Wittenberg began to leave the monastery, he decided to write a book which would at once defend those who abandoned their vows of chastity and attack the institution of monasticism and sacerdotal celibacy. These were the circumstances that led him to write his work On Monastic Vows, *which was probably published in February, 1522. Several months before publication he wrote a dedicatory epistle, addressed to his father, in which he rehearsed his own experiences by way of illustration. Since the letter was written in Latin, it was intended less for Luther's father than for the monks, nuns, and priests who would read it.* [Text in Latin; *WA*, VIII, 564-576.]

To John Luther, my father: greetings in Christ.

Beloved Father:

I have decided to dedicate this book to you, not to make your name famous in the world, nor that we might glory in the flesh contrary to the teaching of Saint Paul,[2] but that I might seize the occasion that has opportunely been offered by our relation to each other to explain to pious readers, in a short preface, the purpose and argument of this book and to illustrate it with an example.

To begin at the beginning, I wish you to know that your son has got so far as to be fully persuaded that there is nothing holier, nothing more important, and nothing more scrupulously to be observed than God's commandment. But here you will say, "Have you been so unfortunate as ever to have doubted this,

---

[1] *WA*, *Br*, II, 397. [2] Cf. Gal. 6:13.

and have you only now learned that this is so?" Unfortunate indeed, for not only have I doubted it, but I had no idea that it was so, and if you will permit me, I am ready to show you that this ignorance was common to both of us.

About sixteen years have now passed since I became a monk,[3] without your knowledge and against your will. In your fatherly love you were fearful about my weakness because I was still a young man, having just entered my twenty-second year; that is, to use Augustine's words, I was still "clothed in hot youth,"[4] and you had learned from numerous examples that this way of life turned out unhappily for some. You were determined to tie me down with an honorable and wealthy marriage. This fear troubled you, and for a time your indignation against me was implacable. Your friends tried in vain to persuade you that if you wished to offer something to God, you ought to give him your dearest and your best. The Lord was meanwhile dinning in your ears that verse of the psalm, "The Lord knoweth the thoughts of man, that they are vanity,"[5] but you were deaf to it. At last you desisted and bowed to the will of God, but your fears for me were never laid aside. For you remember that unforgettable scene when, after we were reconciled and you were talking with me, I told you that I had been called by terrors from heaven and that I did not become a monk of my own free will and accord, still less to gain any gratification of the flesh, but that, blocked by the terror and the agony of sudden death, I took a forced and necessary vow, and then you said, "Let us hope it was not an illusion and a deception." That word penetrated to the depths of my soul and stayed there, as if God had spoken by your lips, though I hardened my heart as much as I could against you and your word. You said something else too. When in filial confidence I upbraided you for your wrath, you suddenly retorted with a reply so fitting and so much to the point that I have hardly ever in all my life heard any man say anything that struck me so forcibly and stuck to me so long. "Have you not also heard," you said, "that parents are to be obeyed?" But I was so sure of my own righteousness that I heard only the words of a man and had very little regard for them, though in my heart I could not despise what you said.

See, now, whether you too were not unaware that the commands of God are to be put before all things. If you had known that I was then in your power, would you not have used your

3 Luther entered the Augustinian monastery in Erfurt on July 12, 1505.
4 Augustine, *Confessions*, II, iii.   5 Ps. 94:11.

paternal authority to take me out of the cowl? On the other hand, if I had known it, I would never have attempted to become a monk without your knowledge and consent even though I had had to die many deaths. For my vow was not worth a fig since by taking it I withdrew myself from the authority of my father and the intent of God's commandment. Indeed, it was a wicked vow and demonstrably not of God, both because it was a sin against your authority and because it was not spontaneous and voluntary. In short, it was taken in accordance with the doctrines of men and the superstition of hypocrites, which God has not commanded. But behold how much good God (whose mercies are without number and whose wisdom is without end)[6] has made to come out of all these errors and sins! Would you not rather have lost a hundred sons than not have seen this good?

It seems to me that Satan must have foreseen from my childhood some intimation of what he now suffers at my hands and that he has therefore raged against me with incredible stratagems in order to destroy or hinder me. Consequently I have often wondered whether I was the only man in the world whom he sought. But it was the Lord's will (as I now see) that I should become acquainted with the wisdom of the schools and the sanctity of the monasteries on the basis of personal and reliable experience (that is, through many sins and impieties) in order that wicked men might not have a chance, when I became their adversary, to boast that I condemned things I knew nothing about. So I lived as a monk—not without sin, it is true, but without reproach, for in the kingdom of the pope impiety and sacrilege pass for the greatest piety and are by no means made an object of reproach.

What do you think now? Will you still take me out of the cloister? You are still my father, I am still your son, and all my vows are worthless. On your side is the authority of God, on my side is human presumption. For that continence of which they boast with puffed up cheeks is valueless without obedience to God's commands. Continence is not commanded, but obedience is. Yet the mad and foolish papists will not suffer anything to be considered the equal of continence and virginity. These they are constantly talking about with such prodigious lies that their very craze for lying and the greatness of their ignorance, singly or together, ought to cast suspicion on everything they do or think.

6 Cf. Ps. 147:5.

What kind of intelligence do they show when they distort these words of the wise man, "There is no price worthy of a continent soul,"[7] to mean that virginity and continence are to be preferred to everything else and [that vows of celibacy] cannot be commuted or dispensed from? A Jew wrote these words to Jews, among whom virginity and continence were condemned, and he was writing about a chaste wife. In like manner they also apply to virgins that eulogy of a modest wife, "This is she which hath not known the sinful bed."[8] In a word, although the Scriptures do not laud virginity, but only give it approval, these men, who are so ready to inflame men's souls for a life that endangers their salvation, dress it out in borrowed feathers by applying to it the praises that the Scriptures bestow on the purity of married life.

But is there nothing that can bear comparison with an obedient mind? It is plain that there is nothing that can bear comparison with a continent mind (that is, with a chaste wife), not only because it is commanded by God, but also because, as the common proverb has it, there is nothing among men that is more desirable than a chaste wife. But these faithful interpreters of Scripture apply what is said about the continence that is commanded to the continence that is not commanded, and then they make a mere human comparison the measure of God's judgment. Hence they grant dispensations from everything, even from the obedience we owe to God. But they grant no dispensations from continence, even from that forbidden continence which is undertaken against parental authority. O worthy and truly papistical little doctors and teachers! Virginity and chastity are to be praised, but in such wise that by their very greatness men are frightened off from them rather than attracted to them. This was Christ's way. When the disciples lauded continence and said, "If the case of a man be so with his wife, it is not good to marry,"[9] he at once disabused their minds of that idea and said, "All men cannot receive this saying."[10] The saying must be received, but it was his will that only a few should understand it.

But let us come back to you, my dear father. I ask again, will you still take me out of the cloister? Lest you should boast of doing so, the Lord has anticipated you and taken me out. What difference does it make whether I retain or lay aside the habit and the tonsure? Do the cowl and tonsure make

---

[7] Ecclus. 26:15.   [8] Cf. Wis. of Sol. 3:13.
[9] Matt. 19:10.   [10] Matt. 19:11.

the monk? "All things are yours, but ye are Christ's,"[11] says Paul. Shall I belong to the cowl, or shall not the cowl rather belong to me? My conscience is free, and this is the most complete liberty. Therefore, I am still a monk and yet not a monk. I am a new creature, not of the pope, but of Christ. For the pope also has creatures and is a creator of puppets and straw men (that is, idols and masks like himself), and I was once one of them, seduced by the various usages of words by which even the wise man[12] confesses that he was brought into danger of death, but was delivered by God's grace.

But am I not robbing you again of your right and authority? Your authority over me remains undisturbed so far as monastic life is concerned, but this life is nothing to me, as I have said. Nevertheless, He who has taken me out of the cloister has an authority over me that is greater than yours, and you see that he has placed me, not in the false service of the monasteries, but in the true service of God, for who can doubt that I am in the ministry of the Word? It is plain that the authority of parents must yield to this service, for Christ says, "He that loveth father or mother more than me is not worthy of me."[13] This saying does not destroy the authority of parents, for the apostle often insists that children obey their parents,[14] but if the authority of parents conflicts with the authority and calling of Christ, then Christ's authority alone must reign.

Consequently (so I am now persuaded) I could not refuse to obey you without peril to my conscience unless the ministry of the Word had been joined to my monastic profession. That is what I meant when I said that neither you nor I realized before that the commands of God must be put before everything else. But very nearly the whole world is now laboring in this same ignorance, for under the papal abomination error rules, as Paul also predicted when he said that men would be disobedient to parents.[15] This exactly fits the monks and priests, especially those who under the appearance of piety and the guise of serving God withdraw themselves from the authority of their parents, as though there were any other service of God except the keeping of his Commandments, which include obedience to parents.

I send you this book, then, that you may see by what signs and wonders Christ has released me from the monastic vow

[11] I Cor. 3:22, 23.   [12] Cf. Ecclus. 34:12, 13.
[13] Matt. 10:37.   [14] Cf. Eph. 6:1; Col. 3:20.
[15] Cf. II Tim. 3:2.

and granted me such liberty that although he has made me the servant of all men, I am nevertheless subject to no one save to him alone. He is himself (to use customary terms) my immediate bishop, abbot, prior, lord, father, and master. I know no other. Thus I hope that he has taken from you one son in order that through me he may begin to help the sons of many others. You ought not only to endure this willingly, but you ought to rejoice with exceeding joy, and I am sure that this is what you will do. What if the pope slay me or condemn me to the depths of hell? After he has slain me he will not raise me up again to slay me a second and a third time. I am willing to be condemned, and I have no desire to be absolved. I trust that the day is at hand when that kingdom of abomination and perdition will be destroyed. Would that we were worthy to be burned or slain by him before that time so that our blood might cry out against him all the more and hasten the day of his judgment! But if we are not worthy to bear testimony with our blood, then let us at least pray and implore mercy that we may testify with our life and with our voice that Jesus Christ alone is the Lord our God who is blessed forever. Amen.

Herewith I bid farewell to you, my dear father. Greet my mother, your Margaret, and our whole family in Christ.

Your son,

The year 1521.   Martin Luther.

TO JOHN SCHOTT. May, 1524

When Luther reached Worms in 1521 to defend himself and his cause before the emperor and the diet, the Saxon nobleman John Schott escorted him to his lodgings. Now the same nobleman had called Luther's attention to a case in which a father had compelled his child to marry someone against the child's will. This provides Luther with the occasion for publishing the following open letter in which he discusses the mutual duties and responsibilities of parents and children. [Text in German; WA, XV, 155-169.]

To the honorable and esteemed John Schott, knight, etc., my dear sir and friend: grace and peace in Christ, our Lord and Saviour.

Honored, dear Sir and Friend:

When I began to write about married life I was afraid that what has occurred would happen, namely, that I would have

LETTERS OF SPIRITUAL COUNSEL

more trouble on this account than with all the rest of my work.[16] If there were no other sign that marriage is a divine estate, this would be demonstrated sufficiently by the fact that the prince of this world, the devil, fights against it in so many ways and resists it hand and foot and with all his powers with the consequence that whoring does not diminish but increases.

I have before written that such obedience to parents is required that a child should not become engaged or be married without parental knowledge and consent, and if this occurs the parents have the power to dissolve the relationship. Now, however, parents are overdoing this and are beginning willfully to hinder and prevent their children from marrying or, as you have recently reported an example to me, to compel their children to take this or that person in marriage without their being attracted to them by any liking or love. Accordingly I feel constrained to publish my opinion and counsel here once again for the benefit of those who may wish to be guided and helped thereby. Herewith I commit you to God's gracious keeping. Amen.

1. Parents Have No Right or Power to Compel Their Children to Marry

To hinder or forbid marriage and to compel or urge marriage are two quite different things. Although parents have the right and power in the first instance—namely, to forbid marriage—it does not follow that they have the power to compel their children to marry. It is more tolerable to obstruct and block the love which two persons have for each other than to force together two persons who have neither liking nor love for each other. In the first case there is pain for a short time, while in the second it is to be feared that there will be an eternal hell and a lifetime of tragedy. Saint Paul says in II Corinthians that the greatest power (namely, to preach the gospel and govern souls) which God has given was given not to destroy but to save.[17] How much less will power be given to parents or to anybody else in order to destroy rather than save? Accordingly it is certain that parental power is so measured and limited that it may not harm or destroy a child, and especially not his soul. If, therefore, a father compels his child to marry somebody for

---

[16] So in Luther's introduction to *Vom ehelichen Leben* (1522), in *WA*, XII, 275–304.
[17] II Cor. 10:3.

whom the child has neither liking nor love, he exceeds and over-
steps his power and the father becomes a tyrant who uses his
power not to help (for which God has given it to him) but to
destroy (for which he takes the power upon himself without God
and even against God).

The same is true when a father prevents his child from
marrying or neglects him with the intention that he should not
marry, which happens in the case of stepfathers in their attitude
toward children or of guardians in their attitude toward
orphans, when greed for the child's property is stronger than
consideration for the child's need. In such a case the child is
indeed free and may act as if his father or guardian were dead.
He may consider his own best interests, become engaged in
God's name, and take care of himself as best he can. However,
this is to be done only after the child has sought the father's
consent, or asked somebody else to plead for consent, in order
that it may be certain that the father or guardian is unwilling
or intends forever to postpone marriage with vain promises. In
such an instance the father surrenders his responsibility and
power and places the child in peril for his honor or soul. It is
his own fault that he is not asked for his consent because he is
not concerned about his child's honor and soul, and it is just.
This is especially applicable to relatives who are even now refusing to help poor nuns to save their honor and who do not
inquire about the nuns' souls and honor. In these cases it is
enough to inform the relatives and then proceed at once and
in God's name to marry, no matter whether the relatives become angry or are pleased about it.

The biggest problem in this whole matter is this: Is a child
obliged to be obedient to a father who compels him to marry
somebody he does not want to marry? It is easy enough to
understand and conclude that a father who does this is unjust
and acts like a devil or tyrant and not like a father, but should
the child suffer such injustice and improper compulsion and
obey such a tyrant? Here we are confronted by the open and
plain command of Christ in Matt., ch. 5: "Resist not evil.
Whosoever shall compel thee to go a mile, go with him twain.
Whosoever shall smite thee on thy right cheek, turn to him the
other also, and if any man take away thy coat, let him have thy
cloak also."[18] From this it is to be concluded that a child should
and must accept and obey such injustice as a tyrannical and
unfatherly father imposes on him.

[18] Matt. 5:39–41.

I conclude, therefore, that in the case of Christians the matter is quickly settled. A true Christian who is an adherent of the gospel will not refuse to enter such an enforced marriage because he is ready to suffer injustice and violence, no matter whether it touches his body, goods, or honor, be it for a short time, a long time, or forever, as God wills, and he would act like a person who has fallen into the hands of the Turk or some other enemy and is compelled to accept whatever conditions the Turk or his enemy imposes on him, whether he is put into prison or shackled to a galley. We have an excellent example of this in the holy patriarch Jacob, upon whom Leah was forced unjustly and against his will, and yet he kept her although he was not obliged to do so in the sight of men even if he had unknowingly cohabited with her. In spite of all this he suffered and endured this injustice and took her against his will.[19]

But where are such Christians to be found? And if there are Christians, where are those to be found who are as strong as Jacob and who have the heart to do what he did? It behooves me not to advise or teach anything, in this matter or any other, except it be Christian. Let him who cannot accept this counsel confess his weakness before God and pray for grace and help— just like a person who fears and shies away from death or some other suffering for God's sake because he feels that he is too weak to do what he ought. There is no getting around it; this word of Christ must stand: "Agree with thine adversary quickly, while thou art in the way with him."[20]

It will not help to offer as an excuse that such an enforced marriage will produce hate, envy, murder, and all sorts of misfortune, for Christ will immediately reply: "Let me take care of that. Why do you not trust me? Obey my commandment and I shall see to it that none of the things you fear will come to pass, but you will enjoy all happiness and good fortune. Will you transgress my commandment with its sure promise of blessedness on account of the uncertain possibility of future misfortune? Or will you do evil in the hope that good will come of it? Saint Paul condemns this in Rom., ch. 3.[21] And even if it were certain that there would be present and future unhappiness, should you on this account omit to keep my commandment when you are in duty bound to put your life and soul in jeopardy, both temporally and eternally, for my sake?"

However, I should give this advice to weak Christians who are unable to keep this commandment of Christ: Let some good

[19] Cf. Gen. 29:23.   [20] Matt. 5:25.   [21] Cf. Rom. 3:8.

friends petition the prince, burgomaster, or other governing authority to bring it about that such a father's outrageous injustice and devilish power is curbed, the child is rescued from his power, and the father is compelled to make a proper use of his parental authority. For although a Christian should suffer injustice, the secular government is also obligated to punish and prevent injustice and to protect and administer justice.

If the government is derelict in the performance of its duty or is tyrannical, the last resort would be for the child to forsake father and state and flee to another country. So in former times some weak Christians fled before tyrants into the wilderness. So the prophet Uriah fled before King Jeroboam into Egypt, and the hundred prophets, including Elijah himself, before Queen Jezebel.[22]

I know no other advice to give to a Christian than these three things. As far as non-Christians are concerned, I leave them to do what they can and what civil law allows.

2. A Child Should Not Become Engaged or Be Married Without the Knowledge and Consent of His Parents

Although I have discussed this in my postil,[23] I must here repeat what I have written before. The Fourth Commandment stands strong and firm here: "Thou shalt honor and obey thy father and mother."[24] Nowhere in all the Scriptures do we read an example of two children entering into an engagement of themselves. It is always written of the parents, "Take wives for your sons, and give your daughters to husbands,"[25] and Moses wrote, "If he have betrothed her unto his son,"[26] etc. In like manner Isaac and Jacob took wives as their fathers commanded them.[27] This is the origin of the universal custom that marriages are celebrated publicly and households are established with feasting and rejoicing. Thereby secret unions are condemned and marriages are confirmed and honored with the knowledge and consent of relations on both sides. Not even Adam, the first bridegroom, took his bride Eve by himself, for the Scriptures expressly state that only after God brought her to him did he take her.[28]

---

22 Jer. 26:20, 21; I Kings 18:4; 19:2 ff.
23 In Luther's treatment of the Gospel for the Festival of the Three Kings
  (1521), in *WA*, VII, 238–245.   24 Cf. Ex. 20:12.
25 Jer. 29:6.   26 Ex. 21:9.
27 Cf. Gen. 24:3 ff.; 28:1 ff.   28 Cf. Gen. 2:22, 23.

All of this pertains only to parents who act paternally toward their child, as I have said above. If they do not act so, they are to be treated as if they were not parents or were dead, and their child is free to become engaged and to marry whomever he pleases. They do not act in paternal fashion if they observe that a child has grown up and is fitted for marriage and inclined to marry and yet do not encourage or help the child to marry but rather postpone the matter or urge and compel the child to live in celibacy, or spiritually, as noblemen have hitherto done in the case of their daughters whom they shut up in monastic houses.

Parents should know that human beings are created for marriage and to bear offspring, just as a tree is created to bear apples or pears, unless by a special grace and miracle God alters or impedes the course of nature. Accordingly parents owe it to their children to help them get married and remove them from the peril of unchastity. If they do not do so, they are no longer parents, and a child of theirs is obliged to engage himself (first, however, informing the parents or reporting their dereliction), to remove himself from the peril of unchastity, and to enter the estate for which he was created, no matter whether it pleases father, mother, friends, or foes.

If things go so far that a child is not only engaged but also becomes involved in clandestine cohabitation, it is proper that the couple be allowed to remain together and that parental authority be held in abeyance. To be sure, according to the law of Moses, God has reserved the child for the father in such a case, for it is written in Ex., ch. 22: "If a man entice a maid that is not betrothed, and lie with her, he shall surely endow her to be his wife. If her father utterly refuse to give her unto him, he shall pay money according to the dowry of virgins."[29] But at that time little weight was laid on virginity. Inasmuch as men in our day have an aversion toward marrying non-virgins and regard it as so disgraceful that the second part of this law of Moses, concerning paternal authority over a deflowered girl, is regarded as dangerous and damaging to such a child, only the first part of the law, which requires that he who deflowered her should keep her, remains in force.

If someone should claim that since a father has the power to prevent or break up his child's engagement and marriage, he also has power to forbid marriage and enforce celibacy, I would answer that this is not so. I have said above that a human being

[29] Ex. 22:16, 17.

is created, not by his father but by God, to eat, drink, procreate, sleep, and perform other works of nature which no man has the power to change. It is one thing, therefore, to prevent marriage with this or that person and quite another thing to forbid marriage altogether. A father may forbid his child to eat or drink this or that or to sleep here or there, but he cannot require his child to do without eating, drinking, and sleeping altogether. On the contrary, he is obliged to furnish food, drink, clothing, a place to sleep, and whatever else is necessary for the child and his best interests. If he does not do so, he is no father, and the child must and ought to provide for himself.

So the father has power to prevent his child from marrying this or that person, but he has no power to prevent his child from marrying at all. On the contrary, he owes it to his child to provide him with a good and suitable spouse or to see to it that he gets one. If the father does not do so, the child must and should provide for himself. On the other hand, the father may without sin waive his right and power and, after faithfully counseling and restraining the child, allow him to have his own way and marry whomever he will without parental consent. For there is no way of preventing wrong if good advice and faithful admonition are disregarded. So Isaac and Rebecca allowed their son Esau to do as he pleased and marry women of whom they disapproved.[30] In such a case the father has done his duty and fulfilled his paternal responsibility without resorting to violence. God will in his time discover and punish the child's disobedience and temerity.

The long and short of the matter is that these things happen according to either Christian or human law. They happen in Christian fashion when there is mutual consent and agreement, when the father does not give his child in marriage without the will and knowledge of the child. So it is written in Gen., ch. 24, that Rebecca was first asked and gave her word and consent before she became Isaac's wife.[31] On the other hand, a child should not promise to marry anybody without the knowledge and consent of his father. However, if the letter of the law and human right are followed, the father may give his child in marriage and the child is obliged to obey, the father has power to break a promise of marriage which his child has made, and the child does not have the right to become engaged behind his father's back. If the father for his part wishes to act in a Christian way, he may waive his right, and let his child proceed in

30 Cf. Gen. 26:34, 35.   31 Cf. Gen. 24:57 ff.

accordance with his disobedience and temerity after the father's conscience is relieved by his paternal restraint, warning, and advice, and the burden has been placed on the child's conscience. Nevertheless, many a patriarch has at times endured more disobedience than this at the hands of his children without sacrificing his own will and the purpose of God.

If things happen in a way that is neither human nor Christian, but devilish—for example, if a father forces marriage on a child who has no heart for it—let the child act as he would if he had been captured by the Turk and was obliged to live according to his enemy's pleasure, or, if he can, let him escape, as I have suggested.

This will have to suffice for an open letter at this time. Perhaps the situation will itself bring out more clearly how one is to act in terms of the law and not merely in terms of the gospel.

Martin Luther.

TO THREE NUNS. August 6, 1524

During the years 1523 and 1524 nuns were leaving various convents to return to the world. It is not known to whom the following letter was addressed, but the advice that Luther offered here was similar to that which he gave to monks and nuns on other occasions, both before and after. [Text in German; WA, Br, III, 326-328.]

Grace and peace in Christ Jesus, our Saviour.

Dear Sisters:

I have now and again received your letters[32] and have gathered from them what is on your hearts. I should long since have replied if a courier had been available and I had had an opportunity, for I am very much occupied with other matters.

Have you thoroughly understood that there are two grounds for abandoning convent life and monastic vows?

The first exists when human laws and monastic works are imposed by force, are not assumed voluntarily, and become burdensome to conscience. Under such circumstances one should flee and let the convent and everything connected with it go. If, therefore, it is the case with you that monastic works were not undertaken of your own free will but were forced upon your conscience, call upon your relatives to help you get out and, if the secular authorities allow it, to provide for you in their homes or elsewhere. If your relatives or parents are un-

[32] Not extant.

willing, let some other good people help you to depart, no matter whether this causes your parents to be angry, die, or rejoice. For God's will and the soul's salvation should come first, since Christ says, "He that loveth father or mother more than me is not worthy of me."[33] But if the sisters grant you liberty in the convent and at least allow you to read or hear the Word of God, you may remain with them and perform and observe such convent duties as spinning, cooking, and the like, so long as you do not put your trust in these works.

The other ground is the flesh. Although women are ashamed to acknowledge this, Scriptures and experience teach us that there is only one in several thousands to whom God gives the gift to live chastely in a state of virginity. A woman does not have complete mastery over herself. God so created her body that she should be with a man and bear and raise children. The words of Gen., ch. 1, clearly state this,[34] and the members of her body sufficiently show that God himself formed her for this purpose. Just as eating, drinking, waking, and sleeping are appointed by God to be natural, so God also wills that it be natural for a man and a woman to live together in matrimony. This is enough, therefore, and no woman need be ashamed of that for which God has created and fashioned her, and if she feels that she does not possess that high and rare gift,[35] she may leave the convent and do that for which she is adapted by nature.

All these things you will abundantly read and sufficiently learn if you come out and hear good sermons. I have proved and substantiated these things again and again in the book on monastic vows,[36] in the tract on rejecting the doctrines of men,[37] in the treatise on the estate of matrimony,[38] and in the postil.[39] If you read these, you will find adequate instruction on all points, be it on confession or something else. It would take too long to repeat everything here, nor is it necessary to do so, for I suspect that you will be leaving the convent, as you threatened to do in your first letter, whether you are affected by both or by only one of these grounds. If it should come to pass that the convent introduces real freedom, those who have the gift and a

[33] Matt. 10:37.   [34] Gen. 1:27, 28.   [35] That is, the gift of celibacy.
[36] *De votis monasticis* (1521), in *WA*, VIII, 564–669.
[37] *Von Menschenlehren zu meiden* (1522), in *WA*, X[ii], 93–158; English translation in *Works of Martin Luther*, Philadelphia ed., II, 427–455.
[38] *Sermon von dem ehelichen Stand* (1519), in *WA*, II, 162–171, or *Vom ehelichen Leben* (1522), in *WA*, X[ii], 267–304.
[39] *Kirchenpostille, Weihnachtspostille* (1522), in *WA*, X[i], 1–739.

liking for that life may enter or return. In just this way the town council of Berne, in Switzerland, has opened the renowned convent of Königsfeld,[40] and is allowing girls, who so choose, to leave, remain, or enter at will, giving back to those who leave what they brought with them when they entered.

Herewith I commit you to God's keeping and ask you to pray for me.

The day of Sixtus, the Martyr, 1524.   Martin Luther.

A friendly letter to be delivered to the three nuns, my dear sisters in Christ.

TO WOLFGANG REISSENBUSCH. March 27, 1525

An early graduate of the university in Wittenberg (1503), Wolfgang Reissenbusch was preceptor in the monastery of St. Anthony in Lichtenberg, Saxony. He had consulted Luther about setting aside his vow of celibacy in order to marry and was apparently familiar with some of Luther's writings on the subject.[41] Yet he hesitated to take the serious step he had been contemplating, and the following letter of Luther was intended to encourage him to proceed with his plan. On April 26, a month after the letter was written, he married Anna Herzog, daughter of a poor tailor's widow in Torgau. Less than two months later, on June 13, Luther himself married Catherine von Bora. Meanwhile the letter, probably intended by Luther as an open letter to encourage others, was printed in Wittenberg. [Text in German; WA, XVIII, 270-278.]

God's grace and peace in Christ.

Reverend and esteemed Sir:

I am moved by several good friends and also by the esteem in which I hold you to write this letter on the estate of matrimony. I have often spoken to you about it and have observed that you are not only suited for and inclined toward marriage but are also forced and compelled to it by God himself, who created you therefor.

I do not think that you should be kept from it by the rule of your order or by a vow, for you should be fully convinced that

---

[40] The decision was made in Berne on June 3, 1524.

[41] For example, *Wider den falsch genannten geistlichen Stand* (1522), in *WA*, X[ii], 93-158; *Vom ehelichen Leben* (1522), in *WA*, X[ii], 267-304; *Dass Jungfrauen Klöster göttlich verlassen mögen* (1523), in *WA*, XI, 387-400; *An die Herrn deutsches Ordens, dass sie falsche Keuschheit meiden* (1523), in *WA*, XII, 228-244, English translation in *Works of Martin Luther*, III, 403-428.

no vow can bind you or be valid except under two conditions.

First, the vow must be possible of fulfillment and within our power to perform. For who will vow an impossible thing? Or who will demand it? All vows are therefore described in the Scriptures in terms that are within our power, such as to give God cattle, sheep, houses, land, and so on. Now, chastity is not in our power, as little as are God's other wonders and graces. But we are all made for marriage, as our bodies show and as the Scriptures state in Gen., ch. 2: "It is not good that man should be alone; I will make him a help meet for him."[42]

Whoever, therefore, considers himself a man and believes himself to be included in this general term should hear what God, his Creator, here says and decrees for him: he does not wish man to be alone but desires that he should multiply, and so he makes him a helpmeet to be with him and help him so that he may not be alone. This is the Word of God, through whose power procreative seed is planted in man's body and a natural, ardent desire for woman is kindled and kept alive. This cannot be restrained either by vows or by laws. For it is God's law and doing. Let him who will be alone abandon the name of man and prove or make himself an angel or spirit, for God does not grant or allow such a condition to a man. Accordingly we do well when we sing of holy virgins in such a way as to indicate that they lived lives that were angelic rather than human and that they were enabled to live in the flesh and yet without the flesh by a special grace of God. Our bodies are in great part the flesh of women, for by them we were conceived, developed, borne, suckled, and nourished, and so it is quite impossible to keep entirely apart from them. This is in accord with the Word of God. He has caused it to be so and wishes it so. Even the impotent, as we know, are full of natural desire. Indeed, the more impotent they are, the more they desire to be with women, which is altogether natural, for we always desire most what we can least have.

Therefore, whoever will live alone undertakes an impossible task and takes it upon himself to run counter to God's Word and the nature that God has given and preserves in him. The outcome is in keeping with the attempt; such persons revel in whoredom and all sorts of uncleanness of the flesh until they are drowned in their own vices and driven to despair. For this reason such a vow against God's Word and against nature, being impossible, is null and void. And God also condemns it,

[42] Gen. 2:18. Luther cites the verse first in Latin and then in German.

L.L.S.C.—18

just as if somebody should vow to be God's mother or to make a heaven.

Secondly, to be valid a vow must not be against God and the Christian faith. Everything that relies on works and not on God's grace is against God and the Christian faith; as it is written in Heb., ch. 12, "The heart must be established with grace, not with meats"[43]—that is, not with works and laws that pertain to food, drink, and the like. Of this sort are all monastic vows; they establish hearts and consciences on works and not on grace, and by this reliance on works men deny Christ and lose faith.

No doubt, reverend sir, you are convinced of what I write and are not hindered by such scruples, but I fancy that human fear and timidity stand in your way. It is said that it takes a bold man to venture to take a wife. What you need above all else, then, is to be encouraged, admonished, urged, incited, and made bold. Why should you delay, my dear and reverend sir, and continue to weigh the matter in your mind? It must, should, and will happen in any case. Stop thinking about it and go to it right merrily. Your body demands it. God wills it and drives you to it. There is nothing that you can do about it.

Besides, your marriage would be an excellent, noble example to help many who are hesitant to broaden their paths and give themselves more scope, and many others may escape the dangers of the flesh and follow you. What does it matter if people say, "So the Lichtenberg preceptor has taken a wife!" Would it not be a great honor and Christian virtue if you, along with others, became an object of reproach? Did not Christ become a reproach for all of us? Do I say reproach? Only those who are ignorant or mad think marriage a reproach; it is those who do not take offense at whoredom who make a mockery of marriage and the Word and work of God. If it is a shame to take a wife, why is it not a shame to eat and drink inasmuch as we have equal need of both and God wills both?

Why should I write more? It is a pity that men should be so stupid as to wonder that a man takes a wife, or to be ashamed of it, when no one wonders at his eating and drinking. Why should this necessity, which is based on human nature, be an object of doubt and wonder? It is best to comply with all our senses as soon as possible and give ourselves to God's Word and work in whatever he wishes us to do, for if we remain under

43 Heb. 13:9.

God's displeasure and wrath, he will punish us by giving us over to sin and hell.

Let us not try to fly higher and be better than Abraham, David, Isaiah, Peter, Paul, and all the patriarchs, prophets, and apostles, as well as many holy martyrs and bishops, all of whom knew that they were created by God as men, were not ashamed to be and be thought men, conducted themselves accordingly, and did not remain alone. Whoever is ashamed of marriage is also ashamed of being a man or being thought a man, or else he thinks that he can make himself better than God made him. Adam's children are and remain men, and hence they should and must let men be begotten by them.

Good God, we see daily how much trouble it takes to remain in marriage and keep conjugal fidelity and yet we undertake to be chaste outside of marriage as if we were not men and had neither flesh nor blood! This is the work of the world's god, the devil, who slanders and shames marriage but lets adulterers, whores, and knaves remain in highest honor. Consequently it is the sensible thing to get married in order to defy and oppose him and his world and to assume and bear his reproaches for God's sake.

Reverend sir, I beg you to receive this faithful Christian counsel of mine in kindly fashion. Act on it quickly so that you may tempt God no longer. If you follow the leadings of God's grace and promise, you will see that you will thereby be honoring his Word and work, and he will honor and glorify you in return. One short hour of shame will be followed by years of honor. May our Lord Christ accompany this letter of mine with his grace in order that by his Spirit it may become a living and powerful force in your heart and bring forth fruit to the praise and honor of his name and Word. Amen.

Your Reverence's willing servant,
Monday after Laetare, 1525.   Martin Luther.

TO JOSEPH LEVIN METZSCH. December 9, 1526

About ten days before Luther wrote the following letter, he wrote one with similar contents to Landgrave Philip of Hesse.[44] *Since only a fragment of the earlier letter is extant, the present letter is here reproduced. The sentiment expressed in it is of special interest in view of the advice which later involved Luther in Philip's bigamy (see below). A graduate of Leipzig University, Joseph Levin Metzsch was an intimate*

[44] See *WA, Br,* IV, 140, 141.

friend of Prince George of Anhalt and was a petty lord residing in his Mylau castle. [Text in German; *WA, Br,* IV, 141, 142.]

To the honorable and esteemed Joseph Levin Metzsch, etc., my gracious lord and good friend: grace and peace.

Honored, esteemed, dear Lord and Friend:

With regard to your first question, whether a man may marry more than one wife, my answer is as follows: Unbelievers may do as they please, but Christian liberty should be so conditioned by love that everything contributes to the service of one's neighbor in so far as this can be done without violating conscience and denying faith. But now everybody is seeking such liberty as will serve and benefit himself without regard for his neighbor's needs and welfare, although Saint Paul says in I Cor., ch. 6, "All things are lawful unto me, but all things are not expedient,"[45] and, "Only use not liberty for an occasion to the flesh."[46] It is allowable to marry or to remain unmarried, but who wishes to do either with a good conscience unless there is necessity? And although the patriarchs were polygamous,[47] this example is not to be followed by Christians because there is no necessity for it, no benefit in it, and no special word of God commanding it. Moreover, great offense and disturbance would result therefrom. Consequently it is my opinion that a Christian is not free to marry several wives unless God commands him to go beyond the liberty which is conditioned by love.

Concerning the baptism of children, I have written at length in the postil[48] for the Sundays after Epiphany; let the fanatics[49] do as they please. It is altogether right that you should engage a preacher[50] for your people, that you should allow him to marry (for this is allowable, necessary, beneficial, and has God's Word to support it), and that you exercise complete power and authority over your subjects. Otherwise you should leave the matter in God's hands and let him decide whether preaching is to be risked or not.

Herewith I commit you to God's keeping. Amen.

Sunday after Saint Nicholas, 1526.   Martin Luther.

---

[45] I Cor. 6:12.   [46] Gal. 5:13.

[47] In the aforementioned letter to Philip of Hesse, Luther wrote: "Some of the old patriarchs had many wives, but they were forced to have them, as were Abraham and Jacob and afterward many kings who were required by the Mosaic Law to take the wives of their deceased relatives."   [48] In *WA,* XVIII, 18, 30.   [49] *Schwärmer.*

[50] Thomas Löscher was perhaps the man engaged.

TO STEPHEN ROTH. April 12, 1528

Stephen Roth had married Ursula Krüger in Wittenberg on May 11, 1524. When Roth entered upon his duties as notary in Zwickau on February 15, 1528, his wife refused to go with him. It is not clear whether she was unwilling to leave her relatives and native town, was dissatisfied with her husband's new position, or was concerned about her health. Whatever the case may have been, Luther was convinced that she had no adequate reason for not moving to Zwickau. She was willful and perverse, he thought, because her husband had spoiled her. Roth was naturally troubled by his wife's refusal and asked her to consult Luther. When she failed to do this, Luther wrote the following letter and had John Bugenhagen cosign it. Roth's wife moved to Zwickau shortly afterward. [Text in Latin; WA, Br, IV, 442, 443.]

Grace and peace in Christ, and authority over your wife!

My dear Stephen:

Your lord and mistress has not yet come to see me, and this her disobedience to you displeases me greatly. Indeed, I am beginning to be somewhat put out with you too, for by your softheartedness you have turned into tyranny that Christian service[51] which you owe her, and you have hitherto so encouraged her that it would seem to be your own fault that she now ventures to defy you in everything. Certainly when you saw that the fodder was making the ass insolent[52] (that is, that your wife was becoming unmanageable as a result of your indulgence and submissiveness), you should have remembered that you ought to obey God rather than your wife, and so you should not have allowed her to despise and trample underfoot that authority of the husband which is the glory of God,[53] as Saint Paul teaches. It is enough that you yield this glory of God to such an extent that you take on the form of a servant,[54] but when it is done away, wiped out, and reduced to nothing, this is going too far.

See to it, therefore, that you act the man. So bear with your wife's infirmity that you do not encourage her malice and that by your excessive submissiveness you do not give a dangerous example and dishonor the glory of God that is in you. It is easy to tell whether hers is infirmity or malice. Infirmity is to be

---

51 The reference is to assuming the form of a servant, mentioned below.
52 For this proverb, see Ernst Thiele, *Luthers Sprichwörtersammlung* (Weimar, 1900), 295, 296.   53 Cf. I Cor. 11:7.
54 Cf. Phil. 2:7.

borne; malice is to be counteracted. Infirmity carries with it a readiness to learn and to listen, at least once in twelve hours; malice is marked by obstinate resistance and persistence. When she observes that you mistake her malice for infirmity, there is no wonder that she gets worse. By your own fault you are now opening a window in this weaker vessel[55] through which Satan can enter at will and laugh at you, irritate you, and vex you in every way. .

You are an intelligent man, and the Lord will enable you to understand what I write. At the same time you will recognize how sincerely I wish you two to come to an agreement and Satan to be driven off. Farewell in Christ.

Martin Luther

Easter, 1528.   John Bugenhagen of Pomerania.

TO GEORGE SPALATIN. October 29, 1528

On the death in 1525 of Elector Frederick the Wise of Saxony, George Spalatin left the electoral court to become pastor in Altenburg, where he married Catherine Heydenreich shortly after. The canons of St. George, who made difficulties for Spalatin in other ways (see letter to Spalatin in Chapter XI), attacked him for abandoning the celibate life and declared that his previous vow made his marriage illegal. On this account, they said, he surrendered his right to a living. [Text in Latin; WA, Br, IV, 594, 595.]

To the esteemed brother in Christ, Master George Spalatin, very faithful servant of Christ: grace and peace in Christ.

My dear Spalatin:

You ought not to grieve because your marriage is called harlotry,[56] but you ought rather to rejoice since you know for certain that this way of life is approved by God, praised by the angels, and honored by all the saints. Now you have this additional seal that it is marked by the cross—namely, that it is evil spoken of by devils and wicked men and even by false brethren—a thing that usually happens to every work and word of God. See to it, then, that you do not regard the sacrilegious words that the wicked hurl against you to be anything else than precious jewels. To be sure, you are befouled by them in the world's eyes, but you are glorified in God's eyes, for you are aware that the world is not worthy to see the honor and glory of this work of God which you see and have. The same

---

[55] Cf. I Peter 3:7.   [56] By the canons in Altenburg.

may be said, and even more may be said, of your ministry. Away with the world and its prince! Away with their foolish, rash, blind, mad condemnations and calumnies! It is written, "The wicked shall be destroyed that he may not see the glory of God,"[57] but "the heavens declare the glory of God."[58] There is no doubt at all that the world belches up dishonor against God.

I do not understand what you write about the danger of your livelihood, for I do not believe that the priests of Bethaven[59] can make you any trouble. But whatever they may be, you now have the office of visitation and the special favor of the elector, who will not allow your living[60] to be taken from you. The Lord Jesus strengthen you with his Spirit and direct you in this episcopal work of yours.[60] Amen. Pray for me, I beg of you.

Yours,
Martin Luther.

Thursday after Saints Simon and Jude, 1528.

TO ELECTOR JOHN OF SAXONY. June 16, 1531

Luther here complained about the scandalous life of John Metzsch and also about a breach in the town walls of Wittenberg which resulted from a plan to reduce their height. Both of these matters were referred by the elector to several councilors, who were instructed to admonish Metzsch "to conduct himself decently and chastely in order that he might give a good example and not give occasion to strangers who study in or travel through Wittenberg to spread bad reports about the town and heap shame and dishonor on the gospel."[61] [Text in German; *WA, Br,* VI, 122-124.]

To my very gracious lord, Duke John, elector of Saxony (to be placed in His Grace's own hands): grace and peace in Christ.

Serene, highborn Prince, gracious Lord:

It is neither my right nor my desire to take a hand in the affairs of secular government or to cast reflections on Your Grace's officials. However, there are widespread and loud complaints, and I believe that Your Grace expects me to be loyal,

---

[57] Cf. Ecclus. 15:7.   [58] Ps. 19:1.
[59] The chapter of St. George in Altenburg.   [60] Words in Greek.
[61] For the elector's instructions to his councilors see G. Buchwald, "Lutherana," in *Archiv für Reformationsgeschichte,* XXV (Leipzig, 1928), 53–56.

as is altogether my duty. If things go wrong afterward, I do not wish it to be said that I kept silence to Your Grace's injury. I have repeatedly admonished Prefect John Metzsch in a kind and earnest fashion that he should leave off his whoring and his vicious relations with women. As a preacher I could not long endure his scandalous conduct or keep quiet about it. But in spite of everything he keeps right on, and he goes so far that everybody's mouth, nose, eyes, and ears are full of his doings. In fact, he has admitted to me privately that he cannot be without women. Accordingly I have refused for my part to have anything more to do with him and have privately forbidden him to receive the Sacrament. But he is tied so tight to the whores' pigtails that he shows few signs of fearing God. Inasmuch as I shall henceforth have to preach against him and condemn his behavior publicly, I humbly pray Your Grace that if it should come to Your Grace's attention that I have come into conflict with him on account of these things, Your Grace will remember what I am now writing. For a continuation of such offensive conduct would in time stop my mouth; it would also give others encouragement to vice. He may be a good soldier, but I do not wish him to protect me in an emergency unless he has some respect for God, who has hitherto protected us wonderfully without the drawing of a sword and who still preserves us.

There is also a second matter in which I desire to express my loyalty to Your Grace. With Metzsch and others I have talked in a friendly way about the breaches in the town wall, but they tell me that I am a writer, do not understand these matters, and ought to let them alone. Nevertheless, if things do not turn out as these master builders expect, no one can say that I have not warned Your Grace. For I know very well how carefully the gates have been guarded heretofore in order that the town might be closed in. But now there is a space of a hundred paces where the town stands wide open day and night. Pigs and all sorts of things run in. It is possible to see, walk, and shoot from the fields to the market place and from the market place to the fields, for the wall is broken down to the ground and there has been no attempt to rebuild it or put something in the breach. If this is as it should be, I am satisfied. I hope that Your Grace will graciously receive this information and give it some attention. It worries me because many honorable people have their sons here[62] and the times are perilous. Something might happen

62 As students in the university.

by God's providence which we would regret when it is too late
to do any good.

Metzsch is headstrong and is causing a great outcry against
himself. It would therefore be well for Your Grace to look into
the matter lest trouble arise. Good people are long-suffering,
but "too much bursts the bag," and it would be easy for a
spark to cause a fire among the impatient who are not content
to endure his swaggering, cursing, and tyranny. Thank God,
this is a good, peaceful, and law-abiding town, but oppression
and obstinacy may change things. People are not minded to
fear an official more than their prince.

I beg again that Your Grace may regard this letter as written
in a spirit of humble loyalty. I have been silent long enough in
a desire not to slander anybody. But unless I am out of my
senses, some people are doing as they please with Your Grace's
money and property. It may be that Your Grace knows all this,
but I wish to do my duty.

God strengthen and comfort Your Grace against all the wiles
of the evil one. Amen.

Your Grace's humble servant,

Friday after Saint Vitus, 1531.   Martin Luther.

TABLE TALK RECORDED BY ANTHONY
LAUTERBACH.[63] October 15, 1538

Inasmuch as he [John Metzsch] haughtily showed his contempt of God, the ministers of the Word, the university, and the
civil magistrates, and inasmuch as he undertook to do many
things against them although he had often been rebuked in
fraternal fashion by Martin Luther, the latter again[64] sent two
deacons[65] to him on November 15, 1538,[66] with a note containing these words, written in his own hand:

"Tell the prefect: First, that the absolution given him last
Sunday by the deacon, Master Fröschel, is null and void because he did not acknowledge his guilt. Secondly, that he
received the Sacrament in his sins, unrepentant. He must bear
this burden himself, not I. (These are harsh words, and he was
terrified by them.) Thirdly, if he wishes to be a Christian,
he must first be reconciled with us preachers, pastors, the

[63] Macaronic text; *WA, TR*, IV, No. 4073 b.
[64] According to a variant, "for the second time."
[65] Anthony Lauterbach and Sebastian Fröschel
[66] Probably should read: October 15.

university, and the town (for he has offended all of these by his tyranny) according to Christ's words in Matt., ch. 5, 'If thou bring thy gift to the altar,' etc.[67] If he is unwilling to do this humbly, I, in the pastor's stead,[68] am content to have him seek his salvation elsewhere, for I do not propose to bear his wickedness and be damned on account of his sins." This was the second admonition according to Matt., ch. 18, "If thy brother shall trespass against thee," etc.[69]

Excusing himself, he [Metzsch] replied to these things by saying that he was innocent and bore no one any hatred. But Dr. Martin Luther had previously, and now again, ordered that he should not receive the Sacrament [of the Altar] or assist at Baptism.[70]

In the same week Martin Luther accused a certain nobleman, Henry Rieder, to his face for being a great usurer and forbade his pastor to admit him to the Sacrament because he took thirty per cent interest a year. For such is the impiety of noblemen that they are without conscience and boast of their wickedness. One of them sired forty-three children in a year. Another said: "Is it not fair for him to take forty per cent interest a year? What good would his eyes be to him if he did not use them to see?"

TO ANTHONY RUDOLF. May 12, 1536

The recipient of this letter was steward of vineyards in Weimar. His son had been a student in Wittenberg since 1531 and had received his master's degree in 1535. At this time he was continuing his studies, and later he became co-rector of a school in Schneeberg, Saxony. Having fallen in love, he failed to secure parental consent for his marriage and asked Luther to write to his father in his behalf. [Text in German; WA, Br, VII, 408, 409.]

God's grace and peace.

Honored, prudent, dear Friend:

Your son Nicholas is attached in bonds of honorable love to a pious girl and wishes to avoid the dangers of passionate youth by marrying the girl according to divine institution. But he complains that in this case you have firmly and harshly opposed him, although it would be more proper for you, as his father, to

[67] Matt. 5:23.
[68] John Bugenhagen, the pastor, was absent from Wittenberg.
[69] Matt. 18:15.   [70] I.e., serve as a sponsor at Baptism.

encourage him to take this honorable step, and especially so since, as an obedient son, he has submissively asked and pleaded for your fatherly consent—just as, I take it, you yourself once sought the consent of your father.

Thank God, the situation is such in the world today that the estate of matrimony is held in honor. No one who really wishes to study and to make something of himself is prevented from doing so by marrying. Accordingly I request you (although you ought in all fairness to be requesting me) that you take a more fatherly attitude toward your son, which is your duty, and that you do not give him occasion to lead a dangerous life against his conscience. God can and will accomplish things in other ways than we think and plan. He has always done this, continues to do this, and will also do it in the future.

Herewith I commit you to God's keeping. Amen.

Friday after Jubilate, 1536.   Martin Luther, Doctor.

TABLE TALK RECORDED BY JEROME WELLER.[71]
About 1536

Dr. Martin [Luther] sighed and said: "Good God, what a bother these matrimonial cases are to us! It takes great effort and labor to get couples together. Afterward it requires even more pains to keep them together. The Fall of Adam so corrupted human nature that it is very fickle. It is as inconstant as quicksilver. Everything is wonderful when a married couple sits down to table together or goes to bed. If they sometimes murmur at each other, this is to be taken as incidental to marriage.

"Adam and Eve must have scolded each other roundly during their nine hundred years together.[72] Eve would have said, 'You ate the apple!' And Adam would have replied, 'But why did you give it to me?' There is no doubt that during their long life they encountered numberless evils as they sighed over their Fall. It must have been an extraordinary regime! And so Genesis is a remarkable book of wisdom and reason."

Someone remarked: "If a woman treated a man like this today, he would hardly forgive her." The doctor replied: "If she acted the fool, what could he do about it? Blessed, therefore, is the man who has a happy marriage, although this is a rare gift." Afterward the doctor added: "That man suffers martyrdom whose wife and maid do not know their way about in the

71 Macaronic text; WA, TR, II, No. 3675.   72 Cf. Gen. 5:5.

kitchen. It is a calamity of the first order from which many evils follow."[73]

TO JOHN WICKMANN. November 2, 1537

Among many letters of similar character, the following is reproduced as an illustration of Luther's recommendation in the case of a man who deserted his wife. It was addressed to a clergyman in Priessnitz, in Thuringia. [Text in German; *WA, Br,* VIII, 136.]

To the worthy John Wickmann, pastor in Priessnitz, my kind and good friend: grace and peace in Christ.

Dear Pastor:

Following is my answer in writing concerning the marriage case about which you have written to me. If the situation is such as you report, namely, that the widow's husband deserted her seven years ago and no one knows where he is, you should first ask the neighbors or the village magistrates, if they have any knowledge of the matter, which of the two is the guilty party. If, according to the testimony of neighbors, it appears that the woman is not to blame, let the pastor in Eisenberg post a public notice on the church door and do the same in your village, citing the man (or somebody else in his behalf) to appear within four weeks. If he does not appear, announce from the pulpit that the deserter has not appeared and that the woman is therefore free to marry again. Thereupon you may unite her in marriage with another man in God's name.

This is the way in which we do it in our churches,[74] although I should prefer to be done with these cases and have the princes take care of them. Accordingly I pray you to suggest to other pastors that they spare me, for I am so overburdened that I can hardly read or write a book. I cannot employ a secretary, for this would lead to a restoration of conditions such as existed in the papacy, and I cannot possibly do everything alone.

Herewith I commit you to God's keeping. Amen.

November 2, 1537.   Martin Luther, Doctor.

TO VALENTINE HAUSMANN. January 27, 1538

Although there is some uncertainty with respect to the addressee, this letter was probably addressed to Valentine Hausmann, the burgomaster

[73] The last two sentences from a variant text.   [74] In Saxony.

in Freiberg, Saxony. Nothing specific is known about the circumstance that called forth Luther's exhortation, but it is evident that Hausmann was contemplating separation from his wife on account of her conduct.
[Text in German; *WA, Br*, VIII, 192, 193.]

Grace and peace in Christ.

Honored, esteemed, dear, and good Friend:

Your dear brother and my especially good friend, Master Nicholas Hausmann, has informed me of the grave misfortune that has overtaken you on account of your wife. I am truly sorry to hear it, and I should like to give you the best advice, as your brother asked me to do, if I were acquainted with the details of your situation as the world sees them.

To speak in spiritual terms, however, you are aware that God has hitherto exalted you and blessed you with many rich gifts. Perhaps this would not be a good sign if it were not relieved by a particular misfortune which serves to humble you and compels you to acknowledge God and seek your comfort in him alone.

You know that according to papal law[75] you may not divorce your wife, and even if you did, you would not be free to marry again. On the other hand, if you were to separate from her according to our teaching (as it is called), everything may not turn out as you think because it appears as if God is tempting you and is testing your patience.

Accordingly I should suggest that, if she behaves uprightly in the future, you should not cast her off. She will have to submit to you henceforth, and you will commit no sin and will not burden your conscience by retaining her, for you will have acted in mercy rather than by the letter of the law. On the other hand, if you proceed strictly in terms of the law, much unhappiness may result and you may ultimately regret it, have a sense of guilt, and suffer heartache. Grace goes before the law, and too strict an adherence to the law will result in a loss of grace both in God's sight and in man's.

Our dear Lord Jesus Christ comfort you and continue to guide you for your own welfare. Amen.

Sunday after Saint Paul's Conversion, 1538.   Martin Luther.

[75] Canon law.

TABLE TALK RECORDED BY AN UNKNOWN
HAND.[76] February 1, 1539

On February 1, 1539, Dr. Martin [Luther] was occupied with a great deal of business and many letters. "Today," he said, "is an unpleasant day, for I have been occupied with letters.[77] This business deprives us of the time for study, reading, preaching, writing, and praying. Yet I am glad that the consistories have been established, especially on account of cases pertaining to marriage."

Then he discussed many things with Dr. [Monner of] Basel. He declared that there are numerous and various matrimonial cases that ought not to be judged by laws but by the circumstances and according to equity[78] and the judgment of a good man. "For," he said, "many parents, especially stepfathers, are unfair to their children and wish, without adequate cause, to prevent their marrying. Marriage should be encouraged in such cases by the judgment of the governing authority and the pastor. I myself have had to do this.

"In short, in the case of young people who are attached to each other by mutual love (which is the basis of marriage),[79] there should be no opposition without grave cause. The example of Samson[80] should be imitated, however, and children should inform their parents. This should be the procedure especially now that the gospel has free course and marriage is held in high esteem. When it was dishonored, as it was under the papacy, marriage was regulated not by equity[78] but by laws which conflicted with conscience. Then a bride could be given to one man and taken from another so that she was adjudged to be married to the first man, with whom she was not living, and to be in an adulterous relationship to the second, with whom she was living. In such cases, therefore, attention must be paid to consciences, and the circumstances must be considered according to equity[78] and the judgment of a good man rather than according to the strict application of rules, laws, etc."

---

[76] Macaronic text; *WA*, *TR*, IV, No. 4736.
[77] No letter written on this date is extant, but the case of John Schneidewein (see the letter below) was probably in Luther's mind.
[78] Greek, *epieikeia*: fair judgment based on the spirit rather than the letter of the law.
[79] *Qui est substantia matrimonii.*
[80] Cf. Judg. 14:2.

TO URSULA SCHNEIDEWEIN. June 4, 1539

John Schneidewein, later a professor of law, had been a student in Wittenberg since 1530. For almost ten years he had been living in Luther's house and had been eating at his table. Consequently the Reformer took a personal interest in him. Now twenty years old, John wished to marry Anna Düring, of Wittenberg. Since his father was dead, he sought his mother's permission. Her silence moved Luther to write to Mrs. Schneidewein in February, 1539. Receiving no answer, Luther now wrote again. In fact, he wrote a third time on July 10.[81] Still receiving no reply, he advised John to marry without parental consent, which he did on July 27. [Text in German; WA, Br, VIII, 453-455.]

To the honorable and virtuous lady, Ursula Schneidewein, widow of a citizen in Stolberg, my good and kind friend: grace and peace in Christ.

Honored, virtuous, dear Madam:

Some time ago I wrote to you that your son John is attached by a great love to an honorable girl here. Since I am sure that you have perceived what my opinion in the matter is, I hoped to receive a favorable reply from you. I too have become impatient with your obstructing your son's marriage, and this has moved me to write to you once again.

Because I too am fond of your son, I am unwilling to see his hope turn to ashes. The girl pleases him very much, her station in life is not unlike his, and she is, besides, a pious girl of an honorable family. Accordingly I believe that you have reason to be satisfied, especially because your son has submitted to you in filial obedience and has asked for this girl like Samson.[82] It therefore behooves you, as a loving mother, to give your consent.

As I have written before,[83] children should not become engaged without parental consent. But at the same time I also wrote that parents should not and can not rightly compel or prevent their children to please themselves. A son should not present his parents with a daughter without their consent. Nor should a father force a wife on his son. Parents and children should come to agreement. Otherwise the son's wife will become the father's daughter against the latter's will. And who

---

[81] The first letter is not extant. The third is reproduced in WA, Br, VIII, 492, 493.   [82] Cf. Judg. 14:2.

[83] See letter to John Schott, May, 1524, above.

knows how much happiness God intends to give your son by means of this girl—happiness of which he might otherwise be deprived—especially because the good girl has given him her promise, she is of a social class not unlike his, and her disappointment might lead to evil consequences.

In short, I pray you not to delay your consent any longer. Let the good fellow have peace of mind. And I cannot wait much longer. I shall have to act as my office requires.[84]

But I request that you keep this letter from your son John. He should not know about it until the matter is concluded, lest he become so desperate as to do something rash. For I love him, as he deserves to be loved on account of his virtue, and so I am unwilling to give him bad advice. Be a mother to him, therefore, and help to free him from the agony of having to proceed without your consent.

Herewith I commit you to God's keeping. Amen.

Wednesday after Trinity, 1539.   Martin Luther, Doctor.

TO JOHN FREDERICK OF SAXONY. June 10, 1540

In 1523, before he was nineteen years old, Philip of Hesse had married Christina, the daughter of Duke George of Albertine Saxony. Although he claimed in a memorandum brought to Wittenberg by Martin Bucer (1491-1551) that "he never had any love or desire for her on account of her form, fragrance, and manner,"[85] he had seven children by her. He also confessed that he "did not remain faithful in his marriage for more than three weeks" and "indulged in adultery and whoredom." In 1538 it became evident that he had contracted syphilis. After he had refrained from receiving the Sacrament for thirteen years on account of his manner of life, he was now conscience-stricken and hoped to solve his problem by taking a concubine after the widespread custom among rulers. Landgrave Philip of Hesse sent the theologian Martin Bucer to Wittenberg to secure approval, and a reluctant and labored approval was given in a statement prepared by Philip Melanchthon and signed by Luther and others.[86] What was intended as private counsel to a wounded conscience was divulged by the landgrave to others, and on March 4, 1540, he married Margaret von der Sale in a public ceremony. A scandal developed, and when inquiries were made of the elector of Saxony by the Albertine Saxon court in Dresden, the elector in turn consulted Luther

---

[84] In his letter of July 10, 1539, Luther wrote, "If the parents are unwilling, the pastor must be willing [to consent to the marriage]."

[85] *WA, Br,* VIII, 631.

[86] Dated Dec. 10, 1539 (*WA, Br,* VIII, 638-644).

*and the following explanation was offered by the Reformer. In arriving
at a just estimate with respect to this complicated and unsavory affair, it
is important to observe that Luther's opinion was in the nature of private
counsel given under the seal of confession, that it was then customary to
allow to rulers privileges that were not accorded to other people, and that
legal provision for divorce was still uncertain and fluid.* [Text in
German; *WA, Br,* IX, 131-135.]

Serene, highborn Elector, gracious Lord:

I have learned that Your Grace has been unfairly molested
by the court in Dresden with reference to the landgrave's case.
Your Grace will know how to deal with those shrewd men of
Meissen.[87] As far as the case is concerned, Master Philip
[Melanchthon] and I were unwilling to report it to you because
it was a confidential matter and it is proper to keep secret both
what is said by way of confession and what is recommended by
way of counsel. If the landgrave had not disclosed this confession and counsel, the unpleasantness and gossip would not
have occurred.

I shall still say that if such a case were to come before me
today, I should not know how to give any other counsel than
that which I gave. I shall not conceal this, even if it is afterward
made public, notwithstanding I am not so clever as those men
of Meissen would have us think they are.

This was the situation at that time: Martin Bucer brought a
certified statement which set forth that the landgrave was unable to remain chaste on account of certain defects in his wife.
Accordingly he had lived so and so, which was not good,
especially for an Evangelical, and indeed one of the most
prominent Evangelical princes. He swore before God and on
his conscience that he was unable to avoid such vice unless he
was permitted to take another wife. This account of his life and
purpose shocked us in view of the vicious scandal that would
follow and we begged His Grace not to do it. We were then told
that he was unable to refrain and would carry out his intention
in spite of us by appealing to the emperor or pope. To prevent
this we humbly requested him, if he insisted on doing it or (as
he said) was unable to do otherwise before God and his conscience, at least to do it secretly because he was constrained by
his need, for it could not be defended in public and under
imperial law. We were promised that he would do so. Afterward we made an effort to help as much as we could to justify

[87] Members of the court of the Duke of Saxony.

it before God with examples of Abraham, etc.[88] All this took place and was negotiated under seal of confession, and we cannot be charged with having done this willingly, gladly, or with pleasure. It was exceedingly difficult for us to do, but because we could not prevent it, we thought that we ought at least to ease his conscience as much as possible.

Both under the papacy and since, I have heard confessions and offered counsel in similar cases. If my counsel were made public, I should either have to deny it or else make the confession public too. Such cases do not belong in a secular court and should not be made public. God has his own court for these cases, and he must counsel the souls of those for whom there is no help in the laws or skills of the world. My preceptor[89] in the monastery, a fine old man who also had many similar cases, once said with a sigh: "Alas, these cases are so confused and desperate that neither wisdom, law, nor reason can be of help. They must be committed to God's mercy." On the basis of such experience I have acted in this case according to divine mercy.

If I had then known what I have recently learned from somebody in Eschweg,[90] namely, that he satisfied his overpowering passion on other women and could continue to do so, certainly no angel could have persuaded me to give him the advice I did.[91] I paid heed to his unavoidable need and weakness, and also the peril to his conscience, which Martin Bucer reported to us. Even less should I have recommended a public wedding or (there was no mention of this either) that the woman should become a princess and wife of the landgrave, which is certainly not to be suffered and is intolerable to the whole empire. I understood and hoped that, because he was compelled by his weakness to satisfy his passion in customary fashion with sin and shame, he might secretly keep an honest girl in a house, have her on account of his dire need and for the sake of his conscience in a secret marriage (although, of course, the world would have considered it adultery), and visit her from time to time, as great lords have often done. In like fashion

---

[88] The opinion prepared in Wittenberg cited the examples of Old Testament patriarchs who had had more than one wife. Cf. Luther's letter to Joseph Levin Metzsch, Dec. 9, 1526, above.

[89] His identity is unknown.

[90] The source of Luther's new information is unknown.

[91] That is, Luther would have recommended that Philip of Hesse take such a woman as concubine rather than a woman of the nobility.

I advised several clergymen under Duke George and the bishops secretly to marry their cooks.

This is my confession. If I had not been forced, I should have preferred to remain silent, but now I cannot. However, by the charge that I have been teaching this for thirteen years[92] the people in Dresden show how friendly their attitude toward us is and how much they are interested in love and concord. As if the scandals and crimes there were not ten times as grave in God's sight as this advice of ours! The world must remove the mote that is in its neighbor's eye and forget the beam in its own![93] If I now had to defend all that I have said and done years ago, especially at the beginning, I should have to worship the pope, and if they had to defend all of their earlier conduct (I shall say nothing of the present), they would have to obey the devil more than God.

I am not ashamed of the counsel I gave even if it should become known throughout the world. Because it is unpleasant, however, I should prefer, if possible, to have it kept quiet.

Martin Luther, with my own hand.

TO JEROME WELLER. September 3, 1540

The Visitation Articles prepared by Jacob Schenk in 1537 for Freiberg and Welkenstein, in Saxony, required the closing of brothels: "Public houses of common women are to be closed by the government. Preachers shall at convenient times teach and preach concerning the natural desire of a man for a woman and of a woman for a man and indicate ways and means of restraining the same until the time comes to marry in order that young people may accommodate themselves thereto and young men may accustom themselves to doing without such horrible houses."[94] Jerome Weller (1499-1572) had been a teacher of religion in Freiberg only a year when he wrote to Luther that some people were urging that the brothels which had been closed should be reopened. [Text in Latin; WA, Br, IX, 228, 229.][95]

To Jerome Weller, servant of Christ: grace and peace.

My dear Dr. Jerome:

Have nothing to do with those who desire that brothels be

92 The reference is to Luther's sermons of 1527 on Genesis, and specifically to his discussion of Lamech's and Abraham's polygamy (*WA*, XXIV, 144, 303).   93 Cf. Matt. 7:3.

94 Emil Sehling, *Die evangelischen Kirchenordnungen des 16. Jahrhunderts*, I (Leipzig, 1902), 466, 467.

95 Cf. parallel text in *WA*, XLVIII, 674, 675.

restored. It would have been more tolerable not to have driven the devil out than to reintroduce and re-establish him now. Let those who wish to restore brothels first renounce the name of Christ and admit that they are pagans who are ignorant of God.

We Christians, if we wish to be accounted such, have a clear word of God, "Whoremongers and adulterers God will judge."[96] This applies even more to those who favor, protect, and support them with their aid and counsel. Besides, how can we preach against fornication if we place ourselves in the position of praising the government which tolerates fornication? They[97] cite the example of Nuremberg, as if the Nurembergers sin only in this respect.[98] "All things are defiled by lusts," they say, quoting words of Augustine.[99] By God's grace there is a remedy for this, namely, marriage or the hope of marrying. But what remedial value will marriage and the hope of marrying have if we allow whoredom to go on unpunished?

Our experience under Satan, when brothels were flourishing, taught us not only that this arrangement is not adapted to the circumstances, but also that, as everyone knows, rape and adultery were greatly increased by the example of unrestricted whoredom. Now that by God's grace prostitution is prohibited, there is less rape and adultery, especially openly. Let the government, if it wishes to be Christian, punish whoredom, rape, and adultery, at least when they occur openly; if they still occur in secret, the government is not to be blamed.

In short, against God we can neither do, nor allow, nor tolerate anything. What is right must be done even if the world perishes.[1] Farewell.

Hastily,

Friday after Saint Aegidius, 1540.   Martin Luther, Doctor.

WARNING AGAINST PROSTITUTES. May 13, 1543

The following was a notice posted by Luther to warn students in the university against prostitutes. Copies made of it have sometimes been included in editions of Luther's correspondence.[2] [Macaronic text; WA, TR, IV, No. 4857 n.]

---

96 Heb. 13:4.
97 That is, those who advocate a reopening of brothels.
98 This sentence was omitted in most editions but is restored in the Weimar edition.   99 Augustine, *De ordine*, II, 4, 12.
1 *Fiat iustitia et pereat mundus.*   2 Cf. Enders, XV, 157–159.

Through special enemies of our faith the devil has sent some whores here to ruin our poor young men. As an old and faithful preacher I ask you in fatherly fashion, dear children, that you believe assuredly that the evil spirit sent these whores here and that they are dreadful, shabby, stinking, loathsome, and syphilitic,[3] as daily experience unfortunately demonstrates. Let every good student warn his fellows. Such a syphilitic whore can give her disease to ten, twenty, thirty, and more good people, and so she is to be accounted a murderer, as worse than a poisoner. In this foul business let everyone offer faithful advice and warning to his brother, even as you would that others should do unto you.[4]

If you pay no attention to this my fatherly warning, we fortunately have a praiseworthy prince, an honest and decent man, who is opposed to all vice and unchastity. He has a strong arm, equipped with a sword, and he will know how to clean out the woods,[5] the fishery,[6] and the rest of the town to the glory of God's Word, which His Grace has received with all seriousness and to which he has hitherto adhered at great danger and sacrifice. Accordingly I advise you students who frequent the woods[7] to make yourselves scarce before the prince learns of your commerce with whores. For His Grace would not tolerate this in his camp near Wolfenbüttel. Even less will he tolerate it in his woods, town, and land.

Begone, I advise you, and the sooner the better! Those who cannot live without whores should go home or wherever else they will. Here we have a Christian church and Christian school where God's Word, decency, and virtue are to be learned. Those who wish to be whoremongers may carry on elsewhere. Our elector did not found this university to serve as a whore house, and so you must accommodate yourselves to the situation.

I must speak plainly. If I were a judge, I would have such venomous, syphilitic whores broken on the wheel and flayed because one cannot estimate the harm such filthy whores do to young men who are so wretchedly ruined and whose blood is contaminated before they have achieved full manhood.

You foolish young men think that you must not suffer, that

[3] *Frantzösisch*; the French sickness.   [4] Cf. Matt. 7:12.
[5] *Speck*, a wooded area northeast of Wittenberg to which the whores and students resorted.
[6] The fishing grounds outside of town, which also served their purposes.
[7] *Speckstudenten*.

as soon as you feel ardent a whore must be found to satisfy you. The old Fathers called it *impatientia libidinis,* inability to endure sexual desire. But it is not necessary to indulge your every passion at once. It is written, "Beware, go not after thy lusts" (Ecclus., ch. 18).[8] Even in the estate of marriage you must restrain yourselves.

In short, beware of whores and pray God to provide you with pious wives. You will have trouble enough as it is.

I have spoken. Whatever you may do, the judgment of God stands: "Neither let us commit fornication, as some of them committed." I Cor., ch. 10.[9] Num., ch. 25.[10]

OPINION. September 13, 1543

Halle, in Saxony, had just recently become Evangelical (Justus Jonas preached the first Protestant sermon there in April, 1541), and Luther was asked whether the bordellos in Halle should be closed at once. It is not known for whom this opinion was prepared, but it was not for the town council, as has sometimes been supposed. A similar opinion was simultaneously prepared by Philip Melanchthon. [Text in German; *WA, Br,* X, 395, 396.]

OPINION OF MARTIN LUTHER CONCERNING THE SUPPRESSION OF BROTHELS IN HALLE[11]

I still believe that for the present, until the gospel is more firmly rooted and the weeds are choked out, it is desirable to be patient with this matter. It may cause injury to the good if this evil is eradicated prematurely, for I believe that there is still a good deal of paganism among the Christians. However, as soon as one well can, severe measures should be taken against the evil. Meanwhile the clergy ought to preach powerfully against it in order that the honorable [town] council may be given opportunity and provocation to suppress such paganism in an appropriate way.

8 Ecclus. 18:30.   9 I Cor. 10:8.   10 Num. 25:1–9.
11 The title is in Latin, the text in German.

X

Suggestions for Problems Facing Clergymen

TO JOHN GULDEN. May 29, 1526

The pastor of St. Peter's Church in Weida, Thuringia, John Gulden caused mischief in his community by quarreling with fellow clergymen, railing against those who disagreed with him, and inciting some people to acts of violence and iconoclasm. Philip Melanchthon described him as one of those "who think that the only way to preach the gospel is to rage with great contentiousness and bitterness against those who differ from us."[1] Complaints about Gulden's preaching and conduct reached Luther and called forth the following rebuke. [Text in Latin; WA, Br, IV, 83-85.]

Grace and peace in the Lord.

My dear John:

It has been reported to me that you are a little too severe in your handling of the Word, and I have been asked to admonish you. If you are receptive to suggestion, I beg you to give first place in your preaching to those things which are of greatest weight, namely, that you urge faith and love upon your hearers. For if these have not struck roots, what is the use of our troubling ourselves about silly ceremonies? Nothing is accomplished by this except that we titillate the unstable minds of the foolish masses who are frivolous and have a mania for novelties. Not only is nothing to be gained by this, but it will result in loss to the glory of God and his Word.

So conduct yourself with your colleagues, therefore, that you may direct and do all things in unity of spirit and form. Do not abuse those of whom you do not know what sort of people they may yet be, but appeal to them gently and humbly, without insisting and boasting that what you propose is right. It will in

---

[1] *C.R.*, I, 898.

time become abundantly clear that "that which thou sowest is not quickened, except it die."[2] Receive this admonition of mine in good part. Farewell.

Yours,

Tuesday after Trinity Sunday, 1526.   Martin Luther.

TO THE CLERGY OF LUEBECK. January 12, 1530

In spite of opposition from the town council, the burghers of Lübeck, Hanseatic free city on the Baltic Sea, succeeded in recalling the two Evangelical clergymen, Andrew Wilms and John Walhoff, who had begun to introduce Reformation teaching there earlier. In accordance with Luther's advice in the following letter, reforms were introduced gradually, beginning with doctrine. It was not, Luther maintained, that traditions and forms of worship required no reform—quite the contrary—but rather that these should grow out of and be based upon the more fundamental reforms in doctrine. [Text in Latin; WA, Br, V, 220, 221.]

To the ministers of the Word in Lübeck: the grace and peace of Christ be with you in faith and patience.

Esteemed Brethren:

We have heard the good and cheering news concerning you, namely, that through your ministry the gospel has begun to be lifted up in your midst. We rejoice over this and thank the Father of mercies.[3] At the same time we confidently pray that He who has begun so good a work among you[4] may guide you by his Spirit in order that the tempter may not hinder you according to his wickedness. Carry on, therefore, in fear and humility, knowing that, since it is the Word of God with which you have to do, this Word must be proclaimed before men and devils with the utmost confidence but it must be dealt with before God with the utmost reverence and fear. He will then bless you so that you will bring forth much fruit and your fruit will remain;[5] as it is written, "His righteousness endureth forever."[6]

Although we believe it to be unnecessary that you be admonished by us, we nevertheless request and exhort you with godly solicitude that you do not begin with innovations in rites, which are dangerous, but that you undertake such changes later. Put first and foremost what is fundamental in our teaching, the doctrine concerning our justification, namely, that we

[2] I Cor. 15:36.   [3] Cf. II Cor. 1:3.   [4] Cf. Phil. 1:6.
[5] Cf. John 15:16.   [6] Ps. 111:3.

are justified by another's righteousness, even Christ's, which is given to us in faith and which by God's grace is apprehended by those who are first terrified by the law and who, struck by the consciousness of their sins, sigh for redemption. It does not help to talk to others of God's grace, for they will perceive only the external change in rites, which will tickle their fancy for an hour or so but will in time cause them to be sated and to loathe all sound doctrine. Reform of impious rites will come of itself when what is fundamental in our teaching, being effectively presented, has taken root in pious hearts. Such people will at once recognize how great an abomination and how sacrilegious a blasphemy that papistic idolatry (namely, the Mass and other abuses of the Sacrament) is, and so it is unnecessary to fish in front of the net, that is, to demolish the traditions before the righteousness of faith is understood. Among the most prominent things that you will wish to impress upon yourselves as well as upon the people are the prayers and litanies, both private and public, for the purity and fruit of the Word, for outward peace and government, and for all other things that you will read in the litany.

I pray that you may be kindly disposed toward these few lines of admonition, coming as they do from one who is a partaker in your benefit and ministry.[7] Christ himself, our only Preserver, will be with you and will teach and accomplish through you what will contribute to his honor and the salvation of men. Amen.

January 12, 1530.   [Martin Luther.]

TO NICHOLAS HAUSMANN. May 19, 1531

There had been friction for some time between the town council and the clergy of Zwickau which seemed to threaten the independence of the church. Without consulting Nicholas Hausmann (1479-1538), chief pastor of the town, the council had removed a clergyman named Soranus on grounds of conduct unbecoming a minister and had called Stanislaus Hoffmann, of Bohemia, in his place. The latter assumed his office on May 1, 1531. Hausmann and his colleague Conrad Cordatus (1475-1546) protested to the council and threatened to air their grievances from the pulpit. They also appealed to the elector of Saxony and to Luther. The Reformer suggested that Hausmann leave Zwickau for a while.
[Text in Latin; *WA, Br*, VI, 101, 102.]

7 Cf. I Tim. 6:2.

Grace and peace.

My dear Hausmann:

I pray you for the sake of Christ our Lord—I write in great haste, for I am very busy—to come to see me as soon as you possibly can. It will be very pleasant to have you here as my dear guest.

Now at last you recognize the reward which your Zwickauers are providing for you, but do not be depressed by their wickedness. I rejoice that such an opportunity is afforded to despise them.

If Cordatus comes with you, everything will be done to provide for him.

Give the scoundrels a full year[8]—not by relinquishing your office entirely but by giving the impression of visiting me and meanwhile leaving them in the hands of that false brother who has wormed his way in[9]—until you see how things turn out. You should indicate this to them in a written protest. Whatever else may be done we can discuss here when you arrive.

Do not be troubled by the scandal which this may produce in neighboring towns. It is not your fault. What can we do about the sects and factions which arise against our will? The rest we can discuss orally.

Meanwhile be strong, and rejoice in the fact that they have struck you in the face for the truth's sake and that you suffer disgrace at the hands of ingrates. The Lord be with you.

Greet Cordatus respectfully for me.

Yours,

Friday after Ascension, 1531.   Martin Luther.

TO CONRAD CORDATUS. May 23, 1531

Nicholas Hausmann having left Zwickau on the advice of Luther (see above), Conrad Cordatus, who had also been involved in the controversy there, scolded the people and attacked the town council from the pulpit. He was therefore asked by the council to refrain from preaching for a while. Rather than be hindered in the exercise of his office by secular authority, Cordatus left Zwickau at once in keeping with Luther's suggestion in the following letter. [Text in Latin; WA, Br, VI, 106, 107.]

8 This part of the sentence in German.
9 *Cum suo idolo intruso*: the reference is to Stanislaus Hoffmann.

Grace and peace.

My dear Cordatus:

I pray you for Christ's sake to leave that Babylon[10] in which you are and give place unto wrath.[11] I see that the people are delivered up to Satan[12] and that God's wrath is come upon them to the uttermost.[13] Indeed, I fear that Satan will stir up some sort of rumpus that will afterward be blamed on you. Let them do as they will.[14] As you see, they are unwilling to endure your counsel of peace, your pains, your ministry.

You have other dangers to worry about, for if you continue to minister to these unwilling, impenitent, and desperate people, you may irritate them even more and give them additional cause to hate you. Flee from that town and shake off the dust from your feet for a testimony against it[15] before matters get worse and it becomes impossible to apply a remedy. The rest we can discuss when you come here.

A short time ago I wrote to the pastor[16] that he should leave there too. As good pastors, you cannot refrain from rebuking people's wickedness. But since they refuse to listen to and heed your reproaches, let them rage on. We have done our duty and can therefore have a good conscience.

Farewell in the Lord. Greet the pastor, Mr. Nicholas [Hausmann]. Do not be sad, but rejoice in the knowledge that you are suffering for Christ's sake.[17]

I do not advise you to shake off the dust from your feet publicly, in the presence of your auditors, lest they ensnare you on the way. Bid them farewell quietly and humbly. Commit the matter to God. Nevertheless, you should tell them that you cannot stay with them any longer with a good conscience. God will judge who is right.

Yours,

May 23, 1531.   Martin Luther.

TO JEROME NOPUS. July 10, 1531

*The friction between the town council and the clergy of Zwickau con-
tinued. This letter appears to have been written to Jerome Nopus, who*

[10] Cf. Isa. 48:20. Zwickau is meant.   [11] Cf. Rom. 12:19.
[12] Cf. I Cor. 5:5.   [13] I Thess. 2:16.
[14] This sentence in German. From this point on in the letter "you" is plural rather than singular and refers to Nicholas Hausmann as well as Cordatus.
[15] Luke 9:5.
[16] Latin: *pastor*. The reference is to Hausmann, to whom Luther had written on May 19 (see above).   [17] Cf. I Peter 4:13.

*since 1522 had been teacher of Greek in Zwickau and who showed a
lively interest in the theological questions of his day. Luther's letter
suggests that Nopus was at this time exercising the office of pastor as well
as teacher. Some versions of the letter which have come down to us
suggest that Conrad Cordatus was the addressee, but in this case the date
would not fit, for Cordatus as well as Hausmann had already gone to
Wittenberg. [Text in Latin; WA, Br, VI, 148-150.]*

To the honorable brother, Jerome Nopus, minister of the Word,
professor of the Greek language in Zwickau, and confessor of
the gospel: grace and peace in Christ.

Dear Brother:

I have read your letter, addressed to your pastor, Mr.
Nicholas Hausmann, and rejoice to learn from it of your faithful
zeal and diligent concern. I also understand the sadness you
feel on account of your pastor's absence. Christ comfort and
strengthen you until, please God, the case is settled. Meanwhile
our godly brethren who are among you do not lack for
anything[18] as long as you and your faithful associates are
there.

It does not behoove your pastor to remain silent in the face
of the outrage and injustice with which your council has confronted him—much less to consent to what it has done—
especially because these men try to justify their sin. Sins can be
forgiven only when they are acknowledged, and wrong should
be borne only by those who profess that they are enemies of
the Word. The sins of those who claim to be brethren are not to
be tolerated, but ought to be rebuked.[19] If, therefore, they wish
to glory in the name of brethren, let them acknowledge their sin
and suffer themselves to be rebuked. On the other hand, if they
wish to justify their sin, let them profess that they are enemies.
Then we shall be content and ready to suffer all manner of
things at their hands, as at the hands of enemies, but not as if
they were brethren, as I have said.

Carry on for the present until the prince reaches a decision.
I trust that Christ will bring this tragic affair to a successful
conclusion if the Zwickauers deserve it, or else he will liberate
us from these madmen. The grace of God be with you.

Greet all the brethren, especially those who are your colleagues in the ministry. Pray for me, for I am weak. Give my

[18] A later version reads: "do not lack for instruction, comfort, and the
Sacraments."

[19] Cf. Matt. 18:15–17.

special greetings to the physician, Dr. Stephan,[20] and admonish him to persevere yet a while.

Yours,

Monday after Saint Kilian's, 1531.   Martin Luther.

TABLE TALK RECORDED BY VEIT DIETRICH.[21] 1532

When somebody[22] asked Martin Luther whether the Sacrament is to be adored, he replied: "No cult is to be made of the Sacrament. I kneel, it is true, but I do so as a mark of reverence. But when I am lying in bed,[23] I receive it without kneeling. For it is a free thing, just as one is free either to kiss the Bible or not to kiss it. This too is an act of reverence. I do not sin by omitting to do it. But if anyone tries to compel me to do it as something necessary for salvation, I should refuse to do it and retain my liberty."

TO MICHAEL STIEFEL. June 24, 1533

A former Augustinian, Michael Stiefel was an early adherent of Martin Luther, and they remained good friends ever after. Stiefel combined with his activity as an Evangelical clergyman a remarkable ability in and love for mathematics. He experimented with the possibility of ascribing numerical significance to letters of the alphabet, and becoming interested in the Second Advent, he believed that he could determine the time of Christ's return from the book of Daniel. His tentative conclusions were published in his Rechenbüchlein vom Ende Christi (*Wittenberg, 1532*), *where he suggested that Christ would return at eight o'clock in the morning on October 19, 1533. Later he also maintained that the Second Advent would occur before Michaelmas (September 29). Luther disagreed with Stiefel's methods and conclusions but would not concur in proposals to punish him.*[24] [Text in Latin; *WA, Br*, VI, 495, 496.]

Grace and peace in Christ.

My dear Michael:

Although you well know the esteem in which I hold you, I hear that you are very much excited because I disagree with

[20] Stephan Wild was town physician in Zwickau.

[21] Macaronic text in *WA, TR*, I, No. 344.

[22] In John Schlaginhaufen's parallel record (*WA, TR*, II, No. 1745) this person is identified as Ignatius Perknowsky, an adherent of the Bohemian Brethren (Hussites) who lived for a time in Luther's home and ate at his table.   [23] In times of illness.

[24] See *New Schaff-Herzog Encyclopedia*, XI, 95.

your computations. I have always said that it is not so much that I disagree as it is that I do not understand, and I do not think that you wish to force me to say that I understand what I do not at all comprehend or grasp. How would it help either you or me to make such a false statement? Certainly I did not suspect that you would become so excited about this indifferent matter. For if that day should come before Michaelmas, you are not a sinner for believing and saying that it will. On the other hand, if it should not come then, we do not sin for believing that it can come at any hour. Anyone who believes that Christ can come at any hour also believes that he can come before Michaelmas. If perchance we are mistaken in what we do not know, and if we confess that we do not know that, as you say, he will come before Michaelmas, then this mistake does not endanger us, just as all your knowledge, if you have it, will certainly not endanger you. Why, then, do you torment yourself so about this matter when either answer is safe and without peril?

I tell you that this excitement of yours causes me to suspect that Satan desires to have you that he might sift you as wheat.[25] For he who so agitates your feelings without cause can also confuse your understanding without evidence. Accordingly, I pray you, put aside this agitation of your mind, come to see us, and do not disregard or disturb our old friendship.

Farewell in Christ.

Saint John's Day, 1533.   Martin Luther, Doctor.

TABLE TALK RECORDED BY ANTHONY
LAUTERBACH.[26] September 28, 1533

On September 28, 1533, Michael Stiefel, pastor in Lochau, came to Wittenberg for a conference with Martin Luther and in twenty-two articles explained his opinion concerning the last day. Silence was enjoined upon him by the elector [of Saxony] and by Luther. He took this ill and said: "Dear doctor, I am astonished that you forbid me to preach and that you will not believe me although my conclusion is certainly true. I do not like to speak thus, but I must."

Martin Luther replied: "Dear master, if you were able to keep and suffer silence for twenty years under the papacy, you can surely keep quiet for four weeks now." O how glad he

25 Cf. Luke 22:31.
26 Macaronic text; WA, TR, III, No. 3360 b.

would have been to have Martin Luther share his opinion! He said: "I regret it very much that you will not believe this."

To this Martin Luther replied by telling of a peasant who was a miller and who predicted that Christ would assuredly come on September 27, the day that had just passed.

Michael Stiefel responded: "When I was on a journey, early one morning, at the rising of the sun, I beheld a beautiful rainbow, and seeing it I thought of the Advent of Christ."

Martin Luther replied: "No, it will not come to pass by rainbows alone. On the contrary, all creation will suddenly be consumed by fire, thunder, and lightning (II Peter, ch. 3).[27] It will happen in one stroke, in a moment. Then all of us will be dead and transformed again. A loud trumpet blast will renew and awaken us. It will not be a sweet sound, like that of a cornet, for those who are in the grave must hear it."

However, Michael Stiefel set a certain time in his book: the 292d day of the 42d week in the month of October and the year 1533.[28]

Martin Luther said: "Let it be so, then. Eighteen weeks ago Michael Stiefel said in my presence that Christ will certainly come before Michaelmas. Michaelmas will be here tomorrow. Get ready, if you will. I shall be glad to give away the baptismal gifts received from the sponsors of my children, but I am afraid that no one will take them, for tomorrow at six o'clock in the evening we are all supposed to be sitting in heaven! Alas, how ashamed we shall be!"

On the vigil of Michaelmas he then said at dinner: "We shall have eight hours to the judgment, for the day begins in the evening according to the Hebrews, and so Michaelmas is upon us."

Master Stiefel also used this argument: "Although according to his humanity the Son of Man did not know when the time would come,[29] he has known this very well during the fifteen hundred years since his ascension and he has revealed it. I am myself the last trump."[30]

Martin Luther replied: "Christ knew the time very well even according to his humanity, but he was not to reveal it to men, for he had not been sent to do this."

I[31] said: "Great offense to the Word will arise after that time."

---

27 II Peter 3:10. Cf. Rev. 11:19.
28 That is, the 292d day and 42d week of the year.
29 Cf. Mark 13:32.   30 The seventh angel in Rev. 11:15.
31 Anthony Lauterbach, the recorder of this table talk.

Martin Luther replied: "It is an error and does not deceive us. Let the papists be afraid. But let those who are prudent look to the godly who rely on the Word, for we think little of this opinion."

TABLE TALK RECORDED BY ANTHONY LAUTERBACH.[32] November 25, 1538

On November 25 there was talk about the perpetual enmity between the clergy and the laity. "It is not without cause," said Martin Luther, "since the untamed masses are unwilling to be corrected and it is the duty of preachers to reprove them. This is a very burdensome and perilous duty. And on this account laymen keep sharp eyes on clergymen. They try to find some fault in them, and if they discover a grievous offense, even if it be in the clergymen's wives or children, they are delighted to have their revenge on them. Except that they surpass other people in power, princes harass clergymen with a like hatred. Let us therefore adhere to the pure Word in order that we may sit in the seat of Moses. Even if life may not be smooth and perfect, God is merciful. Enmity toward clergymen will remain. As the old saying puts it, 'Not until the sea dries up and the devil is taken up into heaven will the layman be a true friend of the clergyman.' "

TO ANTHONY LAUTERBACH. November 26, 1539

Anthony Lauterbach had just entered upon his pastorate in Pirna (where he was also superintendent or bishop) on July 25. He found a custom concerning the administration of Holy Communion to the sick that was different from what he had been accustomed to in Wittenberg. He was expected to communicate with each of the sick even when this might require him to receive Communion several times a day. Luther advised against this and expressed the hope that the practice of private Communion might be discontinued altogether as at once unnecessary and burdensome. [Text in Latin; WA, Br, VIII, 608, 609.]

To the esteemed gentleman, Master Anthony Lauterbach, faithful bishop of the church in Pirna, my brother in the Lord: grace and peace.

32 Macaronic text; WA, TR, IV, No. 4143.

My dear Anthony:

With reference to your question concerning the communication of the sick I think that you have been sufficiently instructed by the custom of our Church with which you have been conversant for such a long time. Yet I wish and am of the opinion that private Communion should be abolished everywhere—namely, that the people should be told in sermons to receive Communion three or four times a year in order that, strengthened by the Word, they may afterward fall asleep, no matter what the cause of death may be. For private Communion will increasingly impose an intolerable and impossible burden, especially in time of pestilence. And it is not right that the Church should be required to peddle the Sacraments, particularly in the case of those who have despised them for a long time and who then expect the Church to be ready to be of service to them although they never rendered it a service of any kind.[33]

However, since this practice has not yet been established, you must do what you can. Meanwhile, as you have done, you should administer Communion to the sick alone when it does not please you to receive Communion with them, but you should explain that you are doing this as a temporary expedient and that you will not continue to do this for them forever inasmuch as something will certainly be decided about this matter.

Katie wants the carved house door to be as wide as the enclosed measure. The craftsmen will themselves know what length or height to make it. She does not need one of the other doors. Do the best you can to take care of this matter.

Herewith I commit you to God's keeping. Amen.

Yours,

Wednesday after Saint Catherine's, 1539.   Martin Luther.

TO GEORGE BUCHHOLZER. December 4, 1539

Elector Joachim II of Brandenburg sent a legation to Wittenberg to secure the opinion of the Wittenberg theologians concerning a draft of an Evangelical church order which was finally published in 1540. The order contained provision for ceremonies which appeared to many to be unevangelical. It seems that the elector hoped to win the support of Catholics among his subjects by making the greatest possible concessions to them. George Buchholzer, dean in Berlin, was one of those who was concerned

---

[33] Luther expressed himself similarly in a sermon on July 18, 1535. See *WA*, XLI, 384, 385.

about these concessions in so far as they involved processions, vestments, and the elevation of the host. Luther wrote to him in a playful way to suggest that the ceremonies in question might be tolerated for the time being. [Text in German; *WA, Br,* VIII, 624-626.]

To the honorable George Buchholzer, dean in Berlin, my dear brother in Christ: grace and peace in Christ.

Dear Dean:

Because of the pain in my head I must be brief. What our opinion is concerning the Church order of your elector, my gracious lord the margrave, you will learn sufficiently from our letters.[34]

With respect to what troubles you—whether a cope or alb is to be worn in the procession during Rogation week and on Saint Mark's Day, and whether a procession around the church-yard is to be held with a pure responsory on Sundays and with the *Salve festa dies*[35] on Easter without, however, carrying the Sacrament about—this is my advice: If your lord, the margrave and elector, etc., permits the gospel of Jesus Christ to be preached with purity and power and without human additions and the two sacraments of Baptism and the Body and Blood of Jesus Christ to be administered and offered according to their institution, if he is willing to abolish the invocation of saints (as if they were mediators, intercessors, and deliverers) and the carrying about of the Sacrament in procession, and if he is willing to discontinue daily Masses, vigils, and Masses for the dead and the consecration of water, salt, and herbs and allow only pure responsories and hymns, Latin and German, in pro-cession, go along in God's name and carry a silver or gold cross and wear a cope or alb of velvet, silk, or linen. And if one cope or alb is not enough for your lord, the elector, wear three of them, as the high priest Aaron did when he put on three vest-ments, one on top of the other and all of them beautiful and attractive[36] (after which ecclesiastical vestments were called *ornata* in the papacy). Moreover, if His Grace is not satisfied that you go about singing and ringing bells in procession only once, go about seven times, as Joshua compassed the city of Jericho seven times with the Children of Israel, making a great shout and blowing trumpets.[37] If your lord, the margrave, de-

---

[34] Luther, Philip Melanchthon, and Justus Jonas wrote letters to Elector Joachim II of Brandenburg on Dec. 5, 1539.

[35] A hymn by Venantius Fortunatus (c. 530–609).

[36] Cf. Lev. 8:7.   [37] Joshua 6:4, 5, 16.

sires it, let His Grace leap and dance at the head of the procession with harps, drums, cymbals, and bells, as David danced before the Ark of the Lord when it was carried into the city of Jerusalem.[38] I am fully satisfied, for none of these things (as long as no abuse is connected with them) adds anything to the gospel or detracts from it. Only do not let such things be regarded as necessary for salvation and thus bind the consciences of men. How I would rejoice and thank God if I could persuade the pope and the papists of this! If the pope gave me the freedom to go about and preach and only commanded me (with a dispensation) to hitch on a pair of trousers, I should be glad to do him the favor of wearing them.

As concerns the elevation of the Sacrament in the Mass, this is an optional ceremony and no danger can come to the Christian faith as a result of it, provided nothing else is added. Accordingly you may lift up the Sacrament in God's name as long as it is desired.

We had ample cause to abolish the elevation here in Wittenberg, and perhaps you do not have such cause in Berlin. Nor shall we restore the ceremony unless some urgent reason requires us to do so, for it is an optional thing and a human exercise rather than a divine commandment. Only what God commands is necessary; the rest is free.

A fuller report will be given to you by your lord's representatives. May God and the Father of Jesus Christ, his Son, whose office you adorn, faithfully support you with his Spirit and cause his name to be hallowed, his Kingdon to come, and his will to be done. I pray for this daily in the Lord's Prayer. Amen.

Farewell and be strong in the Lord,[39] for strength is made perfect in weakness.[40]

Thursday after Saint Andrew's, 1539. Martin Luther, Doctor.

TABLE TALK RECORDED BY JOHN MATHESIUS.[41]
September, 1540

"Dr. Luther, if in time of famine I exhort a rich man in confession to contribute something for the benefit of the poor and he denies that he has anything to give, but I know that he does, ought I to give the Sacrament to such a liar?"

The doctor replied: "If he denies it, what more can you do? Sharpen his conscience. But if he persists in his answer, do

38 II Sam. 6:14, 15.   39 Cf. Eph. 6:10.   40 Cf. II Cor. 12:9.
41 Macaronic text; WA, TR, V, No. 5270.

what Christ did; he gave the Sacrament to his betrayer, Judas."[42]

In opposition to this, somebody else referred to the example of Ananias in Acts and of Peter, who forthwith killed the liar with a word.[43] The doctor replied: "That was something extraordinary. Moreover, I believe that Peter did not do this of himself but by revelation,[44] for God wished to establish the primitive Church by means of miracles."

TO PRINCE GEORGE OF ANHALT. April 5, 1543

Under the same date George Major (1502-1574) wrote a letter to George Held, pastor in Forchheim, which was mistakenly ascribed to Luther in older editions of Luther's works. Since this letter by Major helps to clarify what Luther's letter was about, part of it is quoted here: "Our Joachim [Greff] has asked for my opinion and judgment concerning the presentation of sacred plays, which some of your clergymen disapprove of. This, briefly, is my opinion. All men are commanded to further and extend the Word of God our Father by every possible means, not only by word of mouth but also by writings, paintings, sculpture, hymns, songs, and musical instruments; as the psalm says, 'Praise him with the timbrel and dance: praise him with stringed instruments and organs' [Ps. 150: 4] . . . When produced with good intentions and out of zeal for the extension of gospel truth, such dramatic presentations—done, I repeat, in an earnest and temperate spirit—are by no means to be condemned."[45] The following letter shows that Luther concurred in this opinion. [Text in German; WA, Br, X, 284-286.]

To the serene, highborn prince and lord, George, dean of the cathedral in Magdeburg, prince of Anhalt, count of Ascania, and lord of Bernburg, my gracious lord: grace and peace in Christ.

Serene, highborn Prince, gracious Lord:

The schoolmaster in Dessau[46] has asked me to give my opinion concerning Your Grace's paper (as he calls it) in which it is stated that the rector and preacher[47] are causing disturb-

---

[42] Cf. Luke 22:21.   [43] Cf. Acts 5:1–5.

[44] The reading *revelatio* is here preferred to *relatio*.

[45] De Wette, V, 553.

[46] Joachim Greff, schoolmaster in Dessau, had for some time been active in the writing and presentation of religious plays. In the spring of 1543 he was busy rehearsing an Easter play which he had written the year before.

[47] Severin Star and John Brusch were the men who opposed such use of music and the arts in churches.

ance and agitation among the people by denouncing Palm Sunday hymns and songs and other plays and dramatizations.

It displeases me to hear this. I suspect that an evil spirit is trying to find an opportunity to accomplish something special. Such matters of indifference[48] should be permitted because they are harmless customs and are inoffensive. Moreover, if a change is desired, it should not be undertaken by one man alone but by the considered judgment of all the lords and clergy. Since Your Grace is not only lord but also archdeacon,[49] Your Grace should not suffer it that a fanatic should take it upon himself to denounce these matters of indifference as damnable. He has no authority to do so, and he is still wanting in the necessary learning. One must be careful, for if he is allowed to chew on cloth, he will eventually wish to eat leather.[50] Beyond this Your Grace will know how to deal with the matter.

Herewith I commit Your Grace to God's keeping. Amen.

Your Grace's willing servant,

Thursday after Quasimodogeniti, 1543.   Martin Luther, Doctor.

TO JOHN MATHESIUS. August 19, 1543

Caspar Heydenreich, at the time chaplain to Duchess Catherine of Saxony, informed Luther that John Mathesius (a clergyman in Joachimsthal, Bohemia, who was to become the first biographer of Luther) was frightened by the mandate which King Ferdinand of Bohemia issued on June 19, 1543, and which provided for the exile of all married clergymen. Luther counseled Mathesius to remain calm and see the threat in its proper proportions. [Text in Latin; *WA, Br,* X, 372, 373.]

To the reverend gentleman in the Lord, John Mathesius, in Joachimsthal, very faithful minister of the Word, my dear brother: grace and peace in the Lord.

Master Caspar [Heydenreich] has told me that you are somewhat concerned about the tyranny and the raging of Ferdinand, that most sad and wretched king who issued an edict that all ministers of the Word who are married should be driven out of his kingdom. I wonder if the Bohemians will consent to his raging. But even if they do, what of it? Is Ferdinand's kingdom the only one on earth? Does not Christ have a place elsewhere

---

[48] *Neutralia.*

[49] On George III of Anhalt see letter of July 10, 1545, below.

[50] *Lesst man yhm das Leplin, so wird er fort an lernen, das ledder fressen.*

which is hospitable to his grace? Has he not forsaken the kingdom of Ferdinand as a place of his wrath where kings are
trampled underfoot?

Why, then, do you fear and worry? Be of good courage! Let
your heart be strengthened.[51] Do not overestimate that water
bag[52] who does not know whether tomorrow he will be a king
or a worm. We shall reign forever with Christ; they[53] will burn
in hell with the devil.

Herewith farewell in the Lord.

Yours,

Sunday after the Assumption of Mary.   Martin Luther.

TO JOACHIM MOERLIN. October 2, 1544

*Joachim Mörlin (1514-1571) was the son of Jodocus Mörlin, professor
of metaphysics for some years in the university in Wittenberg, and
assisted Luther after he had completed his own studies leading to the
doctor of theology degree. In 1540 he was made superintendent (or bishop)
in Arnstadt, Thuringia, where his fearless criticism of the government of
the count of Schwartzburg soon led to his dismissal. On May 10, 1544,
he became superintendent in Göttingen. Here as elsewhere he distinguished
himself by his zeal for Christian faith and life, and in the eyes of some
of his contemporaries he overemphasized the law. This probably accounts
for a question he addressed to Luther. [Text in Latin; WA, Br, X,
660, 661.]*

To the esteemed gentleman, the Rev. Joachim Mörlin, doctor
of theology, faithful bishop of the church in Göttingen, my
beloved brother in the Lord: grace and peace in Christ.

Dear Doctor:

I marvel that you think it necessary to consult me, as if you
did not know what you should preach. Do you not have the
Law and the Gospel? According to these the Word of God must
be rightly divided[54] in order that you may wound and heal,
kill and make alive.[55] Perhaps you hope in vain that all will
hear and love the Word, or perhaps you center attention on the
Law to the exclusion of the Gospel, so that the people think
that they are listening to you instead of to God or feel that they
are being subjected to compulsion. Be satisfied if a quarter of
the ground receives the seed[56]—unless you think yourself better

---

51 Cf. Ps. 27:14.
53 I.e., those who oppose Christ.
55 Cf. Deut. 32:39.

52 The king of Bohemia.
54 Cf. II Tim. 2:15.
56 Cf. Matt. 13:8.

than Christ or than Elijah, who was content with seven thousand.[57] Be gentle with those who are gentle, and let those who resist your preaching of the Law quarrel with God about it, just so that you have done your duty. They may read the Scriptures for themselves if they do not believe you. The times are constantly getting worse, and many will turn from the truth.

Beyond this there is nothing that I can write. You yourself know the Scriptures.

Farewell in the Lord, and pray for us.

Yours,

October 2, 1544. Martin Luther, Doctor.

TO PRINCE GEORGE OF ANHALT. July 10, 1545

George III of Anhalt (1507-1553) studied theology in Leipzig and was appointed dean of the cathedral in Magdeburg in 1524. He was at first a bitter opponent of the Reformation, but his studies, pursued in the interest of refuting what he deemed heresy, finally led him in 1530 to embrace the Reformation. In 1544 he was made "coadjutor in religious affairs" to Duke August of Saxony, and in this capacity he made a visitation of parishes in Merseburg. His liturgical inclinations, supported by a desire to make all possible concessions to Catholics, were reflected in a Church order (1545) which he helped to prepare. As the following letter indicates, Luther did not encourage Prince George in his preoccupation with forms and ceremonies. [Text in Latin; WA, Br, XI, 132-134.]

To the reverend father in Christ, most illustrious prince and lord, George, true and genuine bishop of the church in Merseburg, prince of Anhalt, count of Ascania, and lord in Bernburg, my gracious lord: grace and peace in Christ.

Dr. Augustine[58] requested me very urgently that I write to Your Grace about ceremonies. I confess that I am not favorably disposed even toward necessary ceremonies, but that I am opposed to those that are not necessary. Not only have I been (and still am) incensed by my experience under the papacy, but the example of the Ancient Church is also disquieting to me.[59] It easily happens that ceremonies become laws, and after

---

[57] Cf. I Kings 19:9–18. [58] Augustine Schurf.
[59] That is, the extravagant ceremonies of the Medieval Church on the one hand, and the apparent paucity of ceremonies in the Ancient Church (*veteris ecclesiae*) on the other.

they are established as laws, they quickly become snares to men's consciences. Meanwhile pure doctrine is obscured and buried, especially if those who come after are indifferent and unschooled folk who are more concerned about ceremonies than they are about mortifying the lusts of the flesh. We see this even among those who are now living; strife and divisions arise when everybody follows his own opinion. In short, contempt for the Word on our side and blasphemy on the side of our opponents seem to me to point to the time of which John prophesied when he said to his people, "The ax is laid unto the root of the trees," etc.[60]

At all events, since the end is close at hand, it does not seem to me that it is necessary (at least in this blessed time)[61] to be too concerned about introducing ceremonies, making them uniform, and fixing them permanently by law. The one thing that needs to be done is this: the Word must be preached often and purely, and competent and learned ministers must be secured who are concerned above all else that they be of one heart and one mind in the Lord. If this is achieved, it will undoubtedly be easy to secure uniformity in ceremonies, or at least to tolerate differences. Without such internal unity, on the other hand, there will be no end to differences and no way to deal with them, for those who come after us will claim the same right that we exercise, and flesh will be set against flesh, a consequence of corrupt nature.

Accordingly I cannot advise that ceremonies be made uniform everywhere. Diversity may be tolerated—provided that manifestly godless and foolish ceremonies are abandoned. For example, if some ceremonies have been discontinued in certain places, they should not be restored, and if some ceremonies have hitherto been retained, they should not be given up. This applies to the customary location of altars,[62] to the sacred and secular vestments of the clergy,[63] and to other similar things. For if

---

[60] Matt. 3:10.   [61] Apparently ironical.

[62] In his *Deutsche Messe* (1526), Luther had suggested: "In the true Mass of real Christians, however, the altar cannot remain where it is, and the priest will always face the people, as doubtless Christ did in the Last Supper. But let that await its own time" (*Works of Martin Luther*, Philadelphia ed., VI, 178).

[63] In the preface to his *Formula Missae* (1523), Luther had written concerning vestments: "But we think about these as we do about other uses: we permit them to be used without restraint; only let pomp and the excess of splendor be absent. . . . For vestments do not commend us to God" (*op. cit.*, VI, 93).

heart and mind are one in the Lord, one man will readily allow another's ceremonies to be different. On the other hand, if there is no seeking after unity in heart and mind, external agreement will achieve little. Nor will such agreement last long among those who come after us, for observances are subject to places, times, persons, and circumstances. The Kingdom of God does not depend on them. Moreover, they are by their very nature changeable.

No matter what the observances may be, one must beware of making laws of necessity out of them. It appears to me that it would be desirable to act like a schoolmaster or a housefather who governs his school or home without rules but who, by his mere presence, corrects what is wrong and may require discipline according to the law of God. Even so, I should prefer to have everything in the Church governed by personal supervision rather than by inherited laws. For when the housefather's supervision ends, the discipline of the household also ends; as the proverbs suggest, "The horse is beaten by his master's eye," and, "The field is manured by the master's footsteps." All authority resides in able and (as Christ says)[64] faithful and wise persons. Unless we succeed in attracting such men to the government of the Church, it will be useless to try to rule by laws.

After all, why should one wish to make everything uniform when even under the papacy there was great diversity, which reached into every province? And how great are the differences that have always divided the Greek churches from the Latin!

This is why we insist on the establishment of schools, and especially on purity and agreement in doctrine, which will make hearts and minds one in the Lord. But only a few are willing to study, while many are concerned only with their bellies and a place where they might be fed. Hence it has occurred to me more than once that it may become necessary to decrease the number of village pastors and to employ, in lieu of several such pastors, just one learned and faithful man who might visit all the places in a neighborhood several times a year to provide pure preaching and diligent supervision; meanwhile the people might repair to the mother church for the Sacraments or, in case of illness, have the deacons administer the Sacraments to them. Time and circumstances will suggest what cannot be fixed or predetermined by laws.

For the present this will serve to acquaint Your Grace briefly

[64] Luke 12:42.

with my opinion. The Lord direct Your Grace by his Holy Spirit,

> "Without whose power divine
> Nothing is in man,
> Naught but what is harmful,"[65]

into the way of salvation and peace, to the praise and glory of God. Amen.

Your Grace's obedient servant,

July 10, 1545.   Martin Luther, Doctor.

TO JOHN LANG. July 14, 1545

A fellow Augustinian and early follower of Luther, John Lang was pastor in Erfurt until his death in 1548. Through Philip Melanchthon he had sent a copy of his seventy-two theses, "De matrimonio, clandestinis sponsalibus, et de iis quae sine parentum consensu fiunt disputatio," which appear to have been provoked by the secret engagement of a girl who promised herself to a young man without parental consent. In the following letter Luther expresses his approval of the theses and then proceeds to answer a further question which Lang had raised: Whether persons engaged in strife or litigation may receive Holy Communion. Compare Matt. 5:22-24. [Text in Latin; *WA, Br,* XI, 137-140.]

To the venerable gentleman, John Lang, doctor of theology, true and faithful evangelist of the church in Erfurt, my dear brother in the Lord: grace and peace in Christ.

My beloved Lang:

Your disputation concerning clandestine marriage [engagements] pleased me very much, not only because your opinion coincides with ours in this matter, but also because I should long since have been glad to hear that the whole world considers your school[66] to be in agreement with ours, a thing that will undoubtedly be painful to the papists inasmuch as you had previously given no inkling of the position that your school might take. Now that you are expressing your own opinion, the papists will fear that all the rest agree with you. Bravo for this newly found strength, sirs! It points heavenward.[67]

---

65 From the hymn, *Veni sancte spiritus et emitte caelitus*, also quoted at the conclusion of Article XX of the Augsburg Confession.
66 *Schola*: the university in Erfurt.
67 An adaptation of Vergil, *Aeneid*, IX, 641.

Concerning the other question, I have this opinion: Your arrangement is altogether proper. Those who wish to be counted as Christians ought to make this known by acknowledging Christ[68] at least once a year, although, to be sure, they ought to do this all through life. On the other hand, those who indicate that this is not necessary for them, and that they feel no constraint, thereby confess that they have a distaste for grace and a loathing for manna,[69] are manifestly dead within themselves, and have long since returned to the fleshpots of Egypt.[70] Therefore, they are to be regarded as non-Christians.

Others, who excuse themselves on the ground that they are involved in pending litigation, do not have an adequate reason, for we are supposed to be prepared for death at any time. What would they do if they were to die in such circumstances? Litigation may be pending, but their souls must not be left meanwhile without faith, without Christ, without the Word. The fact that they are involved in litigation might also be offered as an excuse for not believing, not hearing [the preaching of] the Word, not having Christ. Therefore, they would have to say that they deny Christ, give up the Word, and cease believing because all these things are similarly prevented by litigation. Why do they not act in this way?

Let them engage in strife over parties and causes and still remain calm and ready to suffer whatever decision may be rendered. I too have had controversies with the papists. In recent years I have also been involved in a case with the jurists which was tried before my prince.[71] But I have not allowed this to disturb me. I was ready to yield my position if the decision was adverse. And I have meanwhile received Communion frequently.

This is my opinion. With your gifts you will be able to improve upon it greatly.

Farewell in Christ. And pray for me, a dying man.

Yours,

July 14, 1545.   Martin Luther.

TO ANTHONY LAUTERBACH. October 19, 1545

Anthony Lauterbach (1502-1569), a diligent recorder of Luther's conversations and sermons, was made superintendent (or bishop) in Pirna,

---

[68] I.e., by receiving Holy Communion.
[69] Cf. Num. 21:5.   [70] Cf. Ex. 16:3.
[71] The case involved the validity of secret engagements.

near Dresden, in 1539. In this position he was compelled to deal with the problems connected with the ordering of public worship. He asked Luther for advice and received from him an answer which was in substance the same as he had given to others again and again: For the present tolerate traditional practices, where they are not manifestly in conflict with the gospel, for the sake of the weak. [Text in Latin; *WA, Br*, XI, 199, 200.]

Grace and peace to the venerable brother in Christ, Master Anthony Lauterbach, pastor and bishop in Pirna and neighboring churches, my very dear friend in the Lord.

Dear Anthony:

I hope that you will be good enough to excuse me for not writing and for not answering your letters—two of them now. You know how very busy I am and that I am a slothful old man who desires to die. Besides, you know very well what my opinion is in this matter, namely, that any sort of ceremony is permissible, not as a right but for the sake of liberty, and especially in the case of so godly a bishop as the excellent prince of Merseburg.[72] (For in God's sight and mine he is a real bishop. It does not matter that this is not his title; that is of no consequence in this situation.)

According to Paul's teaching, everyone must serve his neighbor. Paul was all things to all men, a Jew to the Jews and a Gentile to the Gentiles.[73] But as soon as he noticed that he was being forced into bondage or required to do something as if it were necessary, he refused to yield a whit to anyone.[74]

There is no need to be disturbed about the matter, therefore, or to inquire further about my opinion. Unity of the spirit[75]— which, as you know, pertains to eternal life—is much to be preferred to such temporal and indifferent ceremonies which end with this life. Nevertheless, by submitting to these ceremonies for a little while on account of our neighbors' need and weakness, we can serve them even as parents are obliged to serve little children, the weak, and the sick. The rest you will understand.

I thank you for the apples which you sent. Please ask us for something in return with which we may do you a favor. You put us to shame by doing us so many favors in so obliging a fashion.

---

[72] As in the letter to George of Anhalt, July 10, 1545, above, Luther sometimes addressed the clergyman-prince as "bishop."

[73] Cf. I Cor. 9:20.   [74] Cf. Gal. 2:4, 5.   [75] Cf. Eph. 4:5.

But listen! My niece Magdalene, in whose behalf I asked you to inquire of Ernest Reuchlin's father,[76] seems to be so infatuated with him that she cannot part from him. She declares openly that what you have written about his father is false. So she is infatuated against my will. However, if she will not listen, let happen what may.

Farewell in the Lord Christ to you and yours.

Monday after Saint Luke, 1545.   Martin Luther, Doctor.

[76] Luther's niece, Magdalene Kaufmann, widow of Ambrose Berndt, later married Ernest Reuchlin, of Geising. Luther had written to Lauterbach about his niece on July 5, 1545 (*WA, Br*, XI, 129–131).

XI

Exhortations Concerning Rulers and the State

TO ELECTOR FREDERICK OF SAXONY.

March 5, 1522

*When Luther wrote from the Wartburg to Elector Frederick the Wise of
Saxony that he intended to return to Wittenberg in the hope of counteracting the radical reforms introduced there during his absence,[1] the
elector immediately had word sent to Luther that he should not return.
"If this is your intention, it is the opinion of His Grace that you should
by no means return at this time."[2] But Luther had already made up his
mind to do so, and in this remarkable letter, written while on his journey
back to Wittenberg, he declared that he must obey God rather than his
prince.* [Text in German; *WA, Br,* II, 453-457.]

To the serene, highborn prince and lord, Duke Frederick of
Saxony, elector of the Holy Roman Empire, landgrave of
Thuringia, margrave in Meissen, my gracious lord and patron:
grace and peace from God our Father and from our Lord Jesus
Christ, and my humble service. Jesus.[3]

Serene, highborn Prince, most gracious Lord:

Your Grace's kind letter and opinion reached me Friday
evening as I was preparing to depart the next day. I need not
say that I know Your Grace has the very best of intentions, for
I am as certain of it as a man can be. On the other hand, I am
convinced by more than human means of reckoning that I too
have good intentions. But this does not get us anywhere.

I take the liberty of supposing from Your Grace's letter that
Your Grace was somewhat offended by that part of my letter
in which I wrote that Your Grace should be wise. Yet this impression of mine is canceled by the confidence I have that Your

---

[1] See Luther's letter to Elector Frederick, Feb. 24, 1522, in Chapter V.
[2] Elector Frederick's instruction to Luther through John Oswald in *WA,
Br,* II, 451. [3] Traditional invocation of the name of Jesus.

Grace knows my heart better than to suppose that I would sneer at Your Grace's well-known wisdom in such unseemly terms. I hope that it will always be so that I have a thoroughly unaffected love and affection for Your Grace above all other princes and rulers. What I wrote was done out of concern and to reassure Your Grace, not for my own sake (of that I had no thought), but for the sake of that untoward movement which was introduced by our friends in Wittenberg to the great detriment of the gospel. I feared that Your Grace would suffer great inconvenience from it. Moreover, I was myself so overwhelmed by the calamity that, had I not been certain that we have the pure gospel, I should have despaired of our cause. Whatever I have suffered hitherto for this cause has been as nothing compared with this. I should willingly have averted the trouble at the cost of my life if that had been possible. We can answer neither to God nor to the world for what has been done. It is blamed on me and, what is worse, on the gospel. This hurts me to the quick.

Accordingly, my gracious lord, my letter was directed against what these men are doing in order that Your Grace might see how the devil is at work in the drama now unfolding in Wittenberg. Although the admonition may have been unnecessary for Your Grace, yet it was necessary for me to write it.

As for myself, most gracious lord, I answer thus: Your Grace knows (or, if you do not, I now inform you of the fact) that I have received the gospel not from men but from heaven only, through our Lord Jesus Christ,[4] so that I might well be able to boast and call myself a minister and evangelist, as I shall do in future. I offered to appear for trial and judgment,[5] not because I had doubts about my mission, but out of excessive humility and in order to persuade others. But now that I see that my excessive humility abases the gospel, and that if I yield an inch the devil will take a mile, I am compelled by my conscience to act otherwise. I have served Your Grace well enough by staying in hiding for a year to please Your Grace.[6] The devil knows very well that I did not hide from cowardice, for he saw my heart when I entered Worms. Had I then believed that as many devils were lying in wait for me as there were tiles on the roofs I should nevertheless have leaped into their midst with joy.

---

[4] Cf. Gal. 1:11, 12.   [5] At the Diet of Worms in 1521 and earlier.
[6] After the Diet of Worms Luther had been taken for his own protection to Wartburg Castle, where he remained at his prince's bidding from May 4, 1521, to March 1, 1522.

Duke George[7] is still far from being the equal of one devil. Since the Father of infinite mercies[8] has by the gospel made us daring lords with power over all devils and over death and has given us such an abundance of confidence that we may venture to call him our dearest Father,[9] Your Grace can see for yourself that it would be a great insult to such a Father not to trust him enough to take the measure of Duke George's wrath.

I know myself well enough to say that if the condition that exists in Wittenberg existed in Leipzig,[10] I should go to Leipzig even if (Your Grace will excuse my foolish words) it rained Duke Georges for nine days and every duke were nine times as furious as this one. He takes my Lord Christ for a man of straw. My Lord and I can suffer that for a while.

I shall not conceal from Your Grace that I have often wept and prayed for Duke George that God might enlighten him. I shall pray and weep once more and then cease forever. I beg that Your Grace will also pray and have others pray that the judgment which, alas, daily threatens him might be averted. I should pray Duke George to death if I knew that this would keep the devil at bay.

I have written this in order that Your Grace might know that I am going to Wittenberg under a far higher protection than that of the elector. I have no intention of asking Your Grace for protection. Indeed, I think I shall protect you more than you are able to protect me. And if I thought that Your Grace could and would defend me by force, I should not go. The sword ought not and cannot decide a matter of this kind. God alone must do it, and that without the solicitude and co-operation of men. He who believes the most can protect the most. And since I have the impression that Your Grace is still weak in faith, I can by no means regard Your Grace as the man to protect and save me.

Since Your Grace wishes to know what to do in this matter and Your Grace thinks you have done too little, I humbly answer that Your Grace has already done far too much and should do nothing at all. God will not and cannot suffer your interference or mine. He wishes the matter to be left in his hands and nowhere else. I suggest that Your Grace take a cue from this. If Your Grace believes, Your Grace will be safe and

---

[7] Duke George of Albertine Saxony was threatening to intervene to stop the disturbances in Wittenberg.

[8] Cf. II Cor. 1:3.   [9] Cf. Rom. 8:15; Gal. 4:6.

[10] In the territory of Duke George.

have peace. If Your Grace does not believe, I at least do believe and must leave Your Grace's unbelief to its own torturing anxiety, such as all unbelievers have to suffer.

Inasmuch as I do not intend to obey Your Grace, Your Grace is excused before God if I am captured or put to death. Before men Your Grace should act as an elector, obedient to your sovereign and allowing His Imperial Majesty to rule in your cities and lands over both life and property, as is his right by the imperial constitution, and Your Grace should by no means offer any resistance or present any hindrances in case he decides to capture me or put me to death. No one should oppose or resist authority save him who ordained it; otherwise it is rebellion and an action against God. But I hope they will have the good sense to recognize that Your Grace occupies too lofty a position to be expected to become my executioner. If Your Grace admits and protects those who may come to capture me, Your Grace will have done enough in the way of obedience. They can ask no more of Your Grace than that you do not hold Luther back. I can be taken prisoner without causing Your Grace trouble or danger. Christ has not taught me to be a Christian at another's expense. If they are so unreasonable as to command Your Grace to lay hands on me, I shall at once tell Your Grace what to do. In any case I shall see to it that Your Grace suffers no harm and danger in body, soul, or estate on my account, whether Your Grace believes or not.

Herewith I commend Your Grace to the grace of God. If necessary, we shall speak further of the matter very soon. I have written this letter in haste so that Your Grace may not be disturbed at hearing of my arrival [in Wittenberg], for if I would be a Christian I must help everybody and harm nobody. It is Somebody other than Duke George with whom I have to do. He[11] knows me very well, and I have some knowledge of Him too. If Your Grace believed, you would see the glory of God. But because you do not yet believe, you have not yet seen it. God be praised and worshiped forever. Amen.

Your Grace's humble servant,

Ash Wednesday, 1522. Martin Luther.

TO THE TOWN COUNCIL OF PLAUEN. October 30, 1525

On May 3, 1525, the Dominican monastery in Plauen, Saxony, was closed when most of the friars had abandoned monastic life. Only a few

[11] Jesus Christ.

old and sick friars, who were unable to make a living in the world out-
side, remained. Under these circumstances the town council turned to
Luther for advice concerning the monastic property. [Text in German;
WA, Br, III, 592, 593.]

Grace and peace in Christ.

Honored, wise, dear Sirs:

In response to your request with reference to the monastery
in Plauen, I know of nothing that I might write except what I
have already written and published in similar cases.[12] When a
monastery is deserted, the town or government should take
possession of the buildings and put them to good use. If there
are poor and needy heirs of the founders, the goods and interest
might be turned over to them or partly shared by them.
Accordingly it is my opinion that you should come to a friendly
agreement with the noblemen as to whether they are willing to
surrender all or part of the endowments of their ancestors and
apply them to the work of God. The furniture should in any
case go to the occupants.

Herewith I commit you to God's keeping. Amen.

Monday after Simon and Jude, 1525.   Martin Luther.

TO GEORGE SPALATIN. November 11, 1525

On the death of Elector Frederick the Wise, whom he had served as
secretary, George Spalatin was called to Altenburg, Saxony, where he
became chief pastor or bishop in August, 1525. He invited Luther to be
present at his marriage on November 19 to Catherine, the daughter of
John Heydenreich. In the following letter Luther explained that he was
unable to attend and then proceeded to reply to a question which his
friend had raised. From the start Spalatin had encountered opposition in
Altenburg at the hands of the canons of St. George, who insisted on the
retention of Catholic ceremonies. Faced with this difficulty, Spalatin
wondered whether he might seek help from the State to enforce reforms.
The substance of Luther's reply appears again and again in his writings:
The State has no right to compel anyone to believe or not believe, but it
has the right and duty to suppress sedition and public disorder.[13] [Text
in Latin; *WA, Br,* IV, 615-617.]

---

12 See *Ordnung eines gemeinen Kastens* (1523), in *WA,* XII, 11–30; English
  translation, "Preface to an Ordinance of a Common Chest,"in *Works of*
  Martin Luther, Philadelphia ed., IV, 87–98.
13 See especially his "Secular Authority: to What Extent It Should Be
  Obeyed" (1523), translated in *Works of Martin Luther,* Philadelphia ed.,
  III, 223–273.

To Mr. George Spalatin, new bridegroom and husband, servant of Christ, and my brother in the Lord: grace and peace.

My dear Spalatin:

How I should like to be present at your wedding! I should not allow myself to be hindered in going so that Erasmus' free will[14] might be forced to serve me. But the recent flight of nuns provides me with new troubles, for that ignoble crowd of nobles there is raging against me.[15] It is remarkable that we cannot trust even those who have hitherto seemed most evangelical. Amsdorf himself was lately in peril from those whom, alongside himself, we considered our very citadel and refuge in time of need. Amsdorf said, "Not only God but the whole world sees what scoundrels they are."[16] You would be surprised at their names if I felt it proper to commit them to writing. This is the reason why I cannot visit you, for I am restrained by the tears of my Katie,[17] who believes, as you write, that you desire nothing less than to put me in danger. The argument she uses is that I have high regard for Amsdorf's opinion. Besides, you know that the more zealous for the gospel our present prince is, the less he is feared by his own courtiers, who hope to do what they please with him.

You ask whether princes should suppress religious abominations, and you say that our opponents urge against this, first, that no one ought to be forced to believe or to accept the gospel; secondly, that there is no precedent for so doing; and thirdly, that the princes have power only in externals.

You should answer them thus: Why did they formerly do what they now contend should not be done? For they forced men not only to external compliance with their abominations but also to inward disbelief and impiety of heart. They should, in some measure at least, employ the same rule for us that they apply to themselves. That they used coercion is plain enough from the fact that they invoked the aid of a foreign prince, and for this alone they ought to be expelled. But our princes do not force anyone to believe or to accept the gospel, but only suppress external abominations. When, therefore, they themselves

---

14 Luther is alluding to his controversy with Desiderius Erasmus over freedom of the will; see E. Gordon Rupp, ed., *Luther and Erasmus on Free Will*, Vol. XVII of The Library of Christian Classics.

15 On Sept. 29, 1525, Luther wrote to Michael Stiefel, "This night I had thirteen nuns removed from the power of Duke George and I snatched this booty of Christ from the raging tyrant." *WA, Br,* IV, 584.

16 This quotation in German. Nicholas Amsdorf was a clergyman in Magdeburg.   17 *Katenae,* chains; a play on words.

admit that the princes have power over externals, our opponents condemn themselves. For princes ought to suppress
public crimes like perjury and open blasphemy of God's name,
such as they indulge in, but without forcing those who are
suppressed to believe or not believe, whether they secretly
curse or not. We speak of public slander and blasphemy with
which they curse our God. This, I say, we ought to suppress if
we can; if not, we are obliged to suffer it. By this no one is
forced to believe or to accept the gospel, although our opponents would, if they could, force men to their impious opinions,
and not being able to do it, conspire with and approve of those
who do it and therefore deserve like punishment. (Rom., ch.
1.)[18] We have a sufficient precedent, I think, in Christ's making
scourges and expelling the buyers and sellers from the Temple
with force.[19]

Keep on, therefore, and be not moved by what they say.
Farewell in the Lord to you and your wife. When Master
Eberhard[20] goes I shall send what I can to honor your wedding.
Saint Martin's Day, 1525.   Martin Luther.

TO ELECTOR JOHN OF SAXONY.
September 16, 1527

*In response to repeated requests, the elector of Saxony allowed the town
council of Wittenberg to convert the local Franciscan monastery, which
was now deserted,[21] into a poorhouse. Only such poor people as were
afflicted with diseases like leprosy and syphilis were to be excluded.
Luther's active interest in the project is reflected in the following letter,
which illustrates one of the ways in which monastic property was sometimes applied to the needs of a community during the Reformation. [Text
in German; WA, Br, IV, 248, 249.]*

To my gracious lord, Duke John, elector of Saxony, etc., to be
delivered into his own hands: grace and peace in Christ Jesus.
Serene, highborn Prince, gracious Lord:
Your Grace recently gave the town council of Wittenberg
permission to use the local Franciscan monastery as a refuge for
the sick. Accordingly the council, the pastor,[22] and I inspected

[18] Cf. Rom. 1:32.   [19] Cf. John 2:15.
[20] Eberhard Brisger, Spalatin's associate in Altenburg, was planning to go
to Altenburg from Wittenberg on Nov. 11.
[21] See Luther's letter to Elector John on Feb. 21, 1526, in Chapter VI.
[22] John Bugenhagen.

it and discovered that Gregory Burger[23] has secured from Your Grace the best and most useful parts, such as the well, cistern, bathrooms, brewhouse, and other most important rooms and space, without which the rest of the monastery can be of little use. But when we spoke to him about this, he indicated his willingness to abandon the property for the sake of the poor people and in the hope that Your Grace might grant him another property in return.

Inasmuch as the burial places of both Jews and heathen are held in great honor, this monastery, which was an old burial site for princes, cannot be put to better use than to set it aside for the service of God and of poor people, in whom Christ himself is served. Therefore, it is my humble request that Your Grace will order and give the monastery, including Gregory Burger's space and buildings, to our Lord Jesus Christ to be used as an asylum and home for his poor members, for he says, "Inasmuch as ye have done it unto one of the least of these my brethren, ye have done it unto me."[24] I also humbly request that Your Grace earnestly command the council to put it into usable condition without damaging it, lest in time grasping hands should fall upon it and tear it down. Herewith I commend Your Grace to God. Amen.

Your Grace's humble servant,

Martin Luther.

Monday after the Exaltation of the Cross, 1527.

TO MARGRAVE GEORGE OF BRANDENBURG.
July 18, 1529

Under date of June 15, 1529, the margrave of Brandenburg had written to Luther to report that the churches throughout Brandenburg had been reformed and to request Luther's "faithful, Christian counsel" on the best way to correct "the offensive and unchristian abuses" which still prevailed in the monasteries. "We bear witness before God," the margrave wrote, "that we seek nothing but God's honor, the salvation of our subjects, and universal Christian peace, and that we do not intend to make any profit for ourselves from the monastic property and endowments."[25] The following letter was written by Luther in response to this request. [Text in German; WA, Br, V, 119-121.]

To the serene, highborn prince and lord, George, margrave of Brandenburg, duke of Stettin in Pomerania, prince of Rügen,

[23] Former tax collector, now official escort, in Wittenberg.
[24] Matt. 25:40.   [25] Cf. WA, Br, V, 97, 98.

and burgrave of Nuremberg, my gracious lord: grace and peace in Christ.

Serene, highborn Prince, gracious Lord:

I have long delayed my answer to Your Grace, though unwillingly, for at first, when the courier was urging me, I had no leisure, and afterward I had no trustworthy courier. Your Grace will kindly pardon me. But now that I have got this George Schlegel,[26] who is a reliable courier, I shall tell Your Grace, after having advised with Master Philip Melanchthon, what I consider the best thing to do in this matter.

In the first place, we think it well that the monasteries and foundations should be left as they are until they die out, for so long as the old inmates still live, and they are forced either to introduce or put up with innovations, there is little hope that there will be any peace. Moreover, such worship, established on the foundation of the old manner of worship, will in time become an unprofitable thing, as has occurred before. Whatever of the old, good order of worship it is desired to reintroduce is best put into the schools and parish churches, where the common man too can be present and be touched by it, etc., as we do here in Wittenberg and in other towns.

In the second place, it would be good if in Your Grace's principality Your Grace would establish one or two universities, where not only the Holy Scriptures but also law and all the sciences would be taught. From these schools learned men could be got as preachers, pastors, secretaries, councilors, etc., for the whole principality. To this purpose the income of the monasteries and foundations could be applied so that good scholars could be maintained in the schools at proper salaries: two theologians, two jurists, one professor of medicine, one mathematician, and four or five men for grammar, logic, rhetoric, etc. If studying is to be encouraged, you must have, not empty cloisters and deserted monasteries and endowed churches, but a city in which many people come together, work together, and incite and stimulate one another. Solitary studies do not accomplish this, but common studies do, for where many are together one gives another incentive and example.

In the third place, it is well that in all towns and villages good primary schools be established. From these could be picked and chosen those who are fit for the universities, and men can then be taken from the universities who are to serve your land and people. If the towns or their citizens cannot do this, it would be

26 A student recently matriculated in Wittenberg.

well to establish new stipends for the support of a few bright fellows in the deserted monasteries, and so every town might have one or two students. In the course of time, when the common people see that their sons can become pastors and preachers and incumbents of other offices, many of those who now think that a scholar cannot get a living will again keep their sons in school.

If some of the scholars who are trained in these schools take service and hold office in the dominions of other princes, and the objection is made that you are training people for other lords, it must be remembered that this does no harm, for beyond a doubt these men will promote the founding and endowment of schools in the lands of other princes and peoples, etc.

This is the advice that, in my little wisdom, I have desired to give Your Grace. God grant Your Grace his Holy Spirit to improve on all this and in all things to do his will. Amen.

Your Grace's obedient servant,

Martin Luther.

I also pray, if my gracious lord may be so good, that Your Grace will grant to the messenger George Schlegel, of Gunzenhausen, part of a vacated prebend to enable him to study here with us for a while. In our opinion he has the qualities to make a good pastor or preacher. Moreover, he is a native of your land, etc.

TO ELECTOR JOHN OF SAXONY. November 18, 1529

By the close of the third decade of the sixteenth century Emperor Charles V had a freer hand to deal with domestic problems in his empire and he believed that the time had come to extirpate the German heresy. Faced with the threat of military action, some of the Protestant princes proposed a defensive union. Prominent among these princes was Philip of Hesse, who pressed Elector John of Saxony to make up his mind as to what he would do if there were resort to force. Through his chancellor, Gregory Brück, John asked his four theologians in Wittenberg—Luther, Melanchthon, Jonas, and Bugenhagen—for advice, and the following letter was Luther's reply in behalf of his colleagues and himself. In the situation which then existed Luther may be said to have been more optimistic than realistic, but he could not reconcile himself to the idea of a "religious war."[27] [Text in German; WA, Br, V, 180-183.]

[27] Hans von Schubert, *Bekenntnisbildung und Religionspolitik, 1529-1530* (Gotha, 1910).

To the serene, highborn prince and lord, John, duke of Saxony and elector, etc., landgrave in Thuringia, and margrave of Meissen, my gracious lord: grace and peace in Christ.

Serene, highborn Prince, gracious Lord:

The honorable and learned Dr. Gregory Brück has brought us four a document from Your Grace, and after learning Your Grace's views from him, we have put in writing the best advice we can give. I beg Your Grace to receive our humble opinion kindly.

Our conscience will not permit us to approve or advise any such league, for we remember to what it may lead, and that bloodshed or some other great misfortune may result, so that we might be glad to be out of it and yet be unable to get out. Any such disaster would be intolerable, and we would ten times rather be dead than have it on our consciences that our gospel had become, through any fault of ours, the cause of bloodshed or of harm. It is our lot to be the sufferers and, as the prophet says in Ps. 44, to be "counted as sheep for the slaughter,"[28] and not to avenge ourselves or defend ourselves but give place to the wrath of God.[29]

That this course puts Your Grace in danger does no harm. Our Lord Christ is strong enough and can readily find ways and means to keep this danger from injuring Your Grace. He can destroy the thoughts of the ungodly princes (Ps. 33).[30] For it is our opinion that this undertaking of the emperor is only a threat of Satan which will be powerless and will contribute in the end to the downfall of our opponents; as Ps. 7 puts it, "His mischief shall return upon his own head, and his violent dealings shall come down upon his own pate."[31] To be sure, Christ takes ways—and it is right and proper—to test us and see whether we take his Word seriously and whether we hold it to be certain truth or not. If we really wish to be Christians and have eternal life yonder, we can have no better way than the way our Lord himself and all the saints had and still have. Christ's cross must always be borne. The world will not bear it but lays it upon others. We Christians therefore must bear it so that it may not remain unborne and become of no account. Your Grace has borne it well heretofore, both in the time of the great uprising[32] and in the face of great trials, envy, hatred, and the many evil wiles of friend and foe. God has always helped

28 Ps. 44:22.   29 Cf. Rom. 12:19.
30 Ps. 33:10.   31 Ps. 7:16.
32 The Peasants' War of 1524–1525.

Your Grace and given Your Grace courage, and he has not left Your Grace comfortless, either in body or in soul, but has graciously revealed, broken up, and put to shame all the wiles and snares of the devil. Nor will he make it hard for us in the future if we believe and pray. We know for certain that our cause is not our own but God's, and the manifest help that he has given us has proved it. This is our comfort and our confidence. He has shown himself to be a true Father and has taken up and defended his own cause in such wise that we must confess that it would have been beyond our ability and power, and we could not have directed, defended, and carried on the matter with our own reason.

I therefore humbly beg and exhort Your Grace to be confident and unalarmed at this danger. God willing, we shall accomplish more by our prayers and petitions to God than they with all their defiance of him. Only we must keep our hands clean of blood and violence, and if it were to come to the pass (though I think it will not) that the emperor actually attacks us and demands that I or the others be given up, then by God's help we shall assume responsibility and not put Your Grace in any danger on our account, as I have often told Your Grace's late brother, my gracious lord, Duke Frederick.

For Your Grace ought not to defend my faith or that of any other, nor can Your Grace do so, but everyone must defend his own faith and believe or disbelieve at his own peril and at no one's else, if it goes so far that our overlord, the emperor, attacks us. Meanwhile much water is running by the mill, and God will find a way to keep things from going as they want them to.

May Christ, our Lord and our Defense, bestow on Your Grace the riches of his strength. Amen.

Your Grace's humble servant,

November 18, 1529.   Martin Luther.

TO PRINCE JOACHIM OF BRANDENBURG.
August 3, 1532

On July 15, 1532, Prince Joachim, who had earlier indicated his purpose to participate in an expedition against the Turks, was chosen by the Saxons to be their military leader. He informed Luther of this and asked him for Christian counsel and instruction before he was to set out for war. In the following response Luther indicates in what frame of mind a

Christian might enter battle.[33] [Text in German; *WA, Br,* VI, 343-345.]

Grace and peace in Christ, our Lord and Saviour. Amen.

Serene, highborn Prince, gracious Lord:

I have received Your Highness's letter and learned from it of Your Highness's intention to take the field personally as captain of soldiers of the Saxon district in the war against that accursed tyrant, the Turk. I have also read Your Highness's request for my prayers and for a letter of Christian instruction.

I am heartily glad to hear that Your Highness has so Christian a heart and disposition in such matters and undertakings. Accordingly I am reluctant to omit accompanying you with my prayers to the best of my ability. Apart from Your Highness's request, since I cannot go along bodily, I feel that I am obliged to take the field spiritually with my earnest prayers, join in with my dear Emperor Charles and his soldiers, and help to fight under his banners against Satan and his adherents. God grant that this may be the time when Michael, the prince of God's people, will arise and deliver his people, as Dan., ch. 7, prophesies.[34]

First, and above all else, I wish and I pray God through our Lord Jesus Christ that he may give the pious emperor and all the princes and others who are now to fight against the Turk a courageous spirit that relies cheerfully on God's help. May he graciously keep them from depending on their own power and strength, as do the Turks, for such reliance would be disastrous. Rather let them sing with David, "I shall not trust in my sword."[35] And again, "Lord, thou art the one that giveth victory unto kings."[36] And once again, "Some trust in chariots and some in horses, but we will remember the Lord our God."[37] There are also many other similar verses in the Psalter.

This is what David did when he killed Goliath and said, "Thou comest to me with a sword and with a spear, but I come to thee in the name of the Lord," etc.[38] It is said that the Turkish emperor, when he drew his sword, swore that it was his god. May God help that this idol of his may become a filthy object of ridicule on account of his pride, presumption, and folly. Amen.

[33] Cf. *Vom Kriege wider die Türken* (1529), in *WA,* XXXIII, 81–148; English translation, "On War Against the Turk," in *Works of Martin Luther,* Philadelphia ed., V, 75–123.   [34] Dan. 12:1.
[35] Cf. Ps. 44:6.   [36] Cf. Ps. 144:10.   [37] Ps. 20:7.   [38] I Sam. 17:45.

Secondly, I beg that those on our side may not place their reliance on the Turk's being altogether wrong and God's enemy while we are innocent and righteous in comparison with the Turk, for such presumption is also vain. Rather is it necessary to fight with fear of God and reliance on his grace alone. We too are unrighteous in God's sight. Some on our side have shed much innocent blood, have despised and persecuted God's Word, and have been disobedient, and so we cannot take our stand on our merits, no matter how righteous or unrighteous the Turks and we may be. For the cursed devil is also God's enemy and does us great injustice and wrong. In comparison with the devil we are innocent, and yet we must not boast of our innocence and the superiority of our right, but must fight against him in fear and humility and with God's help alone. This is what David did in his fight against Goliath. He did not boast of his rights, but with God's help he fought and said, "Thou hast blasphemed against God, in whom I put my trust."[39] In like manner we must pray God, not that he may avenge our innocence against the Turk, but rather that he may glorify his holy name against those great blasphemers and meanwhile graciously forget our sins.

Thirdly, I wish and pray that in such a war those on our side may not seek honor, glory, land, booty, etc., but only the glory of God and his name, together with the defense of poor Christians and subjects. For the glory should and will be God's alone. As unworthy sinners we deserve nothing but shame, dishonor, and even death, as Your Highness knows better than I can write. But since Your Highness has so earnestly requested spiritual counsel, I have wished to set down this brief opinion in Your Highness's service. I have no doubt that if Your Highness inculcates such sentiments in others, with the result that the war is conducted on such a high plane, the devil and all his angels will be too weak for our soldiers and the Turks will encounter men who are different from those whom they have fought before, when both sides were insolent and fought without God, which has always harmed God's people more than their enemies.

May Your Highness now go forth in God's name. And may the same God send his angel Michael to accompany Your Highness and help all of you to gain a glorious victory and return home to the praise and honor of God. Amen.

Our prayers shall go with you and follow after you. Please

[39] Suggested by I Sam. 17:45.

God, they will also await Your Highness in the field, that they may be found there. May it please Your Highness to accept these lines which I have written in haste.

Herewith I commit Your Highness to God's keeping. Amen.

Your Highness's willing servant,

August 3, 1532.   Martin Luther, Doctor.

TABLE TALK RECORDED BY VEIT DIETRICH.[40]
About 1533

The question was asked whether a tyrant who persistently acts wickedly and contrary to right and justice may be assassinated. "It is not allowable for a private citizen to do so, even if he can," said Luther, "for the Fifth Commandment, 'Thou shalt not kill,'[41] prohibits it. If I surprise a man, not a tyrant, with my wife or daughter, I could kill him. Likewise if a man took one person's wife, another's daughter, another's fields and goods, and still another's house and means of livelihood, the citizens, unable any longer to endure his violence and tyranny, may form a conspiracy, and it would be permissible for them to kill him, for if it is allowable for a private citizen to do so when he surprises a man with his wife," etc.

TO KING CHRISTIAN III OF DENMARK.
December 2, 1536

When King Frederick I of Denmark died in 1533, his son Christian succeeded to the throne. But he was opposed by the Catholics in Denmark, and it was not until the summer of 1536 that he finally established his authority. Because the Danish bishops opposed the introduction of Evangelical teaching as well as the claims of Christian III, they were arrested on August 20 and were not released until they had renounced their offices. This removal of the bishops (who were later replaced by others) marked the triumph of the Reformation in Denmark. It was accompanied and followed by the confiscation of churches, monasteries, gold and silver, and other valuables. Against such secularization of church property Luther here warned the king. [Text in German; WA, Br, VII, 602-604.]

To the mighty, serene, highborn prince and lord, Christian, elected king of Denmark and Norway, etc., duke of Schleswig

---

[40] Macaronic text; WA, TR, I, No. 1126.   [41] Ex. 20:13.

and Holstein, etc., my gracious lord: grace and peace in Christ, our Lord and Saviour, and also my poor prayers.

Mighty, serene, highborn Prince and gracious King:

I have read Your Majesty's letter with great satisfaction. It pleased me to learn that Your Majesty has wiped out[42] the bishops who were unable to cease persecuting the Word of God and introducing disorder into the secular government. In so far as I can, I shall help to interpret and defend what Your Majesty has done.

At the same time I humbly pray Your Majesty to set aside a sufficient portion of the spiritual properties which are under the jurisdiction of the crown in order that good and ample provision may continue to be made for the churches. For if the properties are taken away and distributed, wherewith will the preachers be supported? I admonish Your Majesty to do this— perhaps unnecessarily, for I have no doubt that Your Majesty will know how to deal with this matter in a wise and Christian way without my admonition. However, I am moved to mention it by the example of our own people, among whom there are many who would like to lay their hands on everything, and many of our pastors would be in a bad way if God had not given us such a pious prince, a man who is faithful and earnest in his intention and in his administration.

If Satan should raise up such persons in Your Majesty's lands, may God help Your Majesty to bear in mind what is needful to the churches, namely, the Word of God, from which all, both now and in the future, should learn how to be saved and to escape from eternal death. For everything depends on the Word of God.

May Christ, our dear Lord, be with Your Majesty here and hereafter. Amen.

Your Majesty's willing [servant],

Martin Luther, Doctor.

Saturday after Saint Andrew's Day, 1536.

TABLE TALK RECORDED BY ANTHONY LAUTERBACH.[43] November 22, 1538

Then Dr. Martin Luther spoke of the boorishness and barbarity of Saxon law. "Saxony," he said, " has very strict laws. It would be best if there were a common, imperial law for the whole

---

42 Luther was laboring under the mistaken impression that the bishops had been put to death.　　43 Macaronic text; *WA, TR,* IV, No. 4139.

empire, but the present laws are so deeply rooted that no change could be made without great confusion. For example, the Saxon law is unfavorable to women. If a husband dies and is survived by a widow who lived with him faithfully for many years, she is compelled to leave her home as a servant woman because the law states that a stool and distaff must be given to the widow or surviving wife. The jurists interpret 'stool and distaff' literally, and so a godly wife is worse off than a servant maid. I, on the other hand, interpret 'stool and distaff' allegorically to mean shelter and food. Even the jurists themselves understand 'four posts' to mean the whole house."[44]

It was then reported that Dr. Fachs[45] was laboring to reduce Saxon laws to an orderly code. Luther replied, "He will work in vain, just as I would if I wished to conjugate the verb *sum* by rule, like this: *sum, sus, sut*."

TO GREGORY BRUECK. January 2, 1540

In medieval Germany debtors' bondsmen were sometimes quartered in inns at the debtors' expense until all debts were paid. What was even worse, debtors were required to entertain and feed the bondsmen's guests. Technically called "einreiten" or "intrare," this right to sponge on unfortunate debtors often produced bankruptcy. Here Luther refers to the case of a Silesian nobleman, Martin List, who paid fifteen times his indebtedness (perhaps an exaggeration) to entertain four fellow noblemen who took advantage of his situation. Luther called upon the government to reform this abuse. [Text in German; WA, Br, IX, 2, 3.]

To the distinguished gentleman, Gregory Henry von Brück, doctor of laws, chancellor and councilor of Saxony, my dear lord and compatriot: grace and peace.

My dear Sir and Friend:

I had hoped that you might visit us during the festival season.[46] Since you have not done so, I must send you this memorandum to request you to intercede with my gracious lord, the elector, that His Grace may forbid the practice of *einreiten* by noblemen in his land. What is the purpose of this shameful harassing, flaying, and robbing of people in public inns, which is carried on legally under princely protection and by which noblemen ruin, destroy, and devour one another?

---

[44] That is, the four walls of a house represent, by synecdoche, the house itself.   [45] Lewis Fachs, professor of law in Leipzig.
[46] Christmas. Brück may have stayed away on account of the plague.

Because Martin List owed twenty florins, four noblemen have just squandered three hundred florins (it is said) by feasting and reveling in an inn at his expense. How much better it would have been if each had contributed five florins to free poor List from his debt!

This is also happening elsewhere. What devil has given the nobility such power to arrest, imprison, and plunder men without the knowledge and against the will of their overlords? If such treatment were accorded an incendiary or assassin like Kohlhase,[47] it might be proper. But here one noble treats another in this fashion with princely permission and protection. If the princes do not forbid and punish this, God will punish the princes, and all of us with them. And who knows why conditions have taken such a bad turn? Perhaps (or should I say, surely?) in the exercise of our offices we have taken a bad turn in God's sight and as a consequence one is incited against another.

Indeed, the princes are obliged to stop this; and you are obliged to counsel and urge that it be stopped, or you too will be responsible for the harm and injury which result. I am thinking of addressing an open letter to the princes on this matter. But what I write will amount to nothing, and it will quickly be tossed aside, unless you actively intervene at the top level, as your office and duty require.

How many are the ways in which the devil can start trouble! If the Turk does not devour us, if the pestilence does not dispose of us, and if the emperor does not suppress us, we shall ruin, exhaust, and devour ourselves with greed and usury. God have mercy upon us. And if this does not help, may the Last Judgment overtake us. Amen.

Herewith I commit you to God's keeping.

Friday after the Circumcision, 1540.   Martin Luther.

TABLE TALK RECORDED BY JOHN MATHESIUS.[48]
September 17, 1540

Dr. Martin Luther was asked whether a pastor or preacher has the power to rebuke the government. He replied: "Yes, indeed! For although it is a divine institution, God has reserved

---

[47] Hans Kohlhase, a merchant in Brandenburg, started a feud against the family of a Saxon nobleman in 1532 and later extended it to the robbing, burning, and pillaging of other Saxons and their property. See also *WA, TR*, IV, No. 4335.   [48] Text in German; *WA, TR*, V, No. 5258.

the right to punish vices and correct wrongs. Accordingly one should rebuke secular rulers if they allow the goods of their poor subjects to be drained off and ruined by usury and bad government. But it is not proper for a preacher to prescribe measures and say at what price bread, meat, etc., should be sold and valued. In general, pastors should instruct every man in terms of his calling in order that he might do, diligently and faithfully, what God has commanded and that he might not steal, commit adultery, fleece, flay, deceive, or take advantage of his neighbor," etc.

TABLE TALK RECORDED BY ANTHONY LAUTERBACH.[49] August 5, 1538

Luther's brother, James Luther, arrived that day with Master Cölius.[50] They said many things about Count Albert [of Mansfeld] and called him a scourge of his people. Luther responded: "I regret that your lot is so unfavorable on account of his wickedness, which stands in the way of God's blessing. For when God grants a blessing to all people, as he does in the case of the mines, etc., and one person tries to appropriate this wealth to himself and so take God captive, God will withhold his blessing. He wishes to remain free in his gifts, not captive."

TO MICHAEL COELIUS. March 9, 1541

A former Roman priest, Michael Cölius (1492-1559) was an early convert to the Evangelical faith. On Luther's recommendation he was appointed chaplain at the court of Count Albert of Mansfeld. He had the reputation of being an earnest and effective preacher who did not hesitate to rebuke evil wherever he encountered it. This helps to explain the apparent confidence with which Luther called upon him to speak to the counts of Mansfeld about their bad government. [Text in German; WA, Br, IX, 334, 335.]

My dear Sir and Friend:

When you have an opportunity to speak to my gracious lords (especially to my gracious lord, Count John George), I suggest that you request, admonish, and urge them for the sake of God's Word that they cease giving such manifest cause for popular

[49] Macaronic text; *WA, TR,* IV, No. 3948.
[50] On Michael Cölius see the following letter.

complaint about their oppression of their subjects. This will assuredly result in the greatest harm to themselves. I am certain that this is so. And I regret that my fatherland[51] may in so wretched a fashion become a plaything of the devil. God is beginning to withhold his blessing.[52] If the mines do not prosper, all Germany will suffer from the loss.

Woe to him who is the cause of such misfortune and injury, who causes so many people distress! No matter what his station, he is bringing a curse upon himself.

Let us pray that God may grant him his Spirit, strength, and help so that my gracious lord may prevent this devilish calamity (or, rather, this calamity which results from God's wrath). If this does not help, at least the devil will not prevail in the end, for the Judgment Day will intervene.

Otherwise you may inform my gracious lord that I am praying faithfully for him and that I offer him my willing service.

March 9, 1541.   Martin Luther, Doctor.

TO COUNT ALBERT OF MANSFELD.
December 28, 1541[53]

Certain mines in Thuringia had for some time been held by individual families as hereditary fiefs. This arrangement was disturbed when, in order to increase his income, Count Albert of Mansfeld began to confiscate the mines and the forges connected with them. Luther had protested against a confiscation of this kind in his letter to Count Albert on May 24, 1540,[54] and had asked the count's chaplain to administer a rebuke (see above). Here he addresses a sharper exhortation to the count. [Text in German; WA, Br, IX, 624-630.]

To the noble, highborn lord, Count Albert of Mansfeld, my gracious and dearly beloved lord: grace and peace in the Lord and my poor prayers.

---

51 Luther was a native of the County of Mansfeld.
52 In an earlier letter to Count Albert of Mansfeld, May 24, 1540, Luther had warned that Mansfeld would be deprived of the blessing of divine grace.
53 This letter, conflated with another on the subject of predestination, has usually been published under date of Feb. 23, 1542. On the problems of text and date see WA, Br, IX, 624-626.
54 See WA, Br, IX, 114-116. The letter of May 23, 1542, below, also deals with this problem.

Gracious Sir:

I desire from the bottom of my heart that you may receive in a Christian and gracious way what I write here. Your Grace knows that I am a native of the territory of Mansfeld.[55] Until now I have naturally loved my native land, for even the books of heathen writers declare that every child has a natural love for his fatherland. Besides, God did many laudable things through Your Grace at the beginning of the gospel[56]: churches, pulpits, and schools were well ordered to the praise and honor of God. And during the peasant uprising[57] God made excellent and glorious use of Your Grace. For these and other reasons I cannot readily forget Your Grace or cease to pray for you and be concerned about you.

But it appears to me, especially from rumors and complaints that have reached me, that Your Grace has fallen away from such good beginnings and has become a very different person. As Your Grace may well believe, this causes me great heartache on your account. Your Grace too must be aware that you have become cold, have given your heart to Mammon, and have the ambition to become very rich. According to complaints Your Grace is also sharply and severely oppressive to subjects and proposes to confiscate their forges and goods and to make what amounts to vassals out of them. God will not suffer this. Or if he does, he will allow your land to become impoverished and go to ruin, for he can take away what is his own gift without giving an accounting for it; as Haggai says: "Ye have sown much, and bring in little; and he that earneth wages, earneth wages to put it into a bag with holes."[58]

I have heard some say that it has been proposed to establish in Germany a government like that in France. I should approve of this if it were first determined whether it would be right and agreeable in God's sight. Meanwhile it is well to observe that the kingdom of France, which was once a golden and glorious kingdom, now has nothing to boast of either in people or in goods. In comparison with the former golden kingdom, it has become a leaden and tinnish kingdom. What before was called a Christian kingdom now is friendly with the Turks. This is what happens when God and his Word are despised.

This is, I believe, the last time that I shall be writing to Your Grace, for I am nearer to my grave than may be supposed. I

[55] Luther was born in Eisleben, County of Mansfeld.
[56] I.e., the beginning of the Reformation.
[57] The Peasants' War, 1524–1525.   [58] Hag. 1:6.

pray again that Your Grace may be more gentle and gracious
with your subjects. Let them remain as before. Then Your
Grace will also remain, if God wills it, here and hereafter.
Otherwise Your Grace will lose both, as the fable of Aesop tells
of the man who killed the goose that laid a golden egg every
day and so lost both the daily eggs and the goose that was the
source of them, or like the dog in Aesop that lost the piece of
meat when he snapped at the shadow of the meat in the water.[59]
This is certainly true, that he who desires too much will have
too little, as Solomon states again and again in the book of
Proverbs.

In short, I am concerned about Your Grace's soul. I cannot
permit myself to cease praying for you and being concerned
about you, for then I am convinced that I would cease being
in the Church. Not only the law of Christian love constrains
me, but also the dire threat in Ezek., ch. 4, that God will
damn us preachers for the sins of others: "If thou givest him
not warning, nor speakest to warn the wicked from his wicked
way, to save his life; the same wicked man shall die in his
iniquity; but his blood will I require at thine hand, for therefore have I made thee a pastor."[60] Your Grace will know how
to take this admonition, for I cannot allow myself to be damned
for Your Grace's sin. I desire, rather, that you may be saved
together with me, if this be possible. If not, I have at least done
my duty and am excused in God's sight.

Herewith I commit you to God in all his grace and mercy.
Amen.

Your Grace's willing and faithful [servant],

Martin Luther, Doctor.

TO JOHN KEGEL. May 23, 1542

*Andrew Kegel (or Kriegel), who had studied in Wittenberg and later
became a gifted schoolmaster, informed Luther that his aged father's
forge in Hettstedt had been confiscated—presumably by an action of
Count Albert of Mansfeld—and asked Luther to console his distressed
father. It is of some interest to observe the contrast in tone between
Luther's reply here and his exhortations in the preceding letters. There he
was rebuking oppressors; here he was consoling the oppressed.* [Text in
German; *WA, Br*, X, 69, 70.]

[59] For Luther's version (1530) of these fables of Aesop see *WA*, L, 442.
[60] Cf. Ezek. 3:18.

Grace and peace.

Honorable Sir and good Friend:

Your dear son Andrew has informed me that you are deeply distressed because you have been deprived of your forge, and he desires that I write you a brief letter about the matter.

My dear friend, I am truly sorry that you have been made to suffer such hardship and loss. May Christ, who is the best consolation of all who are in trouble, and who is both able and willing to help, comfort you. Amen.

Remember that you are not the only one whom the devil torments. Job was sorely vexed. Not only was he stripped of all he had, but he was also made to suffer in his body and soul. Yet God caused everything to turn out well, and Job was abundantly comforted. Learn to do what Ps. 56 suggests: "Cast thy burden upon the Lord, and he shall sustain thee."[61] And do what Saint Peter exhorts when he repeats this injunction: " Cast all your care upon him, for he careth for you."[62]

Even if the loss which you have suffered pains you for a while, God is faithful and may be relied upon to help in his time, as he promises in Ps. 50, "Call upon me in the day of trouble: I will deliver thee, and thou shalt glorify me."[63] For in Ps. 10 he is called "a refuge in times of trouble."[64]

Moreover, what are our sufferings in comparison with those which the Son of God endured innocently and in our behalf? Our weakness intensifies and aggravates our suffering; it would be more bearable if we were stronger.

Herewith I commend you to our dear Lord.

Tuesday after Exaudi, 1542.   Martin Luther.

TO GEORGE VON HARSTALL AND THE TOWN COUNCIL OF CREUZBURG. January 27, 1543

George Spenlein, a former Augustinian friar who had become an Evangelical clergyman, was so sharp and censorious in his relations with his parishioners in Creuzburg, Thuringia, that he caused great offense. Attempts were made to get rid of him, and Luther himself proposed that he be transferred to another parish.[65] Shortly thereafter the town council appealed to the official visitors for relief, but the latter supported and defended Spenlein. It was in this situation that Luther wrote the following letter, which, apart from any merits it may

61 Ps. 55:22.   62 I Peter 5:7.   63 Ps. 50:15.   64 Ps. 9:9.
65 See the letter of Luther and Bugenhagen to the town council in Gräfenhainichen, Jan. 23, 1543, in *WA, Br*, X, 246, 247.

have had in the immediate situation, expressed some of the Reformer's basic views concerning the ministry and its inherent independence from the State. [Text in German; *WA, Br*, X, 252-268.]

To the gracious, honorable, and prudent George von Harstall, bailiff, and to the burgomaster and council of Creuzburg, my good friends: grace and peace in the Lord.

Gracious, wise, and dear Sir and Friends:

Sometime ago I wrote to you, bailiff, and requested you to be good enough to let your parson[66] go. For as I understood the situation, he was a failure and had been dismissed by the visitors. Now I am informed by the visitors that he has not been a failure and that they had neither dismissed him nor intended to do so. On the contrary, they testify to the purity of his teaching and the irreproachable character of his life. But they also report that you have harbored a grudge against him because he rebuked vices, on which account you intended to drive him out. I gather from all this that the devil desires to start trouble and cause you great harm, wherefore I am moved to write this letter to you with the very friendly request that you receive it, as I intend, in your own best interests.

I trust that you have sufficient Christian understanding to know that the ministry and the gospel do not belong to us, or to any men, or even to an angel. The ministry is God's; it is our Lord's, who secured it with his blood, instituted it, and gave it to us for our salvation. Therefore he severely condemns those who despise it and declares, "He that despiseth you despiseth me,"[67] and Peter says, "It had been better for them not to have known the way of righteousness."[68]

Inasmuch as the two excellent men, Mr. Jobst [Menius] and Mr. Frederick [Myconius], the visitors who are responsible for such matters, both testify (and one must believe them) that your parson teaches the Word of God in its purity and lives an honorable life—to which the town of Creuzburg and its neighbors also bear witness—you see, dear sirs and friends, how wickedly and cunningly the evil spirit tempts you to lay violent hands on the chief pastor and bishop,[69] Jesus Christ, God's Son, who out of his great and special grace supplies you so abundantly and purely with his Word and Sacrament (that is, his suffering, death, and blood) through his faithful, godly

[66] *Pfarrher[r]*. George Spenlein had other clergymen under him.
[67] Luke 10:16.   [68] II Peter 2:21.
[69] I Peter 2:25.

minister, your parson. How unwilling the cursed devil is to suffer you to be saved!

Since there is no other cause or reason than that you have developed a grudge against your parson without his deserving it—indeed, because of his great pains and his faithful preaching —you must now consider that it is neither permissible nor possible for you to act unjustly to such a well-attested parson or to slander and violently eject him on account of your grudge and unreasonable prejudice. I do not blame the visitors for refusing to do this, to burden their consciences with such injustice for the devil's sake, and by giving in to your prejudice to go to the devil with you.

Be careful, dear sirs and friends! Be careful! If the devil succeeds in throwing you, he will not be satisfied until you come a cropper.

The first thing the devil will do is this: By making you despise and hate your parson without cause (which is to despise Christ himself, who is the head of all parsons), the devil will make you break yourselves on this stone[70] and be burned in the consuming fire. For in God's sight a godly, faithful pastor is more important than all the unchristian bailiffs, burgomasters, judges, and governments in the world together with all their power and prestige. This is so because the offices of government (if they are not Christian) do not serve God in his Kingdom as does the office of the ministry. Nor did Christ pay such a price (his own blood) for them as he did for the ministry. Accordingly the devil will cause your hearts to be closed and your mouths to be stopped so that you will no longer be able to believe, pray, worship, or lift up your heads before God in time of trouble, even as he says, "First be reconciled to thy brother, and then come and offer thy gift."[71] The result will be that you will no longer be Christians. You will have excommunicated yourselves. And that will be terrible.

In the second place, the devil will bring it about that you will be overwhelmed by other great sins in addition to this sin of your own. That is to say, if you drive out your innocent parson, the church will be deserted, children and other pious people will be deprived of the Word, Baptism, and Communion, and these people will be damned with you on your account. That will be worse than it was under papal rule. How will you answer for it? Moreover, if the common people and the dear youth see such a horrible example—rewarding the

70 Matt. 21:44.   71 Matt. 5:24.

faithful service and labor of learned, godly pastors by heaping disgrace and discredit upon them—who will send his children to school? Who will be willing to study at his own expense? Where shall we get pastors? By such wickedness of yours and of people like you the devil tries to bring these evils upon you. How much better it would be to live under the wicked pope and the cursed Turk—for there schools and churches have remained open to parsons and preachers—than under you, who propose to ruin everything!

In the third place, if you do not watch out, the devil will finally harden your impenitent hearts. That will be the end of you. There will be no more hope. This, in fact, is the cursed devil's intention. Therefore, the sooner you reconcile yourselves with your parson and the churches (that is, with Christ), the better it will be, lest you make an example of yourselves, as has already happened to others.

There are other ways of dealing with the matter. The church door is open to those who are unwilling to listen to the parson; they may stay outside and do without the grace of God. Churches were not built and parishes were not established to exclude those who wish to teach and hear God's Word or, on the other hand, to force those to enter who feel no need for and are unwilling to hear God's Word. They were built and established for the sake of those who gladly hear the Word and cannot do without it.

You are not lords over the pastoral office and over parsons. You have not instituted the office, but God's Son alone has done so. Nor have you contributed anything to it. You have no more right to it than the devil has a right to the Kingdom of Heaven. Accordingly you should not rule over it, dictate to it, or prevent it from rebuking you. For when pastors rebuke you, it is not man's but God's rebuke. And God desires the rebuke to be expressed, not suppressed. Keep to your own office and leave God's rule to him, lest he find it necessary to instruct you. None of you will suffer a stranger to lure or drive away a servant of yours for whom you have need. Indeed, there is no shepherd boy who is so insignificant that he would not resent unjust treatment from another's master. Only God's minister is treated like a no-account who is supposed to endure everything from everybody! No one is willing or able to let him speak, even if it is God's own Word.

I would have you take this admonition as a friendly one. I mean it to be so, for it is God's admonition. But if you will not listen and mend your ways, we shall wash our hands of you. Meanwhile we shall do what we can to resist the devil—at least that our conscience may not be burdened with your sins and that we may not give our consent to the devil's purpose.

We need not excommunicate you. You are excommunicating yourselves. We should be glad and should prefer to release you from the ban.

Even if you could secure another pastor at once, which is unlikely, you would still not be Christians, participants in Christian grace and life. Moreover, no pastor will accept your call against the will and command of the visitors. Who would even wish to go to minister to such treacherous Christians who have a bad reputation for forcibly and unjustly ejecting their pastors and who wish to be called Christians although they have disgraced the name? Such would be your reputation throughout the world that you would be marked as a horrible example.

Finally, I advise you in Christ's name to reconcile yourselves with your parson and live at peace with him. Let him teach, comfort, and chastise as God has commanded him and as his conscience requires; as it is written in Heb., ch. 13, "Obey them that have the rule over you (who are your parsons), as they that must give account."[72] For what you have in mind—that any bailiff, judge, or town councilor can, without right or reason and according to his mere whim, remove a parson—would establish an evil precedent and be a bad thing. God will not and cannot suffer it.

God grant that you may not experience his displeasure, but that you may learn, with fear and humility, to know his will, to honor his Son (that is, his Word) who redeemed you at great cost with his blood, and to respect his servants, the poor pastors, who are so harassed and so deserving of the help and protection which you worldly rulers can give them. If you do this, your work in your calling will be a divine service.

Herewith I commend you to the dear Lord in his grace.

Martin Luther, Doctor.

Saturday after Saint Paul's Conversion, 1543.

TO DANIEL GREISER. October 22, 1543

Daniel Greiser, superintendent (or bishop) in Dresden, seems to have questioned Luther about that section in Duke Maurice of Saxony's new

[72] Heb. 13:17.

constitution of 1543 which provided that the secular authorities should punish crimes with excommunication from the Church.[73] This invasion by the State in affairs of the Church was sharply criticized by Luther, who manifested an awareness of the dangers in State control of churches.
[Text in Latin; *WA, Br*, X, 436, 437.]

To the venerable and honorable gentleman, Dr. Daniel Greiser, very faithful pastor of the church in Dresden, my beloved brother: grace and peace.

My dear Daniel:

I can hope for no good from the form of excommunication which has been taken for granted in your court.[74] If it is to come to pass that courts will rule churches according to their desire, God will withhold his blessing, and the last error shall be worse than the first,[75] for what is done without faith is not good.[76] And what is done without vocation is undoubtedly done without faith and comes to nought. Either they[77] must themselves become pastors and must preach, baptize, visit the sick, administer Communion, and perform all ecclesiastical functions, or else they must cease to confuse callings. Let them be concerned about their courts and leave the churches to those who have been called to them and who are accountable to God for them. It is not to be tolerated that others take actions if we are to be held responsible for them.

We desire that the functions[78] of the Church and of the court be kept separate, or that both of them be given up. Satan continues to be Satan. Under the papacy he caused the Church to meddle in the State. Now he desires the State to meddle in the Church. But with God's help we propose to resist and to do what we can to keep the callings separate.

Farewell in the Lord, and pray for me.

Yours,

October 22, 1543.   Martin Luther, Doctor

TO EBERHARD VON DER THANN. January 10, 1544

In 1539, Elector John Frederick had committed the secularized monasteries in Saxony to several sequestrators who were instructed to visit the

[73] See the chapter "Von dem Banne" in E. Sehling, *Die evangelischen Kirchenordnungen des 16. Jahrhunderts* (Leipzig, 1902), I, 287.
[74] The court of Duke Maurice of Saxony in Dresden.
[75] Matt. 27:64.   [76] Cf. Rom. 14:23.
[77] The courts, i.e., the secular authorities.
[78] *Officia*, literally "offices."

properties semiannually and exercise general oversight over them. Since the individuals who managed the properties under the supervision of the sequestrators were more concerned about getting money out of them than about maintaining the lands and buildings, the elector decided in 1543 to end the arrangement and sell the properties. Luther defends the elector's decision in this letter to a bailiff of Königsberg, in Franconia. [Text in German; *WA, Br,* X, 497.]

Grace and peace in the Lord.

Gracious, able dear Sir and good Friend:

I have of late been so burdened with letters and duties that I have not been able to take care of any one before others. Moreover, all of them must pass through my mind before I put my hand to paper. Accordingly there has been some delay in this answer.

I am not upset by the fact that some people are grumbling because my gracious lord is selling spiritual properties (as they are called). His Grace suffered great losses to the insatiable visitors and sequestrators under the former experiment, and there was no other solution inasmuch as monkery[79] is not to be restored. Besides, the cost to His Grace of supporting the gospel with correspondence, negotiations, etc., is too great to be borne by the land. It must accordingly be accounted a good thing that these properties are transferred to the ruling class, and especially to those who are in need, for the very rich do not require them. Therefore let those who are scandalized by what has happened and who see the mote that is in another's eye first consider the beam that is in their own.[80]

Tell me, of what use to the churches is the whole Würzburg monastery and other foundations like it? There great wealth is spent to serve the devil and persecute the Word of God, while here schools, clergymen, and hospitals are maintained for the sake of God's Word and the churches. There endowments are rich and the canons few,[81] while here the monastery is poor and there are many brothers to support. They must therefore allow us to apply the little that we have to the glory of God (although I am well aware that everything will not be done with clean

---

[79] *Muncherey* (monkery) rather than *Mönchtum* (monasticism).

[80] Cf. Matt. 7:3.

[81] At Luther's table on Sept. 10, 1538 (*WA, TR,* IV, No. 4002), it was reported that six hundred rich parishes in the Roman Catholic diocese of Würzburg were vacant for want of priests.

hands), while we must allow them to employ their full chests in the service of the devil.

This must suffice for the present.

Herewith I commit you to God's keeping. Amen.

Martin Luther.

Thursday after the Feast of Three Kings, 1544.

TO THE TOWN COUNCIL OF KIEL. July 7, 1544

Two monasteries, named Holy Spirit and St. George, were closed in 1530 by King Frederick I of Denmark, and their property was transferred to the city of Kiel, in which they were located. A dispute later arose concerning the ownership of the property, and the town council of Kiel appealed to Luther with a presentation of its own case. [Text in German; *WA, Br*, X, 603, 604.]

Grace and peace in the Lord.

Honorable and dear Sirs and Friends:

I received from your courier the brief which you sent concerning two monasteries, on which you desire that I write a short opinion in accordance with the Holy Scriptures.

It is true that we theologians have taught, and still teach, that such vacated monastic property should be applied to the use, especially and above all, of the churches and of poor people. For this is a fair and godly solution, as you yourselves also state in your brief. But we theologians have nothing to do with determining who is entitled to this property or to whom it shall belong, for we are not commanded to do this, nor are we in a position to know the circumstances. This must be decided by the jurists after inquiring into both sides of the question. We are ready to accept the decision which the jurists may reach in the matter, or have already reached. For this is a worldly matter, and such things have been committed to the jurists.

Our theology teaches that secular law is to be observed for the punishment of evildoers and the protection of them that do well.[82] Accordingly Your Honors should ask the jurists about such and similar things. It is not our function as theologians to give a hearing to two parties in a dispute, and it is not proper to offer an opinion after hearing only one side or party.

Herewith I commit you to the dear Lord's keeping. Amen.

Monday after the Visitation of Mary, 1544.   Martin Luther.

[82] Cf. I Peter 2:14.

TO SIMON WOLFERINUS. September 19, 1544

On two successive Sundays, August 24 and 31, 1544, John Libius, of Eisleben, had preached against corruption and injustice in high places and low. In the course of his sermons he charged that his own ruler, Count Albert of Mansfeld, was guilty of oppressing his subjects by confiscating houses, vineyards, mines, and forges (see letter to Count Albert above), and that in his greed he even debased coins. The count's answer was to charge the preacher with sedition and to remove him from his office. After a passing reference to a marriage case, Luther defends Libius against the count. [Text in Latin; WA, Br, X, 658-660.]

To Simon, minister of the church in Eisleben: grace and peace.

My dear Simon:

The courier has our advice and opinion[83] on the matrimonial case which you described to me. I do not know whether your town council will accept it, but this is the way in which we proceed in our duchy: in order to curb adultery, we banish the guilty party and allow the innocent party the privilege of remarriage.

With regard to Libius, I believe that what he preached was correct. It distresses me greatly that Count Albert is not only troublesome to others, but also—and this is much worse—troublesome to himself. If he hopes to justify himself by stopping the mouth of a preacher or two, he is deceived. For there are too many mouths that speak evil of him (that is to say, his reputation is worse than I like to believe), and unless he reforms, he cannot be useful.

Accordingly he commits a great wrong and offense to charge Libius with sedition. It is not seditious for a preacher to reprove the mighty for the kind of life they live, even if the preacher may be mistaken. It is one thing to make a mistake and sin, and quite another to be seditious.

Consequently Count Albert must not be permitted to call any and every thing seditious according to his whim and wrath. In this case the count has sinned more against Libius than Libius has sinned against the count. If he wishes to be a Christian, the count is obliged to withdraw his charge and ask Libius' pardon. But if he has given himself up to the

---

83 The opinion of the consistory in Wittenberg, to which Luther had referred the case, was delivered by the same messenger who carried Luther's letter to Eisleben.

tempter, he will not listen. I suggest that you let him be, for his bad conscience will not give him peace. God be merciful to him and convert him. Amen.

Yours,

Martin Luther, Doctor.

Friday after the Exaltation of the Cross.

BIBLIOGRAPHIES

TEXTS

The translations in this volume are based on the texts offered by the Weimar edition of Luther's works. The main body of Luther's writings is included in *D. Martin Luthers Werke, kritische Gesammtausgabe*, 58 in 69 vols. to date (Weimar, 1883–). This work is cited as *WA* (Weimarer Ausgabe). The Weimar edition has a separate section devoted to the table talks: *D. Martin Luthers Werke, Tischreden*, edited by E. Kroker, 6 vols., complete with index (Weimar, 1912-1921). These volumes are cited as *WA, TR.* Another section of the Weimar edition is devoted to letters: *D. Martin Luthers Werke, Briefwechsel*, edited by Otto Clemen, 11 vols., with an index still to be published (Weimar, 1930-1948). These volumes are cited as *WA, Br.* There is also a fourth section of the Weimar edition, *Die deutsche Bibel*, 9 vols. to date (Weimar, 1906), which has not been used in the preparation of this book.

The edition of Luther's works that preceded the Weimar edition is occasionally referred to and it is cited as *EA* (Erlanger Ausgabe): *Dr. Martin Luther's sämmtliche Werke*, 67 vols. (Erlangen, 1826-1857), supplemented by *D. Martini Lutheri Exegetica Opera Latina*, 23 vols. (Erlangen, 1829-1841). Two other editions of Luther's correspondence have been used for comparison. The first is *Dr. Martin Luther's Briefwechsel*, 18 vols., edited by Ernst Ludwig Enders, *et al.* (Frankfurt on the Main, 1884-1923), cited as "Enders." The other is *Dr. Martin Luthers Briefe, Sendschreiben und Bedenken*, 6 vols., edited by W. M. L. de Wette (Berlin, 1825-1856), cited as "de Wette."

TRANSLATIONS

A list of Luther's works in English, which now needs to be supplemented, may be had in Roland H. Bainton, *Bibliography of the Continental Reformation: Materials Available in English* (American Society of Church History, Chicago, 1935). There are convenient translations of selected writings in *Works of Martin Luther with*

Introductions and Notes, 6 vols. (Muhlenberg Press, Philadelphia, 1915-1932), often referred to as the Philadelphia edition after the custom of naming editions after places of publication. A revision and extension of·this selection is under way. Only the first volume of a new series, *Reformation Writings of Martin Luther*, by Bertram Lee Woolf (Lutterworth Press, London, 1952), has appeared at this writing, but it is destined to replace the older Henry Cole, *Select Works of Martin Luther*, 4 vols. (London, 1826), and Henry Wace and C. A. Buchheim, *Luther's Primary Works* (London, 1883), in Great Britain.

The best selection of Luther's letters in English, together with letters to and about him, is in Preserved Smith and Charles M. Jacobs, *Luther's Correspondence and Other Contemporary Letters*, 2 vols. (Philadelphia, 1913, 1918), which extends only to April, 1530, and often abbreviates letters. Inferior by comparison is Margaret A. Currie, *The Letters of Martin Luther* (London, 1908), which paraphrases—not always accurately—rather than translates and omits long passages without warning to the reader. Mary Cooper Williams, *Luther's Letters to Women* (Wartburg Publishing House, Chicago, 1930), is a slight volume with wooden translations. All these translations appeared before the *Briefwechsel* of the Weimar edition.

Selections from Luther's table talks were translated by Henry Bell in *Martin Luther's Colloquia Mensalia, or His Last Divine Discourses at His Table* (London, 1652), and were frequently reprinted. The same is true of William Hazlitt, *The Table-Talk of Martin Luther* (London, 1848), a brief extract from which was published by Thomas S. Kepler in *Table Talk of Martin Luther* (The World Publishing Company, Cleveland, 1952). Both of these translations were based on partial and uncritical texts circulated for edifying reading, but a sampling of the table talks which had more recently been found was offered in Preserved Smith and Herbert P. Gallinger, *Conversations with Luther* (Boston, 1915). It is to be observed that even the last collection was translated before the critical texts of the Weimar edition's *Tischreden* were completed.

PERSONS, PLACES, SUBJECTS

The most useful guide for the location of information on persons places, and subjects is Karl Schottenloher, *Bibliographie zur deutschen Geschichte im Zeitalter der Glaubensspaltung, 1517-1585*, 6 vols. (Leipzig, 1933-1940). Standard works of reference are *Allgemeine deutsche Biographie*, 45 vols. with 11 supplementary volumes (Leipzig, 1875-1912); Albert Hauck, editor, *Realencyklopädie für protestantische Theologie und Kirche*, 22 vols. and 2 supplementary volumes (Leipzig, 1896-1912); *New Schaff-Herzog Encyclopedia of Religious Knowledge*, 13 vols. (New York, 1908-1912), with 2 supplementary volumes, edited by Lefferts A. Loetscher, *et al.* (Baker Book House, Grand Rapids, Michigan, 1955); Hermann Gunkel and Leopold Zscharnack, editors, *Die Religion in Geschichte und Gegenwart*, 6 vols. (Tübingen, 1927-1932); Carl Meusel, *et al.*, editors, *Kirchliches Handlexikon*, 7 vols. (Leipzig, 1887-1902). Biographies are also to be found in such older collections as Julius Hartmann, *et al.*, *Leben und ausgewählte Schriften der Väter und Begründer der lutherischen Kirche*, 8 vols. (Elberfeld, 1861-1875), and Moritz Meurer, editor, *Das Leben der Altväter der lutherischen Kirche*, 4 vols. (Leipzig, 1861-1864). The following are recent lives in English of Luther himself: Roland H. Bainton, *Here I Stand: a Life of Martin Luther* (The Abingdon Press, Nashville, 1950); Heinrich Boehmer, *Road to Reformation: Martin Luther to the Year 1521* (Muhlenberg Press, Philadelphia, 1946); James Mackinnon, *Luther and the Reformation*, 4 vols. (Longmans, Green & Co., Inc., London, 1925-1930); E. G. Schwiebert, *Luther and His Times* (Concordia Publishing House, St. Louis, 1950).

THEOLOGY AND SPIRITUAL COUNSEL

Following is a select list of studies in areas that are touched upon in this volume and have in recent years occupied the attention of many scholars in different countries. Y. J. E. Alanen, *Das Gewissen bei Luther* (Helsinki, 1934); Helmuth Appel, *Anfechtung und Trost im Spätmittelalter und bei Luther* (Leipzig, 1938); H. E. G. Barge, *Luther und der Frühkapitalismus* (Gütersloh, 1951); Werner Betcke, *Luthers Sozialethik* (Gütersloh, 1934); Paul Bühler, *Die Anfechtung bei Martin Luther* (Zurich, 1942); Rupert Eric Davies, *The Problem of Authority in the Continental Reformers* (The Epworth Press, London, 1946); Hastings Eels, *The Attitude of Martin Bucer Toward the Bigamy of Philip of Hesse* (New Haven, 1924); August Hardeland, *Geschichte der speciellen Seelsorge in der vorreformatorischen Kirche und der Kirche der Reformation* (Berlin, 1898); H. H. W. Kramm, *The Theology of Martin Luther* (James Clarke & Company, Ltd., London, 1949); Alfred Kurz, *Die Heilsgewissheit bei Luther* (Gütersloh, 1933); Gerhard E. Lenski, *Marriage in the Lutheran Church* (Lutheran Book Concern, Columbus, Ohio, 1936); Svend Lerfeldt, *Den kristnes kamp, mortificatio carnis: en studie i Luthers teologi* (Copenhagen, 1949); Walter von Löwenich, *Luthers Theologia crucis* (Munich, 1929); John T. McNeill, *History of the Cure of Souls* (Harper & Brothers, New York, 1951); Hermannus Obendiek, *Der Teufel bei Martin Luther* (Berlin, 1931); Lennart Pinomaa, *Der existenzielle Charakter der Theologie Luthers: das Hervorbrechen der Theologie der Anfechtung und ihre Bedeutung für das Lutherverständnis* (Helsinki, 1940); Lennart Pinomaa, *Der Zorn Gottes in der Theologie Luthers* (Helsinki, 1938); William Walter Rockwell, *Die Doppelehe des Landgrafen Philipp von Hessen* (Marburg, 1904); Gordon Rupp, *The Righteousness of God: Luther Studies* (Hodder & Stoughton, London, 1953); Paul Schempp, *Luthers*

Stellung zur heiligen Schrift (Munich, 1929); Nathan Söderblom, *Humor och melankoli och andra Lutherstudier* (Stockholm, 1919); Hermann Steinlein, *Luther als Seelsorger* (Leipzig, 1918); M. A. H. Stomps, *Die Anthropologie Martin Luthers* (Frankfurt on the Main, 1935); Gustav Törnvall, *Geistliches und weltliches Regiment bei Luther*, translated from the Swedish (Munich, 1947); Vilmos Vajta, *Die Theologie des Gottesdienstes bei Luther* (Stockholm, 1952); Philip S. Watson, *Let God Be God: an Interpretation of the Theology of Martin Luther* (The Epworth Press, London, 1947); Erich Vogelsang, *Der angefochtene Christus bei Luther* (Berlin, 1932); Gustaf Wingren, *Luthers Lehre vom Beruf*, translated from the Swedish (Munich, 1952).

The following studies came to the attention of the editor after completion of the manuscript: Fritz Blanke, *Luthers Humor: Scherz und Schalk in Luthers Seelsorge* (Furche Verlag, Hamburg, 1954); George W. Forell, *Faith Active in Love: an Investigation of the Principles Underlying Luther's Social Ethics* (America Press, New York, 1954); Johannes Heckel, *Lex charitatis: eine juristische Untersuchung über das Recht in der Theologie Martin Luthers* (Munich, 1953).

INDEXES

General Index

Aaron, 306
Abraham, 68, 87, 234, 275, 276, 290, 291
Absalom, 68, 73, 220, 234
Absolution, 16, 281. *See also* Confession
Adam, 43, 103, 117, 135, 136, 137, 267, 275, 283; old, 69, 70
Adultery, 73, 95, 103, 275, 288, 290, 292, 348
Aesop, 339
Agricola, John, 82, 83, 154; Elizabeth, 82, 83
Ahab, 206
Albert, of Mansfeld, Count (*see* Mansfeld); of Mayence, Cardinal Archbishop (*see* Mayence); of Prussia, Duke (*see* Prussia)
Allegory, 113
Altar, 312
Altenburg, 29, 136, 178, 179, 183, 184, 219, 229, 278, 279, 322, 324
Ambrose, 113
Amsdorf, Nicholas, 167, 168, 191, 323
Amsterdam, 211
Anabaptist, 120, 145
Ananias, 308
Anfechtung, 19. *See also* Anxiety; Cross; Despair; Doubt; Melancholy; Temptation; Trials; Worry
Anhalt, Prince George of, 122, 162, 163, 276, 308, 309, 310–314, 316; Prince Joachim of, 92–95, 98, 181, 182; Prince John of, 163, 164; Princess Margaret of, 162; Prince William of, 92
Annas, 140
Antichrist, 192
Antwerp, 192, 208, 209
Anxiety, 82–108, 138, 150
Apel, John, 144

Apothecary, 17, 83, 235, 239
Arnstadt, 310
Ascania, 162, 163, 308, 311
Asceticism, 92, 93
Ate, 148
Athanasius, 232
Auer, Catherine, 72, 73
Augsburg, 141, 145, 218
Augsburg Confession, 140, 148, 151, 153, 155, 219, 314
Augsburg, Diet of, 60, 140, 144–159, 173
August of Saxony, Duke. *See* Saxony (Ernestine)
Augustine, 112, 113, 232, 259, 292
Augustinian, 109, 112, 123, 132, 186, 192, 194, 197, 208, 259, 314
Aurogallus, Matthew, 245
Austria, 53; Ferdinand of, 56, 150, 309, 310
Authority, 149, 150
Axt, Basil, 173

Baal, 234
Babylon, 195, 299
Baier, Christian, 179
Bamberg, 190
Baptism, 21, 35, 37, 38, 49, 50, 60, 122, 161, 209, 276, 282, 306, 342, 345
Barber, 17, 124, 128, 247
Basel, 286
Baumgaertner, Jerome, 187, 188, 226, 227; Sibyl, 225–227
Bautzen, 74
Bavaria, 150, 190, 213; Duke William of, 199
Beer, 49, 107
Beggar, 185, 188
Belgern, 51, 52
Belgium, 165

355

Horace, 80
Hospital, 237, 247, 346
Huegel, Andrew, 181
Hungary, 57, 88, 150, 209, 211; King
Lewis of, 56, 57; Queen Mary of,
56–58
Hunting, 93
Hunzinger, A. W., 16
Hus, John, 146
Hussite, 194, 301
Hypochondria, 99

Illingen, 42
Illness, mental, 17, 42, 44, 51, 52, 99,
182, 183. *See also* Sick
Impatience, 111, 121. *See also* Patience
Imprisonment, 171, 177, 178, 179, 184,
185, 192–194, 197–199, 211, 214,
215, 216–218, 225–227, 266, 335
Incubus, 43
Indulgences, 13, 153, 197
Ingolstadt, 199
Inheritance, 188, 220, 239
Intercession, 135, 171–189, 335
Interest, 180, 254, 282, 322
Isaac, 40, 81, 87, 135, 267, 269
Isaiah, 14, 275
Israel, 150, 206, 306
Israelite, 186

Jacob, 87, 234, 266, 267, 276
Jacobs, Charles M., 23, 29; Henry E.,
96
Jehoiakim, 234
Jena, 229, 245
Jericho, 306
Jeroboam, 267
Jerome, 112, 113, 125
Jerusalem, 195, 197, 307
Jews, 76, 106, 201, 255, 261, 316, 325
Jezebel, 234, 267
Joachim, of Anhalt, Prince (*see* Anhalt);
of Brandenburg, Elector (*see* Brandenburg)
Joachimsthal, 309
Joerger, Dorothy, 180, 181
John, of Saxony, Elector (*see* Saxony
[Ernestine]); of Anhalt, Prince (*see*
Anhalt)
John Frederick of Saxony, Elector. *See*
Saxony (Ernestine)
John George of Mansfeld, Count. *See*
Mansfeld
Joke, 85, 86, 243
Jonah, 73
Jonas, Justus, 29, 49, 50, 75, 76, 77,
105, 107, 108, 145, 147, 150, 152,
229, 294, 306, 327; Catherine, 75, 76
Joseph, 68, 87

Joshua, 306
Joy, 34, 193
Jud, Leo, 177
Judas, 140, 206, 308
Judgment, Last, 27, 209, 335, 337
Juelich, 104
Julian, 113
Justification, 109

Kaeser, Leonard, 153, 213–215
Kaufmann, Cyriac, 30; Magdalene, 317
Kegel, Andrew, 339, 340; John, 339,
340
Kellner, John. *See* Cellarius, John
Kemberg, 252
Keyser, Leonard. *See* Kaeser, Leonard
Kiel, 347
Kind, Henry, 173
Knudsen, John, 61, 62; Matthias, 61, 62
Koenig, Francis, 222
Koenigsberg, 64, 346
Koenigsfeld, 272
Koethen, 181
Koetteritzsch, Sebastian von, 173, 174
Kohlhase, Hans, 335
Kolditz, 72
Koppe, Leonard, 172
Korner, John, 52
Kreuzbinder, Mrs., 183
Kriegel. *See* Kegel
Krueger, Ursula, 277
Kuenhofer, Helen, 80

Lamech, 291
Lang, John, 314, 315
Latvia, 194–197
Lauterbach, Agnes, 166; Anthony, 43,
45, 46, 73, 130, 164–166, 168, 169,
224, 225, 247, 249, 251, 253, 254,
281, 302, 303, 304, 305, 315–317,
333, 336; Elizabeth, 166; Ursula,
164, 165
Law, canon, 285, 313; civil, 279, 285,
286, 326, 333–335, 347; divine, 86,
179, 269, 270, 273, 276, 310 (*see also*
Commandments); natural, 137, 269
Laymen, 16, 113, 304
Leah, 87, 266
Leipzig, 74, 83, 142, 218, 223, 225, 250,
254, 275, 320
Leisnig, 43
Leprosy, 21, 186, 243, 324
Lewis of Hungary, King. *See* Hungary
Liberty, 276
Libius, John, 348
Lichtenberg, 272, 274
Liegnitz, 211
Lindemann, Caspar, 151
Link, Wenzel, 117, 161, 176, 177

BIBLICAL REFERENCES

CPSIA information can be obtained
at www.ICGtesting.com
Printed in the USA
BVHW071944030821
613436BV00002B/232